*Modernity, Aesthetics,
and the Bounds of Art*

PETER J. McCORMICK

Modernity, Aesthetics, and the Bounds of Art

Cornell University Press

ITHACA AND LONDON

First published 1990 by Cornell University Press.

International Standard Book Number (cloth) 0-8014-2452-6
International Standard Book Number (paper) 0-8014-9740-x
Library of Congress Catalog Card Number 89-71309
Printed in the United States of America
*Librarians: Library of Congress cataloging information
appears on the last page of the book.*

♾ The paper used in this publication meets the minimum
requirements of the American National Standard for
Permanence of Paper for Printed Library Materials Z39.48–1984.

To Moira
Léone and Pierre Bessière
Lisette and John McCormick

Tum pater Anchises: "Animae, quibus altera fato
"Corpora debentur, Lethaei ad fluminis undam
"Securos latices et longa oblivia potant."

"Dicam equidem, nec te suspensum, nate, tenebo;"
Suscipit Anchises, atque ordine singula pandit.
—Virgil, *Aeneid* vi. 712

τὸν δὲ ἀεὶ πιόντα πάντων ἐπιλανθάνεσθαι. ἐπειδὴ δὲ κοιμηθῆναι
καὶ μέσας νύκτας γενέσθαι, βροντήν τε καὶ σεισμὸν
γενέσθαι, καὶ ἐντεῦθεν ἐξαπίνης ἄλλον ἄλλῃ φέρεσθαι
ἄνω εἰς τὴν γένεσιν, ἄττοντας ὥσπερ ἀστέρας. αὐτὸς δὲ
τοῦ μὲν ὕδατος κωλυθῆναι πιεῖν ...

Καὶ οὕτως, ὦ Γλαύκων, μῦθος ἐσώθη καὶ οὐκ ἀπώλετο,
καὶ ἡμᾶς ἂν σώσειεν, ἂν πειθώμεθα αὐτῷ, καὶ τὸν τῆς Λήθης
ποταμὸν εὖ δ;αβησόμεθα καὶ τὴν Ψυχὴν οὐ μιανθησόμεθα.
—Plato, *Republic* 621a–b

Contents

Contents

viii

Preface

IN AN earlier book, *Fictions, Philosophies, and the Problems of Poetics* (Cornell, 1988), I argued that critical appreciation of the nature and role of the arts today requires philosophical reflection. I also argued that doing sufficiently critical philosophical work in some areas requires reflection on the arts. My concerns there centered on the modernist lyric and some strains in both contemporary Anglo-American and contemporary Continental philosophy. And I tried to show that taking appropriate philosophical account of the representations in the modernist lyric of certain poetic fictions—fictional discourse, putative truths, beliefs, feelings, actions, selves, and worlds—requires thinking twice about the adequacy of our habitual philosophical idioms. The background of these systematic reflections was the claim that doing philosophy today takes place in a context of radical cultural change where one paradigm for rationality—the scientific worldview—seems to be ceding its place to a new paradigm so far without name, a postmodern paradigm some want to say.

In this book I step back from my earlier systematic work to explore in a philosophical and historical way the intellectual background to our understanding of the relations between philosophy and the arts. Starting from case studies of the difficult conceptual relations among interpretation, history, theory, and practice in two distinguished representatives of contemporary Anglo-American and Continental philosophies of art, Arthur Danto and Hans-Georg

Gadamer, I show that each is tributary in an important way to competing readings of the seminal period in modern aesthetics, the eighteenth century. The disagreement is between an analytic account of the eighteenth century as progressing to a culmination in the Kantian synthesis and a hermeneutic reading that works backward from Hegel to overcome that synthesis. After detailing these controversies in the Introduction and the first three chapters of part I, while relegating some technical matters to appendixes here and throughout the book, I return to the elements of Kant's aesthetics in chapter 4 before marking out some suggestions for fresh approaches with the help of the largely unnoticed aesthetics of Kant's nineteenth-century critic Bernard Bolzano.

In an Interlude I point to a disagreement within the analytic account itself on whether the key issues in eighteenth-century aesthetics focus on a theory of aesthetic perception or on a theory of taste. This retrospect allows me to underline the importance of Bolzano's critique of Kant in opening the way to a different tradition, what I call the realist backgrounds of modern aesthetics.

In part II, I explore some of the resources of that tradition in chapters centered on largely conceptual issues about the nature of the aesthetic in only one of the arts, literature. I look at questions about aesthetic experience in Dilthey, aesthetic intentions in Brentano, literary psychologism in Husserl, aesthetic entities and states of affairs in Twardowski, aesthetic feelings in Meinong, and aesthetic structures and objects in Ingarden. Finally, in a comprehensive Conclusion I return to my contemporary starting point with the help of my discussion of both the eighteenth-century readings and the realist reflections on the nature of the aesthetic. And I try to formulate in a provisional way, with the aid of a critical discussion of Jürgen Habermas's and Hilary Putnam's recent views on kinds of modernity and realism, several questions that philosophers, art historians, and critics need to address if they are to understand anew the relations between philosophy and the arts at a time of a radical cultural upheaval.

In short, this book focuses sharply on the modernist perspective from which we still view the relations between philosophy and the arts today. It suggests that much representative controversy in such areas follows both from our continuing inability to agree on just how to read the crucial texts of the eighteenth century and from our inattention to the neglected conceptual resources within the realist backgrounds of modern aesthetics. Setting new bounds for art, it turns out, will require rethinking just how our contemporary habits of distinguishing between what is art and what is not, between what is important in art and what is trivial, and between what succeeds as art and what fails remains tributary to the consequences of misreading those eighteenth-century texts as well as of overlooking some of the realist and not just empiricist keys to their understanding.

I thank the Social Science and Humanities Research Council of Canada (Ottawa), the Alexander von Humboldt Foundation (Bonn), and the Taniguchi Foundation (Tokyo) for their support. I owe much to the criticism and encouragement of colleagues and friends, to whom I am most grateful—to Gilles Granger, Shinro Kato, Laurent Stern, Friedrick Kambartel, Francis Sparshott, Megumi Sakabe, William Richardson, Ken-ichi Sasaki, Jürgen Mittelstrass, William Hill, Calvin Seerveld, Ryosuke Inagaki, John Fisher, Robert Czerny, Koichi Tsujimura, Myong-Hwan Jung, and many others. And I owe special thanks to Joseph Margolis, John Ackerman, Tomonobu Imamichi, and Paul Ricoeur.

PETER J. McCORMICK

Modernity, Aesthetics,
and the Bounds of Art

INTRODUCTION

INTERPRETATION
AND HISTORY

The philosophical history of art consists in its being absorbed into
its own philosophy.

—Arthur Danto

In any encounter with art, it is not the particular, but rather the
totality of the experienceable world, man's ontological place in it,
and above all his finitude before what transcends him, that is
brought to experience.

—Hans-Georg Gadamer

ONE VIRTUE among the several vices in recent philosophy of
art, whether in Anglo-American or Continental terms, however
various, is careful work on the interactions between interpretation
and history, theory and practice. Thus, philosophers as diverse as
Arthur Danto, Nelson Goodman, Francis Sparshott, and Richard
Wollheim on the one hand and Hans-Georg Gadamer, Gilles Deleuze,
François Lyotard, and Paul Ricoeur on the other continue to elaborate their sustained reflections on art in the context of repeated and
closely detailed case studies within such individual arts as literature, painting, dance, and cinema.

My purpose here is not to survey the complex character of this
widespread resurgence of interest in a less general and finer-grained
approach to recurring problems in the philosophy of art. Rather, I
will put on exhibit two case studies of this striking new work. My
initial interest is to call attention to its central, repeated, and yet
problematic reliance on what I will argue is an insufficiently
critical grasp of several cardinal notions in modern aesthetics. I
shall take my examples from only two currents in contemporary

philosophical reflection on the arts—analytic aesthetics in the recent work of Arthur Danto and hermeneutic aesthetics in that of Hans-Georg Gadamer. In each case I first present a selective critical reading of their more recent work, then try to suggest briefly, without attempting to demonstrate in detail, that the interpretive practices of these contemporary philosophers of art seriously undermine their theoretical views about both interpretation and history. Specifically I argue that the recurring tension in each account between theory and practice derives largely if not exclusively from very different yet similarly uncritical accounts of both historical and systematic uses of interpretation. Finally, with the help of some little-noticed work on aesthetics in the late Heidegger, I confront Danto's and Gadamer's views briefly in order to generate a series of questions that ask us to reflect anew on both analytic and hermeneutic readings of the seminal period for contemporary philosophies of art and the eighteenth century (part 1), as well as to make an inquiry into conceptual analyses of the aesthetic still largely unexplored in the realist backgrounds of modern aesthetics (part 2). In the concluding chapter, just as in the Interlude between parts 1 and 2, I return to our contemporary starting point with a renewed contrast between recent analytic and Continental philosophy, this time a more general one that allows me to formulate several programmatic conclusions already adumbrated in another form at the end of this introductory chapter.

Interpretation, History, and Theory

In his influential 1964 essay "The Art World," Arthur Danto proposed, among other things, that good reasons were on hand for construing the crucial notion of "the art world" as a conjunction of art history and artistic theory.[1] For once we take "the art world" in this way, we can at last distinguish sharply between what is art and what is not. Since this distinction had been notoriously problematic ever since Duchamp's ready-mades offered putative artworks that were in no perceptual way distinguishable from the mere things that were their physical counterparts, Danto's proposals were of major interest. But the nature of the relations between mere things,

[1] *Journal of Philosophy* 6(1964): 571–84. For all their philosophical importance, it is essential to keep in mind throughout the details of these influential views just how partial a perspective they involve; compare, for example, T. Imamichi's angle of vision in "The Meaning of Night in Aesthetic Experience," in *The Reasons of Art*, ed. P. McCormick (Ottawa, 1985), 185–92.

works of arts, art history, and art theory remained obscure. Danto continued to work on these issues over the next fifteen years while publishing a series of books in analytic philosophy.

Then in his 1981 book about art, *The Transfiguration of the Commonplace*, Danto pulled together some of his previously uncollected work.[2] Moreover, he now focused sharply, and at length, on the relations between the art world and especially artistic theory, claiming that the art world "is logically dependent upon theory" (135). For Danto an art theory has a peculiar power because it can "detach objects from the real world and make them part of a different world, an *art* world, a world of interpreted things" (135). The key point here was the connection between mere things as representations and interpretation. On this view an artwork is the sort of mere thing that requires interpretation. For interpretation, like baptism, Danto claimed, endows a mere thing with "a new identity, participation in the community of the elect" (126). Later Danto wrote more specifically: "The thesis is that works of art, in categorical contrast with mere representations, use the means of representation in a way that is not exhaustively specified when we have exhaustively specified what is being represented" (147–48).

Besides this essential relation between works of art and theory as interpretation, Danto also stressed the connection between works of art and history. For if works of art are essentially connected with interpretation, which changes historically, they will also have an essential connection with history. Some recent comment on Danto's work has brought this connection out clearly.

Whether we talk of languages, pictures, ideas, or beliefs, every representation has two sides, one as an ordinary thing *in* the world and the other as an icon *of* the world. So representations seem to be both inside the world and outside it. The key to this puzzle is interpretation. Interpretation "binds thoughts and symbols to facts and . . . also lifts them into the world of theories, for it is only under some description (thus within the intellectual world of a theory) that facts can be objects of thought at all. . . . but the descriptions available to one time will not and cannot be identical to those available at another."[3] The consequence is a philosophy of art that is both antiformalist and antiaesthetic, a strongly historicist phi-

---

[2](Cambridge, Mass., 1981). Further references to this work are incorporated in the text.

[3]P. Guyer, "When Is Black Paint More Than Black Paint?" *New York Times Book Review*, 1 February 1987, 23. See the very different views of K. Yoshioka, "Reflections on Aesthetics," *Aesthetics* 1(1983): 89–99.

losophy of art that relies on the cardinal notion of interpretation.

Before turning to the historical account that Danto went on to develop in his subsequent work, we need to note several serious questions this initial synthesis raises. One problem has to do with the central talk here of "theory," a term that, despite appearances, remains imprecise in the pertinent domain of art history. Danto thinks of a theory in art as an "interpretation." Yet as Benjamin Tilghman has pointed out in one of the most searching examinations of Danto's initial position, all Danto's examples of theories as interpretations are "examples of what we would ordinarily call artistically relevant descriptions and not theories at all."[4] Moreover, how can "theory" be held to make both art and the art world possible when Danto sometimes includes theory as one of the things that make up the art world (Tilghman 1984:59)? Finally, the logical relationships Danto claims between works of art and theory seem skewed—artworks are said to depend logically on theories, when it seems rather that theories should be said to depend on artworks.

A host of other problems have turned up about other central matters. Thus, important questions have arisen about the satisfactoriness of Danto's distinction between mere things and works of art, about the understanding of such key pieces of evidence for Danto's views as Duchamp's "Fountain," about the analogies between art and language, about the question begging involved in crucial examples in his attempt to provide a new definition of art, and about Danto's various analyses of metaphor, expression, style, rhetoric, and so on. More important for our purposes are several problems not only with the notion of interpretation but with its uses in reading history.

Danto, as we have seen, has argued that "an ahistoric theory of art can have no philosophic defense" because seeing a representation, whether an object or an event, as a work of art requires "an atmosphere of artistic theory, a knowledge of the history of art" (Danto 1981:135). One problem here involves the relations between art and theory at the beginnings of Western reflection on the arts. Danto holds that the key notions of art and reality develop together within a particular culture (cf. 83). Indeed, he claims that a culture that lacks the concept of art will also lack the concept of reality. But as Marcia Eaton has pointed out, Danto here exaggerates the

---

[4]B. Tilghman, *But Is It Art?* (New York, 1984), 61.

connections between art and reality, just as he has elsewhere exaggerated those between art and language.[5]

Part of this exaggeration is on view in the very controversial and strongly disputed reading of Plato's alleged disenfranchisement of art in Danto's 1986 book *The Philosophical Disenfranchisement of Art*.[6] Moreover, his historical views about Kantian philosophy of art, the second attempt he thinks philosophy has made to disenfranchise art, has also raised serious concerns about Danto's historical sense. One contemporary historian of philosophy who has specialized in Kant's aesthetics, writes: "This is implausible history.... when modern aesthetics originated in the eighteenth century, its goal was not to disenfranchise art but to repatriate it from its puritanical exile."[7] Danto's highly controversial readings of Plato and Kant especially, but of other philosophers as well, have also been attacked as unscholarly because they include no documentation. One persistent worry, then, is clearly the reliability of Danto's essential appeals to art history in construing the distinction between what is and what is not art when his repeated discussions in the history of philosophy have aroused such criticism. In turning to Danto's account of art history we need to be just as wary of the historical reliability of that account as of the understanding and role of interpretation within it.

After the initial synthesis of 1981, Danto went on to add nuance to a number of his earlier views. For example, he now argued that we need to distinguish between kinds of interpretation—surface interpretation and deep interpretation—if we are to see the persuasiveness of his view that interpretation is required for a representation to be an artwork. But this clarification as well as

[5]M. Eaton, "Review of Danto, *The Transfiguration of the Commonplace*," *Journal of Aesthetics and Art Criticism* 40(1981): 206–7.

[6](New York, 1986). Further references to this work are incorporated in the text. Talk of Plato and "disenfranchisement" here is peculiar. For a richly different way of reading Plato that opens up a new understanding of the background of Plato's view on art, see S. Kato, *Plato's Earlier Philosophy* (Tokyo, 1988). See Joseph Margolis's major criticisms, still largely unaddressed even though reaching back to Danto's early work, in "Ontology Down and Out in Art and Science," *Journal of Aesthetics and Art Criticism* 46(1988): 451–60. On Danto's art reviews, see J. Brodsky, "Review of *The State of the Art*," in the same issue, 512–18.

[7]Guyer 1987: 23. Similarly, see J. Annas's criticism, the lack of a "serious philosophical engagement with past philosophical thought," in the review of Danto's 1989 book, *Connections to the World* (New York, Harper), in *New York Times Book Review*, 14 May 1989. Part of the problem here is Danto's apparent lack of attention to the cultural contexts of the philosophers he deals with, especially the context of Hegel's philosophy. See L. Dickey, *Hegel: Religion, Economics, and the Politics of Spirit, 1770–1807* (Cambridge, 1988).

others elicited still sharper criticism.[8] More interesting is the remarkable series of essays in art criticism that Danto began to write for the *Nation* in 1984. These essays go far toward settling some quarrels with the peculiar status of certain examples in the early account. Now Danto can point to a wide-ranging series of individual case studies of exhibits devoted to classical and contemporary arts as well as to various movements and moments in art history. Moreover, in his 1986 book and in an important essay published with the collection of his first two years of art critical pieces, Danto addresses himself explicitly to the question of how to read the history of art.

Without trying to follow all the details in the complex story Danto continues to rework, as his more recent essays in the *Nation* demonstrate, we can nevertheless note its major outlines. For Danto, as we saw, the story begins with Plato's reflection on the relations between reality and appearance, which Danto sees as one of the two ways philosophy has tried to disenfranchise art. In claiming that art is no more than an appearance of an appearance, Danto thinks, Plato tried to ephemeralize art. But art resisted this onslaught.

If Plato stands at the beginning, the middle of the story, as Danto would have it, falls into three major periods that are to be understood under the heading of changes in spatial representation. Very roughly, they can be dated 1300, 1600, and 1900. Since this part of the story is very recent, I quote Danto's presentation at length.

> I have lately found it valuable to view the Western pictorial tradition as falling into three main phases, at roughly 300-year intervals: circa 1300, 1600 and 1900. It is possible to think of these as marked by different ways of construing space, though this can be but part of the matter. The first period, beginning with Giotto, is defined by that progressive investigation into natural appearances that culminates in Leonardo and Raphael. Its agenda was to arrange colors and forms on a flat surface so as to engender an illusion of objects in real space. The viewer is strictly excluded from the space into which he or she appears to see, like a disembodied eye. The second phase aspires to a different order of illusion, one which envelopes image and spectator together in what, in his lectures on Caravaggio, Frank Stella somewhat misleadingly terms "working space." We find a good statement of the third phase in some remarks of Maurice Denis, a member of the "Nabi" school of

---

[8]D. Novitz, "Review of Danto, *The Philosophical Disenfranchisement of Art*," *Journal of Aesthetics and Art Criticism* 46(1987): 307–9. Some of Novitz's criticisms here and elsewhere are often immoderate and sometimes unfair.

painting, whose members, including Pierre Bonnard, took their inspiration from Paul Gauguin: "A painting, before being a war horse or a nude woman or an anecdote, is essentially a flat surface covered with colors arranged in a certain order." Under this description, internal and external illusory space are repudiated, and paintings are made almost specifically to stifle the possibility of illusion, as if the work consists only in its own surface.[9]

Danto has important comments to make on just how these periods develop. But his major point for the middle of the story is the distinction between Pre-Raphaelite and "Post-Raphaelite" painting. Most of the latter, he believes, is no more than salon or academy art waiting upon the appearance of modernism in the aftermath of Picasso's fateful visit to the Musée d'Ethnographie at Trocadero in 1907.

But, surprisingly, Danto's story is not open-ended, with the history of art continuing to work out its various latent possibilities while accommodating changing times, technologies, and interests. Rather, Danto sees the history of art somewhat in the way Nietzsche and Heidegger view the history of metaphysics (if not philosophy) —as a history coming to its end. Here, after the alleged second unsuccessful attempt to disenfranchise art—Kant's emphasis on art as no more than an occasion for disinterested pleasure—Hegel's prophetic vision of history as its own time reflected in thought comes true in Duchamp's raising "the question of the philosophical nature of art from within art" (Danto 1986:16) and in the effect of the new art of cinema on artists' attempts at self-justification. The result for Danto is the transformation of the history of art into its own philosophical self-awareness—"the philosophical history of art consists in its being absorbed into its own philosophy" (110). Thus the third of the three-hundred-year phases differs essentially from the others; for Danto 1900 marks the end of the history of art in some sense yet to be fully articulated.

This story, with its clearly marked beginning, middle, and end as well as its continuous retouches and rearticulations, turns on an explicit contrast with other ways of viewing the history of art. Danto owes much to Clement Greenberg in stressing that the evolution of art follows from a curious kind of technology whereby

[9]The *Nation*, 11 June 1988. Danto's reviews since *The State of the Art* are now available as *Encounters and Reflections: Art in the Historical Present* (New York, 1989).

art progresses toward its own self-analysis.[10] In its twentieth-century transformation into theory, art in one sense has come to an end in the postmodern era where theory and cognitive features, rather than taste or sensibility or aesthetic excellence, make artworks of mere things. Thus the history of art ends, like Hegel's history itself, with knowledge and self-consciousness. This Hegelian model "is supposed to be an improvement over Vasari's view that the history of art is the history of perfecting the techniques of presenting visual illusions, over Croce's non-history of art as expression, and over Gombrich's that it is a chronicle of incommensurable symbolic forms."[11] And as an improvement, the implicit claim in Danto's narrative is that it can provide as good an account, if not better, of all that Vasari, Croce, and Gombrich have chronicled while accounting for the one era in the history of art that none of those illustrious scholars could manage—modernism and its peculiar demise.

Now just as in the case of Danto's claims about art and theory as interpretation, the discussion here is far richer and more subtle than my sketch can capture. Moreover, unlike his earlier discussions culminating in 1981, the reflections in both the 1986 book and the five years of art criticism show the sophisticated qualification we would expect from pursuing case studies so continuously. Nevertheless, Danto's new narrative about the course of art history seems to raise almost as many critical reservations about interpretation as his earlier theoretical discussions.

As George Wilson has pointed out, one major difficulty with this story—whatever the many problems that cluster around its beginnings and its middle—is its closure. And the end of this technological story requires particularly close attention. The difficulty is that, like Greenberg, Danto fails to solve the problem of making it "coherent and plausible that the objectives theories of modernism posit were genuinely immanent in the art making of the period."[12] The difficulty consists partly in assigning Duchamp's work an appropriate and not exaggerated role (versus Danto's proclivity for overemphasizing the perceptually indiscernible differences between mere things and some putative artworks) and partly in taking sufficient account of the many ways the countless modernist mani-

---

[10]G. Wilson, "Review of Danto, *The Philosophical Disenfranchisement of Art*," *Times Literary Supplement*, 9 January 1987, 28.

[11]Tilghman, "Review of Danto, *The Philosophical Disenfranchisement of Art*," *Canadian Philosophical Reviews* 7(1987): 99.

[12]Wilson 1987: 28.

festos show real indifference to theoretical issues (versus Danto's neglect of such evidence in favor of a focus on purely intellectualist discussions). Danto cannot persuasively close his story of the history of art without addressing such issues explicitly and cogently, something he has yet to do. Moreover, before arguing for closure he needs to consider those many examples—say, in music to take just one of the arts—where determining the status of a putative work of art does not require appeals to the very special kinds of interpretive "theories" Danto wants to privilege.

Further, Danto's test case is modernism—its appearance, flourishing, and demise. He reads modernism reductively in the sense that he can be said to reduce its enormous international complexities to a largely conceptual movement viewed in retrospect from the standpoint of New York painting of the 1950s and 1960s. And yet, as Flint Schier has insisted, much of the evidence on view in his sporadic discussions of modernism fits better with a nonreductive interpretation, Schier's candidate being an aesthetic one. Danto, the counterclaim goes here, "has the wrong idea of what could possibly constitute an explanation of the works of high modernism. For him these works are so many attempts to solve various puzzles about the identity and essence of pictorial art. But this intellectualist reading of modern art distorts the nature of our concern for these works."[13] Schier's alternative view needs fuller citation.

> The works of high modernism from, say, Manet to Mr Bacon, Frank Stella and Jules Olitski—should not be conflated with the schoolboy jokes of Warhol. Modern art is, indeed, a puzzle to itself. The puzzle is not an intellectual one, concerning the definition of art. It is a crisis of sensibility. Modern art asks how it can possibly stand up against the aesthetic quality of its great predecessors. And the answer to this question cannot be found in a philosophical theory; it must be found in work that can engender the conviction of esthetic excellence induced by the paradigmatic works of the past. The judgment that a work succeeds in carrying this conviction is, irreducibly, one of taste, of sensibility, not a cognitive assessment that some problem has been solved.[14]

---

[13]F. Schier, "Pot, Op, and Modern Flops," *New York Times Book Review*, 5 April 1987, 21.

[14]Schier 1987: 21. For an extended discussion of several key issues here, see P. McCormick, *Fictions, Philosophies, and the Problems of Poetics* (Ithaca, 1988).

Part of the force in this alternative view, I think, comes from the suggestion it raises that Danto's own historicist philosophy of art, in putting such stress on theory as interpretation coupled with what is arguably a tendentious historical interpretation of the so-called transformation of the history of art into its own philosophy, seems to disenfranchise art much more effectively than either Plato or Kant is alleged to have done.

Practice, Theory, and Art Criticism

When we look carefully through Danto's philosophy of art in both its original and its more recent forms, the attempt to answer the question, What is art? remains central. And that question Danto addresses repeatedly across his systematic, occasional, and critical work alike in terms of spelling out the essential links he promotes between artworks, interpretation, and history. But these links remain unsure for a variety of reasons. Even though we must grant that Danto continues to elaborate more critically his historicist philosophy of art, I think those concerned with aesthetics and the philosophy of art are justified in registering serious reservations about the satisfactoriness of this account so far. Before I try to formulate a hypothesis about the grounds of those reservations, however, let me indicate briefly how some of his critical practice undermines his theoretical views, especially about interpretation and theory.

As we have already seen in looking carefully at his views on the history of art, Danto has introduced a great deal of nuance into his previous theoretical positions as a result of his extensive work as art critic for the Nation since 1984. I want to look carefully at his most recent work, which I will take as the critical work from just after The State of the Art[15] for the two years from 27 September 1986 to 3 September 1988.

These essays, like those from the first two years, fall into three unequal groups: those featuring individual retrospectives, whether contemporary like Cindy Sherman's photography or historical, such as Raphael's drawings; those featuring group shows, such as "Vienna 1900" or a Whitney Biennial; and those featuring movements in art history like "The Hudson River School" or "Nineteenth- and Twentieth-Century Chinese Painting." The most frequent subject

[15](New York, 1987).

is the contemporary retrospective, and the least frequent is non-European art.

Such a diverse set of topics leads naturally to discussions of many themes. Some of the recurring ones should be noted as an index to Danto's continuing concern with theory as interpretation. Thus the reviews return regularly to conceptual questions about the senses and significance of such central critical terms as "expression," "representation," "imitation," "portraiture," illusion versus picture, and artifact versus art. Recurring themes include those of art and technology, commercialization and commodification, art and sexuality, modernism and its salient strategies, historicism versus formalism, and mind, eye, and brain. Danto features his favorite critics—Vasari, Panofsky, Gombrich, Greenberg, and others. Occasionally he draws parallels between issues in art criticism and those in literary criticism. And more often he underlines new complexities in his early concern with "the art world" by exploring the politics of exhibitions, "curatorial art," the roles of museums, galleries, patrons, the media, auctions, collectors, and so on. Amid this pleasing diversity, however, and in addition to several of these recurring preoccupations is at least one central theme that requires further critical scrutiny: the nature of theory and interpretation.

I have already noted some difficulties with Danto's earlier discussions of theory in art as interpretation, and these more recent essays in criticism do nothing to answer them in any satisfactory way. We do, however, find some occasional clarifications. In his discussion of the postmodernist paintings of Hans Haacke (14 February 1987)—for example, his piece "Shapolsky *et al.* Manhattan Real Estate Holdings, a Real-Time Social System, as of May 1, 1971"—Danto shows how some theory seems designed not to make a work of art possible (part of Danto's earlier views) but, as in a museum's ad hoc theoretical formulations, to keep a piece out of the art world. Here the Guggenheim saw Haacke's work as a threat to one of its corporate patrons. Again, in his review of the paintings of Morris Louis (15 November 1986), Danto concedes that the ways Louis worked paint onto his cloth canvases with saturated rags and sponges, relying on capillary action, folds, pleats, gravity, and so on, made it impossible to see him as a creator of purely autonomous abstractions—"for in the end the paintings resisted the theory." Here theory, far from making the artwork possible, has not just denied a putative artwork the status of hanging in one of the key spaces of the art world, as in Haacke's case; theory has reversed an artistic reputation. From among the greatest of painters, Louis has fallen for many critics to among the least. In working against the dominant theories of his time, "Louis has betrayed the critical establishment. He has faulted the premisses of its practice." And Danto adds: "The decline is not in Louis. It is in a style of critical address misread as a decline in an artist. Louis is as great as ever."

The incidental comments show Danto's growing awareness of the serious difficulties that continue to plague his still current views about theory in art as interpretation. Although these difficulties are various and some are far from simple, I want to focus on just one of these inadequacies in his view of theory and interpretation, with the help of Danto's own worry about reading "too much into the painting, wanting it to be deep" (see his review of Miro, 20 June 1987, and his "The Hudson River School," 7 November 1987). Three short examples can make the point that Danto's critical practice in important and repeated ways undermines his theoretical views about interpretation.

Consider Danto's comments about the drawings of the last and "the least available" of the great Renaissance triumvirate of Michelangelo, Leonardo, and Raphael (see the 19 December 1987 review). Danto stresses the difficulty for us of gaining access to these drawings—the problems we have of overcoming a modernist perspective on painting, the theories even of the Pre-Raphaelite movement, and the problems with the scarcity of historical information about Raphael, his works, and his stylistic interactions with the works of Perugino, Leonardo, and the Sistine ceiling. Yet despite these obstacles and others, Danto concludes: "It is only at the end, in the magnificent head and hand he drew for the 'Transfiguration'—the masterpiece on which he was working at his death, the greatest drawing in the show and, for all I know, the greatest drawing in existence—that he comes fully into his own as a genius." If Danto is right in this judgment, then how can we explain this view of a connoisseur ("this is a connoisseur's show," he writes as he describes the drawings with the flair of a onetime draftsman and painter become philosopher and critic) on the grounds that theories as interpretations can make artifacts into artworks? Danto's practical appreciation here, with classical rather than modernist work, seems to entail a serious qualification of his theoretical views.

A very similar point emerges when we follow Danto not just outside modernism but outside Western painting—for example, in his review of Chinese painting of the past two centuries (23 April 1988). Once again, in an equally impressive essay, Danto ranges across Renaissance pictorial ideals to cubist principles while citing

Vasari and Gombrich to settle finally with the help of his friends—
the curators Caron Smith and Wen Fong and the now-deceased
calligraphy specialist Chiang Yee—on Wang Yüan's 1871 portrait of
the scholar Chao Chih-ch'ien. Danto views this portrait as exhibiting
"the exact manner of a street artist" and goes on to speculate on
how optical resemblance historically came to be prized as high art
in the China of 1871 in the way that the pop artists raised soup-can
labels to salience in the art world of the 1960s. "What is ironic," he
writes, "is that almost simultaneous with the unseating of optical
criteria in the West, those same criteria began to transform standards of pictorial representation in China." But theory as interpretation in the China of the 1870s is surely not at all the same thing as
theory as interpretation in the 1960s. And the very great care and
sensitivity Danto takes in articulating his view of this body of
Chinese painting, especially the dense historical, technical, and
social details he adduces, once again undercut his philosophical
commitments to an overly general and generous construal of the
role of interpretation in discriminating works of art from mere
things.

Consider finally another Danto subject, this time from neither
the European Renaissance tradition nor non-European painting, but
from Danto's own period of predilection, the modernist era. In his
review of the Soho show of the Japanese painter Chuka Kimura,
whose works he says "are among my greatest enthusiasms," Danto
writes of the extraordinary case of paintings that "could not . . . have
been painted by anyone but a Japanese working in France." Tracing
Kimura's first imaginative perception of the colors and landscapes
of France across the paintings of Bernard that Kimura first saw in
Japan in 1941 to his largely silent life in France since 1951, having
never learned the language, Danto stresses the double vision in his
painting, as in the Latin characters of his Japanese signature, from
which neither the Japanese nor the French perception and gesture
can be excluded. Danto sees Kimura as occupying a third position
rather than either of the two major options of Western art—realism
and expressionism—an alternative rather than an intermediate
position. "It is as though he wanted the landscape to *express itself*,
wants there to come to the surface what does not necessarily meet
the eye: a force, a stirring, a shifting and mildness." Yet after
registering this particularly acute perception and formulating it
sympathetically in terms that borrow much from Kimura's Japanese
culture, Danto moves hastily to a generalization. "Landscapes like
Kimura's," he writes, "reveal the visualistic premises of Western
art, which support the conclusion that nature is something to be

seen, that our relationship to it is external, the stance of responders or witnesses, rather than of participants or beings engaged with it." Now this generalization is vague, for we do not know on the face of such an utterance whether Danto endorses those premises or questions them. His later remarks, however, suggest the latter. And so our question arises again in a new guise. How can we square Danto's theoretical views about interpretation in some strong sense making artworks out of mere things with his sensitive critical appreciation of modernist works like Kimura's? Danto of course can always point to the presence of theory, whether in the case of Raphael, or Chao, or Kimura. But on the evidence of his own most recent and perhaps most accomplished critical practice, I do not think he can sustain his vague, overgeneral, and strongly misleading claim that "theory" in art as interpretation always defines those artifacts we call works of art.

In the double context of this admittedly selective but not unrepresentative reading of one distinguished contemporary philosopher of art, of his theoretical pronouncements and his critical practice, I conclude this section with a working hypothesis. A central gap not just in Danto's philosophy of art but in most, if not all, analytic aesthetics today is the as yet insufficiently critical appraisal of how our various understandings of interpretation are continuing to polarize our theorizing about the arts. For Danto's incautious practice of historical interpretation and overreliance on an indiscriminate notion of theory as interpretation arguably betrays an as yet unacknowledged confusion about the tension between historical and systematic understandings of interpretation.

To put such a working hypothesis into sharper perspective, I turn now to a different current within contemporary philosophies of art, where a similar tension between interpretation in theory and practice is on view—the works of Hans-Georg Gadamer.

History, Truth, and Interpretation

Gadamer's major work on aesthetics is *Truth and Method*, a long and widely read work first published in 1960. Since then he has made numerous revisions and additions in subsequent editions.[16]

---

[16](New York, 1985). A new English translation has recently appeared. Critical work on Gadamer such as G. Warnke's *Gadamer: Hermeneutics, Tradition, and Reason* (Stanford, 1987), as contrasted with more expository work like J. Weinsheimer, *Gadamer's Hermeneutics: A Reading of Truth and Method* (New Haven, 1985), is

But despite the richness of this work and the crucial role it assigns to aesthetics in what originally was a sequence of three independent works, Gadamer clearly subordinates questions in the philosophy of art to the number of other issues arising from his larger concerns with the human sciences.[17] Here, however, I focus, just as with Danto, on his more recent writings.

Although he has not published this later work in as comprehensive and systematic a form as the reflections in *Truth and Method*, Gadamer nonetheless has produced an extended analysis of several issues in aesthetics in a series of essays written after the 1960 work and in his 1975 book *The Relevance of the Beautiful*, both published in English in 1986. Moreover, as in Danto's case, Gadamer has also produced a substantial body of criticism not of painting but of poetry, including numerous essays on Friedrich Hölderlin, Goethe, Stefan George, R. M. Rilke, and Paul Celan. These later essays will also be part of my concern here, especially the essays on Celan, which Gadamer published in book form first in 1973 and then in a revised second edition in 1986.[18]

As in Danto's case, I will sketch sympathetically but critically several of the key issues in Gadamer's later work in aesthetics before confronting these themes with some of the philosophical points that arise out of a reading of his interpretive practices. Instead of starting with how the nature of art is to be understood and then considering his account of the history of art, however, I reverse that order to bring out more sharply both the similarities and the differences between Danto and Gadamer. Thus I begin with Gadamer's later readings of modernist art and its situation in a historical interpretation about the history of art, then move to Gadamer's discussions of the nature of art not in terms of theory as

---

still the exception in English, despite the early criticisms of E. D. Hirsch, *Validity in Interpretation* (New Haven, 1969), which drew strongly on German discussions such as Emilio Betti's. Thus interested readers continue to be confronted with strongly exaggerated and uncritical appreciations: "Gadamer's awareness of the way in which the inheritance of the classical world had become interfused with 'the whole history of Christian interiority' makes almost all other writers on aesthetics seem irrelevant by comparison" (Stephan Bann in *Times Literary Supplement*, 20–26 January 1989).

[17]See Gadamer's remarks in his letter to Strauss (1978) and the comment of Robert Bernasconi in his introduction to Gadamer's *The Relevance of the Beautiful* (Cambridge, 1986), xii.

[18]*Wer bin ich und wer bist du?* 2d ed. (Frankfurt, 1986). On Gadamer's first interpretations of Celan see B. Boschenstein, "Die notwendige Unauflöslichkeit," *Zeitwende* 6(1985): 329–44. For some of the complexities, see W. Hamacher and W. Menninghaus, eds., *Paul Celan: Materialien* (Frankfurt, 1988), and Celan's *Gesammelte Werke* (Frankfurt, 1983).

interpretation, but in terms of interpretation, experience, and truth. I conclude by confronting these views with a series of difficulties that arise from Gadamer's interpretative practices in his extended readings of Celan's poetry.

Gadamer shares Danto's conviction that the modernist period, especially with its works in nonobjective painting, atonal music, and pure poetry, appears to mark a radical break with the earlier course of the history of art. Although he nowhere works as extensively as Danto does to provide a comprehensive reading of the history of art in previous epochs, Gadamer nonetheless puts his major emphasis in *Truth and Method* on the break with the classical traditions of art and beauty in the development of aesthetics in the eighteenth century and then, in the later work especially, on an apparent break with the aesthetic tradition of art as representation in the modernist development of nonrepresentational art. The key philosophical figures in both of these histories seem to be the same—Plato, Kant, and Hegel. But Gadamer brings out much more clearly than Danto the importance of the theories of taste in the eighteenth century. Moreover, he stresses the roles of Schiller, Schopenhauer, Dilthey, Nietzsche, and especially Heidegger in his version of this story, while interpreting modernism largely in literary rather than painterly terms.

More specifically, if we focus on the most recent chapter in this story, as we did with Danto, Gadamer reads modernism as a particular attempt at understanding the general challenge of "the contemporaneity of past and present" (Gadamer 1986:46). In particular, the challenge lies in the fact that paradigm cases of literary modernism, at least for Gadamer in the European and German-speaking world, seem to resist our efforts at interpretating them in terms of art as aesthetic representation. Thus, in the case of Mallarmé's "pure poetry"—which, like Rilke and others, Paul Valéry was to champion in his dialogues, poetry, and Cahiers—trying to construe a particular work like *Le cimetière marin* as a work of art, where art is taken in representational terms, only results in incomprehension. For most of the salient properties of such works, whether directly observable in the language of the poem or indirectly observable in the poem's contexts, conventions, and reception, are not addressed properly in strictly representational or aesthetic terms. So interpreting modernist works of art only in aesthetic terms seems to work for neither Danto nor Gadamer.

Unlike Danto, however, Gadamer does not try to find a way out of this incomprehension by appealing to an overly intellectualist and selective reading of modernism in terms of art's essential dependence on theory as interpretation. Rather, Gadamer focuses on the nature of the apparent revolt of modernist artists against the tradition. He argues, across a series of rereadings of both Plato's philosophy of art and Kant's aesthetics, with their difficult tensions among the central notions of nature, reality, art, taste, and genius, that the challenge of the modernist period to our understanding of the history of art is its requirement that we rethink the relations between continuity and change in the modernist interpretation of tradition. He urges especially that we rethink such traditional concepts as imitation, expression, beauty, play, festival, gesture, sign, and symbol (see, for examples, the 1972 lecture "Art as Imitation" and the 1964 essay "Image and Gesture"). For Gadamer, tradition is to be understood not as a set of artistic conventions irretrievably sedimented in a fixed past, but as horizons of a peculiar sort that are still operative in continuous ways in the present. The task is to reinterpret what is meant by "tradition" and, say, a particular "traditional" concept, in the interest of better comprehending the succession of different epochs in the history of art, and especially the modernist era, in more satisfactory terms than those of "revolt" or "break" or "paradigm shifts."

Such a task, Gadamer believes, can be carried through when we come to understand Plato's philosophy of art in more searching and adequate terms than those of beauty as imitation only, and similarly when we view Kant's philosophy of art not so much as an aesthetics of taste or even of genius but as an aesthetics of the sublime. Such a philosophy of art and such an aesthetics incorporate a different understanding of nature than its rivals do. And it is this understanding of nature that opens up for Gadamer a way of viewing the emergence of modernism as continuous with a construal of tradition and innovation that is larger than merely representational in its openness to nonrepresentational, nonobjective artifacts.

If we return to the notion of modern artists as essentially in revolt against an earlier era in the history of art, we can understand in the light of Gadamer's approach that this revolt "has often had as its real target," as Robert Bernasconi writes, "only the aesthetic definition of art developed in the late eighteenth and nineteenth centuries. Once the philosopher is able to show that the aesthetic definition of art is only a limited and distorted conception of art, then the self-understanding of the contemporary artist as someone in revolt against the tradition is itself open to challenge. It is only by way of the past that we have access to the present, and yet it is in the present and by way of what is most new and unforeseeable in it that we discuss the resources of the past."[19]

Characteristically, Gadamer tries to explain such matters in the series of striking reinterpretations of traditional concepts like imitation, representation, and expression that I mentioned above. Throughout, Gadamer is at work on unpacking some of the conceptual complexity of these concepts, a complexity largely forgotten in post-Kantian philosophy of art. The result is Gadamer's repeated claim that understanding the modernist era as a rejection of such traditional concepts, together with a certain idea of tradition itself, is a superficial reading. For when we retrieve the actual historical and conceptual complexities of these notions, we recognize that much modernist art is continuous rather than discontinuous with them. Hence for Gadamer interpreting modernism as a radical discontinuity is at best a premature verdict. Finally, tradition has nothing essential to do with keeping things unchanged. As Gadamer writes, "tradition means transmission rather than conservation. . . . It means learning how to grasp and express the past anew. . . . the constant interaction between our aims in the present and the past to which we still belong" (1986:49).

Now, before we turn briefly from this very general story about continuity and change in the history of art, and especially in the transition to the modernist period, to a consideration of Gadamer's account of the nature of art, I need to underline several difficulties.

One basic difficulty is Gadamer's exaggerated emphasis on the rejection of tradition in the modernist era. He has no problem with showing how modernist artists define their own innovations with respect to the past. But these innovative features in modernist art, particularly with respect to the arts of literature, which Gadamer himself privileges over painting, music, and the other arts, are arguably not to be understood mainly in terms of rejection. Rather, innovation specifically in the literary realm is very often a matter of creative transformation of a heritage of conventions, styles, institutions, and what not that are challenged implicitly or explicitly. This exaggeration has the consequence, I believe, of making too many of Gadamer's historical points depend on the admittedly problematic notion of "tradition" and how it is to be satisfactorily understood. Accordingly, the picture that emerges on this reading of the modernist period lacks adequate qualification. For besides the crucial issue of tradition, other issues—some of which, like

---

[19]Bernasconi 1986: xviii.

representation, Gadamer himself mentions but does not examine so carefully—are also crucial for our understanding of this period.

A related difficulty with this historical account is the insufficient attention paid to the apparent breaks between the classical period and the eighteenth century. On Gadamer's later readings, despite the extraordinary interest and particularity of his account of the eighteenth century materials by themselves in *Truth and Method*, we are to understand the earlier break as being of the same nature, but perhaps of a lesser degree, than the later break with the appearance of modernism. In short, both shifts are to be taken as discontinuities that, in the light of Gadamer's proposals on what "tradition" properly signifies, are in fact apparent only. But Gadamer's own work suggests, to the contrary, that whatever the difficulties with reading the emergence of modernism in terms of a revised interpretation of "tradition," reading the emergence of the aesthetic in the eighteenth century requires more attention to a range of issues that go beyond the "querelle des anciens et modernes." For as Beardsley, Stolnitz, Dickie, Kivy, and other analytic philosophers of art have been at some pains to show, the transformation of a classical theory of beauty into various theories of the aesthetic across the subtle and extended eighteenth-century discussions of taste involved far more than the tension between artistic permanence and artistic change.

These related difficulties arising from Gadamer's general view of the history of the arts in terms of a preoccupation with one crucial issue leave us finally puzzled as to how we can situate Gadamer's perspective with respect to other general readings such as those of a Vasari, a Wölfflin, a Croce, a Panofsky, or a Gombrich, say, in painting or even those of a Taine, a Reinhold, an Auerbach, or a Curtius in literature. Without close attention to the ways Gadamer's historical interpretation connects with his later reflections not just on tradition but on play, festival, symbol, and truth, we cannot make an intelligent appraisal of that narrative. Let us, then, look briefly at these key terms in the later work before turning to the criticism.

Gadamer's major interest in the later work is to reassert the cognitive role of works of art in the modernist era in the face of what seems to be a radical break with previous traditions. Although these essays do not spell out how Gadamer understands "the cognitive" dimension, his earlier extended analyses in *Truth and Method* make it very clear that "the cognitive" is to be taken in some looser sense than the strictly scientific construal that Kant put on knowledge. Thus the cognitive aspect of art is to include both direct and indirect connections with knowledge. The former had to do with Gadamer's main theme of art and truth, while the latter includes some of the themes mentioned earlier, such as art and expression or art and representation. Here we do well to look briefly at three of these subordinate notions—play, festival, and symbol—before sketching Gadamer's reflections on art and truth. It will prove useful to rely mainly on Gadamer's treatment of these issues in *The Relevance of the Beautiful.*[20]

Gadamer thinks that understanding play, partly after the example of Collingwood, as "non-purposive rationality," "free impulse," and "the to and fro of constantly repeated movement...not tied down to any goal" (1986:22–23), provides us with a means of construing the unity of works of art even in those problematic modernist instances where unity is denied.[21] Although Gadamer had treated this theme earlier, his later remarks focus more on trying to fill out his account of play with an eye on the problem cases of modernist art (see especially the 1973 lecture "The Play of Art"). His later notion includes both an anthropological element, which draws on the work of Gehlen, Plessner, and Max Scheler, and a more speculative element that turns on a conceptual tension between immanence and transcendence.

Play is seen as a phenomenon of "excess," as an "immanent transcendence...that flows over into the realm of freely chosen possibilities" (1986:46). What distinguishes the play of art from other kinds of human and animal play is said to be the relation between the excess of play and the self-imposed discipline and order of human creativity, as well as the permanence its anthropological dimension bestows (1986:47). Further, play exhibits a repetitiveness that indicates that what the player intends is the

[20]References are to the English translation, which I have occasionally modified. Other important Gadamer texts, which I have chosen not to consider here, include several key pieces from the encounter with Derrida, "Text and Interpretation" (1981), "Letter to Dallmayer" (1985), "*Destruktion and Destruction*" (1985), and "Hermeneutics and Logocentrism" (1987), reprinted in *Dialogue and Deconstruction*, ed. D. P. Michelfelder and R. E. Palmer (Albany, 1989).

[21]See Stern-Gillet's 1988 discussion, "Review of Gadamer, *The Relevance of the Beautiful*," *British Journal of Aesthetics* 28(1988): 289–90. Gadamer's understanding of play is one-sided. See, for example, M. Watanabe, "Der Begriff 'Spiel' in der japanischen Kultur," *Aesthetics* 1(1983): 51–59, K. Nishimura's two articles, "Eine Phänomenologie des Spielethos," *Revue Internationale de Philosophie Moderne* (Tokyo) 3(1983): 13–23, and "Über den Begriff der Regel—Spiel, Sprache, Gesetz," *Revue Internationale de Philosophie Moderne* (Tokyo) 6(1988): 39–107, and M. I. Spariosu, *Dionysus Reborn: Play and the Aesthetic Dimension in Modern Philosophical and Scientific Discourse* (Ithaca, N.Y., 1989).

activity itself rather than any particular end beyond it. Play also has a communicative dimension because it invites participation in such a way that "the participant belongs to play" (26). And whatever rules play follows are self-prescribed. In this light Gadamer thinks that modern works of art, even in difficult instances such as improvisation, can be viewed as having a unity—the unity of play—that in turn is linked with the work's unity (cf. Gadamer's remarks on unity in his 1965 essay "On the Speechless Image"). "The hermeneutic identity," Gadamer writes, "establishes the unity of the work...and this identity alone constitutes the meaning of the work" (25). Both, however, require, as play does, the constructive activity of the participant, whether as viewer, spectator, interpreter, or whatever.

A further theme Gadamer explores is the notion of art and festival or feast, drawn from his reflections on Attic tragedy and modern drama, Gregorian music and Western polyphony (cf. his 1954 essay "The Festive Character of Theater"). Gadamer's point is that despite the complexities of these arts, with their dense choral order and medieval notations, they succeed not only in displaying a unity in their aspect as play but in creating a unity in their aspect as "festive celebration"—a festival unites everyone" (1986:49). Moreover, Gadamer thinks this celebratory character of art allows for a certain transcendence. "If art shares anything with the festival," he writes, "then it must transcend the limitations of any cultural definition of art, as well as the limitations associated with its privileged cultural status" (50). Relying on the word of Walter Otto and Karl Kerenyi, he also draws attention to the peculiar experiences of community, temporality, discourse, and even silence that follow from the festive character of art as celebration. The most important of these is temporality (58–59). For just as temporal dimension of festival in which a celebration is enacted forces us to distinguish between a time of busy fulfillment and one of boring emptiness, more generally "every work of art imposes its own temporality upon us." (45). The gist of such experiences, Gadamer thinks, is that works of art invite us "to dwell on the work in a specific way.... the essence of our temporal experience of art is in learning how to tarry in this way" (45).

The last of these salient later themes in Gadamer's more recent work is the notion of symbol. Gadamer thinks it is the symbolic dimension of the work of art that both invites participation in art as play and makes possible community in art as festival. The symbol is basically what allows for recognition. More specifically, "the proper function of the symbol and of the symbolic content of the language of art" is to bring about "recognition which elicits the permanent from the transient" (47). The basis of this interpretation of the symbolic is Gadamer's twofold reminder of how the Greeks used the two halves of a broken object as a token or symbol whereby years later a host might recognize a previous guest, and of how every individual, according to the story in *The Symposium*, is only a part or symbol of the whole that is sought in the experience of love. Similarly, art is symbolic in the sense that the experience of "the beautiful in art is the invocation of a potentially whole and holy order of things wherever it may be found" (32).

Gadamer pushes this analogy further to claim that "in any encounter with art, it is not the particular, but rather the totality of the experienceable world, man's ontological place in it, and above all his finitude before that which transcends him, that is brought to experience" (32–33). Part of the sense of that totality is the recognition through the symbolic that the "work" of art is more properly understood as a "creation" that stands before us independent, unique, and irreplaceable. Thus "the symbolic does not simply point toward a meaning, but rather allows that meaning to present itself," since the meaning is already and actually there (34–35). Gadamer thinks of symbolic reference here as distinct from other kinds of reference in embodying what it points to while at the same time "vouchsafing its meaning" (37). The symbolic character of art understood in this way suggests that no purely conceptualist approach can satisfactorily recover the meaning of a work of art. "The essence of the symbolic," Gadamer concludes, "lies precisely in the fact that it is not related to an ultimate meaning that could be recuperated in intellectual terms. The symbol preserves its meaning within itself" (37).

Besides these three characteristics of art as play, festival, and symbol, as well as a number of related themes, Gadamer has increasingly sought to unify his later reflections on art around one predominant issue, the ancient and perennial question of art and truth. The modern period has revived this issue in very close connection with developments in post-Fregean philosophy, with the consequence that the issue of art and truth has become especially critical. For as Richard Bernstein has pointed out, when truth is restricted to the truth of propositions, "then it appears that art has nothing to do with truth," whereas if Heidegger and Gadamer are right that "truth," can be understood primordially as an openness—a revealing, unconcealing, and manifesting event—the question of art as truth today requires philosophical consideration.[22]

In an important essay published in 1971, "On the Contribution of Poetry to the Search for Truth," Gadamer distinguished two hermeneutic aspects of speech and then went on to ask what connections might hold between the second aspect and truth. The distinction is between speech as dialogue, in which individual utterances acquire their significance from the roles they play in the interaction between question and answer (recall Collingwood's "logic" of question and answer), and speech as utterance that subordinates communicative intentions to the display of the utterance's verbal character as language (see Gadamer's 1961 essay "Making Poetry and Interpretation"). Conversation is a good example of the first, and poetry of the second.

Now if we ask what connections hold between the speech of poetry and truth, we need, Gadamer believes, to recall that the Greeks distinguished between the "truth" we tell one another when we say what we mean and the "truth" something manifests when it shows itself to be what it is. Thus we may say that when we speak of "gold" we mean what glitters, but we may observe that "gold" also exhibits itself as what glitters. In the case of poetry Gadamer argues that language has a peculiar autonomy: what is written "stands written," as Lutherans say, in the sense that, just as in the case of the religious pledge and the legal proclamation, "we subordinate ourselves to it and concentrate all our efforts upon it 'as a test'" (109; see Gadamer's 1978 essay "Aesthetic and Religious Experience"). Against this background Gadamer describes a poetic text as a "statement," an *Aussage*, in the literal sense of a "saying-out," which "expresses a claim to completeness and expresses fully what the given state of affairs is" (110). Such fullness is the basis of the poetic text's autonomy, its requiring no other confirmation or witness to what it says. The strongest examples, Gadamer believes, come from lyric poetry, whose final untranslatability testifies to a striking autonomy of both sound and sense (see Gadamer's 1977) essay "Philosophy and Poetry").

The question of art and truth for Gadamer thus comes down to accounting for the peculiar autonomy of poetic uses of language that "summon up what is 'there' so that it is palpably near. The truth of poetry consists in creating a 'hold upon nearness'" (113). This "nearness," Gadamer continues, has to do with the strange

---

[22]R. Bernstein, "Review of Gadamer, *The Relevance of the Beautiful and Other Essays*," *Journal of Aesthetics and Art Criticism* 46(1988): 422.

character things take on when their natural and ineluctable transience is suspended in the transmutations they undergo in artistic
representation. This change affects their temporality. What the
poem speaks of, unlike all other things, does not fade, "for the
poetic word brings the transience of time to a standstill. It too
'stands written,' not as a promise, nor a pledge, but as a saying
where its own presence is in play" (114). And it is this standing
that holds up the truth of what Gadamer takes, after Hegel, to be
the ideal of the human condition, the striving to achieve a being at
home in the world, whose mark is an abiding rather than a fleeting
familiarity and nearness.

For Gadamer, then, the work of art has an essential relation to
truth in the peculiar sense of the truth of things rather than the
truth of propositions. This notion of truth as something about
things derives from Heidegger's view of truth as what "addresses us
in art through the twofold movement of revealing, unconcealing,
and manifesting on the one hand, and concealing and sheltering on
the other... a showing and concealing that belong to our human
finitude" (1986:34; cf. Heidegger 1971:50–72). And the key idea
here is that the work of art calls attention not just to a meaning but
to the fact that human finitude must leave unaddressed a "something
more" about the very facticity of whatever is on exhibit in a work
of art.

These later reflections on art are full of suggestions about how a
more anthropological approach to the role of art in a society and
culture can open us to a peculiar metaphysical dimension in
individual works of art. But they are far from unproblematic.
Without trying to inventory the many problems Gadamer's later
thought raises in different ways for artists, critics, and philosophers
I will underline several major points.

One problem arises from Gadamer's repeated claim in his discussions of art as play and art as festival or feast that all works of art
both exhibit and create a unity. This point is absolutely crucial for
Gadamer's views, since whatever strictures he wants to put on talk
about the "meaning" of a work of art, he insists rightly that such
works are not without meaning. The difficulty lies not in Gadamer's
linking meaning centrally with the identity of a work of art, a
move that is certainly arguable, but in making the identity of the
work depend essentially on that kind of unity a work exhibits as
play. Whatever unity some modernist works of art display—think of
John Cage's music as an example—the unity is surely very tenuous.
Moreover, the unity that other modernist works exhibit—think of

Virginia Woolf's *To The Lighthouse*—is not properly described in terms of play at all. But if we cannot finally construe some works as unified in terms of play or others as unified at all, then on Gadamer's view these works will lack identity and consequently will lack meaning. But this consequence is highly implausible. Such a view must be judged as unacceptable in its present form, whatever its suggestiveness may be for further work.

Another central problem arises from Gadamer's discussion of art as symbol and truth, focusing on his talk about the "truth" of things. Here the difficulty has to do with a double gap in his account. On the one hand, this account is developed in opposition to a solely propositional theory of truth, without any attempt to consider alternative analytic theories of truth that draw their various strengths from talk of coherence and pragmatic considerations. The result is to leave talk about the "truth" of things up in the air without any suitable connections to traditional theories of truth. On the other hand, Gadamer's theory of the "truth" of things relies on a peculiar understanding of "symbolic reference" that once again develops without any discussion of the greatly extended investigations in the analytic work of a Goodman and even in the hermeneutic work of a Ricoeur.

The result is similar in that even sympathetic critics are left without any critical purchase. As Gadamer writes, "both the poetical and *philosophical* types of speech share a common feature: they cannot be 'false'" (1986:139, my emphasis). What, if anything, could count for or against such a putatively nonextensional account of reference and a putatively noncorrespondence theory of truth? But if we cannot specify, even in weak nonfalsificational terms, what counts for or against such views, just how are we to justify any final acceptance of these speculative recommendations? Provisionally then, on the evidence of Gadamer's later views about art, we need to remain open to the suggestiveness of his speculations while looking further in his reflection and especially our own for the kind of sustained detailed analyses that might support such speculation.

Practice, Theory, and Literary Criticism

Besides his very extensive work on interpretation both in the history of philosophy and in hermeneutics, Gadamer has produced a substantial body of criticism. Most of this work has centered on poetry, though he has also discussed theater, painting, and other arts incidentally. Much remains uncollected, despite the appearance in 1977 of his *Poetica*. One work, however, deserves close attention, his extended commentary on Paul Celan's difficult poetic sequence, *Atemkristall* (1965), published first in 1973 under the title *Wer bin ich und wer bist du? Kommentar zu Celan's "Atemkristall"* and then in a much expanded second edition in 1986.[23] Since this work is Gadamer's most sustained recent attempt at interpretation and one to which he has returned repeatedly in the light of his theoretical work on hermeneutics, I shall focus briefly on this work alone. It will be useful to have in hand a brief description of the book before isolating one of its major themes, the nature of interpretation, and examining this theme critically in the practical context of one of Gadamer's readings.

Gadamer's book is much more of an interpretation than a commentary, but it is an "interpretation" in his sense. For its aim is not so much to provide a thorough guide to understanding these difficult poems as to record a particular experience with a poet's language. Thus, in his preface to the first edition Gadamer talks of his attempts to decipher the poems as if they were an almost unreadable message come to us across the ocean in a bottle (Celan's own metaphor). Gadamer claims to have understood a certain meaning in this message, although he thinks that just what sense it makes to talk of "understanding" needs to be spelled out. And he adds, in the afterword, that he has made his own efforts at understanding independent of any reliance on specialized information about the poet's life, his particular interests such as geology, and his particular sources such as the Cabala. Moreover, he has focused his reading on only one part of a longer work, *Atemwende*, although a part first published independently and representative of Celan's mature work before the onset of the late, extremely obscure poems and Celan's suicide in 1970. In short, Gadamer's extended interpretation of Celan's poetry is highly deliberate in its selection, self-imposed limitations, aims, and major thematic emphasis.

In the course of these very short essays on each of Celan's poems in succession, Gadamer touches on a variety of important interpretive concerns. For example, he repeatedly remarks on such methodolog-

[23]References to the second edition are incorporated into the text. Part of the complex background here includes Gadamer's apologetic stance toward Heidegger's connections with Celan and his poetry, connections that Derrida, J. Lacoue-Labarthe, and others continue to annotate. See, for example, G. Steiner's very informed article, "So Much Darkness Dispelled," *Times Literary Supplement*, 10–16 February 1989.

ical issues as genre criticism, the different roles structure plays in lyric poetry, the only relative pertinence of the poet's self-interpretations, the judicious use of secondary literature and source criticism, and especially how variants of the poetry are to be used appropriately. But just as often Gadamer opposes to these concerns of the professional critic a series of hermeneutic themes he wants to promote—a marked need for patience with poetic language and the recourse to etymologies, the insistence on levels of meaning, a heavy reliance on paraphrase, an attentiveness to the structure of the whole book of poems and not just those of individual poems, reminders of the virtues of the "old philological methods," and regular appeals to authority (Heidegger told me this, Szondi thought that, Bollock, Pöggler, Tschizewsky, Milojcic this and that). These hermeneutic themes coalesce around the major topic of hermeneutic interpretation, which Gadamer brings out especially in his afterword to the second edition as well as in his two prefaces.

Gadamer insists that a hermeneutic interpretation of poetry is less a method whereby one tries to explain one thing in terms of something more general than a particular way of acting on the part of someone who is trying to understand another person by listening or by reading his words. (151). Such an approach is directed toward answering how a reader comes to understand both what the poem says and what is said in the poem. The reader is to make legitimate use of as many scholarly tools as prove useful, but these means alone do not suffice to answer the question of what the reader must know. For a "correct interpretation" of a work of art comes down to having a new experience of that work that integrates the interpretation so completely that the "correct interpretation" is effaced (156).

These views turn on the distinction between a reader of, say, Celan's poetry and an interpreter. For Gadamer a reader, however well informed, needs to become an interpreter if the reading of the poetic work is to result in a new experience of the work as language. This experience consists in the interpreter's becoming open not just to the poetic work's essential themes but to what Gadamer wants to call the unique world of each individual poem. (141). In this context interpretations are always unstable and never static, for one interpretation can become better than a previous one both by incorporating new "correct" information and by articulating more fully the uniqueness of the individual poetic world that the language of the poem reveals and conceals as language continues to change within successive speech communities. The basis of interpretation even in this fuller sense, however, is intuition—"all interpretation...presupposes a mature reflective intuition which precedes the question the interpreter puts to the poem" (11). Some considerations, Gadamer is now willing to concede despite his earlier views, can count against such intuitions (matter of fact, for example—see 96). But the primacy of intuition is at root the generalization of what Gadamer calls here "the old hermeneutic principle" of starting from impressions (113). And intuition most basically is directed to the poetic utterance as a response to a question that the interpreter must divine not at the first level of meaning, but at what Gadamer calls the second level of truth (116).

I have already pointed out several difficulties with the primacy of this notion of intuition in Gadamer's construal of interpretive understanding. Now let me underline a more basic difficulty that arises from a closer look at the most striking change in Gadamer's views between the first and second editions of his Celan book, the radical turnabout in his interpretation of Celan's poem "Harnisch-striemen."

Gadamer recounts how he "succumbed to a first impression" on interpreting this hermetic poem that led him to misconstrue its technical terms—*Harnisch*, *Durchstichpunkte*, and *Kluftrose*—as pertaining to medieval armor rather than to geological formations. Reading a Pöggler article, he was "immediately" persuaded, and now he reports that after "having looked for a better interpretation" (142) he "sees more clearly" (95). Before, he "had gone too far" (95); part of his interpretation was forced, and in the light of the geological uses of these terms "it was therefore false to interpret *Durchstichpunkte*, chisel points, as the piercing points in a suit of armor" (96). And in his preface to the second edition Gadamer writes that he redid his interpretation of this poem in its entirety because "new information had brought me to a better comprehension of the poem."

We need not follow the differences between these two interpretations in their details to be able to notice a basic tension here, just as occurs with Danto, between the doctrine of interpretive understanding as Gadamer propounds it theoretically and its substance as he practices it. Theoretically, such understanding is based on a species of intuition of the whole whose nature remains obscure. Such intuition, Gadamer now concedes, is corrigible, but only as the result of a further intuition as to the final pertinence of whatever new comprehension is in view. Practically, however, the role of new factual information is much more important. Here we need to stress not the further use of intuition but the primacy of certain situations and states of affairs. Thus the critical practice, especially the key instance where Gadamer is forced to change his interpretation, puts into relief a basic unsatisfactoriness in the notion of intuition. On the one hand, intuition seems to be the final court of appeal for hermeneutic understanding—those complex but undifferentiated impressions of the whole. Yet in crucial cases where interpretive understanding is acknowledged to be mistaken, final appeal is made to facts of a certain order—what I am calling situations and states of affairs. Yet without a resolution of this tension, how are we to parse the still controversial notion of interpretive understanding and especially its connections with knowledge and truth?

Without trying to address this matter here, I conclude this selective reading of Gadamer's theory of interpretation and interpretive practice by formulating a second working hypothesis. The cardinal and yet very problematic notion of interpretive understanding in much hermeneutic aesthetics depends on an insufficiently critical reading of kinds of indirect knowledge in eighteenth century aesthetics. In particular, Gadamer's notion of interpretive understanding needs to be situated critically in the context of his attempts in *Truth and Method* to retrieve certain construals of indirect knowledge in pre-Kantian philosophy from the strong exclusions brought about by Kant's construal of all knowledge as scientific. But this second hypothesis, just like the first one, now requires that we take a much closer look at a large range of issues. Instead of pursuing these matters further just now, I will use my conclusion to recapitulate my discussion and to formulate more sharply the specific points at issue about interpretation and history.

Conclusion

When we look back over Danto's substantial achievements within the divese currents of contemporary analytic philosophies of art, we may not unfairly summarize his later views on interpretation and history as follows:

1. What marks the difference between mere things and works of art is interpretation; interpretations define works of art.[24]
2. Interpretations are neither classificatory nor explanatory but are

---

[24]Gadamer 1986: xii, 44.

constitutive in that, as functions, interpretations "transform material objects into works of art."[25]

3. Specifically, interpretations are artistic indentifications that "determine which parts and properties of the object in question belong to the work of art into which interpretation transfigures it."[26]

4. The successful results of a surface interpretation's determination of identity become the interpretanda of deep interpretations.[27]

5. Interpretations change and therefore are essentially historical in character.[28]

Now, Heidegger has reflected throughout his long and newly controversial career on the diverse phenomena of art, both in connection with his own guiding question about time as the significance of the being of beings and in connection with the concerns of such practicing art historians as Meyer Shapiro and such literary critics as Emil Staiger.[29] Almost all of this large and disparate work has been carefully studied,[30] but little attention has focused so far on the suggestiveness of Heidegger's later meditations on art in the context of contemporary philosophical reflections like Danto's. Consequently, I will use a strong contrast between Danto and Heidegger to underline two sets of reflections that merit renewed consideration.

In his later work, for example, the "Dialogue on Language" from *On the Way to Language*, Heidegger distinguishes three senses of interpretation.[31] Interpretation is an art of understanding the peculiar status of the religious language of the Bible. More generally, interpretation is the practice of understanding any kind of work, written, visual, or whatever. And still more broadly, or in what Heidegger calls a more "originary sense," interpretation is "the

[25]Gadamer 1986: 39.

[26]Gadamer 1986: 41.

[27]Gadamer 1986: 48, 66.

[28]Gadamer 1986: 110.

[29]See especially the less noticed discussion with Staiger about Mörike's poetry in E. Staiger, *Die Kunst der Interpretation* (Zurich, 1955), 28–42. Derrida of course has drawn fresh attention to the exchange between Heidegger and Shapiro in *La vérité en peinture* (Paris, 1978).

[30]An earlier excellent work situates Heidegger's reflections on art in a larger perspective. See W. Biemel, *Die Bedeutung von Kants Begründung der Ästhetik für die Philosophie der Kunst* (Cologne, 1959), esp. 182–97. More recent work can be found in W. Biemel and F. von Herrmann, eds., *Kunst und Technik* (Frankfurt, 1989), A. Gethmann-Seifert and O. Pöggler, eds., *Heidegger und die praktische Philosophie* (Frankfurt, 1988), and S. Blasche, ed., *Heidegger: Innen- und Aussensichten* (Frankfurt, 1989).

[31](New York, 1971). For the background here see O. Pöggler, *Die Frage nach der Kunst: Von Hegel zu Heidegger* (Freiburg, 1984).

bearing of message and tidings,"[32] understanding something "hermeneutically, that is, with respect to bringing tidings, with respect to preserving a message."[33] This originary sense of interpretation is the most important for Heidegger, and he links it with his notion of nonobjectifying thinking. Thus interpretation is the practice of an understanding that works in such a way as to resist the insinuation of conceptual representation into what calls for interpretation.[34] Finally, such interpretive understanding also relies on a use of the gestural and exhibitory aspects of the experience of language as utterance—think of conversational dialogue—rather than exclusively on the propositional and referential aspects of a concept of language as statement and representation. Thus for Heidegger interpretation is preeminently a meditative response through the use of language as a showing to whatever antecedently calls for interpretation.

This sketch of Heidegger's later notion of interpretation is admittedly partial and requires a good deal more exposition, qualification, and criticism. Nonetheless, it suggests at least four very important issues that contemporary analytic philosophers of art like Danto need to consider seriously if they are to meet the strong objections their own views have raised. First, a more satisfactory understanding of interpretation itself, the suggestion here runs, must be construed as preeminently a response to what calls for interpretation, not as an imposition of an interpretans on the interpretanda; otherwise we succeed in interpreting only what we are looking for. Second, interpretation needs to be pursued with the symbolic resources of communicative discourse, not just with the representational devices of argumentative discourse; otherwise we restrict interpretation unduly to the domain of the sayable. Third, interpretive understanding requires a transformation not of mere things but of thinking itself into a meditative response to what the linguistic practices of showing allow to become manifest, rather than a descriptive, explanatory, constitutive ratiocination; otherwise we come to understand interpretively only what we have already constructed. Finally, a more satisfactory account of interpretive understanding needs to thematize the historicity of interpretation in other than merely Hegelian terms; otherwise the very disparate

[32]Heidegger 1971: 10–11, 29.
[33]Heidegger 1971: 32.
[34]Heidegger 1971: 25. For a distinguished exploration of some of the many problems here, see K. Tsujimura, "Die Scheinhaftigkeit der ästhetischen Scheinlehre," *Revue Internationale de Philosophie Moderne* (Tokyo) 5(1987): 129–43.

phenomena of the modernist era cannot resist their reduction to an intellectualist dogma. Each of these four points of course requires further comment, and I shall be exploring different aspects of each in part 2. For now, however, we should return to the second current in contemporary philosophy of art, this time Gadamer's Continental views rather than Danto's Anglo-American ones, views that already incorporate some of these suggestions and yet, surprisingly, require serious revision.

When we survey Gadamer's contributions within the different streams of contemporary Continental philosophies of art, we may summarize the elements of history, interpretation, and truth in his later work as follows:

1. The essentially historical character of interpretive understanding lies in a dialectic of innovation with tradition in a fusion of horizons.
2. Interpretation involves rethinking both the cardinal notion of tradition and the traditional character of such central notions as expression, representation, and the cognitive.
3. Such a rethinking needs to award a central place to the distinction between language as utterance and language as dialogue.
4. Deploying the dialogue aspect of language in interpretive understanding helps us take account of the further distinction between the truths of language—truth as what we mean—and "the truths of things"—what things make manifest.
5. Interpretive understanding addresses preeminently the truth of things in the sense of trying to respond to the peculiar way things come to abide as a hold on what is near through the suspension that works of art effect in the natural and ineluctable transience of things.

If we restrict ourselves once again to the "Dialogue on Language," we find Heidegger discussing certain limitations on a number of related concerns. Consider the notion of aesthetics. For Heidegger European aesthetics is part of metaphysics. In its Greek origins aesthetics includes the idea that what can be perceived by the senses, the *aistheton*, in the case of a work of art lets the nonsensuous, the *noeton*, shine through.[35] Such a view, however, results in a double transformation: a thing becomes a work of art, and a work of art becomes "an object for our feelings and ideas."[36] The consequence is a basic understanding of aesthetics in the deeply suspect terms of subject-object relations.

Heidegger opposes to this view the need for a transformation of

[35]Heidegger 1971: 14.
[36]Heidegger 1971: 43.

thinking rather than of the thing, a transformation to be effected through a change in our experiences with language as well as in our practices of a nonobjectifying thinking. This transformation is to be understood neither as a denial nor as a destruction but as an overcoming of metaphysics in the sense of "bringing metaphysics back within its limits" through an "original appropriation" of the history of previous thought, whether in the thinking of philosophy or in that of art.[37] In such an appropriation, Heidegger claims, thinking corresponds to the truth of things that wells up and comes forth from concealment. Interpretive understanding aims to respond to such findings in such a way as to preserve whatever their message manifests.[38] In short, for Heidegger interpretation is not only a meditative responsiveness to whatever calls for interpretation; it is more specifically a dynamic and problematic correspondence to and with the truth of things in their concealment and manifestation within the history of being.

Once again, this sketch of a key notion in Heidegger's later work requires much more detail. For our purposes, however, the notions of interpretation and truth already suggest at least four further issues, this time those that contemporary hermeneutic philosophies of art need to reconsider seriously. First, a more satisfactory understanding of interpretation needs to be freshly construed in broader than merely European ethnocentric terms, perhaps with the help of East Asian reflections on different kinds of contingency;[39] otherwise the genuine sense of what it means to overcome metaphysics will be lost in a hermeneutic but still Eurocentric vision. Second, the aims of interpretation need to be rethought not just in terms of a meditation on tradition and horizon but, to use Heidegger's difficult but strongly suggestive phrasings, in those of what shows itself as holding sway in the bearing of things as the truth of things; otherwise interpretive understanding, however nonobjective in its practices, runs the risk of missing the forest for the trees. Third, the truth of things must be caught up meditatively in an originary appropriation of the history of thinking that would allow some play for the gaps in European philosophy between, for one example,

[37]Heidegger 1971: 20. Cf. D. Kolb, The Critique of Pure Modernity: Hegel, Heidegger, and After (Chicago, 1987).
[38]Heidegger 1971: 32–33, 52. For a fuller discussion of Heidegger's views, especially in connection with some of Rorty's concerns and those of Wittgenstein, see P. McCormick, Heidegger and the Language of the World (Ottawa, 1976).
[39]Cf. a work by one of the thinkers in the background of Heidegger's "A Dialogue on Language," S. Kuki, Le problème de la contingence (Tokyo, 1966).

33

nothingness and emptiness, perhaps along Nishida's and Nishitani's example;[40] otherwise talk of the truth of things will continue to elude the well-disposed efforts at understanding of those even from other Western traditions such as Marxism. And finally, thinking meditatively about the truth of things in and through the practices of a fresh construal of interpretive and historical discourse as more than merely argumentative requires a renewed effort at working rigorously but imaginatively within the limits of metaphysics in order to exhibit those limits; without this affirmation of the neo-Kantian site of our own historical thinking, we cannot preserve the lessons offered for European thinking about the truths of art still obscured for us in the as yet great and still unthought Western tradition of negative thinking.

These eight issues, four that arise from a strong contrast between Danto and Heidegger and four others that arise from a comparison between Gadamer and Heidegger, are of course clearly related. Before testing the satisfactoriness of some of these formulations and investing others in part 2, however, we need to step back to explore in part 1 the different readings of the eighteenth century that underlie them, the seminal period for understanding contemporary philosophies of art. With both the contrastive readings of that century in mind as well as the rich elements for an alternative reading of that century in terms of the realist backgrounds of modern aesthetics, I will return to these issues in another guise in the Conclusion. There with the help of a second contemporary contrast, between Habermas and Putnam on modernity and rationality, the initial questions we have opened up for discussion can be rearticulated in larger and I hope more perspicuous terms.

[40]See especially K. Nishida, *Intelligibility and the Philosophy of Nothingness: Three Philosophical Essays* (Tokyo, 1958), and K. Nishitani, *Religion and Nothingness* (Berkeley, 1982).

PART I

REREADING
EIGHTEENTH-CENTURY
AESTHETICS

IN PART ONE I try to win some critical distance on the strengths and weaknesses of the initial positions we have looked at. The controlling insight behind the move to history is the realization that any contemporary formulation of the problematic relations between theory and practice is necessarily conditioned by the preoccupations of its own times. To what degree these contemporary concerns deform the subject of investigation is difficult to discern from any standpoint. But, so the guiding assumption here would have it, these difficulties may be attenuated if one is able to relativize contemporary formulations by scrutinizing their variations in another historical period.

Not just any historical period will do, however. Although comparisons between contemporary and noncontemporary formulations, whether medieval, Renaissance, or whatever, are of some use, the more careful investigation of such comparisons in the light of eighteenth-century aesthetics is especially pertinent. For in this period, as most historians of the subject agree, what we today call aesthetics assumed its most important characterization. Thus not only the questions we habitually raise about artworks but also in large (but not complete) measure the very way we ask such questions and pose such problems flows directly from the mainstream of eighteenth-century aesthetics. Hence in part 1 I try to develop some critical distance by examining the relevant contexts in which these issues were first explored in the modern period.

Investigating the early modern history of aesthetics as the most appropriate historical setting for questions about theory and practice in contemporary philosophies of art discloses, as we will see, a curious ambiguity on a rather large scale. For there are at least two readings of such a history. However many other readings might be examined—Marxist interpretations, for example (one of which I examine in the Conclusion)—I have chosen to scrutinize only two. And these I have called, somewhat artificially, an analytic and a hermeneutic reading.

In what follows, we must keep in mind three central features of the analytic reading. To begin with, the analytic reading claims that modern aesthetics derives from, roughly speaking, the conjunction of two theories, the theory of art and the theory of beauty. Whereas the first is transmitted essentially unchanged from the ancient period through the medieval period and the Renaissance into the eighteenth century and on to us, the theory of beauty is largely though not entirely transformed in the eighteenth century into a theory of the aesthetic. However tenuous these claims may finally be, and however suspect the distinction between these theories is, at least one consequence for our own concerns is clear. Questions about theory and practice in this reading fall largely within the second, not the first, of these theories, because only the second is centrally occupied with judgment. The difficulty is that this theory is precisely the one that undergoes transformation. Thus questions concerning the objects of some judgments about artworks are now construed as concerning the objects of *aesthetic* judgments.

This cardinal point is reinforced by two further points in the analytic reading, for this reading claims to discern in the development of eighteenth-century aesthetics the emergence of a doctrine about taste that became part of the transformation of the theory of beauty into a theory of the aesthetic. But central to this doctrine is a hesitation about just how aesthetic judgments are to be understood, whether in terms of a peculiar species of objects or of a peculiar species of perception. Finally, the analytic reading concludes that a subjectivization of aesthetics took place in the eighteenth century but views this process in essentially a positive light as making possible, among other things, the emergence of romanticism. Here too the key remains the concept of the aesthetic.

One major consequence of the analytic reading for our concerns is that, whatever other perspectives artworks may need for their understanding, they seem to require examination in some way or other in terms of the aesthetic. But the concept of the aesthetic, for all the vagaries of its uses during this period, remains in the end obscure. Yet this reading of the seminal period in modern aesthetics is not without alternatives, as I go on to show by detailing a number of features in a hermeneutic reading. Again, three of the many features here should be kept in mind from the start.

The hermeneutic reading, we will find, attempts to retrieve several of the largely overlooked conceptual resources of what it calls the humanistic tradition in modern thought. The stress on all of these features—cultivation, common sense, tact, and so on—is without exception on indirect kinds of knowledge. Each humanistic concept selected for discussion is finally taken to be relevant because of its resources when placed in a cognitive context. The result for our purposes is that the difficult relations between theory and practice, if knowable at all, can be known only indirectly. But this thesis only adds to the already considerable difficulties facing us at the outset with the uncertain status of the aesthetic.

Another feature of the hermeneutic reading is its polemical character, for the hermeneutic account is largely engaged in a dialogue with a silent interlocutor, a rather shaky understanding of the scientific tradition that arises in the seventeenth century. The point here is that certain cardinal concepts in the humanistic tradition are understood as providing not so much antagonistic as complementary resources for understanding the relations between theory and practice. The controlling insight of course is that the very way we ask questions of artworks today is, in as yet unthematized ways, determined by the insufficiently criticized paradigms of simple understanding. We will take from this polemical side of the hermeneutic account the caution to build a certain epistemological wariness into whatever reading of theory and practice and the aesthetic we settle for in exploring an alternative view. Our account, that is, should not be couched in terms of an uncritical terminological commitment to only one kind of thinking—the kind that has won the blessings of science.

Finally, the hermeneutic reading, we will see, concurs with the analytic reading in construing eighteenth-century aesthetics as the subjectivization of aesthetics. Here, however, the reasons are different, and of course the appreciation turns out in the end to be a negative one. Aesthetics, that is, is subjectivized in the sense that artworks are no longer understood as sufficiently autonomous artifacts imitating or representing the spatiotemporal world but are seen as above all emblems of consciousness. So whatever the relations between theory and practice may be, their nature is to be understood largely on the model of mental entities rather than nonmental ones.

This concurrence between the two readings about the subjectivization of aesthetics leads again to a convergence on the concept of the aesthetic. Here, however, the stress on the aesthetic is on a species of indirect knowledge—on a kind of understanding rather than on a species of mental object that appears as the object of taste. But the lack of clarity about both leads one ineluctably to the respective interpretations of Kant to the attempt to appreciate the partiality of those interpretations by rereading Kant's work for oneself. However difficult rereading Kant's aesthetics remains, it is not difficult to note very early on the selective character of both analytic and hermeneutic accounts of Kant. Most important, it will turn out, is seeing that what each account leaves out becomes the basis for an emerging realist interpretation of Kant in the much-neglected work of Bernard Bolzano. And Bolzano's criticism of Kant will set the stage for a series of further explorations of the still overlooked realist backgrounds of modern aesthetics. We will go on to explore these in part two as a means of trying to take sufficiently critical measure of the manifold notion of the aesthetic.

Chapter One

Early Modern Aesthetics:
An Analytic Reading

In the eighteenth century's determined effort . . . to understand and explain our experience of art, we can trace two fundamental lines of interest, labeled on the one hand "taste," and on the other "beauty, the sublime, etc."

—Monroe Beardsley

Different theories of beauty as taste exhibit a pattern: two mental faculties, a perceptible object of a specific sort, a mental product which results from the reaction to the perception of a specific kind of object, and finally judgments of taste.

—George Dickie

WHAT FOLLOWS is a sketch of the analytic reading of the history of early modern aesthetics. I do not of course mean to imply that there is any such thing as "*the* analytic reading" of this history or that my version is the only plausible one. Rather, I use this phrase to facilitate later comparisons with a hermeneutic reading of the history of early modern aesthetics, which will be taken up in the next chapter. I also use this phrase to indicate a more particular reading of early modern aesthetics than a merely empiricist one.

Another problem is that my phrase cannot refer to any precise blueprint of what an *analytic* reading of the history of early modern aesthetics should look like. To be sure, some analytic philosophers have done historical work on this period;[1] indeed, one

---

[1]Notably J. Stolnitz. See his influential articles "On the Significance of Lord Shaftesbury in Modern Aesthetic Theory," *Philosophical Quarterly* 2(1961): 97–113;

has written a history of aesthetics.[2] But calling this varied work "an analytic history" does more to link these authors to the stream of current philosophy they identify with than to suggest any clear set of methods and procedures. This is evident when we contrast the richness of detail and variety of treatment this work exhibits[3] with the lack of any satisfying account of just what would define "an analytic reading" of anything whatever.[4]

The work I have in mind includes Gilbert and Kuhn's history, Hipple's book (1957), Beardsley's history, Stolnitz's articles (1960–63), various articles in the *Encyclopedia of Philosophy* (1967), and Dickie's earlier books (1971, 1974).[5] I have relied mainly on Dickie

---

"On the Origins of 'Aesthetic Disinterestedness,'" *Journal of Aesthetics and Art Criticism* 20(1961): 131–43; "'Beauty': Some Stages in the History of an Idea," *Journal of the History of Ideas* 22(1961): 185–201; and "Locke and the Categories of Value in Eighteenth-Century British Aesthetic Theory," *Philosophy* 38(1963): 40–51. See also his book *Aesthetics and the Philosophy of Art Criticism* (Boston, 1960).

[2]M. C. Beardsley, *Aesthetics from Classical Greece to the Present: A Short History* (New York, 1966). See also his major thematic works, *Aesthetics: Problems in the Philosophy of Criticism* (New York, 1958); *The Possibility of Criticism* (Detroit, 1970); his selected essays, *The Aesthetic Point of View*, ed. M. J. Wren and D. M. Callen (Ithaca, 1982); and two editorial collections, *Literature and Aesthetics* (Indianapolis, 1968), and, with H. Schuller, *Aesthetic Inquiry* (Belmont, Calif., 1967). On Beardsley's work see, among many sketches, M. Hancher, "Poems versus Trees: The Aesthetics of M. Beardsley," *Journal of Aesthetics and Art Criticism* 31(1972): 181–89, and especially the articles in the Beardsley Festschrift *Text, Literature, and Aesthetics*, ed. L. Aagaard-Mogensen (Amsterdam, 1986).

[3]Compare, for example, Beardsley's and Stolnitz's work with the earlier history by K. Gilbert and H. Kuhn, *A History of Aesthetics* (New York, 1939), and contrast these with a much earlier work in a different tradition, B. Bosanquet, *A History of Aesthetic* (London, 1892). Beardsley's interests, however, are far wider than Stolnitz's. Cf., for example, Beardsley's article on a still-neglected figure from what I will call later the realist tradition, "Experience and Value in Moritz Geiger's Aesthetics," in *Text, Literature, and Aesthetics*, ed. L. Aagaard-Mogensen and L. de Vos, 13–37 (Amsterdam, 1986).

[4]For further characterization of "an analytic philosophy," see R. Rorty's early outstanding essay, "Metaphilosophical Difficulties of Linguistic Philosophy," in *The Linguistic Turn*, ed. R. Rorty (Chicago, 1969), and H. Putnam's views in *Realism and Reason* (Cambridge, 1983), 179–81. A very different "analytic" approach to aesthetics is on view in A. Savile, *Aesthetic Reconstructions: The Seminal Writings of Lessing, Kant, and Schiller* (London, 1986).

[5]W. J. Hipple, *The Beautiful, the Sublime, and the Picturesque in Eighteenth-Century British Aesthetic Theory* (Carbondale, Ill., 1957); G. Dickie, *Aesthetics: An Introduction* (New York, 1971); G. Dickie, *Art and the Aesthetics: An Institutional Analysis* (Ithaca, 1974). See also G. Aschenbrenner, *The Concepts of Criticism* (The Hague, 1975); and G. Aschenbrenner and R. Sclafani, eds., *Essays in Aesthetics* (New York, 1977). A somewhat different approach can be seen in F. E. Sparshott, *The Theory of the Arts* (Princeton, 1982), and his earlier works *The Structure of Aesthetics* (Toronto, 1963) and *The Concept of Criticism* (New York, 1967). Also note the different orientation in D. Townsend, "Archibald Alison: Aesthetic Experience and Emotion," *British Journal of Aesthetics* 28(1988): 132–40.

because he had taken great care to work through much of the previous writing in a critical way. He has, moreover, usually articulated his ideas first in articles, so that their presentation in book form has already benefited from criticism. Further, questions that his views raise remain near the center of much discussion today. Even though Dickie's influence predominates here, however, what emerges is a composite picture of the central elements of one type of reading of the history of early modern aesthetics. So what I propose as an analytic history is not to be attributed to any one of these thinkers in particular.[6] Similar points will apply to the presentation of an opposed view, the hermeneutic account. I should state plainly that though each of these "readings" is a construct, greater stress has been put on making each as representative as possible than on addressing the not always convincing contrast between them.

An Analytic Reading

The analytic view focuses on the problems central to aesthetics today with the help of a fundamental assumption—that aesthetic problems, as we now understand them, are the consequences of two historical sets of considerations. The first is roughly describable as the theory of art; the second might be called the theory of beauty.[7] In both cases, to do this basic assumption justice, we must construe the term "theory" rather broadly. For what is meant is not so much a unified, consistent, and coherent set of propositions about either art or beauty as a large and not totally inclusive division of the problems of aesthetics between two somewhat overlapping areas.

What is it, according to this assumption, about the character of each of these two theories that separates them? The analytic account stresses a peculiar asymmetry in the historical development of these theories. The theory of *art*, it claims, though subject to detailed and varied formulations, particularly in the Greek

[6]Similarly, no explicit or implicit political orientation is to be assumed for this reading, even though the individual thinkers whose work it is based on have political views. I owe this point to M. Marcussen. For Dickie's more recent works see his *The Art Circle* (New York, 1984) and *Evaluating Art* (Philadelphia, 1988).

[7]See Dickie 1971: 1–3. It is important at the outset to realize how selective a reading this is. Consider, for contrast, the views of T. Kambayashi, "Über das Malerische oder Pittoreske," *Aesthetics* 3(1988): 59–75.

period and in the nineteenth century, has changed rather little compared with the development of the theory of *beauty*. The latter, by contrast, not only has been marked by the usual vagaries that such long-standing concerns undergo, it has suffered definite and extensive changes, particularly in the eighteenth century.[8]

These changes are of four general types. First, in the eighteenth century the theory of beauty comprises for the first time analyses of concepts other than that of the beautiful. Thus we find detailed investigations of notions like the picturesque, the sublime, and the grotesque. Second, eighteenth-century accounts of beauty for the first time begin to investigate not just the concept of beauty but the experience of beauty. Third, as the eighteenth century progresses the concept of beauty gradually cedes its central position in the theory of beauty to the concept of the aesthetic. The "aesthetic," moreover, is construed broadly enough to subsume other concepts such as those already mentioned—including the concept of beauty itself. Finally, this new and encompassing center of the theory of beauty is often analyzed in terms of "disinterestedness." In short, the theory of beauty is no longer a theory of beauty at all, but has become a distinct theory of the aesthetic. Thus the changes affecting the theory of beauty in the eighteenth century are thoroughgoing enough to transform that theory into something quite different.[9]

On the analytic reading, the consequences of this transformation are clear. After the eighteenth century the problems of aesthetics are no longer to be understood in terms of the classical pair of theories. The theory of art remains largely what it had been, but the new theory of the aesthetic now replaces the classical theory of beauty. Although each member of this new pair remains closely related, like the members of the old pair they are distinct theories. For if the theory of the aesthetic can arguably be subsumed under the theory of art, most theories of art cannot be subsumed under the theory of the aesthetic.[10]

---

[8]Dickie 1971: 3–22. See also R. G. Saesselin, "Critical Reflections on the Origins of Modern Aesthetics," *British Journal of Aesthetics* 4(1964): 7–21. To measure just some of the distance philosophers have come since the eighteenth century in their reflections on beauty, compare and contrast the very different views in G. Sircello, *A New Theory of Beauty* (Princeton, 1975), and M. Mothersill, *Beauty Restored* (Oxford, 1984).

[9]For earlier background studies that add nuance to this account see R. Wellek, *A History of Modern Criticism*, vols. 1 and 2 (New Haven, 1955); J. W. H. Atkins, *English Historical Criticism: Seventeenth and Eighteenth Centuries* (New York, 1951); W. J. Bate, *From Classic to Romantic: Premises of Taste in Eighteenth Century England* (Cambridge, Mass., 1946); M. H. Abrams, *The Mirror and the Lamp* (Oxford, 1953); and F. B. Chambers, *The History of Taste* (New York, 1932).

[10]Dickie 1971: 43–46. The qualification is necessary. As an anonymous referee for

The analytic reading then proceeds to relate the dominant contemporary Anglo-American views on aesthetics to this new pair of theories. Thus, on the one hand, aesthetics as a critical examination of the aesthetic attitude, say in Stolnitz's work (1960), is related to the eighteenth-century tradition of the theory of the aesthetic. On the other hand, aesthetics as metacriticism, say in Beardsley's work (1958), is related to the classical and eighteenth-century tradition of the theory of art.[11]

In a preliminary and general way, then, we may note that an analytic reading of the problems of aesthetics discriminates two important and opposed contemporary views. Each is understood as developing from the eighteenth century. But while the theory of art is broadly construed as consistent with its own classical tradition, the theory of the aesthetic is considered discontinuous with its classical tradition, that of the theory of beauty, which was transformed in the eighteenth century. The underlying assumption of such a reading is evident: contemporary understanding of the problems of aesthetics is determined by the conjunction of two theories, one classical and the other eighteenth century.[12]

When presented in summary form, such an account may raise many critical questions, both historical and philosophical. Such a reading, to say the least, is not uncontroversial. Before looking at this reading critically, however, it will prove useful to examine its elements in more detail.

Early Modern Theorists

To pursue these details, I now set aside the theory of art and concentrate on the analytic reading of the aesthetic. For even though the details of the analytic account of Plato and Aristotle

Cornell writes, "If 'expression' is a direct product of eighteenth-century developments of 'aesthetic experience' (and I think it is—see Alison, for example), then any theory of art which relies on expression is subsumed under any theory of the aesthetic."

[11]For references, see notes 1 and 2. I agree with my referee's criticism of Dickie. "What Dickie overlooks in discussing metacriticism is the link provided by Hume who sees that the aesthetic presents major, perhaps insuperable, critical problems, and...initiates the meta-critical move."

[12]Such a view is of course schematic. We need to remember throughout that contemporary aesthetics is marked not only by analytic and hermeneutic strains but, at times, by a bewildering number of other theories as well—Crocean views or Marxist views, semiotics, and phenomenology, to mention just a few. See Beardsley's helpful discussion (1966: 317–98). For an excellent example of a different tradition, see S. Morawski, *Inquiries into the Fundamentals of Aesthetics* (Cambridge, Mass., 1974).

raise many questions in their own right,[13] the cardinal claim this reading turns on concerns the development of a theory of the aesthetic in the eighteenth century from the classical theory of beauty. If we are indeed to do justice to this reading, I think we must above all be attentive to how this particular claim is articulated. Once those details are clearly in view, judging this account on the coherence of its central claim will be sufficient. Whatever contributions and errors the presentation of the other theory involves might then be conveniently left for later examination.

Let us turn to the analytic account of the theory of the aesthetic. A convenient way of grasping its details is to center our attention, however summarily and selectively, on six thinkers: Baumgarten, Shaftesbury, Hutcheson, Burke, Hume, and Kant. The stress will be on those elements that the analytic view finds especially important— for instance, the structure of the theory of beauty as taste. Hence I make no attempt to present a complete or even well-rounded account of all the elements in the aesthetics of these thinkers. Moreover, because of its complexity and achievement, it is well to reserve Kant's work for fuller description in a chapter of its own; Kant figures in this chapter in only a summary way.

The analytic reading begins with Baumgarten's work, especially the *Reflections of Poetry* (1735) and the *Aesthetics* (1750). Starting with Baumgarten not only focuses on the first use of the term "aesthetics," it also sets up a useful though quite schematic contrast between rationalist views of beauty and empiricist views.[14] The contrast turns on a fundamental disagreement about our knowledge of what we call beautiful. For the rationalist tradition, which Baumgarten represents, the beautiful is an object of two faculties, the intellectual and the sensory. For the empiricist tradition, which the eighteenth-century British philosophers epitomize, the beautiful is an object of only one faculty, the sensory. This dispute is easier to formulate than to resolve because the central terms—object and faculty—are difficult to define in a way acceptable to both sides.[15] This problem will carry over into Kant's work.

[13]See Dickie 1971: 32–38 and Beardsley 1966: 30–89.

[14]Compare E. Cassirer, *The Philosophy of the Enlightenment* (Princeton, 1951). Contemporary work in aesthetics, I believe, has yet to draw the consequences of the very strong contrast between Cassirer's views and those of either the analytic or the hermeneutic reading.

[15]For some earlier background here, see C. Davis, "Ut pictura poesis," *Modern Language Review* 30(1935): 159–69; and S. Kjørup, *Baumgarten* (Copenhagen, 1971). See also E. Bergmann, *Die Begründung der deutschen Ästhetik durch A. G. Baumgarten und G. F. Meier* (Leipzig, 1911); B. Poppe, *Baumgarten* (Münster, 1907); and A. Riemzam, *Die Ästhetik A. G. Baumgartens* (Halle, 1928).

Besides this first contrast between two views about the ontological status of the beautiful, the analytic reading urges a second contrast between two views about how the beautiful is perceived. For Baumgarten and the rationalists, what is beautiful is perceived by an internal sense similar in nature to other internal senses such as memory and imagination. For the British empiricists the nature of the inner sense of beauty is controversial. Some deny that there is one; some hold that an inner sense of beauty exists but that it is not distinct; others argue that a distinct inner sense of beauty exists but that it is a composite sense; and still others believe this distinct inner sense is simple, not composite. Most, however, hold some version of the view that there is an inner sense of beauty, which has beauty as its object and which might be called the faculty of taste. Baumgarten thus sets the stage for two philosophical disputes, one about the perception of the beautiful and the other about the nature of the beautiful.[16]

The analytic reading of Baumgarten, besides stressing the origins of these two contemporary problems, is also concerned to link Baumgarten's aesthetics very clearly to the ideas of Descartes. Thus Baumgarten's two major works on aesthetics are consistently viewed in the light of Cartesian interests. Although none of the Cartesian philosophers devoted important reflections to aesthetics, Baumgarten tried to define aesthetics itself in the context of Cartesian theories of both method and truth. Beardsley, for example, when dealing with Baumgarten, exhibits this interpretation clearly. "The object of logic, Baumgarten said, is to investigate the kind of perfection proper to thought...; the object of aesthetics (exactly coordinate with logic) is to investigate the kind of perfection proper to perception.... Aesthetics is 'the science of sensory cognition' (*scientia cognitionis sensitive*)."[17] Baumgarten, on this reading, hoped to demonstrate a basic distinction between scientific discourse (clear and distinct) and poetic discourse (not so clear, and confused). The distinction depended on Leibniz, who had given more precision to Descartes's original discussion of clarity and distinctness by introducing degrees of clarity—for example, the distinction between intensive clarity and extensive clarity. Despite the uncertainties of Baumgarten's achievement, the analytic reading emphasized the concept of "sensate discourse," a discourse that involves confused rather than clear ideas, as a basic contribution to the development of aesthetic theory. Baumgarten is read,

---

[16]Dickie 1971: 9–12.
[17]Beardsley 1966: 157, referring to Baumgarten's *Reflections*, sections 115 and 116 and quoting *Aesthetica*, section 1.

then, not only as the starting point of modern aesthetics; his achievement is understood as a development of Cartesian issues. In this sense, aesthetics is a Cartesian discipline.[18]

By contrast, Shaftesbury's views are taken as transitional. Reading the *Characteristics of Men, Manners, Opinions and Times* (2d ed., 1714), for example, involves accenting both Neoplatonic elements (beauty as an intellectual good) and empirical strains (beauty as the object of the faculty of taste).[19] Besides this mixture, three features of Shaftesbury's theory are especially important in the analytic reading.

First, if the beautiful is the object of the faculty of taste, then that faculty has two functions, not just one. Taste operates morally when practical judgments are made about human behavior, and it operates aesthetically when practical judgments are made about putatively beautiful things. This double function introduces a series of puzzles through analogies between aesthetics and moral philosophy that even Kant's philosophical genius will not be able to resolve completely.

Second, Shaftesbury wants to distinguish the beautiful from the sublime.[20] This distinction, a tentative one at the outset of the eighteenth century, leads later to the new concept of the aesthetic. In Shaftesbury, though, the concept of the aesthetic is not yet in evidence. Rather, beauty is still construed as a genus of which the sublime is a species. Kant, of course, will divide his analysis of aesthetic judgment between the analytic of the beautiful and the analytic of the sublime.

Finally, Shaftesbury introduces the central notion of "disinterestedness." This notion derives from a parallel between selfless motivation in moral behavior as a condition for merit and disinterested contemplation in the aesthetic realm as a condition for beauty. The move is from disinterested, unselfish motives to disinterested contemplation (with no desire to possess). In distinguishing different

[18]Beardsley 1966: 156–59. See for contrast the very different view of H. Matsuo, "Baumgartens Begriff der 'extensiven Klarheit' und die Rezeption desselben durch Kant," *Journal of the Faculty of Letters* (Tokyo) 10(1985): 51–67.

[19]See R. Cohen, ed., *Studies in Eighteenth-Century British Art and Aesthetics* (Berkeley, 1985); D. Townsend, "Shaftesbury's Aesthetic Theory," *Journal of Aesthetics and Art Criticism* 4(1982): 205–13; J. A. Dussinger, "The Lovely System of Lord Shaftesbury," *Journal of the History of Ideas* 42(1981): 151–58; R. L. Brett, *The Third Earl of Shaftesbury: A Study in Eighteenth-Century Literary Theory* (London, 1951); and Stolnitz's Shaftesbury article cited in note 1.

[20]Some of the background here is available in S. H. Monk, *The Sublime: A Study of Critical Theories in Eighteenth Century England* (New York, 1935), and T. Weiskel, *The Romantic Sublime* (Baltimore, 1976).

functions of the faculty of taste and in stressing disinterestedness, therefore, Shaftesbury introduces a basic comparison between moral objects and their perception and aesthetic objects and their perception.[21]

A central passage in this analytic reading of Shaftesbury nicely illustrates the particular themes that account wants to emphasize. Here is an example: "Is there then, said he, a natural beauty of figures? And is there not as natural a one of actions? No sooner the eye opens upon figures, the ear upon sounds, then straight the beautiful results and grace and harmony are known and acknowledged. No sooner our actions viewed, no sooner the human affections and passions discerned ... than straight an inward eye distinguishes, and sees the fair and shapely, the amiable and admirable, apart from the deformed, the foul, the odious, or the despicable?"[22]

Several ideas in this passage are taken to represent Shaftesbury's basic concerns. The tenor of the passage is related to the influence of the Cambridge Platonists, particularly the stress on a reciprocity between the harmony in the created world and the harmony in virtuous character. The "inward eye" here is both the "moral sense" when actions are at issue and the "sense of beauty" when either artifacts or natural objects are concerned. Moreover, Shaftesbury's interest in counting more than just the beautiful as part of the proper sphere of aesthetics comes out in the sequence of contrasts at the end of this passage. And finally Shaftesbury's discussion of "natural beauty," even though the Neoplatonic background is familiar, is singled out as something new in early modern aesthetics. Many of the other issues Shaftesbury discusses in his voluminous though unsystematic work are subordinated in the analytic reading to the particular features illustrated in this kind of excerpt.[23]

Hutcheson, in, for example, his *Inquiry into the Original of Our Idea of Beauty and Virtue* (1725), focuses clearly on the empirical and shows no trace of the transcendental views that were still evident in Shaftesbury. Nevertheless, the connection between aes-

---

[21]Dickie 1971: 12–16; 1974: 59–60.

[22]*Characteristics*, ed. J. M. Robertson, 2 vols. (London, 1900), 2:137; cited in Beardsley 1966: 179. On the difficult textual matters here see R. B. Wolf, "The First Two Editions of Shaftesbury's *Characteristics*," *Publications of the Bibliographical Society of America*, 78(1984): 349–54. The first critical edition appears as vols. 2 and 3 in the new *Complete Works*, ed. W. Benda et al. (Stuttgart, 1989–90); sixteen volumes are projected.

[23]Beardsley 1966: 178–83; the phrase appears on p. 182.

thetics and morals, as Hutcheson's title indicates, is retained.[24] Four points are underlined in the analytic reading.

First, "beauty" is not a thing but a word; this word refers to an idea; and the idea itself arises from our contact with particular kinds of external objects.

Second, those external objects that stimulate the idea that we refer to with the word "beauty" have at least one common property: they are all characterized by uniformity in variety. This property, Hutcheson specifies, causes the idea of beauty to arise; it does not cause beauty itself.

Third, the idea of beauty arises in the sense of beauty, which is an internal sense. Unlike external senses, internal senses such as this are reactive rather than perceptual; they depend for their object on the product of another sense.

Finally, any judgment that an idea of beauty leads to has at least two features. All judgments of beauty are disinterested because the reactions of the inner sense of beauty are not mediated by thought; moreover, they are objective in the sense that they are necessarily related to innate human faculties. Hutcheson's views here are particularly important in that they focus on the nature of aesthetic judgment and thereby set the stage for Hume and Kant.[25]

Although Baumgarten's work is taken, on the analytic reading, as the starting point for early modern aesthetics, the first major contribution to philosophical aesthetics is nonetheless attributed to Hutcheson. This attribution surely is motivated in part by the influence on Hutcheson's work of Locke's theories of sensation.[26] We find Hutcheson searching for those features of objects that cause the idea of beauty to arise. And much of this effort is spent on the issue of whether those features are primary or secondary qualities of the beautiful objects in question, just as Burke would

---

[24]See P. Kivy, *The Seventh Sense: A Study of F. Hutcheson's Aesthetics and Its Influence in Eighteenth Century Britain* (New York, 1976); C. Korsmeyer, "Relativism and Hutcheson's Aesthetic Theory," *Journal of the History of Ideas* 36(1975): 319–30. One idea not developed in this context is the important distinction, as Hutcheson understands the matter, between beauty itself and the idea of beauty.

[25]Dickie 1971: 16–17; 1974: 60–61. See especially P. Kivy, *The Seventh Sense: A Study of Hutcheson's Aesthetics* (New York, 1976), and T. D. Campbell, "Francis Hutcheson: 'Father' of the Scottish Enlightenment," in *The Origins and Nature of the Scottish Enlightenment*, ed. R. H. Campell and A. Skinner, 162–82 (Edinburgh, 1982).

[26]But compare C. D. Thorpe, "Addison and Hutcheson on the Imagination," *ELH: A Journal of English Literary History* 2(1935): 215–34, and E. Michael, "Francis Hutcheson on Aesthetic Perception and Aesthetic Pleasure," *British Journal of Aesthetics* 24(1984): 241–55.

later worry a similar distinction between primary and secondary pleasures. This is just the kind of issue that interests the analytic reader. "Cold, heat, sweetness, bitterness are sensations in the mind," Beardsley summarizes, "which do not correspond to the primary qualities of external objects; and so is beauty, except that, since beauty and harmony are excited by sensations involving 'figure and time,' which are primary qualities, beauty and harmony have a closer resemblance or at least relation to external objects than cold and sweetness."[27]

Similar tributes to the empirical tradition are to be noticed in the care the analytic reading takes to link Hutcheson's work with that of other major figures in the same tradition—for example, Hobbes, whose work Hutcheson criticizes in his *Reflections on Laughter* (1725),[28] and Hume, on whom Hutcheson is understood to have had a "most fruitful influence." When taken together, and especially when focused on Locke, these attempts to situate Hutcheson's work with particular regard for a single tradition amount to a distinctive feature of the analytic reading. Few would contest the links such a reading points out, but at the same time few would fail to notice that the role of such connections in the interpretation of Hutcheson's aesthetics is subject to much critical disagreement.[29]

Burke's seminal work, *A Philosophical Inquiry into the Origin of Our Ideas of the Sublime and the Beautiful* (see the enlarged second edition of 1759), returns to the conceptual problem of distinguishing clearly between the beautiful and the sublime.[30] The basic claim is simply this: the beautiful is not the sublime. Beauty, for Burke, yields pleasure, whereas the sublime yields delight. The first, pleasure in beauty, is positive, namely love; the second, pleasure in the sublime, is only relative, namely delight. The pleasure taken in the sublime is only relative and not positive because it results from the removal of actual pain or the removal of the anticipation of pain. This analysis leads Burke to characterize the beautiful as that quality or those qualities that cause the

[27]Beardsley 1966: 186.

[28]C. D. Thorpe, *The Aesthetic Theory of T. Hobbes*. See also C. Korsmeyer, "The Two Beauties: A Perspective on Hutcheson's Aesthetics," *Journal of Aesthetics and Art Criticism* 38(1979): 145–51.

[29]Beardsley 1966: 185–88. Another perspective can be found in D. F. Newton's "Hutcheson's Moral Realism," in his *David Hume: Common Sense Moralist, Sceptical Metaphysician*, 55–93 (Princeton, 1982).

[30]A helpful article is D. Wecter's "Burke's Theory of Words, Images and Emotions," *PMLA* 55(1940): 167–81. The standard bibliography is C. I. Ganday and P. J. Stanlis, *Edmund Burke: A Bibliography of Secondary Studies to 1982* (New York, 1983).

passion of love or some similar passion. These qualities include smallness, smoothness, clarity, and so on. They are to be contrasted with such qualities of the sublime as largeness, roughness, and obscureness.

Besides this account of the beautiful, the analytic reading finds two other elements of Burke's work particularly important. The first is that Burke holds for no special sense of the beautiful and hence rejects any multiplication of entities. The beautiful is to be based upon pleasure and pain, not upon a theory of special internal senses. And the second is that Burke holds for no necessary connection between the beautiful and disinterestedness. Something may be beautiful even if we desire to possess it.

All three of these elements—the distinction between the beautiful and the sublime, the analysis of pleasure, and the analysis of disinterestedness—move eighteenth-century aesthetics deeper into empiricism.[31]

Further features of the analytic reading of Burke become clear when we notice the particular aspects of his work that elicit praise. Very often these aspects turn out to be just those qualities of philosophical style that are most admired and emulated in contemporary analytic philosophy. Here are some extracts from Beardsley's assessment. "Because of its ingenuity and originality of argument as well as its fresh and vigorous style this work became very popular."[32] Or, more striking, this description of Burke's procedure: "Burke hopes to explain the aesthetic feelings without postulating any autonomous faculty of taste or inner sense. Burke's method of investigation is quite clearly marked out; he is one writer who knows what he is doing. Consider the sublime. There is, first, a certain emotion to be identified and analyzed. . . . the second step is to inquire into those sensible qualities of things that make objects terrible . . . and here Burke is very specific."[33] Economy, clarity, identification, analysis, specificity—these are some of the features that attract the analytic reader. Where Burke is incoherent or where his argument goes astray or where some features of the tradition are passed over in silence—these features go unnoticed and hence elicit no commentary. In short, Burke's many contributions to modern

[31]Dickie 1971: 17–19; 1974: 61–62. Some of the key contexts to Burke's aesthetics can be surveyed easily in C. B. Macpherson's *Burke* (New York, 1980).

[32]Beardsley 1966: 193.

[33]Beardsley 1966: 194–95. Contrast these views with those of K. E. Lokke, "The Role of Sublimity in the Development of Modernist Aesthetics," *Journal of Aesthetics and Art Criticism* 40(1982): 421–29.

aesthetics are taken to include not just his substantial reflections on certain themes but also a style of reflection and argumentative discussion that this analytic reading endorses and thus urges by indirection on its own readers.

Burke's emphasis on the empirical is continued in several of Hume's works, not only in sections of the *Treatise on Human Nature* (1739–40), but especially in the essays first included in *Four Dissertations* (1757) and later republished along with others as *Essays and Treatises on Several Subjects*. In "Of the Standard of Taste" the elements of Hume's views are clearly visible. This essay does not attempt to develop the theory of taste beyond Burke's reflections, but Hume does attempt to explicate the claim that the theory of taste is best understood in terms of an empirical examination of human nature.[34]

Hume refutes one view and asserts another. He refutes the skeptical view that questions of taste cannot be disputed by showing that such an attitude would entail the absurd consequence that we are not in fact able to evaluate one work as better than another. Hume proceeds to assert that the only foundation for any rules that could govern our capacity to evaluate one work as better than another is experience as he contrasts it with intuition.

As for the nature of such rules, Hume first categorizes them and then describes them. These rules are known, Hume says, as the standards of taste. Such standards can be formulated in principle on the basis of an empirical survey of what pleases all true judges (not all persons) in all times and places. Even if rather easy to imagine, such a survey is of course difficult to carry out. Hume stresses the difficulties of meeting the conditions for an adequate survey. Since some persons are pleased because of fashion or envy or ignorance and not just because of what is beautiful, not all cases of persons' being pleased are to count as evidence in such a hypothetical survey. The conditions to be met are serenity, recollection, attentiveness, and so on, so that inferior instances of being pleased

[34]For earlier background, see M. Kellich, "The Argument against the Association of Ideas in Eighteenth Century Aesthetics," *Modern Language Quarterly* 15(1954): 125–36; M. Kellich, "The Associationist Criticism of F. Hutcheson and D. Hume," *Studies in Philosophy* 43(1946): 644–67; and more recently, P. Jones, "Hume's Aesthetics Reassessed," *Philosophical Quarterly* 26(1976): 48–62; R. Cohen, "The Rationale of Hume's Literary Inquiries," *Southwestern Journal of Philosophy* 7(1976): 97–115; and C. W. Korsmeyer, "Hume and the Foundations of Taste," *Journal of Aesthetics and Art Criticism* 35(1976): 201–15; Newton's 1982 book cited in note 29; and for contrast, J. Loughran's "Hutcheson: Benevolence as Moral Motivation," *History of Philosophy Quarterly* 3(1986): 241–55.

may be properly discriminated from genuine ones. These conditions, however, are applied not to experience but only to true judges.

Finally, Hume holds that the beautiful is a property not of objects but of certain qualities in objects. But he does not explain either what those qualities and the necessarily associated feelings are or what kind of necessity is involved.[35]

Once again, the analytic reading presents certain recurring features. The treatment of Hume, however, unlike that of Hutcheson and Burke, stresses neither the empiricist background nor even the importance of philosophical style. Rather, emphasis is put on the unity of Hume's scattered reflections on aesthetics, from the remarks in the *Treatise* of 1739–40 to the revision of book 3 of the *Treatise* in 1751 and the title *Inquiry concerning the Principle of Morals* up to the essay "Of the Standard of Taste" of 1757, construed as "his chief work in aesthetics." One of the issues behind this concern for unity should be underlined here, namely Hume's interest, like that of Burke, to whom he owed much, in what Beardsley calls "an intersubjectively valid standard of taste" in Burke's case and in Hume's "the epistemological problems about critical judgment."[36] Here is Beardsley's revealing summary: "Hume has, then, the concept of a Qualified Observer, in terms of which critical disputes are resolvable within limits, since some judgments can be disqualified or overruled on various grounds—insensitivity, inattention, prejudice, inexperience. Hume's system thus has a non-relativist basis: 'the general principles of taste are uniform in human nature.'[37] Yet there is room for a good deal of explainable variability, since different works of art will appeal to different temperaments or at different stages of life. Hence there is residual range of unsolvable disagreements."[38] What distinguishes the analytic reading here is the insistence on Hume's aesthetics as, in central ways, a criteriology—in short, more an epistemological than a moral inquiry. Both questions will occupy Kant at some length. Before we turn to Kant, however, a summary of the main ideas culled so far from the analytic reading of eighteenth-century aesthetics may be helpful.

This account, I have noted, begins with the contrast between two

---

[35]Dickie 1971: 23–25; 1974: 62–63. For a different view see T. Cohen's articles on Hume and P. Kivy, "Hume's Neighbour's Wife," *British Journal of Aesthetics* 23(1983): 195–208.

[36]The phrases are from Beardsley 1966: 189, 193, and 188 respectively.

[37]Beardsley cites the *Essays*, ed. Elledge, 2:824.

[38]Beardsley 1966: 191.

traditions in order to highlight the kinds of approaches that only one of these traditions adopts. Thus, from the outset the basic questions are assumed to be those that both traditions treat, questions about the nature of a putative set of objects, about the ways such objects are perceived, about the nature of the ideas we entertain of such objects, and about the feelings we experience in entertaining such ideas. The analytic reading then discerns a movement against rationalistic responses to these questions, through the ambiguity of a so-called transitional theory, and into increasingly scanty analyses of both what the beautiful is and the nature of our judgments about beautiful things. Finally, the reading centers on where the criteria for such judgments about the beautiful are to be found, while leaving aside the more partisan struggles for different versions of a theory of taste.

Kant, of course, takes up the question of the nature of aesthetic judgments. Despite its relative obscurity, his work is so persuasive that after Kant the beautiful is no longer construed as the object of a special faculty. Rather, something is beautiful because it is the object of a particular way consciousness is active. What is beautiful no longer is an object in the world perceived by a faculty but is whatever becomes in fact the object of aesthetic consciousness. In the course of the eighteenth century, then, what is beautiful gradually moves away from its connections with a concept of taste toward a relation to aesthetic consciousness.

Kant

Both the richness and the obscurities of Kant's manifold treatment of the beautiful in his *Critique of Judgment* (1790, 1793, 1799) are notorious. Here we are concerned only with those features of that treatment that have found a continuous and central place in the analytic reading of the history of early modern aesthetics.[39] Without exception, these features cluster around Kant's

---

[39]For references to the relevant material on Kant see chapter 4. Several general accounts, however, should be noted here. See especially Paul Guyer's two books, *Kant and the Claims of Taste* (Cambridge, 1982) and *Kant and the Claims of Knowledge* (Cambridge, 1987). See also the useful articles in *Essays in Kant's Aesthetics*, ed. T. Cohen and P. Guyer (Chicago, 1982). A. Hofstadter, "Kant's Aesthetic Revolution," *Journal of Religious Ethics* 3(1975): 171–91; F. O'Farell, "Problems of Kant's Aesthetics," *Gregorianum* 57(1976): 409–58; M. R. Neville, "Kant's Characterization of Aesthetic Experience," *Journal of Aesthetics and Art Criticism* 33(1974): 193–202; S. Kemal, "Systematic Ideas in Aesthetics: Presentation and Expression in Kant's Aesthetics," *British Journal of Aesthetics* 15(1975): 144–58.

account of the nature of aesthetic judgment. Unlike Burke and Hume, however, Kant is not mainly concerned with the empirical bases for our judgments of what is beautiful or even with the empirical bases for the criteria of such judgments. Rather, he chooses to investigate the a priori bases of only those judgments about what is beautiful that are both universal and necessary.[40]

All aesthetic judgments for Kant, the analytic reading goes, are subjective in that they have as their objects some property of the subject. This feature is pleasure. But some aesthetic judgments, Kant continues, are not only subjective but also both universal and necessary. These judgments Kant calls pure aesthetic judgments. All judgments concerned with beauty are for Kant pure aesthetic judgments. An example might be, "This painting is beautiful." Kant's account of these pure aesthetic judgments may be conveniently summarized as follows: "A judgment of beauty is a disinterested, universal, and necessary judgment concerning the pleasure which everyone ought to derive from the experience of form."[41] Each of these attributes is awarded some description.

Judgments of beauty are disinterested on this reading in the sense that they bear no necessary relation to the existence of what is judged, even though the persons making such judgments do have such a relation. But if judgments of beauty are disinterested in the sense just described, then they are also universal. For such disinterested pleasure, on the analytic account, "must derive from what is common to all mankind and not from interests which are peculiar to some persons only."[42] Judgments of beauty are also necessary in the sense that those making such judgments demand that everyone should agree with them even if they do not, since the judgment may derive from something common to all persons and not just to

---

[40]Some background material here is F. Will, *Intelligible Beauty in Aesthetic Thought from Winckelmann to V. Cousin* (Tübingen, 1958); H. Blocker, "Kant's Theory of the Relation of Imagination and Understanding in Aesthetics Judgments of Taste," *British Journal of Aesthetics* 5(1965): 37–45; and especially H. W. Cassirer, *A Commentary on Kant's "Critique of Judgment"* (London, 1938). Notice that Kant is also concerned with the empirical bases of aesthetic judgments, but the view here is not mainly concerned with them. Consider a referee's comment: Why wouldn't Kant be concerned with the empirical bases of our judgments? If the Third Critique is a retrospective attempt to provide a ground for the first two critiques—i.e. if neither pure nor practical reason can operate until given grounds in perceptual judgments, then it is just the empirical basis for our judgments which the Third Critique is about. That this leads to an a priori, transcendental analysis is the result of skeptical problems raised by the likes of Hume; it does not challenge the initial empiricism. That is why the *Critique of Judgment* turns out to be about aesthetics."
[41]Dickie 1971: 27.
[42]Dickie 1971: 27.

whoever makes the judgment. Yet no general rules about taste can be derived, because judgments of beauty are singular. Finally, what evokes the experience of beauty when judgments of beauty are made is the subject's recognition in the artwork not of purpose but of the form of purpose. In brief, this reading finds four key elements in Kant's analysis of the judgments of beauty—disinterestedness, universality, necessity, and the form of purpose.

Besides the judgment of beauty, a second less central feature of Kant's aesthetics that engages the attention of the analytic reader is his transformation of the faculty of taste into the harmonious cooperation of other faculties. This perspective is of interest because it tries to follow Burke's lead of doing away with the multiplication of faculties. A persuasive summary of this feature in Kant's *Critique of Judgment* goes like this: "When a person is aware of a certain kind of object which is devoid of interest and which is represented apart from concepts, the cognitive faculties (common to all men) can engage in 'free play.' This harmony of the cognitive faculties produces the disinterested pleasure characteristic of beauty. Thus for Kant, the apparatus of taste is the cognitive faculties' functioning in a particular way."[43]

This summary, we should note, characteristically places emphasis on the role of disinterested pleasure without examining, at least in the historical accounts, the nature of such pleasure. A second point also needs underlining, and that is the nature of the "certain kind of object" the person is aware of. The analytic reading carefully distinguishes Kant's view of this object from that of the British empiricists. For Kant the object of judgments of taste—namely, the form of purpose—does not exist independent of the experiencing subject as it does for the empiricists. Rather, the form of purpose can exist only because of the structure of cognition in the knowing subject. In this sense Kant's account of the object of judgments of taste is more subjective than the otherwise parallel account of the empiricists. We might formulate this point more concisely as a résumé of the analytic reading of Kant—Kant's analyses of the object of judgments about what is beautiful complete the subjectivization of the theory of beauty that began in the early eighteenth century.[44]

If these two features of Kant's aesthetics—the doctrine of aesthetic judgment and the transformation of the faculty of taste—are

---

[43]Dickie 1974: 70.
[44]Dickie 1971: 26–32; 1974: 69–75.

central to the analytic reading, what other features require at least some notice?

When we look more closely at the description of Kant's aesthetics as it is presented in, say, Beardsley's historical account, we note a division that already parallels the structure of Kant's own exposition in the *Critique of Judgment*. Thus, after describing the quality, quantity, relation, and modality of the judgment of taste, the analytic account takes up the exposition of the sublime in its various kinds (the mathematical and the dynamic) and effects. A shift is then made to accommodate the difficult doctrine of the transcendental deduction of pure aesthetic judgments, which is followed by a summary of the quite diverse materials found in the last sections of the Analytic, and finally a brief treatment of the Dialectic is appended. In short, the sequence of Kant's own exposition is carefully followed.[45]

Three features of this reading need underlining. To begin with, logical matters are stressed throughout. Here is an example:

There is an important logical difference between judgments of beauty and sublimity. The judgment of beauty claims a close and necessary connection between the object and disinterested aesthetic pleasure— that anyone who properly perceives the object will necessarily feel that pleasure. The judgment of sublimity claims a conditional or potential connection, which still has an indirect necessity. It is a necessary truth that if an object can be used by one rational being to evoke a feeling of the grandeur of reason or of man's moral destiny, it can be freely used by all who properly prepare themselves (see section 29). It will not necessarily be so used by all. In the case of beauty, there is, then, a double aspect to Kant's argument: he must first reveal by analysis, what is involved in the meaning of the object of beauty; then he must go on to prove its a priori necessity.[46]

This emphasis on logical concerns is also characteristic of most of the monographic literature on Kant in the analytic tradition.

A second feature is the relatively little space given to the concluding sections of the critique, especially the classification of the arts and the idea of genius. These topics are not totally ignored in the analytic view, which indeed is aware of the role such notions will later play in the development of romantic aesthetics. But when compared with the treatment of aesthetic judgments of taste, these

---

[45]Beardsley 1966: 210–25.
[46]Beardsley 1966: 221.

issues are merely noticed and not awarded anything like the proportionate treatment their importance seems to justify.

A third feature is the similar neglect of the Dialectic. Once again we need to note that the Dialectic is not overlooked but slighted. And the slight suggests here, as in the case of the concluding sections of Kant's Analytic, not so much a lack of comprehension as a lack of interest. In both these cases, then, we have some indication of the lesser role these features are awarded in an analytic reading. Some conclusions will be drawn from this lack of proportion in chapter 3.

We might note in conclusion that these three features of the analytic reading of Kant are secondary in the sense that Kant's aesthetics is viewed centrally in terms of judgments. Such a focus accommodates the epistemological features we already saw stressed in Hume as well as the emphasis on the empiricist tradition noted earlier. We need go no further there. (See, however, appendix 1.)

Beauty as Taste

If these are the central elements in the analytic reading of the history of early modern aesthetics, taking the subjectivization of the theory of beauty as a general movement of this history, can a pattern be discerned in the different theories of beauty as taste?

The analytic reading does claim to discern such a pattern, consisting of five elements: "two mental faculties, a perceptible object of a specific sort, a mental product which results from the reaction to the perception of a specific kind of object, and finally judgments of taste."[47] The presentation of each of these elements needs summarizing.

Perception in the theory of taste is understood as an external sense, a faculty that gives us access to the external world. The work of this external faculty is complemented by the work of the internal faculty of taste, which is oriented to specific kinds of objects in the external world and not to all sensations indiscriminately. The faculty of taste differs from that of perception not only because it is oriented to different kinds of objects, but also because its orientation is reactive rather than cognitive. In this sense the operation of taste is necessarily dependent on that of perception,

[47]Dickie 1974: 55.

since taste reacts to what perception has antecedently presented.

Besides these two faculties and the peculiar nature of the object of taste, the theory of taste includes two final elements, the product of taste and the judgment of taste. The first is discussed under various headings, but the most central concept here is surely pleasure. The faculty of taste, so this controversial view goes, produces pleasure. Finally, the experience of pleasure may take the form of a judgment of taste. This kind of judgment is complicated, as Kant shows, for such judgments refer both to that part of the world that functions as an external stimulus and to the mind, specifically to the pleasure aroused in the mind by the external stimulus. These five distinctions make up the general theory of taste discerned by the analytic reading in the work of eighteenth-century philosophers.

In conclusion, we need to remind ourselves of the highly selective character of such a reading. Not only are a great many theorists overlooked (French and Italian especially), with a consequent overemphasis on the British and German contributions, but much of what is specific to each of the figures treated is left to one side. But at least some if not all of the deficiencies in this analytic reading are perhaps to be understood as a product of the attempt to do something more than write another history of early modern aesthetics. For clearly the emphasis in this account falls squarely on the interpretation of the *movement* of this history—the announcement, succession, interplay, counterpoint, recapitulation, and fresh starts—rather than on the full contents of each element involved. And the movement of early modern aesthetics is taken finally to be uniform: early modern aesthetics is the historical era in which the theory of beauty is transformed into the theory of the aesthetic. Before trying to come to critical grips with such a thesis, we need to achieve some critical distance. I turn next to a different reading of early modern aesthetics—a hermeneutic reading.

Appendix 1: Equilibrium and Semblance

Several points should be added with regard to Kant's relationship with Schiller. On the analytic view, Schiller's reflections in such works as *Letters on the Aesthetic Education of Man* (1793–95) are only transitional. They mark the gap between the end

of a theory of taste and the beginning of a theory of the aesthetic.[48]
Two elements of Schiller's views are particularly important. The
first is his notion of the aesthetic state as one of equilibrium
between opposed forces. The nature of these forces and just what
equilibrium means here are not detailed: the beautiful results from
this opposition; it is enjoyed in the aesthetic state of equilibrium.
The second feature is Schiller's construal of the object of aesthetic
appreciation as appearance in the Kantian sense of "phenomena."
In this sense the pleasures of aesthetic appreciation are pleasures in
what the structuring activity of the mind has itself produced—
namely, appearance or what Schiller calls semblance. What differ-
entiates aesthetic appearance from all others is the disinterested
attitude we adopt toward it. These two aspects of Schiller's theory
are finally taken up into a metaphysics of the will by Schopenhauer.[49]

The analytic reading of Schiller is in some respects surprisingly
nonschematic.[50] Some attempt is made to respond to the many
elements that Schiller brought together in this great work. Thus a
sensitivity is evident in this treatment to the role of Fichte's
pedagogical and political texts as well as to Goethe's reflections on
metaphysics in shaping Schiller's views. There is even an unusual
openness to less easily formulated parts of Schiller's achievement.
Some of this flexibility can be seen in this passage from Beardsley:

> In this work [the *Letters*]—so rich in ideas despite its brevity, and so
> full of the humane spirit, the concern for man and for men, that
> breathes through all his works—Schiller asked a question that no one
> had put so profoundly since Plato: what is the ultimate role of art in
> human life and culture? To give his answer, he brought together his
> own Kantian conception of the cognitive faculties, his deep reflections
> on the history of culture and civilization, and his strong sense of
> living in a time of cultural crisis, for which a constructive resolution
> was needed.[51]

---

[48]See E. Schaper, "Friedrich Schiller: Adventure of a Kantian," *British Journal of
Aesthetics* 4(1964): 348–62; K. Hamburger, "Schillers ästhetisches Denken," epi-
logue to F. Schiller, *Über die ästhetische Erziehung des Menschen* (Stuttgart, 1975),
131–50; G. Baumecker, *Schillers Schönheitslehre* (Heidelberg, 1937); W. Böhm,
Schillers "Briefe über die ästhetische Erziehung des Menschen" (Halle, 1927); E.
Kühnemann, *Kants und Schillers Begründung der Ästhetik* (Munich, 1895); S. S.
Kerry, *Schiller's Writings on Aesthetics* (Manchester, 1961).
[49]Dickie 1974: 72–74.
[50]Beardsley 1966: 225–30.
[51]Beardsley 1966: 225.

The eloquence here is curiously unexpected in the context of a discussion of a German theorist much less central to the general concern of analytic philosophy than, say, a Hume. And the rhetoric itself might be taken by some as an indication of some sensitivity to a wider range of interests than has been at the center of the analytic reading of early modern aesthetics.

But this is an idiosyncrasy at the edge of the analytic reading. At the center remains the grand theme of the subjectivization of aesthetics prepared by Kant, explicated by Schiller, and finally achieved by Schopenhauer[52]—a controversial ending, as we shall see.

[52]See B. Magee, *The Philosophy of Schopenhauer* (Oxford, 1983); P. Gardener, *Schopenhauer* (Baltimore, 1963); F. Copleston, *Arthur Schopenhauer: Philosopher of Pessimism* (London, 1946); and J. S. Adams, *The Aesthetics of Pessimism* (Philadelphia, 1940). A convenient new edition of Schopenhauer's works is A. Hübscher et al., eds., *A. Schopenhauer: Werke in zehn Bänden*, Züricher Ausgabe (Zurich, 1977). See Dickie 1974: 74–77.

Chapter Two

Early Modern Aesthetics: A Hermeneutic Reading

Art is in its essence an origin: a distinctive way in which truth comes into being, that is, becomes historical.

—Martin Heidegger

The experience of the work of art always fundamentally surpasses any subjective horizon of interpretation.

—Hans-Georg Gadamer

I NOW EXAMINE a different reading of the history of early modern aesthetics, a hermeneutic reading.[1] There is of course no such thing as "*the* hermeneutic account." I use the phrase loosely, to refer to *a* hermeneutic account,[2] the one presented here. Moreover, the elements of the hermeneutic account I am concerned with have not been proposed by different philosophers as a hermeneutic history as such. The philosophers I have in mind have not attempted

[1] On the senses of the much abused term "hermeneutic," see A. Diemer, "Die Trias Beschreiben, Erklären und Verstehen," in *Der Theorien- und Methodenpluralismus in den Wissenschaften*, ed. A. Diemer (Darmstadt, 1971); R. E. Palmer, *Hermeneutics: Interpretation Theory in Schleiermacher, Dilthey, Heidegger and Gadamer* (Evanston, Ill., 1969), cited hereafter as *Hermeneutics*; and T. McCarthy, "On Misunderstanding 'Understanding,'" *Theory and Decision* 3(1973): 351–69.

[2] On the history of hermeneutics see especially W. F. Jaeger, "Studien zur Frühgeschichte der Hermeneutik," *Archiv für Begriffsgeschichte* 17(1974): 35–84; J. A. Coulter, *The Literary Microcosm: Theories of Interpretation of the Later Neoplatonists* (Leiden, 1976); H. Jonas, *Gnosis und spätantiker Geist*, 2 vols. (Göttingen, 1934, 1954); H. de Lubac, *Exégèse médiéval: Les quatre sens de l'écriture*, 4 vols. (Paris, 1959–64); W. Bartuschat, "Zum Problem der Auslegung bei Leibniz," in *Hermeneutik und Dialektik*, ed. R. Bubner et al., vol. 2 (Tübingen, 1970), cited hereafter as *HD*; J. Wach, *Das Verstehen: Grundzüge einer Geschichte der hermeneutischen Theorien im 19. Jahrhundert*, 3 vols. (Tübingen, 1926–29).

to present something so grandiose as a distinctive history of early modern aesthetics understandable only in terms of a contemporary philosophical school. Nonetheless, much of this work is oriented in a distinctive way by questions different from those formulated inside the opposed tradition. This definite orientation is sufficient justification to speak in general terms of a hermeneutic account rather than of just one philosopher's individual historical work.[3]

The work I have in mind throughout this chapter stretches from Schleiermacher's hermeneutics, through Dilthey's attempts to construct a critique of historical reason, into Heidegger's formulation of a hermeneutic phenomenology and the more recent work of Lang and Jauss.[4] The major figure, however, is clearly Gadamer, who, somewhat like Beardsley and Dickie, has worked through the previous material in the course of producing his own substantial body of work. Although much other material is available for closer analysis, for reasons of economy I shall rely almost exclusively on the revised and expanded edition of Gadamer's magisterial book *Wahrheit und Methode*.[5] Occasionally some reference to Gadamer's other work will be made, especially to the volumes of his *Kleine Schriften*, now included in the ten-volume *Collected Works*.[6] In short, in what follows the phrase "the hermeneutic reading" refers to the central elements in Gadamer's account, but since most though not all of these elements are drawn from the other thinkers mentioned, I have thought it inappropriate to speak too narrowly of "Gadamer's account."

Here too, as in the previous chapter, I have taken care to get the

[3]For summary accounts, see G. Ebeling, "Hermeneutik," *Religion in Geschichte und Gegenwart*, 3d ed., vol. 3 (Tübingen, 1959); H.-G. Gadamer, "Hermeneutik," in *Wörterbuch der philosophischen Begriffe*, vol. 3 (Stuttgart, 1974); H.-G. Gadamer, "Hermeneutik," in *Contemporary Philosophy: A Survey*, ed. R. Klibansky 360–72 (Florence, 1969); and K. O. Apel, "Das Verstehen: Eine Problemgeschichte als Begriffsgeschichte," *Archiv für Begriffsgeschichte* 1(1955): 74–91.

[4]Hence the earlier history of hermeneutics till the eighteenth century, as detailed in most of the work cited above in note 2, is not taken into account in my use of the phrase "hermeneutic reading." For the period I am concerned with, Palmer's and Wach's works are useful general overviews. A convenient collection of texts is in H.-G. Gadamer and G. Boehm, *Seminar: Philosophische Hermeneutik* (Frankfurt, 1976). An important historical work by one of the main figures is W. Dilthey's *Die Entstehung der Hermeneutik* in his *Gesammelte Schriften*, vol. 5 (Göttingen, 1924). The larger context is very well discussed in D. Sobrevilla, *Repensando... Filosofía, historia y arte en el pensamiento alemán* (Lima, 1986).

[5]2d ed. (Tübingen, 1965), cited hereafter as *WM*. For a list of reviews see that edition, xiii.

[6](Tübingen, 1967–77). A bibliography of Gadamer's work to 1971 can be found in *Kleine Schriften*, vol. 3 (Tübingen, 1972), 261–71. Later bibliographies are found in his *Gesammelte Schriften*, 10 vols. (Tübingen, 1985).

elements in this reading right, even though the contrast I wish to engineer must consequently work more roughly. And again, the reading presented here, even though largely representative of Gadamer's views, should not be ascribed to Gadamer as such. Rather, my concern has been to construct a parallel to the one presented in the first chapter,[7] largely with the help of extensive secondary materials drawn from Continental discussions rather than from more recent accounts in English.

A question might arise at this point about whether the hermeneutic reading is really concerned with aesthetic issues at all, and if so whether dealing with these issues dialectically by contrasting them with the analytic reading makes good enough sense. It is true that hermeneutics is generally concerned with providing a detailed and revisionary account of what makes up the structure of understanding, especially the understanding of normative texts, whether religious, judicial, artistic, or whatever. The main if not the only approach, however, that Gadamer as well as Jauss takes to this theme is through a reading of both the history of aesthetics and particular works in aesthetics. Just as Heidegger attempts to overcome what he takes to be the major metaphysical tradition in Western thought, so too Gadamer tries to "overcome" the history of aesthetics—what he calls its progressive subjectivization. The result is mixed; but an essential part of the hermeneutic project is not just to provide a clearer view of understanding in general, but in particular to reappraise our understanding of artworks and their historical situation in the recurring tension between innovation and tradition. So I think hermeneutics *is* centrally concerned with aesthetics.

Further, bringing out the philosophical interest of Continental hermeneutic approaches to aesthetics should involve, I think, contrasting these views with the much more widely known analytic views. The approach I adopt has all the advantages of calling detailed attention to the hermeneutic views in their own right— the usual approach—plus the additional value of illuminating those ideas from a more familiar perspective. More essential, however, is

[7]For a general bibliography on hermeneutics since Schleiermacher, see N. Henrichs, *Bibliographie der Hermeneutik und ihrer Anwendungsbereiche seit Schleiermacher* (Düsseldorf, 1968). Also useful is the two-part bibliographical article of T. Seebohm, "The Problem of Hermeneutics in Recent Anglo-American Literature," *Philosophy and Rhetoric* 10(1977): 180–99, 263–76. For nonphilosophical hermeneutics, see the many references in the bibliography in A. Diemer, *Elementarkurs Philosophie: Hermeneutik* (Düsseldorf, 1977).

the chance such an approach offers of showing up corresponding gaps and weaknesses in the analytic perspective itself. I call this approach a "dialectic" one, then, because it uses each of two positions to critically illumine the other while refusing for now the opportunity of combining the two, in the interest of providing a subsequent, independent, and more satisfactory view later on. Although both perspectives do contribute to a fuller view of the whole, it is not sufficient to combine these perspectives, because even together, with their many insufficiencies set aside, they still fail to provide an adequate view of not just the empiricist but the realist backgrounds of modern aesthetics.

A Hermeneutic Reading

Before looking at the details of this second reading of the history of early modern aesthetics, it will be helpful to situate more clearly the goals of that reading.[8]

The aim the hermeneutic reading sets itself might be taken as an attempt to conduct a series of inquiries into the kinds of knowledge traditionally operative in the humanities, as opposed to those on view in the natural sciences. These scattered reflections are assembled to provide a suitable epistemological basis for a phenomenological theory of consciousness. In turn, this theory is designed to confirm a daring hypothesis—that beauty is a feature required for any entity to become an object for consciousness at all. The key to this theory of consciousness is a particular understanding of intentionality, the directedness of consciousness toward selected aspects of what presents itself. The emphasis in the theory falls squarely on defining the aesthetic in terms of the disinterestedness of consciousness in the existence and the content of its intentional objects. And of course the major problem for such a theory is whether, and if so in what form, a transcendental theory of consciousness is finally coherent.

A provisional summary of both the general orientation and the specific point of the hermeneutic reading would go something like

---

[8]Several Continental accounts are those of E. Hufnagel, *Einführung in die Hermeneutik* (Stuttgart, 1976); P. Szondi, *Einführung in die literarische Hermeneutik*, ed. J. Bollack and H. Stierlein (Frankfurt, 1975); G. Stackel, *Die neue Hermeneutik: Ein Überblick* (Munich, 1968); M. van Esbroick, *Herméneutique, structuralisme et exégèse: Essai de logique kérygmatique* (Paris, 1968); and Diemer's book, cited in note 7.

this.[9] The hermeneutic reading of the history of early modern aesthetics proposes a series of recommendations that aesthetics, like history, must be rearticulated with its classical sources in the tradition of European humanism. The connection to these sources, according to the pervasive assumption here, has been broken by the subjectivization of aesthetics in the philosophy of Kant. Moreover, the tradition of humanism itself has been distorted by the imposition of a univocal idea of method resulting from the rise and development of the mathematical and natural sciences since the seventeenth century.

The point of the hermeneutic reading comes out most clearly against this background. The hermeneutic reading claims that the humanistic tradition preserves an attentiveness to kinds of knowing that are more appropriate to the experience of art than are those found in the natural sciences. In other words, such a reading attempts to free our appreciation of the humanities from the too narrow model of the early modern concepts of both science and method. The humanistic tradition, in short, is understood as incorporating in a preeminent way of particular understanding of the cultivated consciousness as a mode of knowing.[10] The question behind such a hermeneutic reading hence is this: What can a reconstruction of the humanistic tradition teach us about kinds of knowing other than those preserved in the mathematical and natural sciences?[11]

With these preliminaries in hand, let us look in detail at three central components of this hermeneutic account: the importance

[9]Systematic expositions, each with different assumptions but all from a Continental perspective, are to be found in E. Coreth, *Grundfragen der Hermeneutik* (Freiburg, 1969); E. Betti, *Teoria generale della interpretazione* (Milan, 1955); and Betti's *Die Hermeneutik als allgemeine Methode der Geisteswissenschaften* (Tübingen, 1962). See also the essays in O. Pöggler, ed., *Hermeneutische Philosophie: Zehn Aufsätze* (Munich, 1972).

[10]The most extensive criticism of this approach is found in what has been called "the hermeneutic-criticist controversy," which has developed from Habermas's early criticisms of Gadamer in his seminal article "Der Universalitätsanspruch der Hermeneutik," in *HD*, 1:73–104, reprinted with other early articles in *Hermeneutik und Ideologiekritik* (Frankfurt, 1971), including Gadamer's "Replik," 382–417. Important materials are also found in *Demithizzazione e ideologia*, ed. E. Castelli (Milan, 1973). On the details of this controversy, see W. C. Gay and P. Eckstein, "Bibliographic Guide to Hermeneutics and Critical Theory," *Cultural Hermeneutics* 2(1975): 379–90. I do not treat this criticism here.

[11]Both a critical and in some respects an alternative approach to this view can be found in Paul Ricoeur's extensive writings, especially *Le conflit des interprétations: Essai d'herméneutique* (Paris, 1969); and *La métaphor vive* (Paris, 1976), and the three-volume work *Temps et récit* (Paris, 1983–85). I do not treat this critical alternative here.

of the humanistic tradition, some cardinal concepts in that tradition, and finally the interpretation of Kant.

The Humanistic Tradition

The hermeneutic reading begins by stressing the importance of the humanistic tradition over the scientific.[12] The humanistic tradition here is understood as the immediate background of the development of early modern aesthetics.[13] To the extent that the preeminent role of the inductive method in the development of early modern science permeated this context, this one idea of method easily obscured and in some cases distorted the humanistic tradition. But, the attempt to apply the inductive method in the humanities as well as in the sciences had seemed a natural development for introducing into the humanities the possibility of consensus and progress.[14]

Part of this idea of method included postulating regularities rather than causes as bases for prediction. Since these regularities were matters of observation rather than of speculation, the claim was that the inductive method involved no metaphysical assumptions. Hence the idea of method offered to the humanities promised not only a kind of rapid progress already in evidence in the development of the sciences, but a philosophically neutral instrument that would commit humanistic investigators to no other assumptions than those of their subject matter.

[12]On "the scientific tradition" as understood in hermeneutics, see V. Warnach, ed., *Hermeneutik als Weg heutiger Wissenschaft: Ein Forschungsgespräch* (Salzburg, 1971); H. Kimmerle, "Die Funktion der Hermeneutik in den positiven Wissenschaften," *Zeitschrift für Allgemeine Wissenschaftstheorie*, 5(1974): 54–74; U. Gerber, *Hermeneutik als Kriterium für Wissenschaftlichkeit? Der Standort der Hermeneutik im gegenwärtigen Wissenschaftskanon* (Frankfurt, 1972), and K. Gründer, "Hermeneutik und Wissenschaftstheorie," *Philosophisches Jahrbuch* 75(1967–68): 152–65. For Gadamer's views on science see, among other materials, "Über die Unverständlichkeit der Wissenschaft," *Bücherei und Bildung*, 1(1970): 21–27; "Das Faktum der Wissenschaft," *Sitzungsberichte der Wissenschaftlichen Gesellschaft zu Marburg* 88(1967): 11–20; *Über die Ursprünglichkeit der Wissenschaft* (Leipzig, 1947); and especially *Vernunft im Zeitalter der Wissenschaften* (Frankfurt, 1976).

[13]On humanism and hermeneutics, see the bibliography in Diemer cited in note 7, 269–74, and especially E. Rothacker, *Logik und Systematik der Geisteswissenschaften* (Munich, 1927).

[14]See especially H. Lipps, *Untersuchungen zu einer hermeneutischen Logik* (Frankfurt, 1938), and *Die Verbindlichkeit der Sprache* 2d ed. (Frankfurt, 1958); O. F. Bollnow, "Zum Begriff der hermeneutischen Logik," in *Argumente: Festschrift für J. König* (Göttingen, 1964); J. Berger, "Historische Logik und Hermeneutik," *Philosophisches Jahrbuch* 75(1967–68): 127–51; and G. Buck, *Lernen und Erfahrung: Zum Begriff der dialektischen Induktion* (Stuttgart, 1967).

This promise of course was specious, for too many problems are lumped together in simplistic talk of "the inductive method."[15] The main difficulty, according to the hermeneutic view, concerns the very different aims of the humanities and the natural sciences. When some humanistic disciplines like history use the inductive method as a model for their own investigative methods, they may all too easily distort their proper aims. History and physics, for instance, do not characteristically have the same goals. Unlike a natural science, history does not attempt to increase our knowledge of observed regularities or even our understanding of particular events by subsuming them under general rules. Even when some of the needed distinctions about kinds of induction began to make their way into informed discussion, this disparity in aims between the humanities and the natural sciences remained to condemn as an oversimplification the attempt to impose the same model of inquiry on such different kinds of investigation.

One demonstration of this inadequacy is the inability of theorists to provide a positive account of the methods of the humanities. Helmholtz in 1862, to take Gadamer's example, when trying to distinguish between two kinds of induction, the one logical and the other artistic-instinctive, continued to describe the logic of the humanities in only a negative way. "Both make use of the inductive conclusion," he theorized, "but the conclusions of the humanities are arrived at unconsciously."[16] One of the many problems with this kind of distinction is that it ties the practice of induction in the humanities to particular psychological conditions, such as having a good memory or an appropriate personal attitude toward authorities in the field. In the end, even the attempt to discriminate kinds of induction proved to be insufficient support for extending the inductive model from the natural sciences to the humanities.

In the mid-nineteenth century, after the inadequacies of extending the inductive method to the humanities had been noted, a new attempt was made to find some other unified method. A humanistic discipline such as history, for example, required "a categorical

[15]Some idea of the difficulties in this area can be had by consulting the bibliography on the problem of induction in P. Edwards and A. Pap, *A Modern Introduction to Philosophy*, 3d ed. (New York, 1975), and more recent work in the specialized journals.

[16]Cited in Gadamer, *Truth and Method*, no translator given (New York, 1975), 7. The reference is to H. Helmholtz, *Vorträge und Reden*, 4th ed. (Berlin, 1862), 167 ff. Since the English translation includes as an appendix material not included in the German edition, for convenience I cite this translation as *TM*. However, the translation must be used with caution: see my critical review, "Gadamer on Truth and Method," *New Scholasticism* 51(1977): 423–26. As I indicated in the Introduction, a corrected edition has just appeared.

imperative of history," something, the hope was, a new Kant might provide. In the end, however, Droysen's call went unheeded despite Dilthey's insistence on taking this ill-defined task upon himself.[17] Dilthey's own attempts were imaginative and repeated, and they often demonstrated a magisterial intelligence. But on the hermeneutic reading, Dilthey continued to retain a scientific model of understanding. He defended the epistemological independence of the humanities; but humanistic methods remained modeled on the inductive methods of the natural sciences.[18]

To philosophers of the not too distant past, say the latter half of the nineteenth century, the humanities clearly presented a problematic case. They raised questions about the basis for the psychological "tact" that thinkers like Helmholtz and Dilthey recognized but were finally unable to radicalize in a philosophically persuasive fashion. Like Kant, both thinkers continued to understand the idea of knowledge in terms of the natural sciences. But the counterassertion was that the human sciences (Geisteswissenschaften) are in fact not sciences (Wissenschaften) at all, but nothing less than the true heirs of German classicism. The renewal of criticism and literature in this earlier period moved beyond the rationalism of the Enlightenment.[19]

The basic claim, then, in this hermeneutic reading of the methodological struggle between the humanities and the sciences goes as follows: In the notion of cultivation the humanities sought a different ideal of knowledge than inductive method. And yet this different ideal lacked a sufficient warrant at the epistemological level. The humanistic tradition is important not because it resisted the methodological models of the sciences, but because it insisted

[17]For Droysen's work, see especially *Historik: Historisch-kritische Ausgabe*, ed. P. Leyh, 3 vols. (Stuttgart, 1978). Despite its general importance, I do not think that the opposition here between the *Geisteswissenschaften* and the *Naturwissenschaften* completely transcends a hermeneutic standpoint. Rather, much of our understanding of this distinction arises from the hermeneutic tradition, especially from Dilthey's work.

[18]On Dilthey, see U. Hermann, *Bibliographie W. Dilthey* (Berlin, 1969); R. A. Makkreel, *Dilthey: Philosopher of the Human Sciences* (Princeton, 1975); and Gadamer, *Le problème de la conscience historique* (Louvain, 1963).

[19]Basic texts here include J. M. Chladenius, *Einleitung zur Auslegung vernünftiger Reden und Schriften* (Leipzig, 1742), and S. J. Baumgarten, *Ausführlicher Vortrag biblischer Hermeneutik* (Halle, 1769). Selections from these and other texts both from this period and from the earlier rationalistic period can be found in the work by Gadamer and Boehm cited in note 4. An extremely important alternative to both the analytic and the hermeneutic readings is that of Ernst Cassirer, notably in *The Philosophy of the Enlightenment* (Princeton, 1951), 275–361. I do not deal with Cassirer's view here.

on an ideal of knowledge that it could not justify to the sciences without appealing to that other kind of knowledge that the humanities were trying to complement.

Humanistic Concepts

If this is essentially how a hermeneutic reading of the history of early modern aesthetics understands the importance of the methodological disputes between the natural sciences and the humanities, what then are the operative elements in the humanistic ideal of knowledge? Four notions are primary on this account: the idea of cultivation, common sense, judgment, and taste. We need to look at each in turn.[20]

The first notion, *Bildung* or cultivation, must be understood like the others in terms of its history. The word itself has been studied carefully.[21] Its origins and transformations from medieval times through baroque mysticism have been traced, as well as its development inside the spirituality of Klopstock's vision to the later conception of cultivation as humanistic aspiration in Herder. The deeper senses of this term were operative in the nineteenth century. But earlier in the eighteenth century the central sense had already moved away from its literal suggestions. Thus the earlier connections between external appearances and natural shapes, which previous uses of this word had suggested, were gradually shunted aside in the eighteenth century in favor of a new stress on just how human fulfillment was to be achieved. Wilhelm von Humboldt's later distinction between *Bildung* and *Kultur* reinforces this emphasis. *Bildung*, Humboldt asserted, is "something both higher and more inward, namely the attitude of mind which, from the knowledge and the feeling of the total intellectual and moral endeavor, flows harmoniously into sensibility and character."[22] *Bildung* here means more than *Kultur*, for the word echoes with its earliest uses in medieval mystics like Eckehart, who spoke of the soul as an image (*Bild*) of God. This rich and changing notion of cultivation the hermeneutic reading characterizes as "a genuine historical

---

[20]As I stated earlier, I rely in what follows on Gadamer's account in *WM*.

[21]I. Schaarschmidt, *Der Bedeutungswandel der Wörter Bilden und Bildung* (Königsberg, 1931), as noted in *WM*, 7; *TM*, 11.

[22]W. von Humboldt, *Gesammelte Schriften*, vol. 7 (Berlin, 1860), 30, cited in *WM*, 8; *TM*, 11.

idea," an idea that Hegel appropriates to formulate his understanding of rationality.

With the help of the notion of cultivation, Hegel is able to construe rationality as the capacity to withstand the temptation to reduce oneself to one's own particularity, as "the promotion of the universal." The Hegelian understanding of *Bildung* involves two features: the first is the progressive achievement of a kind of distance, a detachment from possessiveness and interest, and the second is the growing capacity to allow for what is different from oneself. The essence of this idea of *Bildung* is a series of repeated returns to oneself, by means of the necessary and successive distanciations from oneself that the movement from the natural to the universal requires. In short, *Bildung* is a spiritual ideal. It than becomes an ideal not just for individual human beings but for the humanities as well.

Now this spiritual and humanistic ideal, the hermeneutic reading wants to claim, incorporates a distinctive kind of knowledge that might be termed tacit knowledge or "tact." What then is tact as a mode of knowledge? Here is Gadamer's formulation of the way thinkers such as Helmholtz use the word. "By 'tact' we understand," Gadamer asserts, "a particular sensibility and sensitiveness to situations, and how to behave in them, for which we possess no knowledge from general principles. Hence, an essential part of tact is inexplicitness and inexpressibility."[23] Although this citation may suggest that tact is a means or method of knowledge, Gadamer construes tact as a kind of practical rather than theoretical knowledge. Moreover, tact involves some connections with the moral realm of activity. In these respects, what the hermeneutic reading wishes to isolate here under the heading of "tact" is close to the considerations that Aristotle proposes when introducing his discussions of moral reasoning. At least one important difference should be noted, however. Tact is not reasoning of any sort whatever but constitutes what is required for that kind of knowledge we call tacit. This tacit knowledge, as Helmholtz describes it, requires a capacity to make well-founded distinctions and evaluations without *necessarily* being able to provide reasons. Such a capacity thus involves the Hegelian element of a trained receptivity to what is other, a capacity to reach beyond one's own particularity to something more general, a capacity to put oneself in proportion while putting oneself at a distance.[24] The stress on cultivation in the

---

[23]*WM*, 13; *TM*, 16, translation corrected.
[24]Gadamer's important Hegel references are to the *Propädeutik*, the *Phänomenologie*,

humanistic tradition leads to an appreciation for this kind of tacit knowledge.

A second humanistic notion related to kinds of knowledge is common sense (*sensus communis*), a very complex theme. Although this notion is thematized mainly in medieval philosophy, here again the hermeneutic reading addresses the same question to the humanistic tradition. What can a reconstruction of this tradition teach us about kinds of knowing other than those furthered in the development of mathematics and the natural sciences?

The main texts for this reconstruction, besides the pedagogical texts of Hegel, are Vico's writings about humanism, especially the *De nostri temporis studiorum ratione*.[25] In this important work Vico stresses two ideas, common sense and *eloquentia* in the double sense of speaking well and speaking truthfully. Vico is concerned in part to show the limitations of the new sciences. He insists on educating common sense. What nourishes common sense, he holds, is not the true but the probable.

The important idea, according to this reading, is that the *sensus communis* is the sense of the community. The point is that common sense is being understood here not as some species of abstract reasoning that yields successive levels of generality, but as a kind of knowledge instantiating that aggregate of particular judgments that forms the knowledge of a social group. The truths and insights of common sense are not to replace but to complement the truths and theoretical reasoning of the natural sciences.

Like *Bildung*, the notion of a *sensus communis* is close to Aristotle. In fact, for the hermeneutic reading, Vico's common sense is nothing other than Aristotle's *phronesis*. Practical knowledge is directed to circumstances in their infinite variety; it is directed toward concrete situations. What distinguishes Vico's account of this Aristotelian doctrine is the addition of an ethical component. Practical knowledge is required for moral control of

---

and the *Nürnberger Schriften*. Tact as what is required for tacit knowledge, an anonymous Cornell referee notes, recalls Schleiermacher's description of religious knowledge as a knowledge that "cannot be made explicit independently of the situation."

[25]On Vico's work, see G. Tagliacozzo and H. V. White, eds., *Giambattista Vico: An International Symposium* (Baltimore, 1969). Much new work on Vico, including new translations, will require a critical review of Gadamer's interpretations. See especially G. Tagliacozzo, ed., *New Vico Studies*, 5 vols. (London, 1983–87); F. Peddle, "Historical and Transhistorical Tension in Vico's Philosophy of History," *Science et Esprit* 40(1988): 327–49; and P. Burke's useful overview, *Vico* (Oxford, 1985).

the concrete situation to the degree that being able to distinguish between what should and what should not be done involves both pragmatic and moral considerations. Gadamer brings these points together succinctly in his formulation of Vico's idea of common sense. "The *sensus communis*," he writes, "is a sense for the right and general good that is to be found in all men, indeed, even more a sense that is acquired through living in the community and that is determined by its structure and aims."[26]

Operative in Vico's theories of common sense, then, at least as Gadamer reads Vico, is an idea of moral knowledge, an idea that questions the propriety of basing argument in the humanities on universals instead of on circumstances. The hermeneutic reading detects a parallel to this approach in the eighteenth century, specifically in Shaftesbury's reliance on the Latin classics and their interpreters to justify, in terms of the concept of *sensus communis*, the epistemological importance of wit and humor in society.[27] Shaftesbury takes common sense more as a matter of the heart than of the head, however. The basis of his account is the idea of "sympathy." Later on, in Hume's work,[28] sympathy is seen to develop into the moral sense. And it is this moral sense that Kant will take as a foil for his own ethics.[29] Regardless of the final coherence either of Hume's position or of Kant's, what strikes a hermeneutic reader like Gadamer about this development is that sympathetic common sense involves the notion of a capacity to continually adjust one's intelligence to the demands of new concrete situations.

When taken over by the German Enlightenment, however, this early notion of common sense as a kind of practical knowledge of circumstance contracts into an empty and static intellectualization, a theoretical kind of knowledge divorced from any dynamic interaction with the wisdom of a community. But the practical stress is

[26]*WM*, 19; *TM*, 22, translation corrected. Gadamer's reading here, as elsewhere, is controversial. "The individual sense," a referee writes, "does not provide the sole ground for judgments; the *sensus communis* is universal, not individual. At a point when the medieval reliance on universals was in questions, postulation of a *sensus communis* allowed retention of a practical universal."

[27]Shaftesbury, *Characteristics of Men, Manner, Opinions, Times, Etc.*, 2d ed. (London, 1714).

[28]See especially Hume's "Of the Standard of Taste," in *Essays and Treatises* vol. 1 (London, 1784).

[29]References and discussions of these works can be found in M. C. Beardsley, *Aesthetics from Classical Greece to the Present: A Short History* (New York, 1966), chap. 8. See his useful bibliographies, 206–8. Gadamer cites, in addition, a number of other figures.

retained in Pietism. The Swabian Pietist Oetinger, for example, insists that common sense is not just a matter of Scholastic clarity of concepts but involves "anticipations and predilections." Common sense, as Gadamer reads these materials, is the kind of knowledge that enables a father to act without demonstrative proof in claiming to know how to care for his children. Common sense in the Pietist tradition as opposed to the Enlightenment becomes a sense for what is sensible, "a receptivity to the common truths that are useful to all men at all times and places."[30]

Besides the peculiarly practical kinds of knowing that the humanistic tradition has preserved in its emphasis on cultivation and common sense, a third and related notion this tradition retains is that of judgment.

Judgment, in the sense that the hermeneutic reading finds important, is one's capacity to subsume and correctly apply what one knows, the capacity "to recognize something as an example of a rule."[31] What strikes the hermeneutic reader is that learning judgment cannot be done through the mastery of general principles but is possible only through repeated attempts to exercise judgment in individual cases. No conceptual demonstration can impart the capacity to perform this kind of judgment. In this respect, judgment once again is located on the practical side of the distinction between theory and practice.

Two figures stand out here, Baumgarten and Kant.[32] The first wants to hold that the object of such a judgment is always the individual thing, precisely in its degree of perfection or imperfection. The second, however, argues that just as the idea of common sense must be excluded from moral philosophy, so the moral component must be excluded from our understanding of judgment. For Kant judgment gradually becomes the idea of the aesthetic judgment of taste. Such judgments are not made according to concepts; they retain the notion of agreement with something sensuous that is common to different instances of what is beautiful.

---

[30]*WM*, 26; *TM*, 28. Gadamer refers here to F. C. Oetinger's *Inquisitio in sensum communem et rationem...* (Tübingen, 1753). See Gadamer, "Oetinger als Philosoph," in *Kleine Schriften*, vol. 3 (Tübingen, 1972), 89–100. Note again a referee's disagreement. "Even in Pietism, common sense retains the nucleus of the 'universal agreement of the faithful' which makes it epistemologically important in both the Latin and Islamic medieval traditions."

[31]*WM*, 28; *TM*, 30.

[32]Gadamer cites Baumgarten's *Metaphysica* but not the *Aesthetica*, and passages from each of Kant's Three Critiques, not only from the *Critique of Judgment*.

The interpretation of Kant at issue here should be cited. What Kant treats in the transcendental doctrine of judgment, i.e., the doctrine of schematism and the principles, no longer has anything to do with the *sensus communis*. For here we have concepts which are supposed to refer to their objects a priori, and not the subsumption of the particular under the universal. When, however, we are really concerned with the faculty of recognizing the particular as an instance of the universal and we speak of sound understanding, then this is, according to Kant...something that is "common," that is "something that one finds everywhere, but to possess which is by no means any merits or advantages."[33]

The context of this reading will require close scrutiny in the next chapter.

The final notion in the humanistic tradition to which this reading of early modern aesthetics calls attention is the familiar idea of taste. The basic texts, at least for Gadamer, are those of the Spaniard Baltasar Gracián, who held that the differentiation we make in judgments begins in the immediate sensuous discrimination of taste.[34]

This notion of immediate discrimination is to be found in Gracián's ideal of the educated person as the one who achieves the capacity to keep at a distance from the things of the world. This capacity confers on the educated person a freedom to make choices and to formulate distinctions with detachment. Such a person is said to have taste.

What counts as the criteria of taste is curiously subject to the historical changes of different social groups within society. Thus with the rise of a new society after the fall of absolutism, birth and rank are no longer decisive. The capacity to transcend the interests of class and family replaces them.

Taste, the claim here goes, is a kind of knowledge. For taste includes precisely this capacity to stand back from the immediacy of personal opinion and beliefs while moving toward the social. Taste can even be understood as a counter to inclination, as is evident in the experience some people have of liking something that their own taste rejects. Gracián's point might be grasped in

---

[33]*WM*, 30–31; *TM*, 32, translation corrected.
[34]Gadamer's interpretation of Gracián here depends on two basic critical works that he cites, K. Borinski, *Balthasar Gracián und die Hofliteratur in Deutschland* (Munich, 1894), and F. Schummer, "Die Entwicklung des Geschmacksbegriffs in der Philosophie des 17. und 18. Jahrhunderts," *Archiv für Begriffsgeschichte* 1(1955): 230–43.

part by underlining three important properties of taste. Taste is decisive, for though we disagree about taste, we cannot argue about it. Taste, moreover, does not adduce reasons for its pronouncements but is of its essence confident in its verdicts. Finally, like judgments, taste can be learned neither through demonstration nor through imitation. In short, Gracián's ideal for the educated person is more a negative than a positive one. "Taste really seeks, not what is tasteful, but what does not offend it."[35]

An important contrast for the hermeneutic reading of the ideal is that between taste and fashion. These phenomena of course are related, but fashion is changeable because it concerns things that succeed one another and thus are to be dealt with in more than one way. Taste, however, although it changes while it is being formed, is preeminently a static reality focused steadily on the priority of measure, proportion, and harmony. No straining after the requirements of empirical consensus is in evidence here, for what guides taste as opposed to fashion is more of an abstract ideal than a concrete example.

On this account, then, taste is taken as a kind of knowing. For taste interprets individual entities in the light of an abstract ideal and apprehends parts in terms of a harmonious whole. Whenever a whole is intended but not given, taste is required. Whenever rational judgments are unable to grasp individuals as instances of general rules or principles, taste enables one to deal cognitively with the individual in an appropriate way.

Before looking at Kant, we might summarize what we have seen from this hermeneutic reading of early modern aesthetics. The humanistic tradition, we are told, preserves four basic epistemological notions; each is taken as opposed in definite ways to the ideal of knowledge proposed and developed in the scientific tradition. And each notion is taken to be a distinct kind of knowledge. Whether in fact these claims are substantially correct, we must investigate later. For the moment, to complete this hermeneutic account, we need to look at its interpretation of Kant.

Kant

Kant's transcendental analysis, this reading goes, disallowed the claims to independent kinds of knowledge that were part of the

---

[35] WM, 33; TM, 35.

humanistic tradition until his time. The *Critique of Judgment* was
to justify aesthetic consciousness by means of a radical subjectivization, which discredits any kind of theoretical knowledge other
than what the sciences provide. The concept of truth itself was
reserved for conceptual knowledge and was no longer allowed as
possible in relation to works of art.

The hermeneutic interpretation of Kant comprises five major
points: the transcendental quality of taste, the doctrine of free and
dependent beauty, the doctrine of the ideal of beauty, the concern
for the beautiful in nature and in art, and the relation between taste
and genius.[36]

Kant's analyses of the beautiful in the *Critique of Judgment* are
powered by an insight into an a priori element[37] in the phenomenon of taste. This element goes far beyond empirical universality,
which allows no universality beyond that of consensus. To the
degree that this a priori element transcends the empirical order, it
is referred to as the transcendental quality of taste.[38]

Kant's insight has two facets. We are to realize, on the one hand,
that matters of taste in what concerns the beautiful cannot be
demonstrated by proof or by less formal kinds of argument. Good
taste, on the other hand, can never be a matter of appealing to the
taste prevailing at a particular time in history. Taste thus concerns
the particular and the concrete, yet it is not a matter of fashion.

Correspondingly, so this interpretation continues, Kant wants to
base his analysis of taste on the twofold character of the aesthetic
judgment. For aesthetic judgments involve empirical elements and
therefore have a particular character,[39] while they also involve a
priori elements and therefore have a universal character.

Kant's analysis invalidates the claims to knowledge that taste

---

[36]See especially *WM*, 39–56; *TM*, 39–55. A sixth point, the dominance of the idea
of genius, I deal with in appendix 2.

[37]A general bibliographical orientation for most of the technical topics discussed
here—for example, the a priori—can be found in G. Lehmann, *Beiträge zur Geschichte
und Interpretation der Philosophie Kants* (Berlin, 1966); M.J. Scott-Taggert, "Recent
Work on the Philosophy of Kant," in *Kant Studies Today*, ed. L. W. Beck, 1–71 (La
Salle, Ill., 1969); and regularly in *Kant Studien*. Since my aim here is to illustrate
the hermeneutic reading of these themes, the following references are limited to
Gadamer materials. References on these topics from different perspectives can be
found in the extensive notes to chapter 4.

[38]*WM*, 39–41; *TM*, 39–42.

[39]This empirical component is evidence of Kant's debt to the British tradition,
especially to Burke's *A Philosophical Inquiry into the Origin of Our Ideas of the
Sublime and the Beautiful* (enlarged 2d ed., 1759). Kant knew of this work when he
wrote his *Bedeutungen über das Gefühl des Schönen und Erhabenen* (1764), but

was still considered to have within the humanist tradition. Because it becomes only a subjective principle, taste no longer counts as knowledge. Part of Kant's subjectivization of aesthetics is this subjectivization of taste.

Taste thus allows no genuine knowledge at all of whatever entities are judged to be beautiful. It refers, rather, to the occurrence of pleasure in connection with particular acts of consciousness. Taste becomes only a subjective phenomenon, "a free play of imagination and understanding."[40] Yet this phenomenon can be said to have a universality in that the idea of the judgment of taste can be universally communicated. What needs underlining is the hermeneutic emphasis here on the faculty of taste rather than, as in the analytic interpretation, on the judgments of that faculty. Although both elements could be stressed in an interpretation of Kant, neither reading does so.

The second element in this view of Kant is attentiveness to a distinction between things that are beautiful in themselves and things that are beautiful because they are fashioned according to a purpose.[41] What attracts attention, of course, is that Kant considers only the first kind as proper to the pure judgment of taste, whereas the second kind is dependent on human ends. Just because the pleasure this second kind of beautiful thing arouses is a function of particular ends, the pleasure is considered limited. Hence, things beautiful in themselves are free in the sense that the pleasure they arouse is not oriented to such ends. In cases of dependent beauty, Kant thinks that the judgment of taste is imperfect because of the relation between these beautiful things and their purposes.

The consequence is that natural objects that are judged beautiful take precedence in Kant's aesthetics over artifacts judged beautiful. "True beauty," this view goes, "is that of flowers and not of ornament which in our world dominated by ends present themselves immediately and of themselves as beauties and hence do not require any conscious disregarding of any concept or purpose."[42]

One condition for pure aesthetic judgments, then, is that these

---

firsthand contact with Burke's text is evident only in his Third Critique. See J. Boulton's edition of Burke (London, 1958), especially the extended historical introduction with a thorough review of the eighteenth-century British writings on taste. A different reading can be seen in S. Masubuchi, "On 'Sentimental' in Comparison with 'Sublime,'" *Journal of the Faculty of Letters* (Tokyo) 10(1985): 111–17.

[40] WM, 40; TM, 40.
[41] WM, 42–43; TM, 42–44.
[42] WM, 43; TM, 43.

judgments entail no conflict with purposive elements. Imagination must not be bound to the task of providing examples for the general schemes of the understanding, but must be working in free harmony with the understanding. Thus the understanding's desire for unity must not confine the imagination in its activity.

Kant holds that there is an ideal of beauty, that is, something that makes possible the fact that a particular object is universally pleasing.[43] If such an ideal can be made out, Kant goes on to argue, then any particular judgment about some beautiful things must be in accordance with that ideal. Since judgments of taste are not made in accordance with such an ideal, however, aesthetic judgments cannot be understood as merely judgments of taste. In order for something to arouse pleasure precisely as a work of art, then, this something must be somehow more than what is merely the object of a judgment of taste.

The ideal of beauty, at least in this hermeneutic interpretation, is obscure. The doctrine of this ideal is understood as deriving from Kant's distinction between the normative idea and the rational idea of beauty. The former is found in all natural kinds, whereas the latter is to be found in the distinctively human realm alone. As such, Kant associates the rational ideal of beauty with the moral realm. This distinction is said to enable Kant to completely undermine the view that beauty is to be found only "in the complete presence to the senses of every existing thing."[44]

"There is an ideal of beauty only of the human form," Gadamer summarizes, "because it alone is capable of a beauty fixed by a concept of end. This doctrine, propounded by Winckelmann and Lessing, takes up a key position in Kant's foundation of aesthetics. . . . the very recognition of the non-conceptuality of taste leads beyond an aesthetics of mere taste."[45]

The hermeneutic interpretation of Kant takes the distinction between the naturally beautiful and the artistically beautiful[46] as bringing to a focus the major problem of his aesthetics. If the doctrine of the ideal of beauty is adopted, then the artistically beautiful is seen to be superior to the naturally beautiful precisely because it expresses the moral directly. If, however, the doctrine of the pure aesthetic judgment is adopted, then the naturally beautiful is seen as superior because it is free from any necessary

[43]WM, 44–46; TM 44–46.
[44]WM, 46; TM, 45.
[45]WM, 44, 46; TM, 44, 46.
[46]WM, 46–49; TM, 46–49.

dependence on human purpose. Since the naturally beautiful has no content of its own, it can be taken as most perfectly manifesting the aesthetic judgment.

But the problem here is precisely with the naturally beautiful, for Kant holds that the naturally beautiful is also connected with moral sensibility in that the sense of beauty in nature "points beyond itself to the thought that 'nature has produced that beauty.' "[47] The argument in fact is peculiar. Persons find beauty in nature even through there is no purpose in nature. The beauty found there is taken as a disposition in nature that allows "conformity with the goal of our pleasure."[48] In this way nature is taken as manifesting indirectly that persons themselves are nature's ultimate end. Beauty in nature is superior to beauty in works of art because natural beauty brings about an awareness of our own ultimate purpose. The consequence of this doctrine is that the artistically beautiful must be subordinated to the naturally beautiful in a peculiar way: works of art must be considered as natural beauty, that is, independent of their purposes.

The fifth element in this reading of Kant turns on the tension in Kant's thought between the roles of taste and genius.[49] Genius displays originality and invention, while taste brings all such novelty under the constraint of convention. Genius has as its role the invention of aesthetic ideas that bring about the harmony of reason in the play of imagination and understanding. But genius is necessarily limited to the artistically beautiful, whereas taste ranges across both the artistically beautiful and the naturally beautiful.

Now this interpretation of Kant is sensitive to the continuity between the problems of aesthetic judgment and the problems of teleology. Indeed, part of the tension between genius and taste is that the former cannot serve as a bridge to the teleological issues, whereas the latter is precisely that. The critique of taste prepares the way for Kant's teleology, his final effort to construe judgment as a bridge between understanding and reason. Kant's attempt to remove the ambiguity between the competing claims of natural and artistic beauty opens up a way into the teleological issues, for his analysis of the pure judgment of taste turns in the end on the concept of finality. And this is the concept that Kant tries to use in grounding his claims that aesthetic judgments involve an a prior

---

[47] *WM*, 47; *TM*, 47.
[48] *WM*, 47; *TM*, 47.
[49] *WM*, 50–52; *TM*, 49–51.

feature regardless of whether they are about naturally or artificially beautiful things.

If these are the central elements in the hermeneutic reading of the history of early modern aesthetics, then what is the main conclusion this reading reaches?

The hermeneutic reading concludes that Kant subjectivizes aesthetics. But this result, though implicit in Kant's aesthetics, is made explicit only later. Schiller is the one who sets aside the analysis of teleology and takes up Kant's reflection on beauty with different aims. The transcendental idea of taste is dissociated from the problem of adequately accounting for putative a priori elements in judgments about the beautiful. Instead, taste is transformed into an aesthetic imperative so that art can become the practice of freedom. "Adopt an aesthetic attitude to things" is the formulation Schiller proposes.[50] Art and nature are no longer complements of one another; they are rivals in the way that appearance and reality are rivals. Finally, the question of art and truth is no longer raised, since despite the transformation of his aesthetics, Kant's conception of knowledge and truth disallows any genuine cognitive claims for art. So much then for an alternative reading of the history of early modern aesthetics.

This reading takes in figures outside the British and German tradition, giving special attention to such thinkers as Gracián and Vico, although it includes none of the French theorists. Moreover, inside the German tradition in particular a more nuanced treatment is evident in the appeal not just to individual figures such as Baumgarten but to larger currents of thought as well, as in the case of the Pietist movement and the Enlightenment. Particular attention is paid to the tensions between two opposed views of the appropriate methodology for the humanities. And here an even greater stress than in the analytic reading is put on the features of Kant's aesthetics.[51]

---

[50]*WM*, 77; *TM*, 73.

[51]"I think the language/nationality of the sources is perhaps as important as the philosophical school. What is characteristic of this reading is that it is German/classical as opposed to English/empiricist or French/Enlightenment in its texts and orientation. That in itself seems to me more a fact of history than of philosophical methods, though the two are not unrelated in my mind" (referee's comment). This is an important point worth pursuing but, I think, too general; it leaves too little room for alternative readings, like E. Cassirer's (which I favor) that is both German and Enlightenment with a strong but not exclusively empiricist account. Cf. M. Sakabe, "'Historia' et 'Ethica' chez le jeune Kant et Herder," *Journal of the Faculty of Letters* (Tokyo) 6(1981): 119–27.

The details of these summary comparisons and contrasts will occupy us at greater length in the next chapter, but one central difference should be noted now. Whereas the analytic reading of the history of early modern aesthetics stresses the transformation of a theory of beauty into a theory of the aesthetic, the hermeneutic reading emphasizes the idea of aesthetic consciousness, pace Kant, as finally cognitive.

Appendix 2: The Idea of Genius versus the Idea of Taste

Another element the hermeneutic reading emphasizes in Kant's aesthetics should be noted: the dominant role Kant's successors gave to the idea of genius as opposed to Kant's own stress on taste.[52] When, for example, Schiller later set aside Kant's critical aims in his treatment of natural beauty, art itself quickly replaced taste and judgment as the central concept. The priority of taste had become so precarious that the slightest tampering with Kant's larger intentions to argue for teleology was sufficient to subjectivize aesthetics completely. Once art replaces taste at the center of aesthetic inquiry, the idea of genius becomes more comprehensive than either taste or judgment. Just because taste is opposed to the unusual, to the original, to the striking, it must be subordinated to genius at precisely that moment when the artistically beautiful becomes the focus of concern.

Kant's successors reversed the priority of nature over spirit. Nature itself became the work of spirit. The consequences was that the moral interest in the fact of natural beauty ceased to be important. Persons are now understood to encounter themselves not just in nature but preeminently in art. The concept of genius and the related concept of the creative become in turn the cornerstones of romantic aesthetics.[53]

---

[52]WM 52–56; TM, 51–55.
[53]For several of Gadamer's other discussions of Kant, see his "Zu Kants Begründung der Ästhetik," in Festschrift R. Hamann, 31–39 (Burg bei Magdeburg, 1939); and "Einleitung," in his Immanuel Kant: Auswahl (Frankfurt, 1960).

Chapter Three

The Subjectivization
of Aesthetics

It is now no doubt a little ironic that we must begin our examination of seventeenth- and eighteenth-century aesthetics by recalling
the philosophy of Descartes, whose volumes of writings nowhere
present even the sketch of an aesthetic theory.
—Monroe Beardsley

For the development of modern aesthetics it is important to bear in
mind that...speculative idealism has an effect which greatly extends its recognized importance.
—Hans-Georg Gadamer

W HEN WE look through the details of both the analytic and
the hermeneutic readings of the history of early modern aesthetics,
similarities and differences come into focus. Before we try to
formulate such comparisons and contrasts, however, another central feature of these accounts requires brief discussion.

Partialities

Each of these accounts seems to require a number of corrections. A striking inadequacy of each is surely its partiality. This
common inadequacy is immediately evident once one turns to the
actual texts under discussion, whether they are the English
aestheticians so important to the analytic account or the Continental humanists on whom the hermeneutic account concentrates.

Rereading these texts with the analytic and hermeneutic accounts on hand shows up different kinds of difficulty.[1]

To begin with, questions can be raised about accuracy. Are we in fact to read Baumgarten's work only against the background of the overly schematic dispute between rationalists and empiricists so useful to historians of philosophy? Are we in fact correct in opposing the Pietist movement in Germany to the Enlightenment just in terms of epistemology? Much more detailed questions could be formulated not just about the presentation of central ideas of each of the figures treated, but also about the complicated relationships among these figures. For an example of the first, consider the different interpretations of Kant; for the second, consider the relationship between Kant and Schiller.

Besides the accuracy of these accounts, a second difficulty concerns completeness. Why, for example, is Addison's work largely excluded in the analytic account and are Vico and Garcián not mentioned? Why, on the other hand, are the British aestheticians given such short shrift in the hermeneutic account? Again, it is not difficult to multiply such questions once we look carefully at the plethora of important theorists in France, Germany, England, and Italy at this time. To take the case of the literary work of art alone, it is enough to examine Wellek's *History of Modern Criticism* or Zimmermann's *History of Aesthetics* to get some sense for just how incomplete each of these accounts is.[2]

A third difficulty is the lack of balance in the treatment of individual thinkers. Again, recall the scanty attention paid to Baumgarten in the analytic reading and the just as scanty attention given Hume in the hermeneutic reading. I refer here not to the relatively small amount of space awarded to each thinker, but to the fact that only one or two features in their rather elaborate reflections are selected for summary comment. The lack of balance

[1]Important recent orientations with regard to many of the problems about the history of philosophy raised in this section can be found in R. Rorty et al., eds., *Philosophy in History* (Cambridge, 1984). See also such standard works as J. Collins, *Interpreting Modern Philosophy* (Princeton, 1972); A. O. Lovejoy, *The Great Chain of Being* (Cambridge, Mass., 1976); J. H. Randall, *How Philosophy Uses Its Past* (New York, 1963); J. Dunn, "The Identity of the History of Ideas," *Philosophy* 43 (1968): 85–104; and M. Mandelbaum, "The History of Ideas, Intellectual History, and the History of Philosophy," *History and Theory* 4 (1945): 33–66.

[2]R. Wellek, *A History of Modern Criticism*, 6 vols. (New Haven, 1955–86); R. Zimmerman, *Geschichte der Ästhetik*, 2 vols. (Vienna, 1858); see also B. Bosanquet, *A History of Aesthetic*, 2d ed. (London, 1904).

becomes clear when we return to the texts and notice that these concerns are by no means the only important ones for the thinkers in question. In fact, the topics selected in these readings may not even be the central ones.[3]

These three inadequacies suggest that both the analytic and the hermeneutic readings of the history of early modern aesthetics are partial in a definite way. Each aspires to be something more than just a historical account. Each is concerned to use its historical account for philosophical purposes quite outside the usual pale of the historian's craft. Hence, fully aware that not all can be said, each reading places at the center just those interpretations that will serve its larger purposes.

Now the idea of an objective history of early modern aesthetics need not be taken as the opposite of a partial reading, for no philosopher is really sure even today just what understanding of objectivity is suitable in this sort of context.[4] We need to be careful then about at least two points: first, that each of these readings is partial in at least some of the ways I have been describing and, second, that we must not apply to these accounts useless criteria derived from a vague way of talking about historical objectivity.

My aim in this chapter, then, is to notice the similarities and differences between the two readings. Further, I will discriminate the most important common elements. And finally, I hope to identify the shared assumptions behind the most important of the common elements. Accordingly, my purpose is to determine which

---

[3]Some indication of both points can be had quite simply by checking the titles of Hume and Baumgarten scholarship in such bibliographical journals as the *Philosopher's Index* or the *Répertoire bibliographique de Louvain*. Cf. the selection of texts in, for example, K. Sasaki, "L'esthétique d'intérêt: De d'Aubignac à Sulzer," *Journal of the Faculty of Letters* (Tokyo) 10 (1985): 29–51.

[4]Contrast the different approaches to the philosophy of history in such works as W. H. Dray, ed., *Philosophical Analysis and History* (New York, 1966), and P. H. Gardener, ed., *Theories of History* (Glencoe, Ill., 1959), on the one hand, and F. R. Manuel, *Shapes of Philosophical History* (Stanford, 1965) and W. H. Walsh, *Philosophy of History* (New York, 1966), on the other. R. G. Collingwood is an interesting alternative, sharing in some ways features of both analytic and speculative approaches. See his *The Idea of History* (Oxford, 1946). Much recent work in the philosophy of history complements these positions by looking freshly at the various kinds of historical narrative. Cf. an anonymous Cornell referee's comment: "One can be objective and accurate and yet read differently if the issues are different. The context for any text is always dual—its origin and its present location—but that does not imply two different contexts because the present is related to the past by the text itself."

of the several important claims that both readings of early modern aesthetics assume can be properly taken as the cardinal ones.[5]

Differences

Since the basic concern is to identify the common controlling assumptions, it will be useful to begin with the differences between these typical accounts. These differences are many, but I think we do them no injustice to consider them under five headings.

The first group of differences concerns general features. Each account starts at a different point—the analytic account with the beginnings of the use of the term "aesthetics" in Baumgarten, and the hermeneutic with the continuing tension in contemporary thought between the sciences and the humanities. Starting from different points, these readings proceed in different directions. The analytic reading moves forward in more than one sense. Early modern aesthetics is considered as leading up to contemporary aesthetics—more specifically, it flows into the watershed of early modern philosophy, Kant's critical philosophy. And each stage in this development is understood as making some rough progress beyond the previous stage. The analytic reading, in sum, is progressive. The hermeneutic reading, however, largely moves backward. Early modern aesthetics is understood as retaining valuable insights into our understanding of art, and a reading of that history must retrieve these insights. Further, the movement of retrieval must overcome the obstacles that each subsequent stage in the development of early modern aesthetics has erected. The hermeneutic reading, in sum, is retrospective. Thus the hermeneutic reading is, so to speak, an archaeology of aesthetics, whereas the analytic reading is millenarian—it is oriented more to the future.

Closely connected with the different starting points and directions of these readings are their different attitudes to the past, to all that precedes early modern aesthetics. The analytic reading is preoccupied with demonstrating not just continuity in the theory of art, but especially discontinuity in the theory of beauty. The

---

[5]Fuller documentation is available in the notes to the first two chapters. References here will be restricted to the essential. Note that my own standpoint, the angle of vision from which I make these comparisons and contrasts, is of course relative, like any other perspective. I detail that angle of vision more fully in part 2.

hermeneutic reading, by contrast, is exclusively centered on the continuities between the insights of the early modern humanistic tradition, which the predominance of modern science has rendered increasingly difficult to characterize as knowledge, and the abiding values of Greek and Latin reflection on the arts. This different attitude toward the earlier history of aesthetics is more complicated, however, than it first seems, for each reading also shows some concern for the attitude that characterizes its alternative. My point, then, relates to emphasis: the analytic reading stresses the discontinuity while also taking notice of continuities, whereas the hermeneutic account stresses the continuity while also taking notice of its opposite.

One further general difference between these accounts is the different casts of characters they involve and the different roles some of the common figures are assigned. I have pointed out already that Hutcheson, Shaftesbury, and Burke are noticeably absent from the hermeneutic reading, while Vico, Gracián, and the Pietists are missing in the analytic reading. Even more striking, however, is the role that Kant, the central figure in each account, is assigned. In the analytic reading Kant is a philosophical hero (though not for Danto) in the drama of the progressive improvement of aesthetics, whereas in the hermeneutic account (despite Gadamer's debts) Kant turns out, suddenly and surprisingly, to be the villain. The real hero, Hegel, finally shows up in the audience—completely off the stage of eighteenth-century aesthetics.

So much, then, for several rather general differences between these accounts. A second and much more particular difference is one of purposes. Notice that each of these typical readings has a foil, a kind of invisible interlocutor who is constantly imagined in the process of debating a different view with the analytic or hermeneutic reader. In the former case, the foil is clearly the aesthetic attitude theorist who wants to read early modern aesthetics as the development of only one tradition, not two—of the theory of the aesthetic and not also of the theory of art.[6] The

---

[6]Contemporary aesthetic attitude theorists would include the psychical distance theory of E. Bullough, " 'Psychical Distance' as a Factor in Art and an Aesthetic Principle," in *Aesthetics and the Philosophy of Criticism*, ed. M. Levich, 233–54 (New York, 1963); the disinterested attention theory, for instance, in E. Vivas, "A Definition of Aesthetic Experience," *Journal of Philosophy* 74 (1977): 428–34, and idem, "Contextualism Reconsidered," *Journal of Aesthetics and Art Criticism* 18 (1959): 222–40; J. Stolnitz, *Aesthetics and Philosophy of Art Criticism* (Boston, 1960); and the "seeing-as" theory of V. Aldrich, *The Philosophy of Art* (Englewood Cliffs, N.J., 1963).

analytic reading is oriented throughout toward overcoming this one-sided view. In the latter case, the foil is the empirical aesthetician who wants to understand early modern aesthetics as the development of a scientific discipline, a study of artworks founded on an increasingly positivistic understanding of psychology.[7] Each of these foils, I have said, is imaginary: neither is explicitly described or refuted in the two readings. But both are argued against in the positive articulation of its purposes that each reading provides.

The specific aim of the analytic type of reading is to discern the elements of a general theory of taste, most of which can be found in the major stages of the development of early modern aesthetics. The more general aim is to raise convincing doubts about the satisfactoriness of any such theory as an interpretation of the nature of aesthetics today.[8]

The specific aim of the hermeneutic type of reading is to call renewed attention to forgotten and valuable resources of the humanistic tradition in the early modern development of aesthetics. More generally, the aim is to restore to the center of contemporary aesthetics a critical concern with the cognitivity of art. This kind of cognitivity is to be analyzed, however, not with the paradigms of Kantian and contemporary epistemology of science, but with the less quantifiable, more analogical kinds of reflection that are characteristic of Hegel's philosophy and contemporary studies in moral philosophy, politics, and rhetoric.

Besides their general characteristics and their purposes, a third major difference between these readings turns on different approaches to the early modern history of aesthetics.

To begin with, each approach has a different emphasis. In the analytic account the accent falls repeatedly on conceptual issues—

[7]Empirical aesthetics with different emphases would include J. Dewey, *Art as Experience* (New York, 1934), his *Experience and Nature*, 2d ed. (Chicago, 1929), and his "Aesthetic Experience as a Primary Phase and as an Artistic Development," *Journal of Aesthetics and Art Criticism* 9 (1950): 56–58; T. Munro, *The Arts and Their Interrelations* (New York, 1949), and his *Toward Science in Aesthetics* (New York, 1956); W. Köhler, *The Place of Value in a World of Facts* (New York, 1938); R. Arnheim, *Art and Visual Perception* (Berkeley, 1954); and H. Osborne, *Theory of Beauty* (London, 1952).

[8]Note a referee's comment: "The whole analytic/empiricist [approach] is founded on and fundamentally accepts the aesthetic attitude definition of the aesthetic. Metacriticism is a response to the subjectivization which accompanies accepting that foundation—hence the problems of Hume in the 18th c. and Sibley in the 20th. Empiricists escape those problems by turning from the subjectively unmanageable realm of direct experience to the linguistic and critical grounds which can be the subject of investigation and evidence (e.g. Urmson's moves in response to Sibley's re-emphasis on the non-condition-governed nature of the phenomena themselves)."

the concept of beauty, distinguishing between the concept of beauty and the concept of the sublime, the concept of disinterestedness, and so. In the hermeneutic account the repeated accent is on the experiential—the experience of beauty, the experience of the sublime, the experience of nature. Neither account explicates its respective orientation as such, but each orchestrates this stress in a distinctive way.

Another difference in approach arises in the patterns that are outlined. The hermeneutic account dichotomizes the early modern history of aesthetics implicitly by insisting on the recurring opposition between the new sciences and the humanistic tradition in the background of the development of aesthetics. The analytic tradition, by contrast, searches for a unifying pattern, a general structure common to the opposed yet related views that make up the history of aesthetics.

Still another difference in approach appears if we focus on methodological issues. The analytic account consistently aims at presenting the early history of aesthetics in terms of clear ideas working smoothly as hinges in a whole series of arguments about perception, judgment, and entities. Method here is understood in the large contemporary sense as argument and refutation, example and counterexample, even hypothesis and confirmation. The hermeneutic reading, by contrast, is noticeably self-conscious about the assumptions of method. In fact, since part of the intent of this reading is to call into question the adequacy of a strictly argumentative kind of thinking in aesthetics, the hermeneutic account is faced with a central problem about method that has no parallel in its rival. The problem is how to make out a case for the inadequacy of a universal understanding of what is to count as knowledge without making use of precisely those kinds of thinking that are at issue. The result is a methodological quandary in the hermeneutic account as contrasted with the highly structured argumentative character of the analytic account.[9]

A final difference in approach is linguistic. The analytic reading is presented clearly in an expository language that eschews metaphorical expressions while putting a premium on the literal and the

---

[9]For versions of this central problem see H.-G. Gadamer, "Vom Zirkel des Verstehens," in *M. Heidegger zum 70. Geburtstag*, 24–35 (Pfullingen, 1959); J. C. Maraldo, *Der hermeneutische Zirkel* (Munich, 1973); T. Seebohm, *Zur Kritik der hermeneutischen Vernunft* (Bonn, 1972); and P. Reisinger, "Über die Zirkelstruktur des Verstehens in der traditionellen Hermeneutik," *Philosophisches Jahrbuch* 81(1974): 88–104.

explicit. This use of language is especially well suited for detailing the major features in each of the stages in the early development of aesthetics. The language of the hermeneutic account is, by contrast, often vague and even obscure, partly because the task is to exhibit the need for more than just one kind of knowledge. The language is highly evocative, and it deliberately exploits rhetorical effects such as irony and understatement. Metaphor abounds and is used not for ornament but for directing attention to areas that are difficult to conceptualize, areas of indeterminacy and inexplicitness. This linguistic difference is particularly important to keep in mind when questions of evaluation are raised. Appraising the hermeneutic reading seems to require a different kind of approach than appraising the analytic one precisely because these readings are presented in such different terms.

Besides these differences in approach, a fourth general difference between these readings emerges from their interpretations of Kant. The analytic account is concerned from the outset to make plain the sense of each central claim in Kant's analysis of the beautiful. Accordingly, many if not all of the features discerned in the work of earlier figures in the history of modern aesthetics are expounded in such a way as to make Kant's transformation of the particular concept in question all the more comprehensible. Examples are disinterestedness, uniformity in variety, and especially Burke's reflections on pleasure. The hermeneutic account, by contrast, attempts a more rounded and in fact more controversial reading of Kant's aesthetics—not as the synthesis of the earlier history of aesthetics but as, in some important sense, its final breakdown. Thus themes if not concepts and arguments are selected for commentary not just from the analytic of the beautiful but especially from the very difficult sections on teleology—for instance, on the notion of the sublime. Kant's reflections on beauty are continually subjected to scrutiny inside the larger aims of his critical philosophy as a whole. The result, I think, is often more confusing than enlightening. If the analytic account is sometimes too generous in its ordered, neatly proportioned, and perspicuous presentation of Kant's aesthetics, the hermeneutic reading is sometimes too obscure and needlessly implicit.

The final broad contrast between these typical readings, besides these differences in general characteristics, aims, approaches, and treatment of Kant, lies in their different conclusions. The history of early modern aesthetics on the analytic reading ends only with Schopenhauer's formulation of the aesthetics in terms of will. The hermeneutic reading ends much earlier—with Kant's subjectivization of the aesthetic in terms of consciousness. Such a difference is not inconsequential. For by judging Kant the terminal figure in the history of early modern aesthetics, the hermeneutic reading implies a new beginning for aesthetics in the work of Hegel. The analytic reading, by contrast, tends to blur the central distinctions between early modern and romantic aesthetics by making no break at all between the Kantian philosophy and its ultimate transformation in the work of Hegel, Schopenhauer, and Nietzsche.

Similarities

Common points in these two readings have already begun to emerge on the margins of our reflection on contrasts, so this discussion of similarities can be more succinct. I focus on five such similarities.

The first is the stress on the problematic understanding of contemporary aesthetics. Both of these readings are finally anchored in an attempt to do aesthetics at a time when there is no clear consensus either about what aesthetics is or about what the fundamental problems of aesthetics are. Each account consequently looks to the history of early modern aesthetics for resources toward deciding what is to count as philosophical work in aesthetics and how such philosophical work is to be understood. The analytic reading in particular locates some of its historical roots in the continuous tradition of a philosophy of art that reaches beyond the early modern period into the classical reflection of the Greeks. Other roots are claimed in the eighteenth-century transformation of the theory of beauty into the theory of aesthetics. The hermeneutic tradition locates its sources in the humanistic tradition, also going back to the Greeks behind much of the early modern reflection on aesthetics. Each reading, however, seeks to revitalize its own understanding of what aesthetics is by prefacing its present philosophical reflections in aesthetics with an account of the history of aesthetics.

A second similarity is the preoccupation with early modern aesthetics as the critical period in the development of aesthetics. Different reasons underlie this common choice. The hermeneutic view of this period's importance is based on the rise of the new sciences and the gradual spread of a univocal understanding of knowledge. This more formal concept of knowledge reaches its culmination in Kant's philosophy. But already in Leibniz, Wolff, Baumgarten, Meyer, and others the successes of scientific method were undermining the kinds of knowledge characteristic of the humanistic tradition. The implicit claim here is that the kind of thinking the practice of aesthetics requires must be liberated from the dominance of the scientific model for thinking. And this model is taken to be the achievement of the rise of the sciences in the seventeenth century. The analytic tradition finds the early modern period centrally important because one of the two continuous classical theories of aesthetics, the theory of beauty, was entirely transformed then. The implicit claim is that understanding contemporary work in aesthetics requires understanding how and why this transformation of the theory of beauty into the theory of the aesthetics came about.

A third common feature of these two typical readings is the concern for models of aesthetic inquiry. In the analytic reading, as I have noted, particular attention is paid to the structure of the theory of taste. Such a theory is then taken as a paradigm in aesthetic inquiry and scrutinized in its contemporary guise. Alternatively, in the hermeneutic reading there is a heightened sensitivity to the possibility that the scientific model of inquiry has been illegitimately extended to the humanities. The results are taken to be particularly damaging, since one of the most disputed areas in contemporary epistemology has to do precisely with the nature of such paradigms and how they come to be replaced.

A fourth common concern has already been touched on. Both accounts polemicize the history of early modern aesthetics. Each attempts to use an interpretation of this history to advance particular claims or theories inside the quite different historical space of contemporary aesthetics. I stressed earlier that the objects of these polemics differ. Now I am stressing the more important point that each reading is indeed a polemic. What remains to be investigated is the exact nature of the different interests that orient these polemics. Here we may observe only that neither of these readings need make any claim to an ideal of historical objectivity, for both account are to be understood basically as philosophical interpretations and not as historical expositions of their subject matter.

Finally—besides their similar emphasis on the contemporary, the shared conviction about the importance of the early modern period, the similar concern with epistemological paradigms in this history, and the polemical orientation of these readings—both readings agree on at least one fundamental point. Despite their contrasting accounts of just which philosophical theory stands at the end of early modern aesthetics, both accounts claim that the early modern history of aesthetics ends in the subjectivization of aesthetics. All subsequent work in aesthetics begins from that point—the consensus that whatever the aesthetic may or may not be, it must ultimately be understood in subjective terms if not in those of mind. This final similarity is in fact the most important point at which these readings, for all their many differences, ultimately converge. And it is this convergence that we must now try to understand more thoroughly.

Assumptions

It will prove useful to narrow our focus in this final section to just one formulation of this shared claim and to set aside references to the general schemas I have been using so far, the analytic and hermeneutic readings of early modern aesthetics. Let us now look closely at how a contemporary representative of one of these types of views formulates this thesis of the subjectivization of aesthetics. Since Gadamer's account is more extensive than Beardsley's or Dickie's, for the moment I will be content with it. A brief general presentation of Gadamer's major work, *Truth and Method*, should situate the subjectivization claim most conveniently.[10]

Gadamer's title, "Truth and Method," is intended as an ironic summary of a sustained investigation of the uncritical methodological assumptions made in contemporary scientific accounts of the kinds of understanding operative in history, literature, and especially the philosophy of art. Methods, for Gadamer, do not yield truths enough. Accordingly, his essay is not itself one more methodological program for yet another revolution in philosophy. Rather, somewhat in the direction of Feyerabend's phrase "against method," Gadamer is "trying to go beyond the concept of method held by modern science (which [he insists] retains its limited justification) an to envisage in a fundamentally universal way what *always* happens.[11] Since this statement of purpose is not especially clear out of context, we should consider Gadamer's aims, starting points,

---

[10]References are to *Wahrheit und Methode*, 2d ed. (Tübingen, 1965), hereafter cited as *WM*, and to the English translation, *Truth and Method*, no translator given (New York, 1975), hereafter cited as *TM*.

[11]*WM*, 484; *TM*, 466.

and central claim. A suggestion may then follow as to both the limitations of this work and its abiding importance.

Gadamer sees his work as centered on hermeneutics, on what he calls "the phenomenon of understanding and of the correct interpretation of what has been understood."[12] The questions and problems that hermeneutics involves are more extensive than conceptual inquiries into the various understandings of method in contemporary sciences. Hermeneutics has a larger concern for both kinds of knowledge and kinds of truths that are not appropriately describable in terms of scientific method alone. In this respect hermeneutics begins with what Gadamer calls "the resistance within modern science against the universal claim of scientific method."[13] Moreover, the kinds of knowledge and of truth that are the subject of this inquiry are those proper to philosophy, art, and history. Gadamer's basic claim is that whatever knowledge and whatever truths are accessible exclusively in these spheres are to be legitimized by investigating the phenomenon of understanding.

This investigation proceeds in an intriguing way. Gadamer starts with a critical analysis of the inadequacies of aesthetic theory to account for the kinds of truths that artworks, some say, make available in a privileged way. The claim here is that modern aesthetics is based on a double confusion, the mistaken anaylsis of the concept of aesthetic consciousness and the inappropriateness of scientific methods as models for aesthetics. Gadamer then attempts to generalize his criticism of aesthetics into a critique of the humanities as a whole. Here he discusses history and literary criticism at length and more briefly addresses jurisprudence and theology. The generalization is formulated like this: "Just as in the experience of art we are concerned with truths that go essentially beyond the range of methodological knowledge, so the same theory is true of the whole of the human sciences."[14] But the well-foundedness of this analogy remains, to understate the matter, controversial.

In the foreword to the second German edition, Gadamer attempted to inventory the criticisms his work had precipitated and to respond to them. Gadamer stressed, and has continued to stress, that his aim has been neither to describe a new methodological procedure nor to recommend changes in contemporary scientific understand-

[12]*WM*, xxv; *TM*, xi.
[13]*WM*, xxv; *TM*, xii.
[14]*WM*, 95; *TM*, 90. The background here is Hegelian. See S. Bungay, *Truth and Beauty* (Oxford, 1984), and especially R. Pippin, *Hegel's Idealism* (Cambridge, 1989).

ing of method. Rather, he has been centrally concerned to retrieve from disparate sources—Aristotle's practical philosophy, medieval concepts of language, Renaissance investigations of rhetoric, early Enlightenment treatments of common sense, tact, and taste, romantic concerns with imagination, and Dilthey's unsuccessful struggle with the epistemology of the emerging historical sciences— conceptual resources for describing more satisfactorily just what understanding is. Understanding, moreover, is to be described in accordance with other and weaker epistemological canons than those operative in the contemporary self-interpretations of working scientists, mathematicians, logicians, and philosophers of science. In this perspective, as G. von Wright has noted, Gadamer's work, while perhaps most comprehensive, is not an isolated phenomenon.[15] Perhaps Gadamer's most succinct statement of his considered aim gives some indication of this point: "The purpose of my investigation is not to offer a general theory of interpretation and a differential account of its methods...but to discover what is common to all modes of understanding and to show that understanding is never subjective behavior toward a given 'object,' but towards its effective history—the history of its influence."[16]

It is difficult to work one's way through such an essay without balking repeatedly at the many-sidedness of Gadamer's discussion of understanding. Terms are continually pinned down only to come unstuck once again in subsequent reflections. More important, arguments are deployed in many places—against psychologisms, against different concepts of tradition, against inadequate construals of "language"—but a main line of positive argument that such provocative claims about understanding require is tortuously different to make out and to follow. The question remains open whether indeed there is such a central positive argument and not just a series of extraordinarily perceptive and almost always suggestive fragments.

This is, I think, the main question Gadamer's work leaves us with—not in the end issues I discuss in the Conclusion about the critique of ideology that Habermas and Apel have precariously settled on, but something simpler and more elusive, a question about coherence. Can the phenomenon (or, surely better, phenomena) of understanding be construed centrally in terms of such

---

[15]*Explanation and Understanding* (Ithaca, N.Y. 1971), 181–82.
[16]*WM*, xvii; *TM*, xiv. Cf. M. A. Gillespie, *Hegel, Heidegger, and the Ground of History* (Chicago, 1984).

cardinal concepts as language, time, world, and consciousness without succumbing to incoherence? It is not enough, as Gadamer's own argumentative readings of Schleiermacher, Dilthey, Husserl, and Heidegger amply demonstrate, to talk of circles, whether hermeneutic ones or others. Without taking a stand on what self-reference might be and why accounting for the phenomena of understanding seems also to entail addressing issues of truth in an imaginatively philosophical way, the nature of hermeneutics and its intelligibility as an instructive account of understanding must remain obscure. The absence of any convincing account of the problems of self-reference and truth must be acknowledged and then redressed if hermeneutics is to retain our attention as a coherent undertaking.

The effort such attention to issues of self-reference and truth would require seems worthwhile, at least to some. What catches the interest of von Wright, Habermas, Dray, Taylor, and others is in part the controlling, now familiar, and yet still imperfectly conceptualized insight of Gadamer's work. We do philosophy characteristically and unself-critically with an understanding of thinking that (at least in several fundamental areas like metaphysics) continues to obscure from us what it is that provoked our thinking in such a peculiar domain. In his masterly and at times obscure work, Gadamer urges on us strategies other than "understanding understanding" in the light of scientific models only. Whether coherent alternatives are available, and if so, how such alternatives are to be not just suggested but also worked through in the contexts of several paradigmatic problem areas in philosophy itself—after Gadamer's work, these still are open questions.

This general situation of Gadamer's views in his major work helps to make more comprehensible his particular understanding of the subjectivization of aesthetics. Art for Gadamer is a kind of knowledge, and "the experience of the work of art" is a sharing of this knowledge.[17] But how can the truth of the experience of art be accounted for inside the radical subjectivization of the aesthetic that begins with Kant? Gadamer sees Kant as reducing the aesthetic judgment to an element in a theory of consciousness. This reduction is effected by making "a methodological abstraction

---

[17]*WM*, 92; *TM*, 87. The Hegelian background here is especially important. See, for example, M. N. Forster, *Hegel and Skepticism* (Cambridge, Mass., 1989), on Hegel's epistemology, and more generally, Marie McGinn, *Sense and Certainty: A Dissolution of Scepticism* (Oxford, 1989).

corresponding to a quite particular transcendental task of laying foundations."[18] Kant then ascribes a content to this abstraction. The result is that art is understood in terms of the aesthetic.

But how is aesthetics to account for the fact that the experience of art is knowledge of a special kind? Aesthetics cannot furnish such an account if knowledge means, as it did for Kant, scientific knowledge alone. Gadamer thinks that experience must be interpreted more broadly than either the empiricists or Kant would allow. This broader view of experience would in turn make possible a new account of the experience of art as a kind of cognitive experience. Hegel, Gadamer is at pains to argue, provides us with this broader view. The result is that aesthetics "becomes a history of world views, that is, a history of truths, as seen in the mirror of art."[19] Against the Kantian view of aesthetic experience and the neutralization of the question of truth must be ranged the idea that the encounter with artworks is an encounter with elements of a still unfinished process.

Gadamer argues that we need to overcome the subjectivization of aesthetics in the way Heidegger has overcome the subjectivization of metaphysics, by asking what is the truth of aesthetics. "In the experience of art," Gadamer writes, "we see a genuine experience induced by the work, which does not leave him who has it unchanged, and we inquire into the mode of being of that which is experienced in this way. So we hope to understand better what kind of truth it is that encounters us there."[20] But this kind of reflection remains obscure.

What comes clear in this account of the similarities and differences between these alternative readings of the history of early modern aesthetics, particularly in the detailed context of Gadamer's individual project, is that the subjectivization of aesthetics is part of a larger situation. In effect, the construal of the aesthetic in terms of mind is jut part of the construal of everything whatever in terms of mind. For Gadamer, then, and by extension for both the analytic and hermeneutic readings of early modern aesthetics, what calls for explanation is the reversal of the preeminence in classical, medieval, and Renaissance philosophy of the metaphysical over the epistemological. The aesthetic is no longer construed in terms of

---

[18]*WM*, 92; *TM*, 87.
[19]*WM*, 93; *TM*, 87.
[20]*WM*, 95; *TM*, 89. Cf. the related views in K. Tsujimura, "Heideggers Weltfrage in einer ostasiatischen Sicht," *Journal of the Faculty of Letters* (Tokyo) 4 (1979): 19–31.

what is independent of mind because of the final transformation of Descartes's theory of mind into the idealism of Kant.

Before we can raise anew the central questions of aesthetics, then, we need to come to terms both with radical differences and with at least some of the surprising convergence of two ways of reading the history of early modern aesthetics. And to clarify what is being claimed under the programmatic heading of the subjectivization of aesthetics, we must look much more closely at the most controversial level of these readings, their divergent interpretations of Kant. I propose in the next chapter to recapitulate rather than to argue the salient features of Kant's understanding of aesthetic judgments in the *Critique of Judgment*. This investigation might then allow us to determine more critically just what are the most important of the many philosophical issues that separate these two readings of the history of early modern aesthetics.

Appendix 3: Schematizations and Constructs

What has to be emphasized by way of defending these kinds of readings against overly rigorous critics is that, despite their inevitable inaccuracies, they are extremely useful schematizations. They are useful, moreover, precisely because such schematizations help us get a clearer perspective on just where the present—and not necessarily most fruitful—understanding of art and cognitivity comes from, the kind of understanding we saw in the tensions between theory and practice we observed in the opening discussion of Danto and Gadamer.

Thus, if each of these readings is to be understood only as a schematization, and presented with other than exclusively historical intentions, we need to understand my representations of these readings in a similar view. Yet the schematizations differ importantly from my constructs: central elements in the former are attributable to actual positions held by historical personages, whereas central elements in the latter are not so attributable. I call my two renderings constructs in the sense that neither refers in its details to the actual views held by an actual group of philosophers, yet each represents an identifiable perspective that some contemporary philosophers would sympathetically accept as, in part, their own. To understand why these readings types, however, we need to look more closely at their interrelationships.

Chapter Four

Rereading Kant on
Aesthetic Judgments

A judgment of taste is aesthetic.

—Immanuel Kant

The necessity of the universal assent that we think in a judgment
of taste is a subjective necessity that we present as objective by
presupposing a common sense.

—Immanuel Kant

Kant's major work on aesthetics is found in two places—in
the *Observations on the Feeling of the Beautiful and the Sublime*[1]
and in the *Critique of Judgment*.[2] Commentary has generally
neglected the first of these works to concentrate on the second,[3]

---

[1](Königsberg, 1764, 1766; Riga, 1771). See Kant, *Werke in zwölf Bänden*, ed. W.
Wieschedel (Frankfurt, 1968), 2:825–87 (this edition is cited hereafter as *Werke*).
Here I rely on the more familiar translation by J. C. Meredith, *The Critique of
Judgment* (Oxford, 1952) (cited as M), rather than on the new translation by W. S.
Pluhar (Indianapolis, 1987).

[2](Berlin and Libau, 1790; Berlin, 1793; Berlin, 1799) (the *Critique of Judgment* is
cited hereafter as *KU*). See Kant, *Werke*, vol. 10. This edition includes both the
"Erste Einleitung" (that is, "Erste Fassung der Einleitung in die Kritik der Urteilskraft,"
9–68) and the "Introduction" (78–109). See Weischedel's editorial comments for the
relations between this edition and the earlier Akademie Ausgabe. See also Kant,
Opuscula selecta zu Kants Kritik der Urteilskraft, ed. G. Tonelli, 3 vols. (Hildesheim,
1978), G. Lehmann, *Kants Nachlasswerke und die Kritik der Urteilskraft* (Berlin,
1939), and especially V. Mathieu, *Kant Opus postumum*, ed. G. Held (Frankfurt,
1989).

[3]See, however, the important earlier discussions of the development of Kant's
aesthetics in P. Menzer, *Kants Ästhetik in ihrer Entwicklung* (Berlin, 1952); A.
Bäumler, *Kants Kritik der Urteilskraft: Ihre Geschichte und ihre Systematik* (Halle,
1923); and O. Schlapp, *Kants Lehre vom Genie und die Entstehung der Kritik der*

but this concentration has now always yielded the comprehension desired. The Third Critique is notorious for its myriad difficulties, which derive partly from its place in the system of Kant's philosophy as a whole and partly from the search for a unified account of his practical philosophy in particular.[4] A careful rereading of at least parts of that work brings out, I believe, serious gaps in both the analytic and the hermeneutic readings of early modern aesthetics.

Restrictions

In light of our quite specific aim here, to understand more clearly the central issues that separate the analytic and the hermeneutic readings of the history of early modern aesthetics, we may restrict our consideration of Kant's aesthetics to the Third Critique and in particular to part 1, "the critique of aesthetic judgment."[5] Both readings disregard the early treatise as premature because precritical; furthermore, the second part of the Third Critique is mostly concerned with problems in the philosophy of religion and the philosophy of science rather than in aesthetics.[6] Important connections link both works and both parts of the Third Critique,

---

Urteilskraft (Göttingen, 1901). In general I have used these notes to call attention to some of the very valuable work not in English as well as to the occasional older study in English that some of the most recent work carelessly overlooks. For other general references see chapter 1 notes 39 and 40.

[4] A further problem is continuing lack of attention to the debates that make up part of the context of Kant's work. See, for example, T. Tsunekawa, "Lessings *Laokoon* und Herders Kritik," *Journal of the Faculty of Letters* (Tokyo) 10 (1985): 67–83. For several general commentaries besides the Guyer cited in chapter 1, note 39, see J. Kulenkampff, *Kants Logik des ästhetischen Urteils* (Frankfurt, 1978); H. Mertens, *Kommentar zur Ersten Einleitung in Kants Kritik der Urteilskraft* (Munich, 1975); W. Bartuschat, *Zum systematischen Ort von Kants Kritik der Urteilskraft* (Frankfurt, 1972); G. Lebrun, *Kant et la fin de la métaphysique* (Paris, 1970); H. W. Cassirer, *A Commentary on Kant's Critique of Judgment* (London, 1938; 2d ed. 1970); M. Souriau, *Le jugement réfléchissant dans la philosophie critique de Kant* (Paris, 1926); M. Horkheimer, *Über Kants Kritik der Urteilskraft als Bindeglied zwischen theoretischer und praktischer Philosophie* (Frankfurt, 1925).

[5] Some larger perspective can be gained from K. Vorländer, *Immanuel Kant: Der Mann und das Werk*, 2 vols. (Leipzig, 1924; 2d rev. ed., vol. 1, Hamburg, 1977), 343–405. For an excellent selective bibliography on central points see Pluhar's translation (Indianapolis, 1987), 443–59. His glossary and index are valuable working tools.

[6] On the second part, see especially J. D. McFarland, *Kant's Concept of Teleology* (Edinburgh, 1970); K. Düsing, *Die Teleologie in Kants Weltbild* (Bonn, 1968); P. Baumanns, *Das Problem der organischen Zweckmässigkeit* (Bonn, 1965); and the older work of A. Stadler, *Kants Teleologie und ihre erkenntnistheoretische Bedeutung* (Berlin, 1874).

but elucidating these connections is usually the task of monographs on Kant's aesthetics as such and is not typically a concern in the more general readings of an entire era in the history of aesthetics.[7]

A second restriction is also in order. The structure of the Third Critique is elaborate.[8] Thus, not only does the treatise include two parts, one on aesthetic judgment and one on teleological judgment, but the first part itself divides into two sections, the first comprising two of what Kant calls "books." A schematic and abbreviated outline thus looks like this:

First Part: Critique of Aesthetic Judgment

Second Part: Critique of Teleological Judgment

First Section: Analytic of Aesthetic Judgment

Second Section: Dialectic of Aesthetic Judgment

First Book: Analytic of the Beautiful

Second Book: Analytic of the Sublime

We should recall that in the history of early modern aesthetics a clear relation exists between the beautiful and the sublime.[9] Indeed, one might argue generally, as we have already seen, that the classical concept of the beautiful holds the center of critical reflection on aesthetics until the early modern period; at the outset of the romantic period it is gradually replaced by the concept of the

[7]Several exceptions are the earlier works of V. Basch, *Essai critique sur l'esthétique de Kant* (Paris, 1896); H. Cohen, *Kants Begründung der Ästhetik* (Berlin, 1889); H. Lotze, *Geschichte der Ästhetik in Deutschland* (Munich, 1868); and R. Zimmermann, "Kant: The Aesthetic Judgment," in *Kant*, ed. R. P. Wolff (London, 1968).

[8]See R. K. Elliott, "The Unity of 'Kant's Critique of Aesthetic Judgment,'" *British Journal of Aesthetics* 8(1968): 244–59; G. Tonelli, "La formazione del testo della Kritik der Urteilskraft," *Revue Internationale de Philosophie* 8(1954): 423–48; and K. Kuypers, *Kants Kunsttheorie und die Einheit der Kritik der Urteilskraft* (Amsterdam, 1972).

[9]Note the discussion in P. Crowther, *The Kantian Sublime* (Oxford, 1989), and particularly several others of the classic English discussions already considered earlier, notably in A. Alison, *Essays on the Nature and Principles of Taste* (4th ed., 1815; New York, 1968); H. H. Kames, *Elements of Criticism* (1762; New York, 1971); and of course E. Burke, *A Philosophical Inquiry into the Origin of Our Ideas of the Sublime and the Beautiful*, ed. J. T. Boulton (New York, 1958).

sublime. Consequently Kant's division of his treatise is somewhat misleading, for a clear distinction is suggested between the two concepts of the beautiful and of the sublime while in fact such a distinction remains the subject of increasing controversy as the history of early modern aesthetics develops. But since this controversy and its many related problems—such as the nature of the sublime—are not the subject of our concern here, and since the basic concept remains that of the beautiful, it will prove useful to limit our considerations still further to the analytic of aesthetic judgment.[10]

One final restriction is called for. The analytic of aesthetic judgment falls roughly into two uneven parts, what we might call an analysis of the nature of aesthetic judgments and then what Kant calls a transcendental reduction, that is, a justification of the possibility of aesthetic judgments. The latter is especially important for understanding the interconnections between Kant's aestetics and his moral philosophy, as well as his treatment of the sublime.[11] But since the deduction is not naturally concerned with the nature of the beautiful and since each of the five stages of the deduction requires extensive critical commentary that is irrelevant to our primary concern with the nature of aesthetic judgment, we may set aside any detailed consideration of the deduction.[12] In what follows, then, neither Kant's early treatise, nor the critique of

---

[10]On the nature of aesthetic judgment, besides Souriau's work cited in note 4, see two older articles in English: H. Blocker, "Kant's Theory of the Relation of Imagination and Understanding in Aesthetic Judgments," British Journal of Aesthetics 5(1965): 37–45; and R. L. Zimmermann, "Kant: The Aesthetic Judgment," Journal of Aesthetics and Art Criticism 21(1962–63): 333–44. For more recent, and controversial, views see G. Nagel, The Structure of Experience: Kant's System of Principles (Chicago, 1984), and M. A. McCloskey, Kant's Aesthetics (London, 1987).

[11]There are important literary studies on these topics that are too often ignored by philosophers. See notably M. Nicholson, Mountain Gloom and Mountain Glory: The Development of the Aesthetic of the Infinite (Ithaca, 1959); E. Tuveson, The Imagination as a Means of Grace: Locke and the Aesthetics of Romanticism (Berkeley, 1960); D. B. Morris, The Religious Sublime: Christian Poetry and Critical Tradition in Eighteenth-Century England (Lexington, Ky., 1972); A. Wlecke, Wordsworth and the Sublime (Berkeley, 1973); and especially T. Weiskel, The Romantic Sublime: Studies in the Structure and Psychology of Transcendence (Baltimore, 1976).

[12]The deduction is a central piece in the understanding of the details of Kant's aesthetics, but it requires far more attention in its own right that I am able to award it here. A careful study should begin with the recent excellent collection by R. Förster, Kant's Transcendental Deductions (Stanford, 1989); a lucid exposition and criticism of the deduction is to be found in D. W. Crawford, Kant's Aesthetic Theory (Madison, Wis., 1974), and should be compared with Guyer's views. R. A. Makkreel, Imagination and Interpretation in Kant (Chicago, 1990), also undermines Guyer's position. See also A. C. Genova, "Kant's Transcendental Deduction of Aesthetic Judgments," Journal of Aesthetics and Art Criticism 30(1971–72): 459–75.

teleological judgment, nor the transcendental deduction of aesthetic judgment will be examined. I do, however, treat both the Preface and the Second Introduction in a brief appendix to this chapter.[13]

Unlike the procedure in the previous exposition of the major figures in the history of early modern aesthetics, it will be useful here to set aside secondary accounts and try to formulate briefly Kant's reflections on the beautiful. With these elements in hand, it will be necessary to focus on the major defects in Kant's treatment before finally turning to the particular features of his account that I will take as central in the analytic and hermeneutic interpretations.

Aesthetic Judgments

Kant begins his analysis of the beautiful by attempting to show that judgments of what is beautiful are valid not just subjectively, but also intersubjectively. His basic procedure is an analysis of the forms of these judgments, judgments that have been, as it were, emptied of empirical content. In the *Critique of Pure Reason* Kant believed he had established four basic forms of understanding; in the *Critique of Judgment*, he presupposes the well-foundedness of that previous analysis and proceeds to treat judgment under the same four headings. Similarly, each heading here, as in the First Critique, involves four "moments": thus judgments must have a quantity, a quality, a relation, and a modality. The quantity must be universal, particular, or singular; the quality affirmative, negative, or infinite; the relation categorical, hypothetical, or disjunctive; and the modality problematic, assertoric, or apodictic. Kant chooses to begin his analysis of aesthetic judgment with an investigation of quality rather than quantity because, as he says in a footnote, "this is what the aesthetic judgment on the beautiful looks to in the first instance."[14] Beginning with quality, moreover, enables Kant to

---

[13]Other approaches are carefully examined in J. Taminiaux, "Des interprétations de la *Critique de la faculté de juger,*" in *Actes du Congrès d'Ottawa sur Kant,* ed. P. Laberge et al., 124–142 (Ottawa, 1976). Early readings of Kant's aesthetics may be examined in the convenient collection of J.Kulenkampff, *Materialien zu Kants Kritik der Urteilskraft* (Frankfurt, 1974), which includes, besides selections from precursors of Kant such as G. F. Meier, Baumgarten, Hume, and Burke, further materials from Kant followed by selections from Schiller, Hegel, Goethe, and Schopenhauer.

[14]*KU,* section 1, note; M, 41, note 1. In general, I use the earlier, more familiar translation. After reflection I have thought it preferable to present a summary of Kant's views and then a series of criticisms rather than integrating the criticisms into the summary. Since my criticisms often overlap the important divisions in Kant's own exposition, I have tried to pay roughly equal attention to those divisions and to the criticisms.

determine the quantity of the aesthetic judgment more easily by arguing from the disinterestedness to the universality of aesthetic pleasure.

The quality of the aesthetics judgment is affirmative. Kant's point here is that aesthetic judgments are disinterested in that they do not depend on the representation of the existence of the object in question. Moreover, aesthetic judgments are not logical in Kant's special sense of judgments that attribute some property to the object in question, because the representation of the object in aesthetic judgments is always referred to the feelings of pleasure or displeasure in the subject. Furthermore, pleasure and displeasure, Kant says simply, are parts of the subject's "feeling of life."[15]

If we are to comprehend his characterization of aesthetic judgment as "disinterested," we must grasp what he means by "interest." "The delight," he writes, "which we connect with the representation of the real existence of an object is called interest."[16] Kant thus does not deny that in aesthetic judgment delight is taken in the presence of the object so long as "the mode of existence" is clearly understood to be strictly mental. This means that contemplation of the object must abstract from the question whether, in addition to existing mentally as representation, the object also exists in the spatiotemporal world. Disinterestedness then concerns the independence of aesthetic judgments: not simply independence from the existence of the object under consideration but, more precisely, independence from its real existence.

Kant proceeds to distinguish aesthetic judgments both from judgments about what is agreeable and from judgments about what is good where "good" is taken in the sense of useful. Judgments about what is beautiful differ from judgments about what is agreeable in being disinterested. The two are similar, however, for both concern objects in their relation not to objective sensation but to subjective sensation. But unlike aesthetic judgments, judgments of what is agreeable are interested. These judgments generate a desire to possess such objects, a desire for gratification.

Aesthetic judgments differ also from utilitarian judgments in being disinterested. These two kinds of judgments, however, are also similar. A certain delight accompanies each. Yet utilitarian judgments presuppose that the person judging already has a concept of "what sort of thing the object is intended to be,"[17] whereas aesthetic judgments presuppose no such concepts. "Delight in the

[15] *KU*, section 1; M, 42.
[16] *KU*, section 2; M, 42.
[17] *KU*, section 4; M, 46.

beautiful must depend upon the reflection on an object precursory to some not definitely determined concept."[18] Kant concludes that, although all three judgments are accompanied by delight, each is a different kind of judgment. Each exhibits a different relationship between its representation and the feelings of pleasure. Moreover, aesthetic judgments alone are disinterested.

In short, Kant argues here that aesthetic judgments are "indifferent" to the real existence of the objects in question. Further, the contemplation of these objects or modes of representation in aesthetic judgment is, he claims, neither "*grounded* on concepts, nor yet intentionally directed to them,"[19] but always accompanied by either delight or aversion. The emphasis thus falls squarely on the subject and on a negative characterization of the beautiful as what the subject takes disinterested delight in, not on any presumed properties of the objects actually judged. Thus the beautiful is linked with pleasure, but these pleasures are disinterested ones. And aesthetic judgments as to their quality are affirmative judgments. But such a characterization remains partial, for Kant insists that we can speak of a pure aesthetic judgment only to the degree that all four aspects of an aesthetic judgment are properly determined.

Kant now specifies the quantity of aesthetic judgments as universal. Although he proposes a series of considerations to justify this conclusion, not all are of equal value. Some, indeed, seem fallacious. The most important reflection, however, is persuasive. For Kant argues that if what is beautiful is represented in association with disinterested feelings of pleasure, then the reasons for the delight the subject takes in the beautiful are not particular to the subject himself. Hence they cannot be presupposed as available to all subjects. "Accordingly," Kant writes, "he will speak of the beautiful as if beauty were a quality of the object and the judgment logical (forming a cognition of the object by concepts of it) although it is only aesthetic, and contains merely a reference of the representation of the object to the subject."[20] But since this universality is not based on concepts, Kant speaks of a subjective rather than an objective universality.

The subjective universality of aesthetic judgments is, besides their disinterestedness, a further feature that distinguishes them both from judgments of what is agreeable (Kant now calls these

[18]*KU*, section 4; M, 46.
[19]*KU*, section 5; M, 49.
[20]*KU*, section 6; M, 51.

judgments of sense) and from utilitarian judgments. Neither makes any claim to be valid for all persons. What is useful and what is agreeable is relative to the individual in question; what is beautiful, however, is such regardless of individual preferences. Kant concedes that some things may be agreeable or useful to many persons. But even in these cases we are dealing at best only with empirical rules and not with something of genuinely universal validity.

In his discussion of subjective universality Kant stresses again that aesthetic judgments have to do with the form, not the contents, of our representations of things. An aesthetic judgment "imputes" to everyone the delight that the subject takes in the representation of something. This representation is not a concept itself, nor is it based upon a concept, as is the case when judgments are made about what is good. Thus in an aesthetic judgment the representation is referred directly to the feelings of pleasure or displeasure without the mediacy of concepts. Since no concepts are involved, such judgments cannot serve as the basis for knowledge of objects. Kant summarizes his point as follows: "The judgment of taste i.e., aesthetic judgment itself does not *postulate* the agreement of every one (for it is only competent for a logically universal judgment to do this, in that it is able to bring forward reasons); it only *imputes* this agreement to every one, as an instance of the rule in respect of which it looks for confirmation, not from concepts, but from the concurrence of others."[21] Aesthetic judgments, Kant adds, may be erroneous; but no aesthetic judgment lacks the claim to universal, that is, intersubjective validity.

Kant next describes the relation between the feeling of pleasure and the judgment of the object. The priority here is not on the side of pleasure. Rather, the "subjective condition" for an aesthetic judgment is its communicability or, as Kant puts it, "the universal capacity for being communicated incident to the mental state in the given representation."[22] What determines the aesthetic judgment, then, is not a concept but a particular mental state, "a feeling of the free play of the powers of representation in a given representation for a cognition in general."[23] In short, what characterizes the aesthetic judgment is the free play of both imagination and understanding in the nonconceptual presence of a particular

---

[21]*KU*, section 8; M, 56.
[22]*KU*, section 9; M, 57.
[23]*KU*, section 9; M, 58.

representation. Such a harmonious interplay is antecedent to feelings of pleasure just because this harmony is what generates the feelings.

In an aesthetic judgment, then, the delight the subject feels refers to the harmonious interplay of both imagination and understanding. Moreover, we are aware of this delight not intellectually through concepts but by what Kant calls minor sensations. An aesthetic judgment makes a claim on subjective universality. For such a judgment, though subject to error, involves the claim that what is beautiful pleases all persons by being able to affect their harmonious mental interplay without the mediacy of concepts.

Aesthetic judgments thus are not private but public; they claim subjective universal validity. The delight that accompanies these judgments is a pleasure not in particular material contents, but in the form of a representation. These feelings must of course be consistent with one another in order to be universalizable. When consistent, however, these feelings are also disinterested. Thus, as Kant titles one of his sections, "the beautiful is that which, apart from concepts, is represented as the object of a universal delight."[24] The aesthetic judgment, though singular in form, claims universal assent.

Purpose and Necessity

In the third section of the analysis of the aesthetic judgment, Kant turns to determining the judgment's relation. The problem here is reconciling two claims. According to the first, aesthetic judgments, unlike cognitive and moral judgments, are not based upon concepts. According to the second, aesthetic judgments are based upon the purposefulness of the object under consideration. Kant assumes throughout his discussion that the "relation" of aesthetic judgments is categorical.

Kant begins by reminding his readers that purposefulness is part of every mental act of judgment. Thus every judgment is performed to some end. But the particular end at issue cannot always be identified unequivocally, even when it is clear that the mental act itself exhibits the form of finality. "Finality therefore," as Kant says, "may exist apart from an end, insofar as we do not locate the causes of this form in a will but yet are able to render the

[24]*KU*, section 6; M, 50.

explanations of its possibility intelligible to ourselves only by deriving it from a will."[25] For Kant, the basis of aesthetic judgment is not any end whatever, either subjective or objective, because ends involve interest and a judgment thus based on interest would contradict the disinterested character of aesthetic judgment argued in the first moment. Rather, the basis of aesthetic judgments is the form of finality—what Kant describes as "the subjective finality in the representation of an object exclusive of any end (objective or subjective)... the bare form of finality in the representation whereby an object is *given* to us so far as we are conscious of it."[26]

Aesthetic judgments, moreover, in being grounded on the form of finality, are grounded on an a priori basis.[27] Thus the pleasure experienced in aesthetic judgments is not the effect of a cause but something disinterested and hence merely contemplative. The pleasure is "the consciousness of mere formal finality in the play of the cognitive faculties of the subject attending a representation whereby an object is given."[28] Nonetheless, although not an effect, this pleasure involves an inherent final causality. In other words, the pleasure involves a pleasure in preserving the representation, a pleasure in dwelling on what is being contemplated while the mind remains inactive.

Two kinds of aesthetic judgment must be distinguished: material aesthetic judgments predicate the agreeableness or disagreeableness of an object or its mode of representation, whereas formal aesthetic judgments predicate beauty of an object. Only the latter are proper, that is, pure aesthetic judgments. Since, however, both charm and emotion involve empirical elements, neither is characteristic of a pure aesthetic judgment. Kant's emphasis on form is part of his concern with making aesthetic judgments universalizable. He holds that only formal determination can be universally communicated because of variations in the sense capacities of different individuals. Hence he writes, "It is not what gratifies in sensation but merely what pleases by its form that is the fundamental prerequisite for taste" and therefore for aesthetic judgments.[29]

Pure aesthetic judgments not only are independent of charm and

[25]*KU,* section 10; M, 62.
[26]*KU,* section 11; M, 63.
[27]Note, however, the nuance that Kant discusses not only the form of finality of an object but also the form of finality of the mode in which the object is represented. See *KU,* section 5; M, 50; and *KU,* section 11; M, 62.
[28]*KU,* section 12; M, 64.
[29]*KU,* section 14; M, 67.

emotion, they are also independent of the concept of perfection. The argument is familiar. Kant again appeals to the subjective basis of aesthetic judgments in preconceptual feelings of pleasure in order to show that concepts are irrelevant here. "Beauty therefore as a formal subjective finality," Kant writes, "involves no thought whatsoever of the perfection of the object."[30] And further on he stresses again the noncognitive character of the aesthetic judgment, claiming that it "refers the representation by which an object is given solely to the subject and brings to our notice no quality of the object but only the final form in the determination of the powers of representation engaged in it."[31] A similar argument underlies Kant's related claim that any authentic judgment that characterizes something as beautiful with reference to a definite concept must be a material judgment and not a pure aesthetic judgment.[32] What determines the ground of pure aesthetic judgments are feelings of subjects, not concepts. These feelings are the basis of the universal communicability of what is correctly judged as beautiful.

Kant concludes by redescribing the beautiful as "the form of finality in an object so far as perceived in it apart from the representation of an end."[33] The example he provides is significant in referring to natural beauty rather than to the beauty of an artifact. "A flower . . . is regarded as beautiful," Kant writes, "because we meet with a certain finality in its perception which in our estimate of it is not referred to any end whatsoever."[34]

In the fourth and final part of his analysis of aesthetic judgment, Kant tries to determine the modality of this judgment. He had argued in the First Critique that there are three kinds of modality, depending on just how an affirmation or denial is made. Thus when what is affirmed or denied expresses logical possibilities, the mode is problematic; when what is affirmed or denied is considered real or true, the mode is assertoric; and when what is affirmed or denied is logically or necessarily true, the mode is apodictic. In the Third Critique the task is to determine whether the mode of aesthetic judgment is problematic, assertoric, or apodictic. More specifically, Kant wants to reconcile the view that an aesthetic judgment as

---

[30]*KU,* section 15; M, 70. See I. Stadler, "Perception and Perfection in Kant's Aesthetics," in *Kant: A Collection of Critical Essays,* ed. R. P. Wolff, 339–84 (New York, 1967).

[31]*KU,* section 15; M, 71.

[32]*KU,* section 16; M, 72.

[33]*KU,* section 17; M, 80.

[34]*KU,* section 17; M, 80.

subjective must be autonomous and based upon subjective feelings of pleasure or displeasure with the opposed view that aesthetic judgments may claim universal assent. He argues finally that the modality of aesthetic judgments is apodictic, but of a subjective kind.

Kant holds that aesthetic judgment involves a necessary reference to delight. The difficulty is to make the kind of necessity here explicit. He argues that the necessity is neither a "theoretical objective necessity" nor a strictly practical necessity, but an exemplary necessity. "In other words," Kant writes, "it [this exemplary necessity] is a necessity of the assent of *all* to a judgment regarded as exemplifying a universal rule incapable of formulation."[35] In short, like the feelings of pleasure accompanying aesthetic judgment, the peculiar necessity of an aesthetic judgment is also of a subjective kind. Hence this necessity is conditioned by the correctness or incorrectness of the particular aesthetic judgment in question.

Kant tries to describe in more detail just what conditions the necessity of aesthetic judgment by searching for a suitable principle that governs aesthetic judgment. He argues that some principle must be operative, for otherwise aesthetic judgments would not be pure and hence universally communicable. And yet this principle cannot be a definite objective one, for in that case the necessity of the aesthetic judgment would not be conditioned at all. He therefore claims the existence of a subjective principle, "one which determines what pleases or displeases by means of feelings only and not through concepts but yet with universal validity. Such a principle however could only be regarded as a *common sense.*"[36] Such a common sense, however, needs to be distinguished from the more familiar cognitive common sense governing practical judgments, which are made on the basis of concepts (although not clear ones). The common sense at issue here is based on feeling and is noncognitive.

With this hypothesis in hand, Kant goes in search of reasons that might justify the actual existence of such a principle as the subjective condition on the exemplary necessity of aesthetic judgments. Kant's central argument here is characteristic of his philosophical strategies elsewhere. Briefly, he assumes a common sense "as the necessary condition of the universal communicability of our knowledge."[37] The conclusion to such a common sense is reached

[35]*KU*, section 18; M, 81.
[36]*KU*, section 20; M, 82.
[37]*KU*, section 21; M, 84.

by showing how it follows from the universal communicability of "the way the cognitive powers are attuned for cognition generally,"[38] which itself follows from the universal communicability of cognition and judgments *tout court*.

Kant summarizes his position in the title of section 22: "The necessity of the universal assent that is thought in a judgment of taste [an aesthetic judgment, that is] is a subjective necessity which under the presupposition of a common sense is represented as subjective."[39] Kant's point is that when we judge something to be beautiful, we are advancing a public and universal claim that what we judge here and now to be beautiful ought to be (not will be) judged as such by all persons. The norm for the necessity of the judgment is not determinate, however, because it is merely subjective. But such an indeterminate form is precisely what the nature of aesthetic judgments presupposes.

With the considerations as background, Kant concludes by redescribing the beautiful as "that which apart from a concept is cognized as object of a necessary delight."[40]

Criticisms

Kant's analysis of aesthetic judgment has provoked much critical comment and scrutiny. My purposes, however, do not include an exhaustive evaluation of this complicated doctrine, with its many assumptions and frequent confusions. Rather, I am interested in just which of the varied controversial features of this doctrine might fairly be taken to centrally characterize the divergence between the alternative readings of the history of early modern aesthetics. I begin by underlining several of the disputed elements in Kant's theory.

One problem is the ambiguity in Kant's account, in the Third Critique and elsewhere (most notably, perhaps, in the distinction in the First Critique between analytic and synthetic), between the act of judging, the contents of that act, and a spatiotemporal correlate for these contents.[41] Although Kant takes great pains in his account of aesthetic judgment to draw on the analysis of mental acts that he developed in his two previous critiques, nowhere does he remove

[38]*KU*, section 21; M, 83.
[39]*KU*, section 22; M, 84.
[40]*KU*, section 22; M, 85.
[41]See, among others, Crawford 1974: 177–78.

the ambiguities that continually play around his use of the word "judgment." This is unfortunate, for unless we can determine in each of the four moments of his analysis of aesthetic judgment just which of these different senses is preeminent, we continually risk interpreting Kant's account as psychologistic or, at the other extreme, taking it as nothing more than a prelude to a more adequate linguistic treatment of the same matters. Are we to construe aesthetic judgments, in other words, as empirical events in individual minds, or are we to understand them as a species of mental sentences? In the first case any claims about universality and necessity would be definitively excluded, while in the second whatever necessity might at least be claimed could unsympathetically be argued away as analytic only.[42] Even on the basis of the general summary presented here, I think it is clear that neither of these interpretations does justice to Kant's aims in the Third Critique. His analysis of aesthetic judgment must not be taken as either merely psychologistic or merely linguistic. But exactly how we are to mediate between these extremes while giving Kant's own expressions their due is not obvious.

A second and related difficulty pervades Kant's account here. We have already noticed how ready Kant is to develop arguments against opposed interpretations of the nature of aesthetic judgments. It is striking that so many of these arguments turn on his insistence that aesthetic judgments are indeterminate. In other words, as reflective judgments aesthetic judgments do not function with the help of antecedent concepts.[43] This doctrine is central to Kant's treatment of the basically disinterested character of aesthetic judgments. The difficulty, of course, is trying to account at the same time both for the lack of any determinate control exercised over aesthetic judgments by clear and perspicuous concepts and also for the nonetheless somewhat specific nature of aesthetic judgment. Again, Kant's way of making his point can be confusing. Thus he speaks as if there were no conceptual control at all in aesthetic judgment while still recognizing in the practice of art the

[42]See B. Dunham, A Study in Kant's Aesthetics: The Universal Validity of Aesthetic Judgment (Lancaster, Pa., 1934); and W. Henckmann, "Über das Moment der Allgemeingültigkeit des ästhetischen Urteils in Kants Kritik der Urteilskraft," in Proceedings of the Third International Kant Congress, ed. L. W. Beck, 295–306 (Dordrecht, 1972).

[43]See G. Weiler, "Kant's 'Indeterminate Concept' and the Concept of Man," Revue Internationale de Philosophie 16(1962): 432–46; and F. Williams, "Philosophical Anthropology and the Critique of Aesthetic Judgment," Kantstudien 46(1954–55): 172–88.

role of what Plato construed as exemplary causes. Kant provides us with no graduated range of conceptual possibilities to draw on as an effective means for dealing with his puzzling talk. We are not sure at places if Kant wants us to think of preconceptual rather than nonconceptual modes of thinking. And more specifically in the case of conceptual thought itself, he allows us no distinction of confused versus clear concepts, or complete versus incomplete and justified versus nonjustified concepts, and so on. In short, just as in the case of his talk about judgments, we are left with no more than our own rough approximations to Kant's intentions as a way of arguing our merely felt conviction that he wants to retain at least some preconceptual control over the contents of aesthetic judgments. Some conceptual control is necessary for the well-foundedness of aesthetic judgments, but just what kind of control remains inexplicit.

A third difficulty in Kant's account is the link between the feelings of pleasure and displeasure and the nature of aesthetic judgment. For Kant the link is essential. And of course in holding out for some sort of relation between pleasure and aesthetic judgment he is doing no more than following a remarkably consistent pattern in the history of aesthetics. For not only do Plato and Aristotle both insist on this connection (each drawing different conclusions from the conjunction), Augustine and Aquinas also make a central place in their aesthetics for pleasure. The problem is rather that, unlike his classical and medieval predecessors in this matter and unlike his habitual practice with almost all of the other cardinal concepts in the Third Critique, Kant takes virtually no interest in explaining to his readers just what he understands by his highly varied uses of the word "pleasure." This silence is disconcerting, for one of the cornerstones of Kant's doctrine of aesthetic judgment is the idea of disinterested pleasure.[44] And as we have noted already, it is from the well-foundedness of this idea that Kant wants to derive, in a loose sense of this logical term, his further characterization of aesthetic judgments as having universal import. To make this point Kant even varies the usual order of the four moments as he expounded them in the First Critique, electing here in the Third to take quality before quantity. If then we remain unclear as to the sense of Kant's use of the term "pleasure," we must remain even more unclear about the sense of his phrase "disinterested pleasure."

---

[44]See S. Axinn, "And Yet: A Kantian Analysis of Aesthetic Interest," *Philosophy and Phenomenological Research* 25(1964): 108–16.

But if confusion remains on this point, how are we to comprehend the connections that Kant repeatedly insists hold between disinterested pleasure and universalizability?

Such reflections are not simply quibbles about the inevitable obscurity involved in any attempt to define central terms. Kant's various uses of the word "pleasure" here—some commentators have described at least seven distinct senses of the term[45]—leave us in a peculiarly difficult position to assess the validity of his arguments for the necessity of the connection between pleasure and aesthetic judgments. This defect in Kant's analysis is all the more consequential in that without such clarification for his defense even sympathetic critics are left with little reason to resist the conclusion that Kant's insistence on a necessary connection is quite simply misplaced. Thus many would hold that we can properly speak of aesthetic judgments not only in those cases where feelings of pleasure or displeasure accompany such judgments, but just as well in cases where the putatively beautiful object leaves us either indifferent or with no feelings of pleasure or displeasure at all. Consider the indifference and sometimes complete lack of feeling that often assail even the careful critic who spends too long an afternoon in an outstanding museum.

In his helpful book *The Harmony of Reason*, Francis Coleman puts this important point well:

> Like many other objects in the world, a work of art can hold the attention without likes or dislikes being summoned to the scene.... aesthetic judgment is broader than feeling pleasure or displeasure, judgments of aesthetic mediocrity or indifference are no less aesthetic judgments for being concerned with what is neither pleasurable nor unpleasurable. Moreover, aesthetic judgment is often engaged in discernment or detection just as much as in enjoyment and delectation. If one is interested in something—even "disinterested" in Kant's sense—it does not necessarily follow that we must be interested hedonically.[46]

How are we to deal with appraisals such as these when Kant himself, like so many of the eighteenth-century aestheticians, forgoes defining more carefully one of his central terms?

---

[45]F. X. J. Coleman, *The Harmony of Reason: A Study in Kant's Aesthetics* (Pittsburgh, 1974), 66–74. Coleman's work has been of help throughout my reading of Kant.
[46]Coleman, 1974: 76.

A fourth difficulty with Kant's doctrine of aesthetic judgment concerns his account of the free play of imagination and understanding.[47] Kant holds that the harmony of this play of our intellectual faculties is precisely what generates the feelings of pleasure that are said to be the necessary concomitants of aesthetic judgments. We need not insist here on the easily remedied confusion that Kant's habitual talk of faculties involves. Like both his predecessors and his contemporaries, Kant continued to speak of the mind in terms of separate faculties regardless of several consequences his epistemology seems to entail as to the existence or nonexistence of such entities. Moreover, in formulating his views of aesthetic judgment, Kant never felt the need to avoid the intermediacy of a faculty of taste.[48] We need not follow Kant in these practices, however. When Kant speaks of the faculties of understanding, imagination, and taste, we may talk instead of understanding and imagining and judging something to be beautiful.

But when we try to parse what Kant means by the "free play" of understanding and imagining, a difficulty appears. Part of the difficulty is related to the earlier problem of whether or not all aesthetic judgments unify their contents in terms of concepts, and if so in terms of just what kinds of concepts. For the "freedom" Kant has in mind here, at least in the case of imaginings, has to do basically with a freedom from at least some kinds of clear conceptual constraints. But this is not all of the difficulty; what needs still further clarification is his perspective. When he speaks of "free play" and "harmony," does Kant have in mind the aesthetic judgment of artists in the throes of artistic creation or audiences in the tangles of artistic appreciation? The difference is important. For if we focus our attention on the role that exemplarity plays in artistic conception, Kant's account seems fine. In fact, this case appears to be the central one for Kant. But if we turn to the vagaries that accompany the making of aesthetic judgments by an individual patron or an audience as a whole, then little if any role for exemplary causes seems left. And if we set aside such entities, then

[47]See H. Blocker's article cited in note 10; R. D. Hume, "Kant and Coleridge on Imagination," *Journal of Aesthetics and Art Criticism* 28(1969–70): 485–96, and R. Park, "Coleridge and Kant, Poetic Imagination and Practical Reason," *British Journal of Aesthetics* 8(1968): 335–46.

[48]S. Körner, "Kant's Theory of Aesthetic Taste," in his *Kant* (Baltimore, 1955), chap. 8; see also B. Lang, "Kant and the Subjective Objects of Taste," *Journal of Aesthetics and Art Criticism* 25(1966–67): 247–53, and J. Fisher and J. Maitland, "The Subjectivist Turn in Aesthetics: A Critical Analysis of Kant's Theory of Appreciation," *Review of Metaphysics* 27(1974): 726–50.

just which features of audiences' experience are relevant to Kant's talk of the free play of understanding and imagination? Kant assumes the relevance of his analysis to the case of the artist. But in leaving on the margins of his account the nature of the free play of imagination and understanding in the audiences' aesthetic judgments, Kant invites criticism of the universality he claims for this feature. In short, more than just artists make aesthetic judgments. And with regard to nonartists, Kant leaves obscure whether their aesthetic judgments also involve a harmony of the faculties generating feelings of pleasure or displeasure.

A final difficulty with Kant's account concerns his analysis of form.[49] Kant, we have seen, wants to distinguish between temporal form, which he calls "play," and nontemporal (mostly spatial) form, which he calls "figure." Unlike the immediately perceived features of nontemporal form, those of temporal form require the work of the imagination to produce some kind of synthesis for the operation of judgment. Kant takes pains to insist that the aesthetic use of the word "form" is not meant to include "shape" as such, or even a particular "fixed form" such as is a necessary feature in certain genres of, say, the literary arts—for instance, the sonnet. Although each of these may be associated with aesthetic forms, peculiarly distinctive of aesthetic form is rather its connection with the individuality of the object that is judged beautiful. For this reason, of course, Kant holds that aesthetic judgments are singular even though they are universalizable. Note further that Kant does not construe this individual form with the help of abstraction from the material contents of aesthetic judgment. Aesthetic judgments have content, and some of this content includes what Kant wants to call aesthetic form. This aesthetic form, as Coleman has noted, "arises out of the interplay" of the different ways the contents of the aesthetic judgment are organized—of the varieties, we might say, with which certain aesthetic constraints in a medium are interrelated.[50]

Kant goes on to distinguish between pure form and mere form. Mere form is linked with Kant's idea of dependent beauty. Like dependent beauty, mere form relies upon a concept of what the beautiful thing must be in its perfected state. Pure form, on the other hand, is linked with Kant's idea of free beauty. Like free

---

[49]See T. E. Uehling, Jr., *The Notion of Form in Kant's "Critique of Aesthetic Judgment"* (The Hague, 1971), and D. Barrows, "Kant's Theory of Aesthetic Form," in *The Heritage of Kant*, ed. G. T. Whitney and D. F. Bowers (New York, 1939).

[50]Coleman 1974: 61.

beauty, pure form does not involve this dependence on a concept. Again, the talk of concepts is disconcerting for its lack of specificity. The basic problem, however, is making sense of what Kant means here by pure form or aesthetic form properly speaking.

Some have suggested that aesthetic form "is either what the artist imparts by the workings of his own subjective schematism, or what the perceiver, in aesthetic judgment, recognizes as what would be an expression of his own subjective schematism."[51] But this interpretation is complicated by the further difficulty of sorting out Kant's earlier and difficult doctrine of schematism. The basic idea of a schema is the capacity to articulate in a temporal mode both categories and concepts, a capacity to articulate models that include categories and concepts. "Although the schemata of sensibility," Kant writes in the First Critique, "first realize the categories, they at the same time restrict them, that is, limit them to conditions which lie outside the understanding, and are due to sensibility. The schema is, properly, only the phenomena, or sensible concept of an object in agreement with the category."[52] Kant applies this doctrine to the imagination in "The Analytic of the Sublime" in the Third Critique. He holds there that imagination involves a kind of spontaneity that is associated with our feelings of pleasure and displeasure.[53] This spontaneity appears to impose an individual form on the central contents of the aesthetic judgment.

The idea, then, seems to be this: In making aesthetic judgments, artists do so in light of their own previous experience of styles, conventions, traditions, and whatnot—in short, in terms of a schema. They continually call on this standard individually when they come to make particular judgments about beautiful things. The schema thus is a general and somewhat but not completely indeterminate framework or open set of regularities that functions as principles in accordance with which aesthetic judgments are made. Such an influence on the contents of the aesthetic judgment might then be construed as an imposition of form. The form imposed on the contents, however, is not at all the classical correlate of matter in the Aristotelian and later Scholastic metaphysics. Rather, form is a subjective schematism to which contents of individual aesthetic judgments are spontaneously referred through what Kant calls "the free play of the imagination." A similar schematism may be

---

[51]Coleman 1974: 62.
[52]*Critique of Pure Reason*, trans. N. Kemp Smith (London,1933), A 146, B 185–86; cited in Coleman 1974: 63.
[53]*KU*, Allgemeine Anmerkung, 191; M, 121.

taken as operative in aesthetic judgments made by audiences. Such schematism Kant holds to be produced by the pure categories when they are subsumed under space and time.[54]

When we reflect again on at least these five kinds of difficulties that threaten the final satisfactoriness of Kant's aesthetics in the *Critique of Judgment*—on the difficulties, that is, with such major themes as judgment, concepts, pleasure, harmony, and form—I think a fuller understanding of what both the analytic and the hermeneutic readings call "the subjectivization of aesthetics" comes into focus. The subjectivization of aesthetics in Kant's work is nothing more or less than the preeminence of the form and contents of aesthetic judgments over their spatiotemporal correlates. The central theme of early modern aesthetics is not the transformation of the theory of beauty into the theory of the aesthetic, as the analytic reading would have us believe. Nor is this theme the gradual eclipse of the cognitivity of the artwork, as the hermeneutic reading would urge on us. Rather as an attentive reflection on precisely that figure where both of these readings converge and diverge suggests, Kant's subjectivization of aesthetics is his leaving finally unresolved the ambiguities of aesthetic judgments. The issue is whether aesthetic judgments properly speaking are cognitive or not. Kant says they are not, and analytic philosophers have mainly been content to follow him without noting his nuance: aesthetic judgments are precognitive. But given these difficulties, is Kant finally right? Hermeneutic philosophers think not. But neither the analytic nor the hermeneutic reading is detailed enough to justify the respective positions. For in the first case the possibility that Kant might be mistaken about the noncognitivity of aesthetic judgments does not seem to arise seriously enough, while in the second the possibility seems to be taken for a certitude but the demonstrations are still outstanding. I suggest in the next chapter that we look for some further light on this dispute in an unusual place, Bernard Bolzano's criticisms of Kant. In his preoccupations with both logical rigor and the primacy of consciousness, Bolzano, although almost forgotten, is an appealing figure for both analytic and hermeneutic readers alike.

---

[54]On the complicated doctrine of the schematism and the imagination, see especially W. H. Walsh, *Kant's Criticism of Metaphysics* (Edinburgh, 1975), 72–77.

Appendix 4: Judgment, the Finality of Nature, and Imagination

In the Preface and Second Introduction to the *Critique of Judgment*, Kant situates the analysis of judgment with respect both to his views about the nature and divisions of philosophy as a whole and to his separate but related tasks in the two previous critiques.[55] The general question he proposes for his work here is whether the judgment, like the understanding and reason, has a priori principles.[56] If so, the question is, "Are they constitutive, or are they merely regulative . . . and do they give a rule a priori to the feeling of pleasure and displeasure."[57]

The subject mater here is difficult, particularly the problem of finding at least one a priori principle specific to judgment. Such a principle, Kant says, may not be derived from a priori concepts, since these belong in the domain of understanding, but only from the judgment itself. Moreover, whatever a priori concept can be identified in the domain of judgment must not be constitutive in the sense of providing cognition but must be merely regulative in the sense of providing a heuristic. And finally, this concept must not be applicable as objective rule, because in that case an infinite regress would be generated, since "another faculty of judgment would again be required to enable us to decide whether the case was one for the application of the rule or not."[58] The principle peculiar to judgment thus must be derived from a regulative, subjective, a priori concept.

"Judgment in general," Kant writes, "is the faculty of thinking the particular as constrained under the universal."[59] Judgments, moreover, are of two kinds, determinant when the judgment subsumes the particular under a given universal, and reflective when

[55]See P. Heintel, *Die Bedeutung der Kritik der ästhetischen Urteilskraft für die transzendentale Systematik* (Bonn, 1970); R. Odebrecht, *Form und Geist: Der Austeig des dialektischen Denkens in Kants Ästhetik* (Berlin, 1930); and A. C. Genova, "Kant's Three Critiques: A Suggested Analytical Framework," *Kantstudien* 60(1968–69): 135–46.

[56]For citations, I refer first to the relevant sections or paragraphs of the German text cited in note 2, then to pages in the English translation by J. C. Meredith (New York, 1952). The commentary in Meredith's first edition is sometimes helpful—see *Kant's Critique of Aesthetic Judgment* (part 1 of the *Critique of Judgement*), trans. J. C. Meredith (Oxford, 1911). J. Bernard's earlier English translation (London, 1892) sometimes repays comparison with the usually better version of Meredith.

[57]Vorrede; M, 4.

[58]Vorrede; M, 5.

[59]Einleitung, section 4; M, 18.

the universal for a given particular must be found. Only the latter requires a principle, since the universal or principle or rule or law is already given for the former. The reflective judgment, further, requires not an empirical but a transcendental principle, because no empirical principle alone suffices to establish the unity of all empirical principles, a unity that systematic subordination presupposes. "Such a transcendental principle therefore the reflective judgment can only give as a law from and to itself."[60] This principle Kant identifies with the finality of nature: "The argument for this identification is an argument by analogy.... as universal laws of nature have their ground in our understanding, which prescribes them to nature..., particular empirical laws must be regarded, in respect of that which is left undetermined in them by these universal laws, according to a unity such as they would have if an understanding...had supplied them for the benefit of our cognitive faculties, so as to render possible a system of experience according to particular natural laws."[61] The basic idea is that nature in its multiplicity is presented in the concept of natural finality as if all of its empirical laws constituted a unity capable of being understood by some intelligence.

When Kant terms the finality of nature a transcendental principle, he wants to distinguish it from any merely metaphysical principle. The former, but not the latter, enables us to "represent a priori the universal condition under which alone things can become objects of our cognition generally."[62] The concept of those objects cannot, unlike those at issue in metaphysical principles, be determined empirically. Rather, these concepts are pure concepts of "objects of possible empirical cognition generally."[63] Moreover, such a transcendental principle dissolves neither concepts of nature, because the basis of the transcendental principle is by definition not empirical, nor concepts of freedom, because reflective judgments, Kant claims, do not attribute anything objective to their contents. In light of transcendental a priori principles, reflective judgments prescribe for themselves regulative laws that are adopted, as Kant says, "in the interests of a natural order."[64] Thus the general law is called the law of the specification of nature, that is, the law by which nature is considered in reflective judgments to

---

[60]Einleitung, section 4; M, 19.
[61]Einleitung, section 4; M, 19.
[62]Einleitung, section 5; M, 20.
[63]Einleitung, section 5; M, 21.
[64]Einleitung, section 5; M, 25.

constitute a basic unity in all the diversity its known and unknown empirical laws involve. In short, the finality of nature is its harmony.

Kant now turns, in section 6 of the Introduction, to deal with the association between this harmony and the feelings of pleasure and displeasure. Something, he writes, "that makes us attentive in our estimate of nature to its finality for our understanding—an endeavor to bring, when possible, its heterogeneous laws under higher, though still always empirical, laws—is required, in order that on meeting with success pleasure may be felt in their accord with our cognitive faculty, which accord is regulated by us as purely contingent."[65] Judgment attributes to nature a unity that understanding cannot impose. Attaining such a purposefulness in nature generates feelings of pleasure that are subjective. But since the judgment is governed by a transcendental principle, the feelings of pleasure are also governed by something that is more than merely subjective.

The core of Kant's treatment of judgment in the Introduction is to be found in his distinction in section 7 between the subjective and the objective aspects of representations. The subjective aspect he calls "aesthetic quality," the objective "logical validity."[66] Some features of the subjective aspect can serve as the basis for knowledge, and Kant gives as examples spatial qualities and qualities of external sensation. But other features of the subjective aspect cannot provide a basis for cognition—in particular, the feelings of pleasure and displeasure. Kant goes on to claim that the finality of nature is, like the feeling of pleasure associated with it, a feature of the subjective aspect of representation that cannot be constituent of knowledge because it is prior to cognition. This claim allows him to describe aesthetic judgment more fully. If, he writes, "imagination (as the faculty of intuitions a priori) is undesignedly brought into record with understanding by means of a given representation and a feeling of pleasure is thereby aroused, then the object must be regarded as final for the reflective judgment. A judgment of this kind is an aesthetic judgment upon the finality of the object which does not depend upon any present concept of the object and does not provide one."[67] The basis of the feelings of pleasure thus is not the contents of the object judged, but its form. And when in a reflective judgment the feelings of pleasure are

[65]Einleitung, section 6; M, 28.
[66]Einleitung, section 7; M, 19.
[67]Einleitung, section 7; M, 31. For a helpful account here cf. M. Sakabe, "Kant on *Verstand, Vernunft,* and *Einbildungskraft,*" in *The Reasons of Art,* ed. P. McCormick, 250–56 (Ottawa, 1985).

associated with the form of the object, the representation of the object in the judgment accords with the law of the specification of nature. And this law is governed by an a priori transcendental subjective principle, the harmony of nature.

Kant's central conclusion for our purpose is also to be found here in section 7. "When the form of the object... is in the mere act of reflecting upon it," he writes, "without regard to any concept to be obtained from it, estimated as the ground of a pleasure in the representation of such an object, then this pleasure is also judged to be combined necessarily with the representation of it, and so not merely for the subject apprehending the form, but for all in general who pass judgment. The object is then called beautiful." [68]

The subject for the analytic of aesthetic judgment is then announced—the analytic of the beautiful. And the beautiful remains the center of Kant's aesthetics because of its logical priority over all other aesthetic terms. Before pursuing Kant's discussion further, however, we need to return briefly to the key element of harmony. The question is whether Kant's understanding of artistic creativity much later in the *Critique of Judgment* requires a different notion of imaginative capabilities than the account he provided in the *Critique of Pure Reason* and elsewhere of both productive and reproductive imagination. [69]

One way of exploring such a challenging thesis is to look more closely at the discussion of those peculiar indeterminate products of imaginative play that Kant calls aesthetic as opposed to rational ideas. And this involves looking further ahead in the *Critique of Judgment* than the Preface and Second Introduction we have been discussing so far in this appendix, and paying fresh attention to the cardinal yet sketchy notion of "aesthetic ideas."

Immediately after using the example of Jupiter's eagle in section 49, "On the Powers of the Mind Which Constitute Genius," to distinguish an object's aesthetic attributes from its logical ones, Kant goes on to assert that aesthetic attributes "yield an *aesthetic idea*" whose role is "to quicken [*beleben*] the mind by opening up for it a view into an immense realm of kindred presentations." [70] In works of fine arts such aesthetic attributes, Kant continues, "accompany the logical ones and... give the imagination a momentum which makes it think more in response to those objects

[68]Einleitung, section 7; M, 31.
[69]See B. Sassen's excellent discussion, "Imagination and Artistic Genius: Kant's Theory of Originality," forthcoming.
[70]Akademie Ausgabe, V.315.

[*dabei*], though in an undeveloped way, than can be comprehended within one concept and hence in one determinate linguistic expression."

Recognizing perhaps that some of this doctrine is hardly transparent, Kant immediately presents this example from a French poem by Frederick the Great:

> Oui finissons sans trouble, et mourons sans regrets,
> En laissant l'Univers comblé de nos bienfaits.
> Ainsi l'Astre du jour, au bout de sa carrière,
> Répand sur l'horizon une douce lumière,
> Et les derniers rayons qu'il darde dans les airs
> Sont ses derniers soupirs qu'il done à l'Univers.

> Let us part from life without grumbling or regrets,
> Leaving the world behind filled with our good deeds.
> Thus the sun, his daily course completed,
> Spreads one more soft light over the sky;
> And the last rays that he sends through the air
> Are the last sighs he gives the world for its well-being."[71]

Realizing that his readers may not be clear as to exactly what is being exemplified, Kant comments: "The king is here animating his rational idea of a cosmopolitan attitude, even at the end of life, by means of an attribute which the imagination (in remembering all the pleasure of a completed beautiful summer day, which a serene evening calls to mind) conjoins with that presentation, and which arouses a multitude of sensations and supplementary presentations for which no expressions can be found."[72] After using a one-line example to illustrate a different but related notion, Kant formulates what the aesthetic attribute is said to yield—namely, an aesthetic idea—as "a presentation of the imagination which is conjoined with a given concept and is connected, when we use imagination in its freedom, with such a multiplicity of partial presentations that no expression that stands for a determinate concept can be found for it. Hence it is a presentation that makes us add to a concept the thoughts of much that is ineffable, but the feeling of which quickens our cognitive powers and connects language, which otherwise would be mere letters, with spirit."

In this context Kant says little more about the nature of aesthetic

---

[71]Pluhar's translation; see note 1.
[72]Akademie Ausgabe, V.316.

ideas, except to add that genius involves, besides the talent to discover ideas, the talent "to communicate to others, as accompanying a concept, the mental attunement that those ideas produce," what Kant here calls "spirit." Why, we ask, is spirit required? Kant replies: "In order to express what is ineffable in the mental state accompanying a certain presentation and to make it universally communicable . . . we need an ability (viz., spirit) to apprehend the imagination's rapidly passing play and to unite it in a concept that can be communicated without the constraint of rules (a concept that on that very account is original, while at the same time it reveals a new rule that could not have been inferred from any earlier principles or examples)."[73]

Now Kant's discussion of aesthetic ideas in this passage raises some key questions about at least three matters: (1) whether the role the imagination is said to play here requires recognizing capabilities other than those Kant has already included in his distinctions between productive and reproductive imagination; (2) if so, then just how we are to describe these capacities more explicitly; and (3) just where the limits of the freedom of imagination are to be found. I will conclude by indicating briefly how these questions might be understood.

As to the first question, do we require a third kind of imagination, or may we simply revise Kant's account of productive imagination to include the three closely related notions of aesthetic attitude, aesthetic idea, and spirit? The revisionary move would come to reconstruing Kant's earlier notion of productive imagination from the *Critique of Pure Reason* with the help of the related but somewhat fuller and later discussions from the *Critique of Judgment.*

As to the second question, even were we to concede both the propriety and the utility of taking Kant's later discussions as implying a kind of imagination fully distinct from either the productive or the reproductive imagination, can we characterize such reflective imagination in other than metaphorical terms without in fact providing a fuller, more mature description of productive imagination?

And as to the final question, if indeed Kant's later texts provide sufficient grounds for distinguishing a third, logically independent kind of imagination, and if such a reflective imagination can be properly characterized only in metaphorical terms, then what qual-

[73]Akademie Ausgabe, V.317.

ifications must we attach to our metaphors so as to properly restrict the freedom of reflective imagination?

When Frederick the Great chose to complement a particular idea of the cosmopolitan attitude with what is after all a rather trite extended metaphor, are post-Kantian readers justified in claiming that this kind of aesthetic presentation requires something distinctly different from a fuller account of Kant's earlier notion of productive imagination?

Chapter Five

Bolzano, Kant's Aesthetics, and a Realist Tradition

We call an object beautiful if its mere consideration provides us with pleasure, a consideration which we carry out with such a facility that we need not in even a single case become conscious of the consideration.

—Bernard Bolzano

Even the simplest object has an endless set of characteristics.

—Bernard Bolzano

BERNARD BOLZANO's outstanding work in mathematics, philosophy of science, and philosophy of logic is fairly well known.[1] In this chapter, however, I recall his almost forgotten reflections on

[1]Besides the *Wissenschaftslehre*, latest edition, 4 vols. (Stuttgart, 1985–88), see *Paradoxien des Unendlichen*, 2d ed. (Hamburg, 1962), and *Grundlegung der Logik*, 2d ed. (Hamburg, 1978). For a brief overview of Bolzano's work, see Y. Bar Hillel's article in *The Encyclopedia of Philosophy*, ed. P. Edwards (New York, 1967). A bibliography of Bolzano's works can be found in volume 2.1 (with a supplement in 1988) of the *Bernard Bolzano Gesamtausgabe*, ed. E. Winter et al. (Stuttgart, 1969–), which also contains many of the mathematical works. About fifty volumes are planned. Good working bibliographies of material about Bolzano may be found in J. Berg, *Bolzano's Logic* (Stockholm, 1962), and in E. Herrmann, *Der Religionsphiloso-phische Standpunkt Bernard Bolzanos* (Uppsala, 1977). The best biography is that by J. Louzil, *Bernard Bolzano* (Prague, 1978; in Czech); see also E. Winter, *B. Bolzano* (Stuttgart, 1969). To situate Bolzano's work with respect to Kant's, see the Kant chapter in L. W. Beck, *Early German Philosophy: Kant and His Predecessors* (Cambrige, Mass., 1969), 426–505, and F. C. Beiser, *The Fate of Reason: German Philosophy from Kant to Fichte* (Cambridge, Mass., 1987). An excellent alternative to Beiser's approach is D. Jähnig, *Welt-Geschichte, Kunst-Geschichte: Zum Verhältnis von Vergangenheitserkenntnis und Veränderung* (Cologne, 1975). A useful selection is *Bernard Bolzano: Philosophische Texte*, ed. U. Neeman (Stuttgart, 1984), with a selected bibliography.

aesthetic, specifically his criticisms of Kant.[2] After sketching further those themes that are peculiar to Bolzano's work alone, I suggest several critical questions about Bolzano's own theory that should help us better understand the central differences between the two readings of early modern aesthetics we have been examining here. A larger and related point is that Bolzano's investigations into the concept not of the aesthetic but of the beautiful are more than just an important and unduly neglected criticism of Kant's well-known views;[3] these investigations provide a basic link between Kant's aesthetics and the work of Dilthey, Brentano, Meinong, Husserl, and Ingarden. In short, Bolzano's aesthetics include the initial elements of what might be broadly called a "realist" tradition in modern aesthetics, an alternative I go on to examine in some detail in part 2.

Four Definitions of the Beautiful

Bolzano's most important work on aesthetics in his *Über den Begriff des Schönen: Eine philosophische Abhandlung*, which first appeared in Prague in 1843 as a separate publication and was then reprinted in the Transactions of the Royal Bohemian Academy of Science in 1845, three years before his death at the age of sixty-seven.[4] This essay of little more than a hundred pages falls

---

[2]Bolzano's aesthetics, although in active preparation as volume 13, has not yet appeared in the *Gesamtausgabe*. My discussion here will be limited to his most important work in aesthetics, *Über den Begriff des Schönen: Eine philosophische Abhandlung*, which can be found in a modernized edition in B. Bolzano, *Untersuchungen zur Grundlegung der Ästhetik*, ed. D. Gerhardus (Frankfurt, 1972), cited hereafter as Bolzano. Besides his other essay, "Über die Einteilung der Kunst," which is also reprinted in Gerhardus, there is virtually nothing else of great importance. Very little has been written about Bolzano's aesthetics, and what we have is sketchy. The one exception is the best work so far on the aesthetics, the thorough survey article by K. Svoboda, "Bolzanova estetika," *Rozprovy Ceskoslovenské Akademie Ved* 64, Rada sv, 2(1954): 1–62, which includes a German translation.

[3]For other aspects of Bolzano's relation to Kant, see the work by his most gifted student, F. Prihonsky, *Neuer Anti-Kant oder Prüfung der Kritik der reinen Vernunft nach den in Bolzanos Wissenschaftslehre niedergliederten Begriffen* (Bautzen, 1850); M. Palagyi, *Kant und Bolzano* (Halle, 1902); and U. Neeman's two articles, "Analytische und synthetische Sätze bei Kant und Bolzano," *Ratio* 12(1970): 1–20; "Bolzanos Kantkritik," in *Akten der Internationalen Kant-Kongress*, ed. G. Funke, vol. 2 (Berlin, 1974), 842–47.

[4]Besides the works mentioned in note 2 above, there are a number of manuscripts in the Pamatnik Narodniho Pesennictvi (National Literature Archives) in Prague. A complete catalog of the Bolzano manuscripts, mainly mathematical, in the Austrian National Library has been prepared and published in the *Gesamtausgabe* by Jan

conveniently into roughly six parts: an introduction (section 1), an initial characterization of the beautiful (sections 2–13), a formulation of the concept of the beautiful (sections 14–15), consequences and corollaries of this formulation (sections 16–18), objections (sections 19–25), and a lengthy historical discussion (sections 26–57). Kant appears almost midway in the long historical part. And Bolzano's discussion consists almost exclusively of an exposition of Kant's treatment of the four "moments" we recalled at some length in chapter 4: quality, quantity, relation, and modality.

Bolzano begins on a critical note. He observes that, far from providing us with a single definition of the beautiful as he himself does in section 14, Kant has left us with four definitions. Moreover, each of these is supposed to represent the beautiful in terms of the four categories in which any object whatever, whether beautiful or otherwise, can be exhaustively described. Bolzano is ironic here about Kant's attachment to the doctrine of the categories ("Aus Liebe zu seinen Kategorien...beschenkte uns Kant"),[5] but he is also plainly dissatisfied with several of the proposed definitions, for three reasons. The last three definitions are not clearly separate definitions at all. The second deals with universality rather than, as Kant claims, with "quantity." And the third definition Bolzano reads as relevant to "relation" in only the narrowest sense. Because of these difficulties, Bolzano examines each of the four definitions more closely.

Bolzano paraphrases the first definition from Kant's Third Critique as "the beautiful is what pleases disinterestedly."[6] He reminds us that what Kant means by "interest" here is the feeling we associate with the representation of the existence of an object. In the case of something beautiful, our feeling is bound up only with the representation of the object, not with the representation of its existence. Bolzano, however, finds this account unacceptable. He points out that Kant's use of the term "interest" does not correspond to any of our everyday uses of the term, uses that Bolzano

Berg. Similarly, a complete catalog of the Prague manuscripts has for several years also been completed, prepared by P. Krivsky and M. Pavlikova for publication in the *Gesamtausgabe* as volume 2.2. However, the present Czechoslovakian authorities have repeatedly refused permission for the publication of this catalog. Bolzano's other incidental references to aesthetics are discussed very helpfully by Svoboda 1954: 27–33, 44–56.

[5]Bolzano, section 37, 65.

[6]Kant, *Kritik der Urteilskraft*, in *Werke*, ed. W. Weischedel (Frankfurt, 1968), B17 (cited hereafter as *KU*).

goes on to describe. When we find something interesting we usually mean that the thing merits our attention or that we can expect some advantage from it. But in neither sense is it true that when we find something "interesting" we must find in ourselves some kind of feeling related to the existence of the object. Rather, Bolzano argues, when what is at issue is a beautiful object, then we surely have an interest in the beautiful if we take "interest" in either of its two usual senses. In short, Kant's first definition depends on adopting his unusual and merely stipulated sense of the definition's key term. But Kant gives us no reasons to do so, and besides, his unargued construal of this term seems in some of the centrally interesting cases to result in a false account.[7]

The second definition, which Bolzano paraphrases as "the beautiful is what without concepts pleases generally," is supposed to be a consequence of the first definition.[8] Citing other texts, Bolzano tries to specify the precise relation between the two definitions as Kant sees it.[9] But Kant does not succeed in making the relation precise. What pleases generally is what pleases everyone, says Kant. Bolzano tries to clarify the sense of the *jedermann* Kant refers to and concludes that not only God but many other persons must be excluded. For Kant has in mind every person who enjoys a certain level of cultivation. His definition thus is too broadly construed and hence, Bolzano concludes, the general proof of this definition must be false because it would have to prove too much.

A more interesting objection is based on Bolzano's distinction between concepts that are required if certain judgments are to be effected and concepts we are conscious of when effecting such judgments. Bolzano uses this distinction to challenge the first reason Kant adduces for his claim that judgments of taste are judgments without concepts. He cites Kant's own repeated remarks about the imagination and the understanding (B28) as well as Kant's own example (B49) against him. He also rejects the second justification Kant provides for his claim, that there is no transition from concepts to feelings of desire or lack of desire (B18). Bolzano cites as a counterexample the feelings that arise in someone who becomes acquainted with a particular kind of object solely by means of theoretical concepts. Thus, since neither justification withstands criticism, the second definition must also be set aside.

---

[7]Bolzano adds here further interesting comments on "good."
[8]From *KU*, B32; in Bolzano, section 38, 68.
[9]*KU*, B17, B21, B49, and B18, respectively.

The third definition Bolzano paraphrases as "the beautiful is what seems to us purposeful without having nevertheless a representation of its purpose."[10] Kant holds that something beautiful that is the object of a judgment of taste cannot have either a subjective or an objective purpose and yet may and must have a form of purposefulness. Bolzano rejects this doctrine because he claims that it finally depends on two previous contentions he has already rejected—that the feeling of beauty has to be connected with the representation and not the existence of an object, and that there can be no transition from any kind of concept to a feeling for something beautiful.

Again, however, a more interesting objection is put forward. Bolzano holds that Kant's doctrine of a "form of purposefulness without purpose" involves substantive and not just verbal contradictions. In the many circumlocutions Kant uses to convey this doctrine, the question arises just how, if there is no purpose, the form of purposefulness is to be recognized. For Bolzano "the perception of purposefulness... always presupposes perception of a definite purpose."[11] If there is no purpose, there can be no form of purposefulness. What we find in beautiful things is not purposes at all, but rules and concepts. When we consider a rose as something beautiful, we find a series of regularities that lead to our taking a kind of pleasure in the rose. We go on then to judge the rose beautiful. Accordingly, Bolzano also rejects Kant's third definition of the beautiful.

The final definition Bolzano paraphrases as "the beautiful is what without concepts is recognized nonetheless as an object of a necessary feeling of well being."[12] Bolzano concurs with Kant that the necessity at issue here is not objective so long as the judgments of taste under discussion have empirical objects as, for example, this rose. But in those cases where the objects at issue are pure concepts, such as virtue, then Bolzano thinks we cannot get away from objective necessity. Moreover, although Bolzano is willing to follow Kant in speaking of a distinction among objective, theoretical, and practical necessity,[13] he finds Kant's talk of "exemplary necessity" almost incomprehensible. He has the same problem with Kant's talk of certain kinds of universality.[14] Most interesting,

[10]From *KU*, B61; in Bolzano, section 39, 72.
[11]Bolzano, section 39, 75.
[12]From *KU*, B68; in Bolzano, section 39a, 78.
[13]See *KU*, B62.
[14]See, for example, *KU*, B65 and B67, and Kant's talk of "universal communicability."

perhaps, is Bolzano's observation that Kant's peculiar use of the word "feeling" clearly indicates that he is not talking about feeling at all but is dealing with a kind of knowing.[15]

Simples and Complexes

Let us now consider Bolzano's alternative account. In his short treatise on the beautiful Bolzano's aim is to clarify, or to define in the broad sense of the term, the concept of the beautiful. His main concern is to determine whether what we usually call the beautiful refers to something simple or something complex. If the latter, then a further task involves determining just which of the several referents is most appropriate.

When Bolzano proposes to formulate a clarifying definition of the beautiful, he aims at providing one and not several articulations of an objective concept that, if complex, must include all and only those components and relations that are proper to it alone.

Once these four preliminary points have been made, Bolzano begins his analysis of the beautiful by effecting several exclusions. The beautiful is not to be confounded, Bolzano holds—as does Kant—with the good, the pleasant, or the charming. Bolzano's reasons, however, are not the same as Kant's. Although many good things can rightly be called beautiful, Bolzano claims that not all beautiful things are properly to be called good; they often are called good simply from custom. As regards the pleasant, as long as we use the word in its habitual sense as what gives rise to pleasurable feelings and therefore refuse to follow Kant's usage, which Bolzano considers unjustified, we can agree that there is a connection between the pleasant and the beautiful. But Bolzano finds an asymmetry here: everything beautiful either gives or can give pleasure, but not everything pleasurable can be considered beautiful. For some things that do not affect the senses at all are rightly to be judged beautiful. And as regards the charming, which Bolzano takes as what arouses a certain desire in us, a further asymmetry is to be found. For again the beautiful turns out to be the broader concept in that beautiful things are charming but not all charming things are beautiful.

Bolzano's comments are all too brief to be finally convincing. But once we recall that the point of these exclusions is to allow us a

[15]Bolzano, section 39a, 81.

more unobstructed view of the concept of the beautiful rather than to enter into the kind of detail about the peculiar overlaps between the beautiful and less general concepts already investigated by Kant, I think Bolzano's brevity here is unobjectionable.

Bolzano's next move is to isolate the relevant characteristics of the beautiful. What features of the object our thoughts are directed to when we perceive this object as beautiful is not the first Bolzano wants to raise. Rather, he is initially concerned about just how something beautiful brings about a feeling of pleasure in the perceiving subject—about the kind of consideration going on in the perceiving subject's consciousness that results in, rather than is just accompanied by, a feeling of pleasure. And the phenomenon he settles on is the lightness and rapidity with which certain thoughts occur, so that we experience no need to make ourselves clearly conscious of these thoughts in any strictly conceptual manner. Bolzano's point is that considering something beautiful is accompanied by a sequence of thoughts that moves so quickly and lightly that we can follow those thoughts through without needing to explicate their contents precisely as concepts. By contrast, consider a complex mathematical proof where the sequence of thoughts must be explicated conceptually if the proof is to be grasped at all. Pleasure occurs in both cases, but only in the first case, Bolzano holds, are we properly dealing with pleasure in the beautiful. Thus two components of the beautiful may be articulated as follows: "We call an object beautiful if its mere consideration provides us with pleasure, a consideration which we carry out with such a facility that we need not in even a single case become conscious of this consideration."[16]

Universality and Pleasure

To find further components of the beautiful, Bolzano now returns to the question he had earlier postponed—just what our thoughts might be directed to when we find ourselves considering something beautiful. Whatever this feature or features may be, Bolzano, like Kant, wants to hold that our judgment that something is beautiful includes a certain claim to universality. Bolzano tries to specify, though in a different way than Kant does, just what kind of universality is involved. And he insists on the observation

[16]Bolzano, 16.

that persons differ in their receptivity to what is beautiful as a function of their education, their powers of understanding, and the use they make of these powers. These qualifications, he holds, must be kept in mind if we are to answer the question about where our thoughts are directed in the consideration of something beautiful.

When we judge something beautiful, Bolzano suggests, we are involved in asking what kind of thing this something is. In other words, we are looking for a particular concept or a particular representation or a particular rule that would allow us to deduce the properties of the thing in question. Since intuitions are insufficient by themselves, the kind of representation sought cannot be a simple one; it must be complex. When something is considered beautiful, not just intuition but all our intellectual powers must be involved. And as remarked earlier, memory, imagination, understanding, judgment, and reason must all be already developed to some degree and have been already exercised on beautiful things.

Besides the content of our considerations—particular concepts, representations, or rules—Bolzano tries to specify the source from which our pleasure in the consideration of beautiful things arises. Here he holds that whatever increases our natural powers is perceived as pleasure, whereas whatever decreases these powers is perceived as pain. Even our becoming conscious of some natural powers is to be considered pleasure. The stronger a particular natural power is, the more pleasure we derive from its increase. The pleasure we derive from the consideration of something beautiful, Bolzano continues, arises not from its utility, but from the activation of our various natural and especially intellectual powers. Something beautiful sets these powers to work in such a way that they are neither too little nor too much engaged for us not to be able to notice their growth in power. What we feel, then, is an increase in our natural intellectual powers. And this feeling brings pleasure.

Bolzano is especially careful to support this part of his theory, as if he were ready to acknowledge just how important a role his analysis of the course of aesthetic pleasure will play in his clarifying definition of the beautiful. Thus, besides providing an interesting description of how this pleasure process is supposed to work, and besides detailing three extended examples (which aim to show why we find a spiral, a fable, and a riddle beautiful), Bolzano offers what he calls two proofs for his view. The first[17] is simply the

---

[17]Bolzano, section 12, 1.

assertion that our pleasure in the beautiful can be explained on no general grounds other than the ones he has cited, for there are numberless cases where no other explanation can be found. Bolzano challenges us to explain his previous examples in an equally satisfying way with the help of some theory other than his own. And the second proof he offers[18] is that the degree of pleasure afforded by considering something beautiful increases directly in proportion to the demands it makes on our intellectual powers. Although each of these "proofs" invites closer attention, and though the apparently psychologistic character of parts of his description here needs examination, nonetheless, when put with Bolzano's formulations, descriptions, and examples they do serve well as reinforcements for the well-foundedness of his views.

With a series of components worked out, and having reassured himself that the synthesis of just these features will lead to neither too narrow nor too broad a concept, Bolzano now moves to formulate his definition of the beautiful. His conclusion might be paraphrased as follows: A beautiful object is one whose consideration by any person with developed intellectual powers results in pleasure. The basis of this pleasure is that it is neither too easy not too difficult for such a person—who at the moment does not in fact take the trouble of reaching conceptual clarity in this matter, once some of the object's properties have been grasped—to form a concept that would eventually allow working out, through further consideration, the remaining perceptual properties of this object. At the moment, however, the readiness of the intellectual powers allows the individual to arrive at "a dark intuition."[19]

This account itself, of course, is not transparent. But once we recall the earlier reflections that have led Bolzano to this formulation, even some of the more obscure elements become, I think, reasonably clear.

Bolzano now completes his account with two further steps. He first draws out the consequences of his definition and then tries to anticipate objections his definition may provoke. I will deal here with the first only, leaving the second for closer scrutiny in the final section of this chapter, where the question of the adequacy of Bolzano's theory must be raised.

The major consequences are four. This theory is said to allow us to account for why we often cannot express the reasons we find

18Bolzano, section 13, 32.
19Bolzano, section 14, 33.

something beautiful. For it is the very facility and alacrity of our thinking when considering the beautiful object that in part gives rise to the pleasure we experience. Moreover, the theory is also said to allow us to account for why, especially, our two highest senses, seeing and hearing, provide us with representations of perceptual beauty. For the senses of smell and taste are too uniform to allow us to observe the workings of a particular rule whose discovery sufficiently engages our intellectual powers. A third consequence is that this theory allows us to understand why a beautiful object can bring us pleasure by offering aspects of itself that we have not previously noticed. For some beautiful things—Bolzano mentions paintings and long poems—require varied, prolonged, and repeated consideration for all their relevant parts and relations to be grasped in an appropriate way. And finally, the theory is said to allow us to understand why different individuals are responsive to different kinds of beautiful things. For an individual's response to beautiful things is a function of the development of his or her intellectual powers. So much for the major elements of Bolzano's theory of the beautiful.

Dark Judgments

Bolzano details and responds to seven objections against his theory. Since one deals with the ugly, a topic omitted from my description of Bolzano's theory, I will attend to only six of these objections.

The first objection is that the theory presupposes that all beautiful objects are complexes that comprise dependent parts and their interrelations. But some beautiful objects, a single tone or a color, for example, are simples. Hence the theory is too narrowly construed. Bolzano's replies include a number of interesting incidental remarks about perception and the science of his day. Although, as he points out, the existence of simples is a controversial topic for his contemporaries, in any case neither a single note nor a color can be taken as without parts. Therefore, since the examples fail, it remains an open question whether the theory is in fact too broad. But another issue is concealed here, to which I will return later.

A second objection is that Bolzano's theory implies that some complexes are so difficult to grasp that they cannot count as beautiful objects. Yet the history of the humanities offers counterexamples. For instance, classical scholarship shows that some understanding of the proper sense of archaic lexical items in Greek epigrammatic poetry allows us finally to perceive this poetry as an instance of something beautiful; and yet this program may require several generations of arduous scholarly work for its realization. Again, the theory seems to be too narrowly construed in taking as beautiful only those objects that can be grasped without much difficulty. Bolzano replies with a distinction between those considerations that lead up to an apprehension of the object as beautiful and those that accompany that apprehension. The first, indeed, as his favorite examples from mathematics show, may require prodigious and protracted effort. But the second, he insists, must be neither too facile nor too difficult if the object is to be apprehended as beautiful.

A third objection turns on the claim that Bolzano's theory confuses the beautiful with the regular. Although many rule-governed things, such as complicated astronomical clocks, may indeed be beautiful, some beautiful things are not regular at all. Again, the theory seems too exclusive. Bolzano replies that not every kind of regularity is a condition for beauty, but only that kind that can be grasped in an anticipatory way without going through with the complete conceptual analysis of the object in question. Consequently, the theory does leave room for some kinds of beautiful complexes that show themselves after analysis not to be rule-governed in the sense specified. What is necessary is an initial apprehension of the possibility of rule-governedness such that a person's intellectual powers are sufficiently engaged to arouse the feelings of pleasure, which is precisely the sense of the increase of those powers in the continuation of their present activity.

A related objection holds that Bolzano's theory construes the beautiful object to be the result of the rule-governed activity of the artist or creator. But since art must arise out of the free interplay of the artist's perceptual, emotional, and intellectual powers, Bolzano's theory effectively subjects all artistic activity to the exaggerated constraints of determined rules. And any object that consequently exhibits such overdetermination will displease rather than please. Bolzano replies once again with a distinction, this time the familiar one between the production of a beautiful object and the properties of the object produced. He argues that what is at issue in the definition of the beautiful is not the first (how much rule-governed activity goes into the production of the beautiful object), but only the second. Although regular relations must subsist among the parts of the beautiful object, these regularities must not be manifest in such a way that they detract from the perfection of the work—for example, where they are too obviously apparent, or where one series of rules has been abandoned halfway through the work for another series. This objection, then, although it raises several important issues, is basically irrelevant; what is at issue is how an object appears to us and not finally the related but different question of how the object has been produced.

A fifth objection focuses on the key terms in Bolzano's theory, facility and alacrity. Here, the claim is, the theory leads to the unwelcome, even absurd conclusion that the more easily and quickly we grasp the regularities that govern the beautiful object, the more beautiful that object must be. The example cited is that of a play: the more easily and quickly we can anticipate its conclusion, according to the theory, the more beautiful the play. Such a consequence is unwelcome because it would privilege the most pedestrian of our dramas—say, early nineteenth-century sentimental comedies— and devalue the best of our tragedies, such as Sophocles' Oedipus plays, where an unforeseeable turning point is part of the essence of the play's success. Bolzano replies with a simple denial that this consequence follows from his theory. To the contrary, he argues, such a result could not follow from a theory that required above all that a person's intellectual powers first be sufficiently engaged. Dramas whose opening scenes allow us infallibly to predict their outcomes are insufficiently complicated to allow of the peculiar kinds of pleasure that arise from our considerations of beautiful objects.

The last objection to be considered here is that the concept of the beautiful is too widely employed for its definition to include so many elements organized in such a complicated way. For it seems that virtually all human beings employ some kind of a distinction between the beautiful and the ugly. Moreover, this distinction is learned by almost everyone at an early age. So either the beautiful is a simple concept, or it is at least less complicated than the definition Bolzano has so painstakingly elaborated. Bolzano replies that the mere fact that the concept is used by almost all persons does not entail that it is less complicated than his theory makes it out to be. And he cites in support of his denial the even more widely employed concepts such as horse, dog, bird, and so on, whose definitions are at least as complicated as the concept of beauty if not more so.

These, then, are the objections and the replies that Bolzano imagines with regard to his own theory. Before commenting on them, I will make several points about his criticisms of Kant in the light of what we have now seen of his own theory.

Recall that Bolzano criticizes Kant generally for offering more than one clarifying definition of the beautiful. We know from what Bolzano says at the outset of his own treatment of the beautiful that, unlike Kant, he aims to provide only a single account. Each correct attribution of the beautiful is finally an instance of an objective, not a subjective, concept. And objective concepts are to be provided with one definition, not several.

Now this criticism is perhaps more instructive for what it shows us about Bolzano's intentions than for what it calls attention to in Kant's own theory. In either case, however, Bolzano is relying here on a complicated discussion in the *Wissenschaftslehre* of both the nature of concepts and the nature of definition. But when we reread that discussion in view of our own contemporary accounts of such difficult matters, it is not self-evident that Bolzano himself provides a satisfactory rendering either of the distinction between subjective and objective concepts or of the nature of definition. This makes his general criticism of Kant inconclusive.

More specifically, we need to recall Bolzano's criticism of Kant's use of the cardinal term "interest." The point was that Kant's discussion of disinterestedness depends on an idiosyncratic use of that term for which Kant nowhere argued convincingly. But Bolzano here is using a two-edged sword. His criticism of Kant is on this point, I think, well-founded. But the same criticism also cuts in the opposite direction. Hence a further question arises whether Bolzano's own key terms carry generally accepted meanings. When we scrutinize afresh his own definition of the beautiful, we quickly find ourselves stumbling on such unfamiliar and unexplained terms as "dark intuition" and the critical phrase that keeps turning up in the objections Bolzano himself anticipated, "die Mühe des deutlichen Denkens." I have tried to shed light on both these terms through paraphrase of what Bolzano has said about them; the result, however, is not wholly satisfactory. For Bolzano himself, so insistent on tying his own technical terms down and so critical of Kant and others in precisely this respect, does not—at least in the case of his own definition of the beautiful—seem finally to have done the job that needed doing. Unlike the first criticism, then, Bolzano's second criticism of Kant does seem well-founded; in fact, it suggests at least one serious difficulty with Bolzano's own theory.

Recall further Bolzano's criticism of Kant's repeated references to *jedermann* in his discussion of the judgment of taste and universality. Bolzano's basic claim was that Kant does not mean what he says about "everyone," for what he says does not seem to be true. That everyone ought to find beautiful what is correctly judged to be beautiful is false, since children and, Bolzano could have added, mentally disturbed persons are not always able to concur and cannot be described as persons who should concur. Hence Kant must have meant by "everyone" only those individuals who have the full use of their natural and especially intellectual powers. And this provision, of course, is just the one that Bolzano builds into his own theory.

But whether Bolzano has gotten Kant right on this point is open to question. Kant probably does not mean that something that is correctly judged beautiful will in fact always be correctly judged beautiful by anyone whomever. Kant would make room not just for erroneous judgments of taste but also for some persons' not being able to concur with proper judgments of taste. The point of Bolzano's remarks should be taken less as a criticism than, especially where Bolzano speaks of "developed intellectual powers," as an explication of something Kant has already seen.

More interesting is the question whether Bolzano's insistence in his own theory on "developed intellectual powers" as a prerequisite for finding something beautiful does not preclude the Kantian requirement of universality. The problem, as I see it, is with the ambiguity in Bolzano's (but not in Kant's) use of the term "developed." If Bolzano means, as Kant does, simply the proper functioning of all the intellectual powers in the mature or potentially mature individual, then the universality claim for the correct judgment of taste cannot be excluded in principle. But if Bolzano goes beyond Kant to the additional sense of mature intellectual powers as those that have been further formed, exercised, and refined in the various activities associated with the knowledge, practice, and pursuit of the arts, then it is very doubtful that Bolzano can maintain a claim to universality. On this second sense of "developed," which Bolzano seems to hold at least on the evidence of his own repeated discussions of how necessary are the use and exercise of these powers for finding something beautiful, no one except the cultivated individual will be able to correctly judge something to be beautiful.

Recall finally Bolzano's criticism of Kant's discussion of purposefulness. We remember that according to Kant we find purposefulness in the beautiful object, whereas Bolzano asserts to the contrary that we find not purposefulness but regularities and rule-governedness. Bolzano's criticism of Kant's talk of the form of purposefulness is cogent. What calls for reflection, however, is just what additional reasons there may have been, if not these only, for Bolzano's abandonment of a quite similar view. For in a definition of the beautiful that he made in 1818 as well as in one of his published academic talks to his students, Bolzano himself talked of purposefulness; in his definition of 1843 all trace of this talk has gone. But this is largely a historical question, and however interesting in its own right for our understanding of the development of Bolzano's philosophical views, it need not detain us just now. Rather, against the background of these questions about the adequacy of Bolzano's own theory of the beautiful, I shall take up two further critical points before concluding with a brief general assessment.

One difficulty with Bolzano's theory, I believe, arises out of his initial discussion of the four preparatory points he wants us to keep in mind when judging his own efforts to provide a clarifying definition of the concept of the beautiful. This discussion is particularly interesting not only because of its manifest opposition to the then dominant school in German philosophy—idealism—but also because of the succinct form it imposes on several of the key ideas of the *Wissenschaftslehre* of 1837. Thus there is the untimely insistence on clarity, the aim itself of trying to articulate a definition, and the suggestive but hardly explicated contrast between two kinds of concepts, subjective and objective. Each of these features can be taken to generate some critical questions in its own right, yet most if not all such questions can be resolved by closer attention to related discussions in the *Wissenschaftslehre*. But the related theme that does not allow of such a quick resolution, and that continues throughout Bolzano's major exposition of the concept of the beautiful and even in his extended and critical review of other historical theories of the beautiful, is the distinction between simples and complexes.

Recall that this distinction underlies Bolzano's insistence that a clarifying definition of the beautiful is subject to different evaluatory criteria depending on whether the beautiful is a simple or a complex. Ultimately, of course, Bolzano will hold for the second, that the concept of the beautiful is the concept of a complex. And we recall also Bolzano's appeal to this distinction in a more complicated context when he tries to show that one of the objections that his theory is too narrowly construed—that it cannot account for pure tones or colors—is mistaken. But there is a problem here, as indeed the second case suggests. And the problem is whether there are any simples at all.

In the discussion of color, Bolzano intimates that the empirical issues remain open for him as he writes this treatise. But whatever importance the empirical issues might finally have, the philosophical point that such a distinction can indeed be made remains controversial. Some evidence for Bolzano's hesitation on this issue may be found, for example, in his discussion of André, Hutcheson, and several followers of the Leibniz-Wolff school. Bolzano criticizes their various uses of the terms "manifold" and "unity." "Even the simplest object," Bolzano writes, "has an endless set of characteristics." [20] But if Bolzano is right on this central point, the question inevitably arises whether any simples exist. If he has doubts about the answer, as I think he does, then the various and especially the cardinal uses of the distinction between simples and complexes also become questionable. Since this very distinction stands at the foundation of Bolzano's theory of the beautiful, final judgment on that theory must await clarification of Bolzano's understanding of what simples are. One general difficulty with Bolzano's theory, then, is the uncertain ontological status of simples. [21]

A second general difficulty concerns the content of a correct judgment of the beautiful. Recall that Bolzano is adamant in his criticism of Kant's discussion of purposefulness as the content of the judgment of taste. The content of this judgment, Bolzano asserts, is rule-governedness. He is careful to add that this kind of regularity is not apprehended with any clarity in the judgment of taste; rather, it is apprehended confusedly or "darkly." The problem is understanding just what Bolzano is referring to in his metaphorical talk about dark apprehensions.

Some help may be found in two places: an early definition of the beautiful, already alluded to, that provides an interesting contrast to Bolzano's definition in the present work; and a critical discussion of a similar concept in Mendelssohn's *Briefe über die Empfindungen*.

Bolzano's earlier definition of the beautiful is found in unpublished notes from 1818. [22] The relevant passage reads as follows: "The

[20]Bolzano, section 28, 55.

[21]This problem, largely but not exclusively centered in Bolzano's philosophy of logic, recurs throughout the realist tradition and of course is notorious in the Wittgenstein of the *Tractatus*.

[22]These notes, now lost, served as the source material for the entry on "The Beautiful" in the 1821 glossary, "Bolzanos Begriffe 1821," available as a lengthy appendix to E. Winter's essay "Die historische Bedeutung der Frühbegriffen Bolzanos," in *Sitzungsberichten des Deutschen Akademie der Wissenschaften zu Berlin*, 22–101 (Berlin, 1964), cited hereafter as Glossary.

beautiful object is one whose purposefulness is of such a nature that it can be recognized even confusedly. This purposefulness is objective. It is related to just what we think of as what brings to the fore the same thoughts that possess this purposefulness.... but purposefulness must not be too deeply hidden because otherwise it would only be recognizable through a strenuous reflection which would result in clear judgments." [23] In other words, a judgment of taste is an unclear judgment, a "dark" judgment.

What should be added here is a gloss from Bolzano's early letters on the notion of a confused or dark judgment: "A confused judgment is one which cannot be recalled even after the smallest interval and which one could not, even in the very moment of making such a judgment, say 'I have it.' For this judgment does not remain in consciousness long enough to require a transition from the judgment which just preceded it to the new judgment 'I have it.' Briefly, a dark judgment is one which is not accompanied by the consciousness of having it." [24] In other words, the judgment of taste is unclear or confused in the sense that it is not accompanied by a consciousness of its having been made.

There are several problems with this doctrine. Does Bolzano, like Kant, want to attempt to clear distinction between the form and the contents of judgments of taste? If so, how would the distinction be made? [25] Further, do the contents of a judgment of taste require for their completion an accompanying act of consciousness—that is, a simultaneous awareness on the part of the individual while making a particular judgment of taste that it is just this judgment that is being made? And of course our uncertainty increases in view of the substitution of rule-governedness in the definition of 1843 for purposefulness in the definition of 1818, which could entail further changes in what is to be understood as a "confused judgment."

If we turn for help to the second set of materials, the discussion of Mendelssohn, some clarity does emerge, but not quite enough. There Bolzano suggests that when Mendelssohn spoke of the unity

[23]Glossary, 76.
[24]Glossary, 89–90.
[25]Part of the problem here touches on how to construe the differences between epistemology and psychology, a problem that one of Bolzano's strongest admirers, Edmund Husserl, took up in a systematic way and that I treat in part 2. Note the comment of an anonymous Cornell referee: "Bolzano, like other mathematicians at this point, has not distinguished between the logical form and the psychological form of understanding sufficiently to get clear about how 'concepts' and 'judgments' can be described in other than psychologistic terms."

of the manifold apprehended in the judgment of taste, he ought to have referred to "a clearly recognizable unity" rather than to "a darkly recognized" one.[26] This suggests that the judgment of taste has as its content not purposefulness but the rule-governedness of a unity whose components, despite their unity, could be grasped discursively were one to take the trouble. But since in practice one does not take on that analytic task, this unity in its rule-governedness is said to be apprehended confusedly, that is, in a not completely explicated way.

This kind of talk, though difficult enough, improves on the 1818 doctrine, but it still should fall short of convincing even Bolzano's sympathetic readers. For we face again the many difficulties that confound our attempts to talk of simples. As one of Bolzano's own objections spelled out, this doctrine of "the dark judgment" assumes that something beautiful is always a complex manifold, a rule-governed whole whose regularity, though apprehended in a confusing way, can ultimately be made out. But the specter keeps coming back, the thought that some beautiful things, despite Bolzano's disclaimers, may well turn out to be, if not simples, then not rule-governed manifolds of just the type his theory must presuppose. And this possibility is not too difficult for us to entertain, especially today, when extensive work in the philosophy of science on different models of explanation has made us chary of assuming without argument that any kind of talk about regularity, lawlikeness, or rule-governedness makes plain sense as it stands. Bolzano himself would recognize the difficulties facing any attempt to construct, if not what he calls an "objective concept," at least what some today might call a satisfactory account. Another difficulty is our obscure but persistent suspicion that just as there may well seem to be things with more than one essence or with no essence at all, so too there may be things that, though ordered in some way, cannot be characterized as conspicuously rule-governed. As such, things too—Why not?—may be the objects of some judgments of taste.

Notwithstanding our recourse to several of the few places where Bolzano tells us more about such matters, I am afraid we must conclude here, as we did with the talk of simples and complexes, that Bolzano's doctrine of the dark judgment is a dark doctrine.

I end with the suggestion that Bolzano's aesthetics, for all its

[26]Bolzano, section 29, 56.

difficult terms and distinctions, be taken as a different reading of Kant from that provided either by analytic philosophers like Beardsley, Dickie, Coleman, or Guyer, or by hermeneutic philosophers like Gadamer, Ricoeur, Biemel, or the early Apel. On the one hand, there is an extraordinarily persistent concern for conceptual clarity, argumentative thoroughness, and systematic development, which has often been claimed by analytic philosophers. On the other hand, there is a reliance on a dark doctrine of intuition, apprehension, judgment, and finally consciousness, which has many echoes in hermeneutic philosophy. In no way do I claim that Bolzano's work is characteristic of the best of these two philosophical worlds. Rather, I suggest that his reading of Kant, which in many ways generates the peculiar features of his aesthetics, is importantly different from each of the two dominant interpretations we have before us today of the formative period in modern aesthetics, the eighteenth century and its watershed, Kantian aesthetics. It is this other reading of aesthetics—the beginnings of a realist tradition, if you will—that begins in Bolzano's theory of the beautiful and leads on to the further investigations found in Dilthey, Brentano's posthumous works, Husserl's preoccupations with various versions of psychologism, Twardowski's struggles with ontology, and finally the aesthetics of Roman Ingarden.[27]

In light of both the analytic and the hermeneutic readings of early modern aesthetics and the central disagreement about the interpretation of Kant's philosophy when viewed from the standpoint of Bolzano's careful considerations, before turning to those elements of another tradition let us reflect in an Interlude on the course of this book so far.

Appendix 5: Clarifications as Elucidations

To help his readers understand just what is to count as a clarification, Bolzano makes four preparatory points. He begins by recalling that philosophers often change their minds about what they mean by certain key words and phrases. What Bolzano himself is aiming at here, however, "objective propositions and truths" and "objective concepts and representations,"[28] do not allow for any

---

[27]The analysis of these texts is the work of part 2.
[28]Bolzano, section 1, 6.

subjective changes at all in their meanings. Bolzano develops this contrast between objective and subjective in great detail in the first two volumes of his *Wissenschaftslehre,* which he alludes to here.[29] But the point of the distinction may be seen more succinctly in his example in the present text of a contrast between objective concept (*Begriff an sich*) and concept or idea (*Begriff oder Vorstellung*). In philosophical discourse the word "God," Bolzano claims, refers to a single objective concept, even though there may well be an indefinite number of individual concepts and ideas of God. In the case of the beautiful, then, Bolzano's clarification is to consist in formulating the objective concept of the beautiful—the unchangeable sense, Bolzano adds (in a reference to the practice of his own times, which still retained the schoolbook tradition of Leibniz, Baumgarten, Wolff, and Kant), that is and should be found in university manuals in aesthetics.

A second feature of what Bolzano calls a clarification is the rule that each objective concept is to be provided with only one definition or clarification. The same words are to be used in the same senses, and above all the same objective concepts are not to be defined in more than one way. This requirement, which today seems overfamiliar, was much more important to stress in Bolzano's time as an antidote to the speculative concoctions of the idealist epigones. The examples Bolzano wants to reject are those like I. H. Fichte's definition of the absolute, while examples that he wishes to retain are those like the mathematicians' definitions of a square.[30]

A third point about clarification is the need for a certain kind of simplicity. Bolzano concedes that some objective concepts may indeed be complex; he insists, however, that each complex be

---

[29]The *Wissenschaftslehre,* Bolzano's masterpiece, first appeared in 1837 after many vicissitudes with the subtitle, "Versuch einer ausführlichen und grösstenteils neuen Darstellung der Logik mit steter Rücksicht auf deren bisherigen Bearbeits," in four volumes outside his own country, in Sulzbach (Bavaria). It has been reprinted three times: Vienna 1882, Leipzig 1914–31, and Aalen 1970. Two selections have been translated into English, one by R. Georg (Oxford, 1972) and one by B. Terrell (Dordrecht, 1973). Jan Berg's introduction to the latter is an excellent overview. A summary of the first two volumes, by one of Bolzano's collaborators (probably but not certainly Prihonsky), is *Kleine Wissenschaftslehre,* ed J. Louzil, Sitzungsberichte der Österreichischen Akademie der Wissenschaften 299 (Vienna, 1975). A shorter summary of the main points can be found in the rare book Bolzano wrote anonymously under the title *Bolzanos Wissenschaftslehre und Religionswissenschaft in einer Beurtheilenden Übersicht* (Sulzbach, 1841), which can be consulted in the Prunk Saal of the Austrian National Library. The new multivolume edition in the *Gesamtausgabe* referred to in note 1 is indispensable.

[30]Bolzano polemicizes often against German idealism. See especially his criticism of Hegel's aesthetics in section 54, 98–108.

clarified in such a way that we can see just how it is built up from the connection of simple components. This procedure, Bolzano thinks, not only contributes to clarity, but reflects both some of the ways we actually use objective concepts and some of the ways we have learned their use. Yet Bolzano is cautious here also, for he does not want to commit himself to the false view that "any component which can be found in the objects of a concept would have to be an actual component of the concept."[31] If the beautiful is an instance of a complex concept, then a clarification of the beautiful must include all the components of this complex but not all the properties its objects have.

Finally, Bolzano raises the question of just how a putative clarification is to be justified and thereby made persuasive for oneself and others. If the clarification is of a simple objective concept, then the only final justification consists in showing the inadequacies of alternative suggestions. If, however, a complex objective concept is at issue, then both the component parts and their relations must be specified, and the concept must be shown to be neither too narrow nor too broad. This second case Bolzano underlines as much more difficult than the former. For finally the justification of a putative clarification is to be found only through repeated acts of introspection. Bolzano does not speak explicitly here of intuition, but he insists on the need for repeated attempts to direct our attention to those mental acts that both consist of and accompany our thinking about the beautiful.

[31]Bolzano, section I, 9.

INTERLUDE

RETROSPECT
AND PROSPECTS

WE BEGAN with important contradictions between theory and practice in the work on interpretation and history of two contemporary philosophers of art, one representative of Anglo-American reflection and the other of Continental thought. In each case, despite the very great differences between their approaches, a close look at critical practice showed up common central strains in philosophical theory. At least one strong thread held these different thinkers together, and that thread was not so much the shared tension between theory and practice in dealing with at least one common theme as a shared commitment to a historicist philosophy of art. However different in conception and execution, this historicist commitment united these two bodies of work in their reliance on different understandings of Hegel. But those understanding themselves derived from very different readings of the seminal period in the modern history of aesthetics, the eighteenth century. The initial task, then, was to explicate those hidden differences behind the shared historicism of two of the most important contemporary approaches to the philosophy of art.

Before turning in part 2 to a critical exploration of a very different tradition, deriving from neither an analytic nor a hermeneutic reading of the Kantian philosophy, I return to contemporary philosophies of art and narrow our focus to several of the key disputes within the analytic reading, where the cardinal concept of the aesthetic that we will investigate in part 2 is especially in evidence.

With a sharper grasp of the disagreements not just between analytic and hermeneutic readings of the eighteenth century but also within the analytic reading itself, we will be better able to appreciate some of the central resources in the little-studied development of an alternative approach.

In 1984, in the pages of the most important journal in the field, the *Journal of Aesthetics and Art Criticism*, a long-smoldering dispute flared up once again.[1] The general issue had to do with how to understand the conceptual connections between contemporary discussions of art and the aesthetic and the seminal eighteenth-century works of such thinkers as Shaftesbury, Addison, Hutcheson, Hume, Burke, Gerard, Alison, and Kant. The particular quarrel was whether a major line of reflection running through the writings of these thinkers was properly characterized as the precursor of modern aesthetic attitude theories or as the forerunner of modern preoccupations with taste and other aesthetic predicates. Other questions were also at issue in the 1984 exchange—for example, how to read philosophical classics, how to interpret the sometimes tangled strands of both Platonism and empiricism in the eighteenth century, and especially how to take the critical measure of Kant's extraordinary achievement with respect both to the questions of his predecessors and to the preoccupations of his successors. But the basic quarrel had to do with understanding the eighteenth century's sustained reflections on art and beauty either mainly in terms of disinterestedness or mainly in terms of taste.

In 1960 Jerome Stolnitz published *Aesthetics and the Philosophy of Art Criticism*, which set out in some detail the lineaments of a modern aesthetic attitude theory of the arts. Something is to be understood as beautiful when it becomes the object of a "disinterested and sympathetic attention . . . and contemplation . . . for its own sake alone" as, for example, "the 'look of the rock,' the sound of the ocean, the colors in the painting."[2] Now the key to this view was the notion of "disinterestedness," a cardinal term in eighteenth-century aesthetics.

In a much remarked series of articles, Stolnitz went on to offer a reading of those texts, purporting to show the details of the eighteenth-

---

[1]G. Dickie, "Stolnitz's Attitude: Taste and Perception," *Journal of Aesthetics and Art Criticism* 43(1984): 195–203 (cited hereafter as Dickie 1984), and J. Stolnitz, "'The Aesthetic Attitude' in the Rise of Modern Aesthetics," *Journal of Aesthetics and Art Criticism* 43(1984): 205–8 (cited hereafter as Stolnitz 1984).

[2](Boston, 1960), 34–35.

century accounts of disinterestedness as well as to suggest their central connections with his own version of twentieth-century aesthetic attitude theories such as those of Bullough and Vivas. Thus, in " 'Beauty': Some Stages in the History of an Idea," Stolnitz tried to show how our contemporary neglect of the notion of beauty is a direct consequence of "the demotion of 'beauty' " in the eighteenth-century thinkers and their substituting for it the "logically prior" notion of the aesthetic.[3] In a second article, "Of the Origins of Aesthetic Disinterestedness," Stolnitz put at the center of his argument a claim that earlier had remained somewhat in the margins. He began his second article: "We cannot understand modern aesthetic theory unless we understand the concept of 'disinterestedness.' If any one belief is the common property of modern thought, it is that a certain mode of attention is indispensable to and distinctive of the perception of beautiful things."[4] This concept Stolnitz took to be the "motive idea" that enabled eighteenth-century British thinkers to articulate the idea of a general and autonomous philosophical discipline called aesthetic theory. And once again Stolnitz took his readers on a careful survey of the central reflections on disinterestedness to be found in the now familiar sequence of Shaftesbury, Addison, and Hutcheson in the early part of the century, to Burke and Gerard in the middle, all the way to Archibald Alison at the end. Hume, curiously, was slighted, and Reid's very important work was overlooked.

The focus narrowed in the third of the 1961 articles "On the Significance of Lord Shaftesbury in Modern Aesthetic Theory," where Stolnitz tried to show that "British aesthetics was directed above all to the descriptive analysis of aesthetic experience," that the linchpin of this analysis was the notion of aesthetic perception, with the result that " 'art' comes to be defined in terms of the attitude of disinterested perception, either in the spectator, e.g. Bell, or transposed to the mind of the creative artist, e.g. Croce."[5] Stolnitz took this to be the characteristically "modern" view, and he was at pains to spell out the peculiar and manifold understanding of "disinterestedness" in Shaftesbury's transitional work, where

[3]*Journal of the History of Ideas* 22(1961): 185–86, 189.
[4]*Journal of Aesthetics and Art Criticism* (1961), reprinted in G. Dickie and R. J. Sclafani, eds., *Aesthetics: A Critical Anthology* (New York, 1977). I cite the pagination in this reprint, 607. This anthology includes in its excellent bibliographies references to other nonhistorical articles of both Stolnitz and Dickie. A second edition, substantially revised, appeared in 1989.
[5]*Philosopical Quarterly* 2(1961): 98–99.

elements of the Renaissance, medieval, and ancient views of harmony coexist in an uneasy opposition with Shaftesbury's own attempts to articulate the innovative notion of disinterestedness. This transition was completed, Stolnitz claimed in the fourth and final article in the series, "Locke and the Categories of Value in Aesthetic Theory," in Hutcheson's argued repudiation of Locke's' understanding of perceiving beautiful things and of beauty as a complex idea. But Hutcheson stopped short of developing a "phenomenalist analysis" of beauty, Stolnitz argued, and pointed his readers instead to Addison's "Essays on the Pleasure of the Imagination." [6] For Stolnitz, however, it was not Addison but Burke who managed not just to complete the critique of Locke's legacy for aesthetics but to transform the value categories of the eighteenth century.

This transformation most simply came down to establishing the notion of aesthetic perception at the center of the experience of art whereby the aesthetic came to displace the beautiful as the cardinal notion of philosophical reflection on the arts. In short, the movement of eighteenth-century thought about the arts from Locke to Kant is, on Stolnitz's reading, a progressive transformation on the notion of the beautiful to that of disinterestedness. And disinterestedness itself is to be understood as aesthetic perception, the precursor of the modern notion of the aesthetic attitude. Thus the historical roots of the characteristic note of modern reflection on the arts are to be found in the eighteenth century's gradual articulation of the notion of aesthetic perception.

Now, this bold and detailed body of work—comprising a theory of the arts in the 1960 book supported by a historical genealogy of the thought for the four articles between 1961 and 1963—did not go unchallenged. Although a number of articles appeared in the sixties, especially on the controversial issues connected with modern notions of the aesthetic attitude, it was not until 1970 that the link between the conceptual difficulties with aesthetic attitude theories and the putative genealogy of these theories was addressed critically. Drawing on some of his earlier systematic articles, George Dickie challenged Stolnitz's comprehensive views in the historical sections of his 1971 book *Aesthetics: An Introduction.*[7] Here

[6]*Philosophy* 38(1963): 47–48.
[7](Indianapolis, 1971) (cited hereafter as Dickie 1971). For some of the underlying earlier work see Dickie, "All Aesthetic Attitude Theories Fail: The Myth of the Aesthetic Attitude," *American Philosophical Quarterly* 1(1964): 56–66, which discusses other systematic essays by Stolnitz.

Dickie began to propose an alternative reading of the eighteenth century, which after many broken lances would bring him to the renewed quarrels of the 1984 controversy. The basic claim Dickie finally came to was that "my main conclusion that Stolnitz's attributing of aesthetic perception to the eighteenth-century British philosophers is wrong."[8] He qualified this view partly by allowing that Stolnitz was right in focusing on disinterestedness as the cardinal notion in the eighteenth-century theories and its links with the notion of beauty. But Dickie insisted that, pace modern aesthetic attitude theorists like Stolnitz, there was no such links between disinterestedness and perception.

In the 1971 book Dickie was to begin his critique much more broadly and sympathetically with an attempt to show how the problems of aesthetics as we consider them today, despite their diversity, share close logical and historical relations. Instead of beginning like Stolnitz with the eighteenth century, however, Dickie began with Plato's concerns for both the theory of beauty and the theory of art. The former was to undergo a sea change in the eighteenth century, he argued, whereas the latter was to survive almost unchanged until the twentieth. This initial thesis pushed Dickie to telescope his early discussions of ancient, medieval, and Renaissance reflections into several short paragraphs on Plato and Plotinus (no Aristotle until a later systematic discussion of imitation), on Thomas (no Augustine), and on Ficino and Alberti. His "Historical Introduction to Aesthetics" thus arrives rather quickly at the eighteenth century. There Dickie slowed the pace and, after a nod to Baumgarten, charted the decline of beauty and the rise not of aesthetic perception but of "taste." He divided his discussion, however, very much as Stolnitz did in awarding the key roles in his story first to Shaftesbury, then to Hutcheson and Burke, and— unlike Stolnitz—to Hume also. But before moving on he focuses on three thinkers Stolnitz chose not to emphasize—Gerard, Knight, and Stewart—and then resumed his story with Alison and Hume, to finish the eighteenth century with Kant.

Throughout, Dickie eschewed more chronology and chose, as in the juxtaposition of Hume with Kant, to highlight contrast. The historical introduction ended with Kant, although a glance was allowed of Schopenhauer's views. But however condensed his story, Dickie went out of his way to emphasize repeatedly that its theme was the rise of the theory of taste. Each thinker in the eighteenth

[8]Dickie 1984: 195.

century was taken to subjectivize beauty while still tying taste to some objective feature in the world. And the appearance of "aesthetic" theories (Dickie's scare quotes) was taken to be subsequent to the heyday of taste theories: "As the philosophy-of-taste approach was abandoned, 'aesthetic' theories began to take hold."[9] Dickie concluded: "before the eighteenth century beauty was a central concept; during the century, it was replaced by the concept of taste; by the end of the century, the concept of taste had been exhausted and the way was open for the concept of the aesthetic."[10]

In this first book Dickie had split his historical introduction into two parts, one for the theory of beauty, which gave way to the theory of taste, and one for the theory of art, which was taken to continue into the twentieth century largely unchanged. In a second book, however, *Art and the Aesthetic* (1974),[11] Dickie was to go back over the first part of this history by incorporating his 1973 article "Taste and Attitude: The Origin of the Aesthetic."[12] The starting point this time was a polemical reading of the 1961 Stolnitz articles, to which he had acknowledged a debt in his 1971 book. Dickie now claimed that Stolnitz was wrong in taking both Addison and Alison as aesthetic attitude theorists. Although asserting that his major concern was to describe the structural differences between aesthetic attitude theories and theories of taste, Dickie nonetheless made a series of historical claims. In particular, he argued that the first aesthetic attitude theorists were not the eighteenth-century British theorists but certain nineteenth-century German thinkers. The basis of this claim was his description of what he called the five-part structure of the theory of taste,[13] which he then used to criticize Stolnitz's attributions of aesthetic attitude theories to the British thinkers. Finally, in this second book Dickie extended his earlier history beyond Kant to discuss both Schiller and Schopenhauer,[14] a move that was to prove both incautious and unproductive. This second historical discussion nonetheless clearly brought Dickie to his 1984 view that the major explanation of Stolnitz's alleged misreadings of the British thinkers as aesthetic attitude theorists was "the fact that he [Stolnitz] does not fully understand the nature of the aesthetic attitude theory that he himself holds."[15]

[9]Dickie 1971: 31.
[10]Dickie 1971: 32.
[11](Ithaca, 1974) (cited hereafter as Dickie 1974).
[12]*Theoria* 39(1973): 153–71.
[13]Dickie 1974: 55 ff.
[14]Dickie 1974: 72–77.
[15]Dickie 1984: 195.

After the initial proposal of this reading of the eighteenth-century British thinkers in Stolnitz's 1961 to 1963 articles and its cautious acceptance and then radical challenge in Dickie's books of 1971 and 1974, the third chapter of this story was not difficult to anticipate. Stolnitz formulated a critique of Dickie's views as well as a defense of his original position in a 1978 article, "'The Aesthetic Attitude' in the Rise of Modern Aesthetics."[16] This article seemed to put the controversy to rest until Dickie's belated response in 1984, "Stolnitz's Attitude: Taste and Perception," together with Stolnitz's immediate rejoinder, "'The Aesthetic Attitude' in the Rise of Modern Aesthetics—Again," the dispute we began with.

In his 1978 reply Stolnitz took sharp aim both at Dickie's claim that aesthetic attitude theories are not stated fully until Schopenhauer and at its putative justification by an appeal to the apparently different structures that nineteenth-century German theories reveal when compared with eighteenth-century British theories. Specifically, Stolnitz challenged the satisfactoriness of Dickie's crucial distinction between theories of taste (the British contribution) and aesthetic attitude theories (the German contribution). The point of the challenge was to underline, by Dickie's own admission, that both theories share the cardinal notion of disinterestedness and then to demonstrate that the most plausible interpretation of that notion "erases the distinction on which Dickie's argument rests."[17] After a thorough review of the details of Dickie's' argument in the context of repeated returns to the particulars of the key historical texts, Stolnitz concluded that "the theory models formulated by Dickie are both raggedly stated and internally inconsistent, and that, furthermore, they fail to carve at the joints the thought both of the British and of Schopenhauer."[18] Stolnitz added the corollary that if he was right then Dickie had both misrepresented the thought of these major figures and provided "a lop-sided account of the 'historical priorities.'"[19] Some six years later, in the 1984 rejoinder to Dickie's reply, Stolnitz reasserted his earlier conclusions in even stronger terms when he categorized Dickie's distinction as "merely conceptual and wholly unhistorical," with the result that "the metatheory which Mr. Dickie advanced for the understanding of modern aesthetics...lies in shambles."[20]

[16]*Journal of Aesthetics and Art Criticism* 36(1978): 409–22 (cited hereafter as Stolnitz 1978).
[17]Stolnitz 1978: 412.
[18]Stolnitz 1978: 409.
[19]Stolnitz 1978: 409.
[20]Stolnitz 1984: 206, 205.

In his half of the 1984 exchange, however, Dickie, as we saw at the outset, put on record several serious changes that Stolnitz did not address directly in his strongly worded but largely familiar rejoinder, where he was mainly content to reaffirm the main lines of his 1978 criticism and defense. Thus Dickie's claim that Stolnitz was wrong in attributing not disinterestedness but disinterested perception to the British thinkers was not finally countered. And since Dickie went on to argue that it was precisely the presence or absence of this peculiar understanding of perception that distinguished the two kinds of theories—the British taste theories lacking this component and the German attitude theories incorporating it—Stolnitz's view that Dickie's was a distinction without a difference remained controversial.

Now of the two principals here, each has had his supporters. Thus Stolnitz has been able to cite the interesting work of Sushie Saxena from 1978 and 1979 in his favor as well as Joseph Margolis's criticisms of Dickie.[21] But Dickie has had supporters too. Thus, besides defending himself against Margolis, he has also called attention to related views in Peter Kivy's work and in that of John Fisher.[22] The dispute, then, has not continued just because of the obstinacy of two philosophers whose views are equally idiosyncratic.[23] Rather, much remains to be done both in formulating the types of theories we find in the British and German thinkers and in articulating their respective contributions to our modern understanding of philosophical problems concerning the arts.

And here, I believe, rather than just in the important details of this protracted dispute, lies its major interest. For the issue here

[21]See S. K. Saxena, "The Aesthetic Attitude," *Philosophy East and West* 28(1978): 81–90, the criticisms of this article in E. Coleman, "On Saxena's Defense of the Aesthetic Attitude," 29(1979): 95–97, and M. H. Snoeyenbos, "Saxena on the Aesthetic Attitude," 29(1979): 99–101, together with Saxena's "Reply to My Critics," 29(1979): 215–20. See also J. Margolis, "Review of Dickie's *Art and the Aesthetic*," 33(1975): 341–45, together with Dickie's "A Reply to Professor Margolis," 34(1975): 229–31.

[22]See especially P. Kivy, "Recent Scholarship and the British Tradition: A Logic of Taste—the First Fifty Years," in Dickie and Sclafani 1977: 626–42, and J. Fisher, "Review of Wolterstorff's *Art in Action*," 39(1980): 209–10. Kivy has written an important comparison piece, "The Logic of Taste: Reid and the Second Fifty Years," in *Thomas Reid: Critical Interpretations*, ed. S. F. Barker and T. L. Beauchamp (Philadelphia, 1976).

[23]Several other pieces need to be noted for the record without trying to document everything. See R. Arnheim's "Reconsiderations 2: Review of Langfeld's *The Aesthetic Attitude*," 39(1980): 201–3, and Dickie's "Reconsiderations 6: Review of Prall's *Aesthetic Judgment*," 42(1983): 83–85, as well as his book *The Art Circle* (New York, 1984).

finally is not just which, if either, of the two disputants is right about both the structure of these two theories and their histories. Those interested in philosophy and the arts today want to know as well whether our modern understanding of what count as philosophical problems of the arts is finally to be explained by reading the seminal eighteenth-century thinkers in terms of either taste theories or aesthetic attitude theories or of something else entirely.

This important and protracted contemporary dispute about modern aesthetic theory and its eighteenth-century conceptual and historical roots can be construed in a number of ways to reflect a number of interests. But at least one general conclusion seems relatively noncontroversial. In some strong sense, how we understand philosophy and the arts today largely springs from the flourishing of aesthetic theory in the various thinkers of the eighteenth century, and how we construe those eighteenth-century theories is closely tied to our modern philosophical concerns. We read the eighteenth century from the perspective of our modern interests, and conversely these very interests themselves exhibit the various concerns of the eighteenth-century thinkers. Thus, to take one example, the general problem of how to characterize the peculiar judgments we find in the domains of the arts—"this X is beautiful"—remains caught today between the tensions of various interpretations of the subjective and the objective. Philosophical consensus is still lacking on whether such judgments refer preeminently to objective properties of the artifact in question or to subjective impressions of its perceivers. But this problem first moved to the center of critical reflection on the arts in the eighteenth century, when the classical doctrine of beauty gave way, under the impact of the empiricist philosophies of Bacon, Hobbes, and especially Locke in the preceding generations, to doctrines of the aesthetic.[24]

In this context, then, my central concern so far has been to show that, just as there is more than one modern set of philosophical interests, so there is more than one plausible reading of the seminal theorists of the arts in the eighteenth century. Further, I hope to suggest, though not to argue in detail, that the plurality of such plausible readings has central consequences for how we are to continue to think critically about philosophy and the arts. In particular, just how we construe the philosophy of art, how we

[24]See especially M. Beardsley's very influential narrative, *Aesthetics: From Classical Greece to the Present* (New York, 1966).

identify its characteristic problems, how we differentiate the central problems of the philosophy of art from the peripheral ones, what we are ready to count as satisfactory formulations, discussions, and solutions of such problems, and just where such pursuits connect with our nonphilosophical questions and concerns, whether scientific, ethical, political, or religious—each of these radically important matters, I believe, can be seen afresh when we draw the philosophical consequences of such a plurality in our readings.

My approach so far has been to pursue the backgrounds of this contemporary dispute in the larger context of the differences between analytic and hermeneutic readings of the eighteenth century. Thus it is germane to my larger purposes to set aside for now any self-imposed task of trying to adjudicate finally between Stolnitz and Dickie on the structures of taste theories and aesthetic attitude theories. Instead, I have tried to counter the shared features of such readings, the many similarities on which both parties have continually commented, with the features of a very different reading. The common ground between Stolnitz and Dickie, with some qualifications, I have referred to as "an analytic reading" of the eighteenth-century thinkers. And to this I have opposed a different composite reading from another contemporary tradition I have referred to, again with some qualifications, as "a hermeneutic reading."

Accordingly, after examining in the Introduction a shared historicism in two representative contemporary philosophies of art from apparently very different contexts, in chapter 1 I began by detailing the similarities rather than the differences between Stolnitz and Dickie that I have been sketching in this Interlude, while adding some important material from other views within the same tradition. In chapter 2 I turned to detailing the very different reading of the eighteenth-century thinkers that we find in the hermeneutic tradition. This contrast brought me in chapter 3 to specifying comparisons and contrasts with a view to isolating the central questions at issue. And just as with the sketch here of the crucial disagreements between Stolnitz and Dickie on aesthetic versus disinterested perception, with the moral general differences between analytic and hermeneutic readings of the eighteenth century we also found a critical juncture in the discussion. The crux turns out to be the interpretation of Kant's aesthetics either as the culmination of eighteenth-century aesthetics or as a premature synthesis, to be set right only in the aesthetics of Hegel. In chapter 4 I rehearsed some of the detail in Kant's aesthetics in order to open up the possibility of an interpretation that is more critical than the analytic account and yet less dismissive than the hermeneutic story. This possibility I then set out to associate in chapter 5 with Bernard Bolzano's attempt to construct a critical aesthetics that arguably exhibits both the characteristic preoccupation with argumentative rigor one appreciates in many analytic accounts and the characteristic concern with relatively intractable and therefore often ignored themes such as "subjectivity" that one finds in many hermeneutic accounts. I treated Bolzano's work as the beginning of an alternative tradition in reading the difficult relations between philosophy and the arts, a reading that runs at least through Dilthey, Brentano, Husserl, Twardowski, Meinong, and Ingarden. In part 2, I look in turn at each of these successors to Bolzano's readings of Kant.

This material is of course very diverse. I do not claim that such diversity is to be unified in any one way. Rather, in different ways I think each of these thinkers belongs in a tradition that is properly characterized as neither analytic nor hermeneutic. For each is in similar ways a beneficiary of Bolzano's critique of Kant—a critique that avoids both the progressive reading of Kantian aesthetics as the culmination of eighteenth-century thinking and the regressive reading of Kantian aesthetics from a later Hegelian perspective as a strongly cognitivist program that must be overcome. I do not center my readings on the debts each of these disparate but related thinkers owes to the kind of approach to Kant, which Bolzano initiated. Rather, I want to give this work a clearer, more argumentative focus by examining what its considerations of problems in only one of the arts contributed to the concept of the aesthetic. Accordingly, I shall try to explicate and make newly available to contemporary work in the aesthetics of literature some relatively overlooked yet remarkably stimulating reflections on aesthetic experience, the role of intentions in the description of literary works of art, kinds of literary psychologism, aesthetic contents and feelings, and questions about the nature of putative aesthetic structure. My aim throughout will be to put on exhibit some elements from a substantial and still neglected tradition that lies behind contemporary work in the philosophy of art. This tradition is not historicist in the way some of the best work in both analytic and hermeneutic aesthetics is. Nor is it properly speaking a formalist tradition. For want of a better description, I shall call this tradition the realist backgrounds of modern aesthetics.[25]

_____

[25]The term "realist," of course, is deliberately vague, since here I do not want to distinguish sharply between epistemological, metaphysical, and other versions of "realism."

PART II

REALIST
BACKGROUNDS OF
MODERN AESTHETICS

W HEN WE look back on the larger details of the eighteenth-
century contribution to aesthetics, after the more particular concerns I have exhibited in the Interlude, at least one general conclusion becomes clear. We cannot resolve problematic issues in
contemporary philosophies of art simply by an appeal to previous
historical reflections on aesthetics, even to those of the most
important period for the understanding of aesthetics today. For the
plain fact is that we disagree about the details, the cardinal elements, and enduring significance of eighteenth-century aesthetics.
Nonetheless, one positive result is a new sensitivity to the problematic status of the concept of the aesthetic and to the realist
backgrounds of modern aesthetics.

Wilhelm Dilthey's poetics, as we will see, is suggestive in many
ways. For one thing, his criticisms of previous understandings of
critical theory provide important elements toward constructing an
alternative reading of the seminal eighteenth century. Moreover, as
a not inconsiderable student of Kant and as someone who structured
much of his own philosophical development in terms of Kantian
concepts and intellectual ideas (recall his project for a critique of
historical reason), anchoring at least some of Dilthey's historical
views in his reading of the *Critique of Judgment* is not difficult.
Like Bolzano's early attempts and the later efforts in the same
direction to be found in the posthumous aesthetics of Brentano,
Dilthey's work may be viewed as part of neither an analytic nor

even, pace Gadamer, a hermeneutic tradition, but rather as belonging to an arguably independent realist tradition. As such, the issues Dilthey's work first thematizes in a general way are ones I have chosen to pursue further in subsequent chapters by examining their role in the work of other realist thinkers such as Brentano, Husserl, Twardowski, Meinong, and Ingarden.

More specifically, we will need to be alert to how Dilthey's poetics in its central doctrines about the imagination and lived experience seem to involve in summary form virtually all the central topics that touch on the aesthetic. If we reconsider this work and sharpen our attention by considering not just any work of art but literary works of art in particular, as I shall do throughout part 2, it becomes evident that talk about the aesthetic requires clarity about both aesthetic intentions and aesthetic objects. For put most generally, what appears for Dilthey to make experiences precisely into aesthetic ones involves both a peculiar kind of directedness on the side of consciousness and the consequent constitution of a peculiar kind of object. If, however, as I will argue, Dilthey's own account of lived experience falls prey to at least some of the pivotal objections against aesthetic experience theories, it still is not evident that just because of that fact there is nothing more to either the doctrine of aesthetic intentions or that of aesthetic objects.

Consequently, the sympathetic yet critical considerations of Dilthey's views will set us a series of tasks that can be viewed as falling under two traditional, though quite ambiguous, headings. Thus, investigating the idea of aesthetic experience leads to the isolation of both "subjective" components, such as the aesthetic intentions and aesthetic feelings mentioned above, and to "objective" components such as aesthetic contents and structures. Each of these components is looked at in turn, though deliberately in a different order. Thus, by alternating "subjective" and "objective" aspects of the aesthetic, I try to keep a certain distance from that unsatisfactory distinction while respecting a roughly chronological sequence in my discussions of the realist tradition.

I try to deal perspicuously with the subjective components by investigating the role of intentions in the description rather than in the interpretation or evaluation of literary artworks in particular. After identifying the relevant texts in Brentano and examining both weak and strong forms of descriptive intentionalism, I then test in a second chapter on intentions the persuasiveness of the strong form, with the help of an analogy based on Husserl's arguments against logical psychologism. And I conclude that, whatever points for further reflection might remain about the final well-foundedness of such arguments by analogy, not even strong forms of descriptive intentionalism are finally convincing. Aesthetic intentions thus need to be excluded at least provisionally as a promising standpoint from which the nature of the aesthetic in general and of literary artworks in particular can be well understood.

I then turn to Twardowski's much neglected reflections on aesthetic contents and states of affairs. Specifically, the task will be to provide an account of what could pass muster as putative aesthetic entities and aesthetic situations. And here again the important goal will be the larger one of examining critically the suggestion that there may well be kinds of entities that could be factored into a more objective account of literary works of art than aesthetic intentions and aesthetic objects alone would allow. The conclusion, however, will remain tentative. Twardowski's discussion is filled with a variety of intriguing distinctions. But these distinctions, both in their detail and especially in their profusion, raise many questions in their own right that would require a far more searching appraisal. So Twardowski's suggestive ontology will remain suggestive; I will not be able to take it further here. Instead, before coming to Ingarden I will explore briefly another element that will figure in his own views about aesthetic structure, the ways works of art invite emotional interaction.

Meinong's account of emotional presentation will prove instructive here. For Meinong's extraordinary work on emotional presentation will provide a series of ideas and distinctions that will enable us to push a bit further the idea of what we might call literary showables. The basic insight, of course, is the distinction taken over in contemporary philosophy from Wittgenstein between what a literary work says and what it is only able to exhibit. And the problem is to arrive at a more informative account of these literary showables than a too strict allegiance to finally misleading analogies between the formal semantic features of texts and their stylistic features would allow. Fregean kinds of analyses are, despite their suggestiveness for other areas of aesthetics, not always of equal interest in this particular context. And it is Meinong's account that will sharpen our attention for some of the features in the final discussion of Ingarden.

As Ingarden himself repeatedly stressed in his analysis of schematized aspects, the literary artwork is always the result of an interaction between a text and a person. This interaction in part is the result of an imaginative response by readers to both the stated and nonstated particulars of a text. But it is not just the imagination that is active in such an exchange. For as Meinong understood, the emotions are also at work. On this level, however, what is imagined elicits from readers an emotional response that imbues the artwork itself with the appearance of an extraordinary quality. Through the operation of both imagination and feelings readers are occasionally able to endow the artwork with a fullness of valuational qualities the text alone does not exhibit. And it is this imagined sense of participation in a world of centrally important values that elicits the sense of having come to know a peculiar species of truth.

In the final chapter of part 2, I come back to another "objective" aspect of the aesthetic, this time that of structure. A comparative investigation of literary structure in the work of both Roman Ingarden and Monroe Beardsley will serve several purposes. On the one hand, it will enable us to identify some of the main requirements a theory of literary structure will need to satisfy. And on the other hand, it will carry further our dealings with the nature of the aesthetic. This second purpose is the more important. Specifically, the investigation of aesthetic structure in the case of literary artworks locates within the literary artwork the level at which much talk about the aesthetic in literature must be situated. It will of course be no surprise to learn that such talk, to have a sense at all, must be at the semantic level. What may prove somewhat novel is the observation that the semantic level is only one of a series of such levels, each of which may be understood as a relevant perspective in the task of articulating the relation between literary artworks and the aesthetic. This will be less the case with the phonological level, as it will be with the levels of schematized aspects and represented objectivities. The larger suggestion, then, will be that talk about the aesthetic, at least in the case of the literary arts, will have to be perspicuous in a different way that will talk about, say, the scientific. Although both take place at the semantic level, only the former involves the essential task of accounting for putative aspects of the work of art in terms of schematized aspects and represented objectivities as well. There may, of course, be features involved in a perspicuous account of aspects of the literary work of art that accommodate scientific analysis. But here I claim that there need not be, whereas an account of whatever aspects may properly be called aesthetic requires and not just accommodates description of these other levels as well.

When we look ahead to the work in part 2 on key elements in both the subjective and objective aspects of our experience of the aesthetic in the particular case of the literary work of art, it is clear that accounting for the nature of the aesthetic will have to involve more than the correlation between aesthetic intentions and aesthetic objects. For the thematic inquiries to be pursued suggest that further clarity can be had only in the pursuit of both a more systematic kind of understanding than that deployed so far and a fresh reading of the seminal texts of the eighteenth century. In both cases, as we will see in the Conclusion, the realist background of modern aesthetics must be thoroughly explored.

Chapter Six

Dilthey and
Aesthetic Experience

Even the first expression of the imagination is regulated by
rules.... And all these rules are finally grounded in the rational
order of the universe.

—Wilhelm Dilthey

In understanding we proceed from the context of the whole as given
in its vitality, in order to make the parts comprehensible on the
basis of it.

—Wilhelm Dilthey

Sɪɴᴄᴇ ᴛʜᴇ crystallization of hermeneutic theory in 1960
with the publication of Hans-Georg Gadamer's *Wahrheit und
Methode*, Dilthey's work on the arts and especially literature has
attracted new attention.[1] For many years, thanks to the criticisms
of an entire school of German critics whose main theorists were
Viëtor, Kayser, and Staiger, this theory suffered neglect.[2] The charge

---

[1] (Tübingen: Mohr, 1960). The particular direction of Gadamer's work on Dilthey
can be gleaned from "Portée et limites de l'oeuvre de Wilhelm Dilthey," in his *Le
problème de la conscience historique* (Louvain, 1963), 21–37. See also P. Redding,
"Action, Language and Text: Dilthey's Conception of the Understanding," *Philosophy and Social Criticism* 9(1982): 227–44; and B. E. Jensen, "The Recent Trend in
the Interpretation of Dilthey," *Philosophy and Social Science* 8(1978): 419–38.

[2] See Vietor's authoritative survey, "Deutsche Literaturgeschichte als Geistesgeschichte: Ein Rückblick," *PMLA* 60(1945): 899–916. For W. Kayser's views see his
widely read *Das sprachliche Kunstwerk*, 6th ed. (Bern, 1960). Staiger's views are
spread out. A convenient summary is in his *Grundbegriffe der Poetik*, 4th ed.
(Zurich, 1949), a book that is also well known. René Wellek and Austin Warren in
their *Theory of Literature* (New York, 1956) follow the German view closely. For
other texts see K. Müller-Vollmer, ed., *The Hermeneutics Reader: Texts of the*

was that Dilthey had exaggerated the historical and psychological aspects of texts to the neglect of their formal features. Gadamer's work showed the now forgotten lessons Dilthey had learned during his exhaustive work on Schleiermacher. The publication of the first complete bibliography on Dilthey,[3] together with an early interesting study in German on Dilthey's aesthetics,[4] showed clearly that the stereotypes attached to Dilthey's views were no longer viable. But, in 1963 a book was already available that destroyed these

---

Tradition from the Enlightenment to the Present (New York, 1985), and Heinz Malorney, "Wilhelm Dilthey—a Representative of the Philosophy of Life at the Turn of the Nineteenth and Twentieth Centuries," *Filozoficky Casopis* 29(1981): 377–81. For a historical perspective see Theodore Plantinga, *Historical Understanding in the Thought of Wilhelm Dilthey* (Toronto, 1980), and Michael Ermarth, *Wilhelm Dilthey: The Critique of Historical Reason* (Chicago, 1978).

[3]U. Herrmann, *Bibliographie Wilhelm Dilthey* (Weinheim, 1969). This bibliography, easily supplemented especially since 1983 with the continuous bibliography in *Dilthey-Jahrbuch* (Göttingen), provides a chronological listing of all of Dilthey's publications, plans, lectures, letters, diaries, and posthumous writings. There is a list of translations into six languages. The detailed chronological list of Dilthey's own writings involves ninety pages, whereas the bare list of secondary literature runs to eighty-four pages. Only Dilthey's *Einleitung* of 1883 and volumes 5, 6, and 8 of the *Gesammelte Schriften* have been translated into French. Princeton University Press is in the process of publishing a six-volume *Selected Works* in English and has published the first English translation of the *Einleitung* as *Introduction to the Human Sciences* (Princeton, N.J., 1989). Dilthey's *Gesammelte Schriften* is in nineteen volumes (Göttingen, 1913–82), cited hereafter as *GS*. An interesting early review is H. L. Friess, "W. Dilthey: A Review of His *Collected Works,*" *JP* 26(1929): 5–25; a more recent survey is that of F. Rodi, "Zum gegenwärtigen Stand der Dilthey Forschung," *Dilthey-Jahrbuch* 1(1983): 260–68.

[4]F. Rodi, *Morphologie und Hermeneutik: Zur Methode von Diltheys Ästhetik* (Stuttgart, 1969). For a more general survey of Dilthey's work viewed from the contemporary German perspective, see M. Riedel's lengthy introduction to his enlarged edition of Dilthey's *Der Aufbau der geschichtlichen Welt in den Geisteswissenschaften* (Frankfurt, 1970), 9–81, and the same author's previous, more specialized articles, "W. Dilthey und das problem der Metaphysik," *Philosophisches Jahrbuch* 76(1968–69): 332–48, and "Das erkenntniskritische Motiv in Diltheys Theorie der Geisteswissenschaften," in the Gadamer Festschrift *Hermeneutik und Dialektik*, vol. 1 (Tübingen, 1970), 233–57. O. F. Bollnow's much earlier 1933 work remains very helpful, *Dilthey: Eine Einführung in seine Philosophie*, 2d ed. (Stuttgart, 1955). More recently, see especially R. A. Makkreel's three articles: "Dilthey and Universal Hermeneutics," *Journal of the British Society for Phenomenology* 16(1985): 236–49; "Husserl, Dilthey and the Relation of the Life-World to History," *Research in Phenomenology* 12(1982): 39–58; and "Dilthey and Universal Hermeneutics: The Status of the Human Sciences," in *European Philosophy and the Human and Social Sciences*, ed. S. Glynn, 1–19 (Hampshire, 1981). Also note T. J. Young, "The Hermeneutical Significance of Dilthey's Theory of World Views," *International Philosophical Quarterly* 23(1983): 125–40; I. N. Bolhof, *Wilhelm Dilthey: A Hermeneutical Approach to the Study of History and Culture* (The Hague, 1980); and T. Plantinga, *Historical Understanding in the Thought of Wilhelm Dilthey* (Toronto, 1980).

stereotypes for good—K. Müller-Vollmer's *Towards a Phenomeno-logical Theory of Literature: A Study of Wilhelm Dilthey's Poetik*.[5] Given the importance of hermeneutic theory in the interpretation of the history of early modern aesthetics, and especially the importance of Bolzano's rereading of Kant, it is essential to look critically at some of the views this important work disseminated. We may then step back from those views and look in more detail at the central elements in Dilthey's post-Kantian aesthetics. First, however, a brief description of Müller-Vollmer's book will prove useful.

MV starts from a widely held conviction that the present state of literary study is highly problematic because the diversity of interpretive approaches to literature lacks a coherent philosophical center. "A theory of literature is needed," he writes, "which would avoid the philosophical pitfalls of the great number of today's onesided and exclusive types of criticism and which would yet accommodate their rich—though often isolated—empirical insights. We believe that in his writings on aesthetic and literary philosophy Dilthey actually succeeded in providing a basis for such a theory" (19). Given this starting point, Müller-Vollmer wants to prepare for a fresh examination of Dilthey's theory of literature by providing an accurate genetic and systematic study.

This theory is found mainly in *Die Einbildungskraft des Dichters* (1887) and in a number of related writings. A detailed study involves at least three steps. First, Dilthey's views are discriminated from the similar but importantly divergent writings of such theorists as F. Gundolf, R. Unger, O. Walzel, and J. Petersen.[6] Second, Dilthey's own views are explored, together with the original intentions that led to their formulation. And third, the principles and essential features of Dilthey's literary theory are systematically restated.

Müller-Vollmer's study is organized as a function of these three steps. In an introductory section, the book stresses the importance of Dilthey's philosophical writings for understanding his literary theory and shows how his central ideas of *Erlebnis*, *Weltanschauung*, and *Zeitgeist* had been misunderstood by his followers. In the second part the accent falls on Dilthey's reasons for requiring a new

---

[5](The Hague, 1963); cited hereafter as MV. References incorporated in the text are to this work.

[6]The basic works are F. Gundolf, *Goethe* (Berlin, 1916); R. Unger, *Herder, Novalis und Kleist* (Frankfurt, 1922); O. Walzel, *Gehalt und Gestalt im Kunstwerk des Dichters* (Potsdam, 1923); and J. Petersen, *Die Wissenschaft von den Dichtern* (Berlin, 1939).

aesthetic theory, his criticism of three previous theories, and the double orientation of Dilthey's own approach along both transcendental and historical lines (roughly, Kant plus Vico). Finally, in the third and most important part an attempt is made to show the starting point of Dilthey's analysis, Dilthey's view of the creative imagination, the ontopsychological bases of art and literature, the genesis of the concepts of "essence," "type," and "symbol," the ontological status of the literary work, categories of literary analysis, and the historicity of poetic technique. With this summary in mind, let us take up some issues more directly.

Literary Theory

To begin, consider Dilthey's basic criticisms of previous aesthetic theories. Confining himself to post-Renaissance theories, Dilthey distinguished three basic types: the rationalistic, the psychologistic, and the idealistic. The rationalistic theory, first introduced in the Cartesian theories of Boileau and D'Ambignon, culminated in Leibniz's system. This system was to reach down as far as Mendelssohn and Lessing for its final adherents. Dilthey thought the core of this theory was in Leibniz's use of the notion of force and instinct to explain mental representations, and in the Leibnizian conception of cosmic harmony. Art became a "sensuous representation of the harmony of the world order" (sinnliche Vergegenwärtigung des harmonischen Weltzusammenhangs). The problem with this theory was its reduction of aesthetic impressions to rational correlations between mind and cosmos. Yet the rationalistic emphasis on constitutive norms for all art gave Dilthey one of the keys to his own program.

Dilthey believed that the psychological theories of the succeeding century derived from the empirical methods Locke and Hume had adopted. This approach culminated in Lord Kames's (Henry Home) Elements of Criticism (1762), which founded modern experimental aesthetics. Although Kames's work is largely neglected in both the analytic and hermeneutic readings, Dilthey held that Kames effectively opened the way for Kant's theories by proposing that aesthetic impressions be linked with definite objective qualities. Two basic ideas emerge here. First, since a distinction can be made between the pleasure a person derives from a particular object and the desire felt for that object, aesthetic experience can be linked with disinterestedness. Second, the aesthetic object is able to dissociate

167

pleasure from desire by its being the "ideal presence" of an object. Dilthey viewed Kames's work on the descriptive analysis and correlation of motive impressions with particular objective qualities as establishing the methodological framework for dealing with aesthetic experience. Nonetheless, Dilthey urged against the psychology of aesthetic impressions a number of arguments: the circularity of psychologistic interpretation, the distortion empirical methods work on the historically conditioned aspects of aesthetic experiences, and the necessary misconstrual of a sympathetic phenomenon by analysis into diverse impressions.

On the third group of theories, the idealistic type of German classicism and romanticism, Dilthey was able to bring to bear the insights he had gained from his exhaustive study of Schleiermacher.[7] It is not surprising, then, that Dilthey saw the final defeat of the objectivist Aristotelian theories of mimesis in the culmination of the subjectivist turn that rationalistic and analytic aesthetics had already taken in German classicism and romanticism.

Dilthey saw this movement as effecting three substantive achievements. First was Schiller's descriptive account of aesthetic creativity as an active reciprocal correlation between life and form, between lived experience and artistic form. "Schiller's Law," as Dilthey called this active reciprocity, although it led through Schelling to Hegel's late system, nevertheless blurred the essential distinction between aesthetic appreciation and philosophical understanding. The second achievement was Kant's analysis of aesthetic pleasure as independent of conceptual intermediacy, with the consequence that beauty could no longer be construed as an embodiment of "the true." Kant freed the role of feeling in aesthetic theory from an

[7]See the third edition of this massive and incomplete work. Wilhelm Dilthey's *Das Leben Schleiermachers*, ed. M. Redeker (Berlin, 1966–70), makes up volumes 13.1 (1970), 13.2 (1970), and 14.2 (1976) of *GS*. Gadamer has called this work the single classic in hermeneutic practice (personal communication). For Schleiermacher's poetic see *Werke*, ed. L. Jonas et al. (Berlin, 1836–64), part 3, vol. 7 (*Vorlesungen über die Aesthetik* [1842]—these are the lecture notes from 1832 to 1833), vols. 8 and 9 (*Literarischer Nachlass* [1845 and 1849]), and the earlier 1819 and 1825 lectures, which can be found in *Schleiermachers Ästhetik*, ed. R. Odebrecht (Berlin, 1931). See also his *Hermeneutics*, ed. H. Kimmerle (Heidelberg, 1977). Considering the importance of Schleiermacher's work for interpretation theory, the lack of any critical edition of his works or any reliable studies on his aesthetics is regrettable. Nevertheless, see Schleiermacher's *Ästhetik* and his *Über den Begriff der Kunst* (Hamburg, 1984), and R. Wellek, "Schleiermacher," in his *A History of Modern Criticism: 1750–1950*, vol. 2 (New Haven, 1955), 303–8. See also *Schleiermacher: Hermeneutik und Kritik*, ed. M. Frank (Frankfurt, 1977). Some background is also given in H. P. Richman, *Wilhelm Dilthey: Pioneer of the Human Studies* (London, 1979).

overdependence on mistaken conceptual primacies. The difficulty here was the incompleteness of Kant's analysis. Dilthey intended to explore the role of feeling throughout the entire range of affective life. The third achievement was Herder's stress, in opposition to the universalism of Kant and Schiller, on the historicity of aesthetic experience. Ideals of beauty and taste necessarily change with changing historical conditions. Here the problem was Herder's insensitivity to whether such a necessary historical conditioning of aesthetic norms might not allow at the same time for the existence of some universal characteristics.[8]

Behind these three achievements that Dilthey identified with Schiller, Kant,and Herder lay a controlling methodological insight: "The attempt to establish a close relationship between the intellectual and spiritual constitution of the artist and his work, i.e., between the creative faculty and its product, the created work" (77). These achievements, however, were obscured because of the metaphysical direction the idealist movement took, which ended in the illuminating confusions of romantic theory. Dilthey's own analysis of literary aesthetics was to substitute a historical and phenomenological account of human life as a natural succession to those achievements, thus restoring the continuity of aesthetic theory with the interrupted themes of its past.

Literature and Statements

If this is the substance of Dilthey's dialogue with the post-Renaissance tradition, what were the major aims of his own work, specifically his literary aesthetics? In the 1880s Dilthey saw that a breakdown of communication was taking place between public and artists, artists and critics, critics and philosophers. This breakdown was not to be ignored. If the artist's work was to be more easily understood by the audience, the artist would require the help of critics. And if the critics in turn were to keep their own conceptual confusions from burdening their interpretive tasks, they would

[8]For a literary perspective on Kant and Schiller see Wellek, 1955, 1:227–57; and on Herder see Wellek, 1955, 1:176–201, but especially *Sprachphilosophische Schriften*, ed. E. Heintel (Hamburg, 1960). Two key articles here are H. Ineichen, "Diltheys Kant Kritik," and H. P. Richman, "Kant's Criticism of Dilthey," both in *Dilthey-Jahrbuch* 2(1984): 51–65 and 159–71, respectively. See also R. Makkreel, "The Feeling of Life: Some Kantian Sources of Life-Philosophy," *Dilthey-Jahrbuch* 3(1985): 83–105.

require the help of philosophers. Moreover, the breakdown indicated the failure of previous aesthetic theories. For classical and postclassical aesthetic canons were no longer applicable to the distinctive concern of the modernist movement for social and political problems, for truthfulness and sincerity, and for the detailed experimental fascination with new techniques. Hence, Dilthey's task became that of elaborating a new aesthetic for the modernist movement. His initial question was: "Considering the obsoleteness of the traditional theories of aesthetics and the absence of universally recognized evaluatory principles, how could the philosopher go about restoring the 'natural relationship' between aesthetic theory and creative art?" (56). And Dilthey was to elaborate his answer to this question inside an enormously well-read critique of previous approaches to aesthetics, especially Kant's and Vico's, an approach that Gadamer was to use later in his *Wahrheit und Methode*.

Dilthey undercut the traditional distinction between extrinsic approaches (biographical, sociological, historical) and intrinsic ones (the work itself as a world of its own). He accepted the arguments of the formalist critics against extrinsic approaches, but he rejected the formalist position itself in favor of his own thesis. This thesis goes: "The nature of the 'literary work' itself cannot be determined without a prior investigation of its position in and relationship to the world of human experience" (81).

What justification does Dilthey give for this thesis? His argument (on MV's account) is the following. (A) "If a poet does present an independent world in his work, then the statements he makes must be true insofar as they relate to this poetic world. (B) Poetic statements share therefore in the general notion of truth; in other words, they cannot carry meaning differing from ordinary statements. (C) If this were not so, poetic statements could not be understood for lack of common reference. (D) Consequently, in order to determine the specific truth character of poetic statements, to understand what is really meant by the 'structure of signs' or the *Bedeutungsfüge*, we must relate the poetic truth to other truths known to us through experience" (81). But this argument does not establish what it is designed to establish. For while (A) is an unobjectionable premise, (B) is extremely confused. The result is that (C) is beside the point. In the end, the conclusion does not follow. It will prove instructive later for our critical appreciation of Dilthey to see why this argument fails.

"The general notion of truth" is simply too vague a characterization of that class to which "poetic truth" is supposed to belong.

Moreover, the implicit conjunction in (B) between the truth of poetic statements and the truth of ordinary statements, and between the meaning of poetic statements and the meaning of ordinary statements, is a double confusion. First, these conjuctions equivocate with the terms "truth" and "meaning"; second, they assert an equivalence between the truths of some statements and the meanings of the same statements. But it is by now a commonplace that the truth of a statement is to be distinguished from its meaning, a distinction already clear in Husserl's *Logical Investigations* (not to mention in Frege), the first edition of which Dilthey used repeatedly in his seminars.

Suppose we attempt a reconstruction of the argument. One possibility might go along these lines. (A') Determining the nature of any sign system requires reference outside the sign system itself. (B') For if the nature of a sign system were a function only of its self-referential character, the sign system would be undeterminable by anyone not already inside the system. And not everyone (e.g., some readers) is necessarily inside the sign system of a particular artwork. (C') But the "literary work itself" is a sign system. (D') Hence determining the nature of "the literary work itself" requires reference to factors outside the literary work.

This argument is an improvement but, as it stands, still unsatisfactory. The reason is that we remain unclear just how we are to understand the term "sign system." It is clear that we *can* call some things "sign systems," because we in fact do so. Some examples of sign systems might be traffic signs, semaphore, Boolean algebra, Wordsworth's "The Solitary Reaper," the French language. But it is also clear that not all of these items are "sign systems" in the same sense. Hence we remain vague about whether the justification adduced for (A'), namely (B'), is both necessary and sufficient, since the argument nowhere specifies how the term "sign system" is to be understood. It may in fact be possible that there are some sign systems (a particular set of linguistic universals, say, in phonology) of such a scope that no discourse outside that system is either possible or necessary. But in any case, neither the original argument nor a sympathetic reconstruction in support of Dilthey's important thesis will do. What this thesis really comes down to requires that we move further into the details of Dilthey's theory.

In the context of his concern to avoid the limitations of an intrinsic viewpoint on the work of art, Dilthey restates his task as a double question: Are there "principles of universal validity" that can function normatively for both artists and critics? And if so, what relation do these principles have to various historical styles, techniques, and forms (82)? These two questions are concerned with a single problem, the possibility of making universally valid statements. To deal with this problem Dilthey makes two moves: he classifies critical statements as normative statements, and he then searches for universal normative statements. These moves do not succeed. Let us consider each in turn.

Here is the first move. In his *Einleitung in die Geisteswissenschaften* Dilthey distinguished three kinds of statements, each correlated with a different kind of noetic attitude: assertions, theoretical statements, and practical prescriptive statements. The first kind, for example, historical statements, is concerned with stating perceived facts. The second kind, for example, psychological or sociological statements, is concerned with stating relations between facts. And the third kind, for example, ethical or educational statements, is concerned with stating value judgments. Dilthey then goes on to assert that though different disciplines must employ predominantly one kind of statement or another, no such separation among *attitudes* correlative to these statements can hold.

Now for Dilthey the theory of literature predominantly employs normative statements while involving not just normative attitudes but factual and theoretical attitudes too. This point bears remembering in light of the frequent criticism of Dilthey's alleged historicizing. In fact, Dilthey sees criticism as making use preeminently of the same kind of statements that are used in ethics and educational theory over against either historical statements or sociological statements. The problem with these distinctions, of course, is that they are very rough indeed. For we notice immediately that critical statements, while unlike either historical or sociological statements, are not like ethical or educational statements either. We need not elaborate further on this point. But the weakness of Dilthey's classification of statements underlines the important fact that a more adequate theory of critical statements is one of the still unaccomplished tasks of contemporary literary theory.

Here is the second move. After classifiying critical statements as normative statements, Dilthey goes in search of universal normative statements "under a double aspect, namely by connecting the concrete investigations in the cultural and humanistic studies with the transcendental analysis of the conditions which make these studies possible" (87). The program has been summarized in the phrase "Dilthey's transcendental historicism," a blend of Vico's thesis on the intrinsic intelligibility of human history (human

beings can understand history because human beings make history)
and Kant's concerns with analyzing the conditions of possibility of
experience.[9] Dilthey's poetic theory was to provide the foundations
for the transcendental conditions of human history. In this sense
poetic theory was to be part of Dilthey's unrealized project to
elaborate a "critique of historical reason."

These two moves, a theory of statements and a concept of
transcendental historicism, are the context for the empirical method
Dilthey attempted to develop for his new poetic theory. Rhetoric was
in a state of disrepair. Hermeneutics remained where Schleiermacher
had left it. Only comparative linguistics offered inspiration, for
linguistics was a field where Dilthey had the benefit not only of
much knowledge but also of friendship with Lazarus and Steinthal.

One problem with the comparative method of linguistics, however, was the impossibility of inferring a general theory of literature
on the basis of a detailed examination of the morphological and
syntactic aspects of an individual natural language. The critic must
be able to account for the frequent experience of the relation
between the inner aspect of speech and the outer linguistic feature,
a relation unobservable by the linguist. Both linguist and critic are
concerned with the same kind of object, but they view this object
differently. The first has only a generic interest in the particular
qualities of an individual phenomenon, whereas the second is
concerned with the same qualities precisely insofar as he or she has
a lived experience of their individuality. Hence the comparative
method needed supplementing.

Dilthey turned to the new empirical psychology of his time in
hopes of adapting a second empirical method to the analysis of the
creative process itself. His basic strategy was to attempt a new
poetic with the double help of a linguistic analysis of poetry and a
psychological analysis of poeticizing. Practically speaking, Dilthey
was to forget the first and to transform the second into an ontology,
his *Lebensanalyse*. From the latter sprang his poetic. The transformation was in the end regrettable. What Dilthey did was lose
himself in the task of reconstructing the psychology of his times, a
psychology that was still in its infancy.

[9]See R. Makkreel, "Vico and Some Kantian Reflections," *Man and World* 13(1980):
99–120; and *Giambattista Vico: An International Symposium*, ed. G. Tagliacozzo
(Baltimore, 1969), including H. Hodges, "Vico and Dilthey," 439–47; H. Read, "Vico
and the Genetic Theory of Poetry," 591–99; S. Hampshire, "Vico and the Contemporary Philosophy of Language," 483–97; and H. P. Richman, "Vico and Dilthey's
Methodology of the Human Sciences," 447–57.

Imagination and Experience

We can find the record of this confusion in Dilthey's theory of the imagination and especially in his theory of aesthetic experience. Dilthey first tried to analyze the distinctive features of poetic imagination by comparison and contrast with ordinary imagination. He noted, however, that although poetic imagination was mainly different from ordinary imagination, it was remarkably similar to the kind of imagination dreamers and insane persons manifest. To distinguish poetic imagination further, he was forced to elaborate a more comprehensive theory than the ones psychological theorists like Wundt had put at his disposal. This task led him to reject the mechanistic assumptions of the behaviorist psychology of his time.

His theory may be understood as involving four major elements. The first is Dilthey's obscure concept of *seelischer Zusammenhang*, or psychic continuum. Sometimes Dilthey speaks of this continuum naturalistically and biologically as an "empirically verifiable fact" underlying all mental phenomena. At other times he speaks of it psychologically as what is present in any given "formative process": conditioning perceptions, representations, and feelings, a psychic *Gestalt*. At still other times Dilthey describes this continuum ontologically as a "crystalization of our total understanding of, and orientation in the world" (110).

Now on the basis of this concept, Dilthey wants to insist that an object is always experienced initially in an undifferentiated unity of cognitive, emotive, and volitional acts and not as a perception of a particular knowing subject. The unity of this multiple awareness is a function of the gestalt that regulates this awareness. The gestalt evaluates the present, interprets the past, and projects the future. Now this regulative unity of the consciousness continues "as the product of an individual's personal history and development, but it also embodies to some extent the ideas, beliefs, modes of feeling and thinking which prevail at his time and place" (113).

A second element of Dilthey's poetics is his distinction of mental acts into representations (*Vorstellungen*), affections (*Gefühle*), and volitions (*Willensäusserungen*). Every mental act, while in some measure all three, is nonetheless preeminently of one kind rather than another. Each of these kinds of mental acts demarcates a particular sphere, and within each sphere Dilthey claims he can distinguish a particular kind of imagination. Hence to the cognitive sphere belongs the scientific imagination whereby Dilthey characterizes the mind's capacity to produce hypotheses. To the volitional sphere belongs the practical imagination whereby Dilthey characterizes the mind's capacity to produce goals, purposes, and ideals. And to the affective sphere belongs precisely the poetic imagination whereby Dilthey characterizes the mind's capacity to produce images and representations of life. An affective state of mind is properly aesthetic only when it is distinct from any kind of volitional activity. Hence "an aesthetic state of mind ... may only occur when projection of one's self toward a future goal or purpose has ceased" (117). Dilthey also uses the term "mood" (*Stimmung*) to denote this felt awareness that dominates both representations and volitions. Dilthey goes on to maintain that such aesthetic moods can often generate particular images that in turn mediate the affective content of this aesthetic mood to other persons. Poetic imagination is the power to produce such images.

Since the affective was the domain of poetic imagination, Dilthey hoped a further analysis of this domain might shed further light on the nature of poetic imagination. Hence a third element is his division of the affective domain into a system of six spheres of affective life. These groups can be enumerated as follows: (1) feelings of physical pleasure and pain (warmth); (2) feelings related to simple sensory qualities and their intensities (sound); (3) feelings arising from relating different sensory perceptions (harmony); (4) feelings associated with the cognitive acts through which these relations are effected (wit); (5) feelings connected with instinctual drives (hunger); and (6) feelings connected with individual awareness of potentialities (courage). From this sixth sphere of the affective life the poet formulates a life ideal that becomes the center of an entire poetic oeuvre.

Dilthey thought these theories enabled him to distinguish how the poet creates images from how dreamers and the insane produce images. All three produce images, but the acquired psychic gestalt that regulates this production operates only in the instance of poetic activity. The poet never loses the capacity to distinguish the images produced from the real world, whereas the dreamer's images and the hallucinations of the insane person often fuse with their conception of the real. The psychic gestalt affects the relation between the imagination and the real. In addition, it structures the artistic unity that organizes the imagined.

The fourth and final element of Dilthey's theory of the imagination was his account of the poetic imagination in particular. He believed that an explanation of the psychological genesis of poetic imagery could clarify the nature of poetic imagination. A poetic image was "a (verbal) representation of a (mental) representation" (133). These images were produced in much the same way as memory images. A particular conscious state controls the expansion or reduction of a particular state of affairs. The same process takes place when the future is anticipated. Hence remembering the past and anticipating the future in some measure depend on transcending the present through the construction of mental images. What is distinctive about the poetic construction of images is not that verbal images are then substituted for mental ones. Rather, original representations not only are heightened or contracted, they are also added to. But "adding new elements to the original components is not a process of accumulation or association. It is rather the images themselves, as they emanate from the inner nucleus of the creative act, that carry with them a transmutational energy imported to them from the life stream of the poet" (135). Thus Dilthey wanted to hold that the poetic process is characterized by "the 'nuclear unfolding of images' against the background of the poet's psychic gestalt, and under the impact of a particular affective state or 'mood' " (136).

In a famous phrase Dilthey maintained that art is "an organ for the understanding of life" where "life" was to be understood as the historical world of human beings. The underlying claim here is that art can represent essential aspects of the human world and hence be a way of understanding the world. The larger claim is that contact with art, together with scientific and philosophical ideas, is an independent resource for human beings concerned with understanding both themselves and the world. Art is even more important than science and philosophy, however, because contact with art and literature enlarges our horizon on existence as no other kind of experience can. For the poet is able to represent what is essential to human beings. The essential is understood here as the values revealed to us inside the felt awareness of objects. And value is always understood as a function of a particular object's significance for an existing individual's life. Now Dilthey wants to hold that "the essential" cannot be formulated in assertion statements because no body of assertions can translate the significance that an individual, through reflection, has come to attach to certain qualities of personal experience. Only the poetic work can present "the essential," what is individually significant, because only poetic statements are able to avoid making assertions. But "the essential" is always the essential of a particular lived experience (*Erlebnis*). What, then, does Dilthey mean by *Erlebnis*?

Five senses of *Erlebnis* have been distinguished: (1) someone's personal experience; (2) someone's inner experience; (3) an interpretive category that denotes a particular type of experience; (4) everyday experience in the sense of *Erfahrung*; and (5) someone's immediate experience of a general significance.[10]

This last sense is centrally important here because Dilthey maintains that this kind of significance cannot be conceptualized. The literary work of art represents this unconceptualizable essence of someone's lived experience of a general significance. The task of the poet is to recreate an *Erlebnis* through the imagination. The poet's *Erlebnis*, however, cannot exist independent of its artistic expression, which can always remain incomplete. *Erlebnis* and the work of art are inseparable. "The nature of literary art," according to Dilthey, "consists in the expressive verbal articulation of a significant experience (*Erlebnis*) in a concrete work through which an essential aspect of human reality is disclosed" (145).

This definition leads to the problem of universality in art. How can the expression of a particular experience (*Erlebnis*) at the same time express something universal (*Wesen*)? Dilthey tries to answer this question by analyzing how "essentiality" (*das Wesenhafte*) is perceived. "Essentiality" here means "whatever the existing individual perceives and accentuates as being characteristic and necessary in a particular lived relation" (146–47). Perceiving what is essential means perceiving what is typical. Where the scientist and the philosopher produce concepts, the poet produces types. Like *Erlebnis*, however, the term "the typical" has more than one meaning in the course of Dilthey's development. Dilthey uses the term to mean: (1) the ordinary, something characteristic of a person; (2) the scientific, something belonging to a definite class or species; (3) the ontological, something necessarily connected with existence.

The last sense again is the relevant one. Dilthey wants to hold that "all our acts of apprehending and understanding are typologizing acts before they become conceptual (148). Thus Dilthey is talking about a kind of preconceptual schematization of sense impressions. This connection leads to a discrimination of two further senses of "typical": (4) a common trait in a variety of phenomena: (5) an

[10]On *Erlebnis* see K. Cramer, "Erleben, Erlebnis," *Historisches Wörterbuch der Philosophie* 2(Basel, 1971): 702–11; and K. Sauerland, *Diltheys Erlebnisbegriff* (Berlin, 1972). For a thorough account of the related concept of *Lebenswelt* see G. Brand, *Die Lebenswelt: Eine Philosophie des konkreten Apriori* (Berlin, 1971). See also "The Dilthey-Husserl Correspondence," in *Husserl: Shorter Works*, ed. P. McCormick and F. Elliston, 203–9 (Notre Dame, Ind., 1981).

ideal case, model, or norm. Now, Dilthey insists that ideal types are spontaneously produced by the mind. He insists further that such types are operative not only in perception but in all kinds of mental acts. Moreover, such types are concrete representations of the essential significance of particular states of affairs. This leads Dilthey to another and final sense of "type" as (6) a concrete representational image of the general in the particular—"the essential in the particular."

But how is the essential to be perceived in the particular? It must be understood that types are not simply internal preconceptual images of the external world. Dilthey holds that the internal/ external dichotomy is inappropriate here because a type arises from the contact between a phenomenon and not simply the knowing subject but the totality of consciousness. A typical representation is the unity between the phenomenon and the lived totality. Hence the artist does not represent the objective but represents the typical as the convergence of phenomena and consciousness. In the end Dilthey's solution to the problem of generality and universality in art is an appeal to the nondiscursive presentation of meaning through the symbol.

How does Dilthey understand symbol? Basically, the same way Cassirer and Langer do[11]—which means for all practical purposes the way Wilhelm von Humboldt did.[12] The historical connection between Dilthey and Humboldt runs across Dilthey's Berlin professors, the historian Droysen and the linguist Steinthal. In Humboldt's view the mediation between the inner and the outer is realized in language. Language hence is not merely objectively oriented as a means of conveying information; it is also subjectively oriented as a means of symbolizing reality. Language both refers to objects and expresses a speaker's mind.

[11]E. Cassirer, *The Problem of Knowledge* (New Haven, 1950), and *The Philosophy of Symbolic Forms*, 3 vols. (New Haven, 1953–57). S. Langer, *Philosophy in a New Key* (New York, 1958), and *Mind: An Essay on Human Feeling* (Baltimore, 1969).

[12]See Steinthal's edition and notes, W. von Humboldt, *Die sprachphilosophischen Werke* (Berlin, 1884). Von Humboldt's central influence on Heidegger's theories of language can be seen in the last and most important chapter of Heidegger's *Unterwegs zur Sprache* (Pfullingen, 1959). A good presentation of Humboldt's theories is R. Brown's *W. von Humboldt's Conception of Linguistic Relativity* (The Hague, 1967). For a solid presentation of the complementary theories of B. L. Whorf, see M. Black, "Linguistic Relativity: The Views of B. L. Whorff," *Philosophical Review* 68(1959): 228–38. On two central concepts in Humboldt's theory see E. Stolte, "W. von Humboldts Begriff der inneren Sprachform," *Zeitschrift für Phonetik und Allgemeine Sprachwissenschaft* 2(1948): 205–7; and L. Weisgerber, "Zum Energeia Begriff in Humboldts Sprachbetrachtung," *Wirkendes Werk* 4(1954): 374–77.

For Dilthey the symbol is the sensuous fusion of the inner and the outer. Symbols, then, are ambiguous depending on whether one stresses their referential or their expressive aspect. Yet regardless of how we interpret a symbol, some symbols are based on the conventional correlations existing between inner and outer. These conventions are historical. Hence the essential ambiguity of a symbol is to be understood in two dimensions: that of the timeless present (conventional correlations) and that of both the past and the future (the historicity of conventional correlations). Art can be universal because it "is essentially symbolic, an outgrowth of man's symbol-making faculty, which is an integral part of his nature and thus provides a root for language, methodology, and all the arts" (165). This means that art is universal in a complex way, since its symbolic character can function either historically (making use of previous symbols) or creatively (fashioning new symbols). Thus, for society there are two correlative spheres of universality—the universality of the historical-cultural cosmos and the universality of human nature.

What is distinctive about literary symbolism? Dilthey answers, poetic symbolism is necessarily verbal. Moreover, the coherence of this verbal symbolism requires both temporal organization and a perceivable order among the various images employed. Further, the treatment of time, space, and causality in poetic symbolism is distinctive in that completeness is always handed over to the work of the reader's imagination. Time, space, and causality in the literary work of art cannot exist independent of the interrelationships between fictional characters and fictional events. "The literary work ... takes its origin from the poet's articulation of an *Erlebnis* by means of words; he thereby transforms this *Erlebnis* into a total coherence of images which exists merely in his mind and that of his readers or listeners" (171).[13]

[13]For a philosophical account of some of the problems that this theory of literary symbolism completely ignores see M. Beardsley, "Metaphor," *Encyclopedia of Philosophy* (New York, 1967), 5:284–88. See also Paul Ricoeur, *The Rule of Metaphor,* trans. R. Czerny (Toronto, 1977). On Dilthey's theory of the constitutive elements of literary works, it is instructive to review the classical theories. See, for example, M. McCall, *Ancient Rhetorical Theories of Simile and Comparison* (Cambridge, Mass., 1969).

Aesthetic Experience

Although there are many features both of Dilthey's theory of the imagination and of his theory of *Erlebnis* that are distinctive of his general philosophical position alone, I will argue here that some of these features can be taken to make up a general position that Dilthey shares with other theorists such as John Dewey, Clive Bell, or more recently Monroe Beardsley. In short, I will show that Dilthey's position implies the existence of aesthetic experiences. Dilthey's theory of *Erlebnis* I construe as a theory of aesthetic experience; moreover, the *Erlebnis* theory itself depends on a theory of imagination that is not itself a theory of aesthetic experience but nonetheless implies such a theory.[14] Here, now, are some details.

Dilthey's theory of *Erlebnis*, as I have sketched it above, comes to nothing less than the view that an artifact is an artwork if it is at least produced, even if not appreciated, as the result of an aesthetic experience. This formulation allows us to incorporate a distinction that Dilthey himself overlooks, the distinction between the aesthetic experience that Dilthey holds takes place in the creation of the artwork and the one that occurs in the subsequent appreciation of the artwork, whether by the artist or by an audience. For Dilthey's theory to be fairly classifiable as an aesthetic experience theory, it is sufficient that we speak of the creation of the artwork, since its appreciation is necessarily dependent on that prior fact.

We have already noted that the revelant sense of the polyvalent term *Erlebnis* for Dilthey is "someone's immediate experience of a general significance," say here at least the artist's. This experience, we recall, is peculiar to the experience that only artworks involve, because such an experience cannot be conceptualized but can only be presented by the artwork. An artifact that arises out of the contemplation of such an immediate experience thus becomes an artwork to the degree that the artist succeeds in imaginatively recreating this immediate experience in the artifact itself. The

---

[14]For more commentary on this central doctrine of Dilthey's see M. v. d. Groeben, *Konstruktive Psychologie und Erlebnis: Studien zur Logik der Diltheyschen Kritik an der erklärenden Psychologie* (Stuttgart, 1934), and E. Paczkowski-Lagowska's two articles, "Dilthey's Reform of Psychology and Its Contribution to the Philosophy of Human Sciences," *Reports on Philosophy* 7(1983): 13–40, and "Human Studies and Psychology: Analysis of the *Einleitung in die Geisteswissenschaften*," *Reports on Philosophy* 6(1983): 3–16. See also J. Scanion, "Empirio-criticism, Descriptive Psychology, and the Experimental World," in *Psychology and Archaic Experience*, ed. J. Sallis, 185–88 (Pittsburgh, 1982).

"general significance" at issue Dilthey takes to be something essential about human nature, something typical in the sense of an ideal type, an image of the general presented through the particular. The artwork, then, not the artifact, embodies the immediate experience of general significance to the degree that it presents symbols of what is humanly typical, sensuous manifolds that involve both the subject and the object.

Such a theory has its own difficulties, whether terminological or otherwise. The epistemology here, with its commitment to an immediate kind of knowledge and to entities such as concrete universals, to mention just two issues, is problematic. But however tractable these difficulties may prove, others arise precisely in our attempts to understand just what kind of experience is at issue when Dilthey centers his treatment of *Erlebnis* on the idea of an immediate (i.e., nonconceptualizable) experience. However we finally articulate Dilthey's view here, I think we must conclude on any account that for him artworks are the products of this immediate experience. If we go on to say that whatever immediate experience of general significance results in an artwork deserves the description "aesthetic experience," we need to conclude that Dilthey's theory of *Erlebnis* comes down to a theory of aesthetic experience. Just which kind of aesthetic experience theory we are dealing with becomes clear on closer examination of Dilthey's previous discussion of the imagination. Dilthey's aesthetic use of the *Erlebnis* theory depends on his view of the imagination, because the artist is able to recreate the immediate experience of general significance through the imagination alone.[15]

But to see this, we need to bring into focus a distinction that Dilthey continually blurs. Two experiences are at work here—the artist's immediate experience and the recreation of that experience in an artwork. The aesthetic experience is preeminently the result of the immediate experience, not the immediate experience itself. It follows that the artwork is the result of the aesthetic experience. We have then a progression from (1) an immediate experience to (2) an aesthetic experience to (3) an artwork. Dilthey's understanding

[15]On the general background to the theory of the imagination see the standard work of M. H. Abrams, *The Mirror and the Lamp: Romantic Theory and the Critical Tradition* (New York, 1958), basic sources in S. T. Coleridge, *Biographia Literaria*, vol. 1, ed. John Shawcross (London, 1958), and G. E. Lessing, *Laocoon: An Essay upon the Limits of Painting and Poetry*, trans. Ellen Frothingham (Boston, 1898), as well as the German study of A. Nivelle, *Kunst- und Dichtungstheorien zwischen Aufklärung und Klassik* (Berlin, 1960).

of the imagination is an attempt to account for the nature of (2). Ordinary experience becomes aesthetic experience because of the transformations worked upon it by imagination.

Each of the four elements of Dilthey's account of the imagination contributes to this conclusion. In the first place, the continuum of consciousness is realized by the synthetic effect of the imagination on the differentiated manifold of past, present, and future sensible particulars. In other words, the unity of aesthetic experience is the achievement of the imagination. Second, the threefold distinction of mental acts enables Dilthey to specify the idea of poetic imagination in the particular terms of what he calls affection or moods rather than in terms of representations or volitions. Affective awareness produces an affective state of mind. Some but not all of the feelings we experience while in this affective state of mind are themselves constitutive of aesthetic experience. Third, the division of the affective sphere into six kinds of feelings specifies just which feelings are the constitutive ones. Thus the feelings relative to different sensible qualities and their respective intensities—(2) and (3) in the earlier enumeration—as well as those associated with cognitive acts through which these feelings are effected (4), are the relevant ones for the constitution of aesthetic experience, and not those feelings distinguished in numbers (1), (5), and (6). Finally, in the specific instance of the literary work of art, experience of these artifacts becomes aesthetic (as opposed to textual, critical, grammatical, etc.) to the degree that readers center their affective awareness of the work on precisely those symbolic images that mediate the author's recreation of the immediate experience of general significance.

But such an account comes to the same view we noted a moment ago in the discussion of Dilthey's account of *Erlebnis*—what makes an artifact an artwork is experiencing the artifact aesthetically. And experiencing the artifact aesthetically is unifying the disparate sensory perceptions imaginatively by centering affective attention on the general symbolic constructs of the work, with the help of precisely those feelings that are associated with the different sensible qualities of the work.

This theory of *Erlebnis* again implies the thesis that a work of art in necessarily a result of an aesthetic experience, and in several senses: first, because a work of art must incorporate something of general significance that itself can be appreciated only through a special state of mind, that is, affectively; second, because this general significance can be embodied only if the artist first recreates it through personal aesthetic experience or inner state; and third, because this general significance can function essentially only to the degree that it arises to the level of the typical, which also demands an aesthetic experience.[16] I conclude, then, with the view that Dilthey's account of imagination implies a theory of aesthetic experience and that in Dilthey's work this theory can be identified with his theory of *Erlebnis*.

Now we need to ask whether Dilthey's theory of aesthetic experience can provide a satisfactory account of the artwork. I argue that it does not. The reasons I insist on, however, are importantly different from those we might wish to urge against other theories of aesthetic experience mentioned previously.

There are, of course, different kinds of theories of aesthetic experience. Thus an aesthetic experience may be construed in different ways. Reading through the representative literature on this topic[17] shows that aesthetic experience is sometimes taken as a reaction to a special kind of experience, or as a report about a special kind of experience, or as an instrument whereby a special kind of experience affects others, or as the kind of experience itself—whether unified, or harmonious, or pleasurable, or beautiful, of disinterested, or whatever. The same literature not only provides accounts of these different views but furnishes arguments against all of them without exception. But Dilthey's account, on my understanding, does not fall under any one of the variations just mentioned. Rather, for Dilthey an experience is aesthetic depending on whether it is or is not a product, an effect, a result, a consequence of some prior experience he terms *Erlebnis*, in the sense, as we have seen repeatedly, of an immediate experience of general significance.

Now, regardless of the complications that follow from the *Erlebnis* doctrine, the construal of aesthetic experience as a product of some other experience is subject to extremely serious objections that have repeatedly been sharpened, notably by G. Dickie and E.

---

[16]See G. Dickie's article, "Aesthetic Experience: Affective Unity?" in his *Art and the Aesthetic* (Ithaca, 1974), 182–200, and the very different perspective in the Japanese account of A. Omori, "Hermeneutik des Lebens und Ästhetik bei W. Dilthey," *Bigaku* 35(1985): 14–25.

[17]See, for examples of two traditions, M. Dufrenne, "Is Art Language?" *Philosophy Today* 14(1970): 190–200, and W. Tartakiewicz, "Aesthetic Experience: The Early History of the Concept," *Dialectics and Humanism* 1(Autumn 1973): 19–30, and "Aesthetic Experience: The Last Stages in the History of the Concept," *Dialectics and Humanism* 2(1974): 81–91.

Zemach.[18] The basic objection is that the descriptions used to characterize the observation of whatever objects or works are in question properly apply to the objects or works themselves. In Dilthey's case the basic objection thus assumes the following form: the description of those properties that are taken as characteristic of the immediate experience of general significance properly apply to the work itself. The force of this objection is clearly formulated in Zemach's summary dilemma. "If aesthetic properties do not exist, aesthetic experiences cannot exist; but if aesthetic properties do exist, aesthetic experiences are irrelevant for the explication of aesthetic judgments. In either case instrumentalism [the view that aesthetic experience is the product of valued experience or objects] is false."[19] And the instrumentalist version of the theory of aesthetic experience is the view I have been concerned to ascribe to Dilthey.

There is, however, a more interesting reason why Dilthey's view is unsatisfactory, and this reason is specific to Dilthey's view alone. As I have shown, Dilthey's instrumentalism is consequent upon a theory of the imagination, and this theory fatally collapses the distinction between intentions and objects into overgeneral talk of "affective awareness." Dilthey's theory of aesthetic experience in fact cannot adequately account for the nature of the artwork because, besides the general difficulty it shares with other instrumentalist accounts, it involves the specific difficulty of allowing us no way of distinguishing between the properties of the artist's intentions and the properties of the works that incorporate those intentions. And without this kind of distinction the question whether something is an artwork or merely an artifact founders on inconclusive analyses of putative features of an insufficiently defined manifold. About the merits of such analyses, whether Dilthey's or someone else's, we cannot reach a conclusion just because we are unable to decide on Dilthey's account, at least, whether these analyses apply to mental entities or to material ones. Often we do not agree on the putative features of what we are attempting to analyze, and in the case of disagreement we do not have procedures available for resolving such disagreements. In short, Dilthey's aesthetics seems to be built upon an instrumentalist version of

[18]Besides Dickie's book cited in note 16, see his earlier book *Aesthetics* (New York, 1971). See also E. Zemach, "Farewell to the Aesthetic Experience," *PTL: A Journal for Descriptive Poetics and Theory of Literature* 2(1977): 65–72.

[19]Zemach 1977: 67.

aesthetic experience theories. This adds to the usual problems of such theories the particular weaknesses of a radical ambiguity in the formulation of its central expression, "affective awareness."

In several of the following chapters, I examine in turn elements of this ambiguity between intentions and objects with the help of other major figures in the realist backgrounds of modern aesthetics, especially Brentano, Husserl, Twardowski, Meinong, and Ingarden. For part of the task Dilthey has left to contemporary aesthetics is the conceptual work of making clear in just what senses an aesthetic object can be both particular and universal and, more particularly, in what senses the historicity of the literary work of art makes any elaboration of "objective interpretive norms" necessarily futile. It is especially the second of these problems, the "objectivity" of interpretive norms, that arises when we attempt to survey critically Dilthey's literary aesthetics. And central to this problem is the notion of "type," particularly in relation to Dilthey's unsatisfactory theory of statements. What remains to be investigated at length and by more than one researcher, is the general theory of statements that will accommodate not just the statements of literary theory but the statements of poetic texts, and that will do so precisely in the context of a perspicuous treatment of the Diltheyan concept of "type." To the degree that the various elements of Dilthey's rich aesthetic reflections raise such issues about language and art in the context of a persistent concern with history, those reflections can be seen as part of a fresh philosophical tradition stemming from Bolzano's critical readings of Kant. But these reflections of even so accomplished a reader of Kant as Dilthey himself remain quite general. For a more detailed development of some of these issues, we need to follow this tradition another step into the work of Brentano.

Appendix 6: Theory in Literature

One basic problem in attempting to present an accurate and constructive account of "Dilthey's literary theory" (say, T) is deciding whether such a phrase has a referent. Here is a schematization.

1. T is identical with that part of Dilthey's writings most concerned with literature. This is the general view of both Dilthey's disciples and his critics. But this view is inadequate for two reasons. In practice this view concentrates on only three works, to

the exclusion of much of Dilthey's earlier work on literature.[20] In principle this view denies the possibility of any important connection between the literary and mainly historical and philosophical aspects of Dilthey's work. But this denial is unnecessary, and this connection is demonstrably true.

2. T is identical with the literary theory contained in all of Dilthey's works. But this view is also inadequate for two reasons. For in fact an exhaustive reading of Dilthey's work shows that nowhere is there any presentation of his literary theory that can be taken as complete. Moreover, some of the many different presentations of his literary theory are inconsistent.

3. T is identical with the literary theory that can be inferred from Dilthey's actual practice as a literary critic. But this view is inadequate because of the second reason given above against (1).

4. T is identical with the set of Dilthey's enduring terminological contributions (e.g., *Bildungsroman*, "literary generations"). This theory also fails because there is disagreement over what criteria define this set and what terms fit these criteria. Hence it seems that T has no identifiable referent at all. But Müller-Vollmer has his own proposal, which reads:

5. T is identical with Dilthey's *Einbildungskraft* essay, its sequel *Die drei Epochen der modernen Aesthetik und ihre heutige Aufgabe* (1892), parts of four other works,[21] and views contained passim in parts of the works after 1900.[22]

He writes: "The clue to the theory of literature ... lies in the philosophical studies written in the last decade of his life, in which he strove for clarification and systematization of earlier views and insights" (43). And the value of this clue purportedly is that it provides a way of overcoming the arguments brought against (1) to (4) above. In effect (5) would amount to holding that T is not to be

---

[20]These works are three collections of essays: the well-known *Das Erlebnis und die Dichtung* (1905), *Von Deutscher Dichtung und Musik*, 2d ed. (posthumous 1957), and *Die grosse Phantasiedichtung und andere Studien zu vergleichender Literaturgeschichte* (posthumous, 1954). Almost all of Dilthey's writings in aesthetics now appear in English translation in the *Selected Works*, vol. 5 (Princeton, 1985).

[21]*Ideen über eine beschreibende und zergliedernde Psychologie* (1894), GS, 5:139–240, *Beiträge zum Studium der Individualität* (1896), GS, 5:241–316, *Eine Einleitung in die Geisteswissenschaften* (1883), GS, 1:3–429, and the monograph *Das Leben Schleiermachers* (1867–70), references to which are to be found in note 7 above.

[22]MV, 45–46. For these works see the detailed listings in Herrmann. Compare M. Ermarth's discussion in *Wilhelm Dilthey: The Critique of Historical Reason* (Chicago, 1978), with H. U. Lessing, *Die Idee einer Kritik der historischen Vernunft* (Freiburg, 1984).

found mainly in Dilthey's literary writings at all. Rather, T must be sought mainly in the combination of the late philosophical writings, and precisely those literary writings (the 1887 and 1892 essays) where the breakthrough occurred toward a new philosophical outlook which culminated in the phenomenological writings of the years after 1900" (44). Such a breakthrough is assured on the basis of G. Misch's remarks in 1923 and those of L. Landgrebe in 1928.[23]

To the negative consideration that (5) avoids the disadvantages of (1) to (4) must be added a positive argument. Müller-Vollmer maintains that T must include at least some of Dilthey's philosophical works because "literary theories... have been essentially and of necessity philosophical" (46). The assumption is that to look for T outside the philosophical works is to neglect the truth of this claim. But that the essential and necessary philosophical character of T need not be found in the philosophical works is overlooked. Thus the positive argument is unconvincing because it assumes without sufficient evidence that the philosophical character of T is to be found mainly in the philosophical works.

We fall back, then, on the negative argument. But this argument is also unconvincing. For it mistakenly assumes, first, that Misch and Landgrebe are correct in their interpretation of Dilthey's philosophical development, and second, that this breakthrough privileges the later philosophical works for any investigation of T. For the sake of the argument, let us grant the first assumption. The second, however, needs demonstration. The author provides none. Müller-Vollmer's proposed solution to the difficulties of the other attempts to specify Dilthey's theory is inadequate because the assumption that the philosophical breakthrough in the *Poetik* of 1887 privileges that work over others as a sufficient basis for Dilthey's literary theory is argued both insufficiently and unconvincingly. Here is the major difficulty with this early and pioneering

---

[23]Müller-Vollmer see the interpretations of G. Misch and L. Landgrebe as basic. Misch's introduction to *GS*, vol. 5, "Vorbericht des Herausgebers," in *GS* (Göttingen, 1914), 5:7–117, and his later article "Die Idee der Lebensphilosophie in der Theorie der Geisteswissenschaften," *Kant Studien* 31(1926): 536–48, must be sharply distinguished from his turgid book *Lebensphilosophie und Phänomenologie: Eine Auseinandersetzung der Diltheyschen Richtung mit Heidegger und Husserl* (Leipzig, 1931). Landgrebe's excellent article appeared in Husserl's famous *Jahrbuch*, "Wilhelm Diltheys Theorie der Geisteswissenschaften: Analyse ihrer Grundbegriffe," *Jahrbuch für Philosophie und Phänomenologische Forschung* (Halle) 9 (1928): 238–366. Important background material, including Mische and Landgrebe, is in R. Rodi and H.-U. Lessing, eds., *Materialien zur Philosophie Wilhelm Diltheys* (Frankfurt, 1984).

study in English—it fails to solve the extremely important problem it raises: just how we are to specify what is to count as Dilthey's literary aesthetics. We need, I suggest, to backtrack, with the help of studies like Müller-Vollmer's and others, and try to get our bearings again.[24]

[24]Despite some inaccuracies, R. Wellek's article remains very helpful—"Wilhelm Dilthey's Poetics and Literary Theory," in *Wächter und Hüter* (New Haven, 1957), 121–32. The best general book is R. A. Makkreel, *Dilthey: Philosopher of the Human Sciences* (Princeton, 1975). Other important material can be found in T. E. Seebohm, "Boeckh and Dilthey: The Development of Methological Hermeneutics," *Man and World* 17(1984): 325–46; S. Corngold, "Dilthey's Essay *The Poetic Imagination: A Poetics of Force,*" *Interpretation* 9(1981): 301–38; and H. P. Richman, *Wilhelm Dilthey: Pioneer of the Human Studies* (Los Angeles, 1979). For an excellent discussion of the larger issue here—just how we are to understand "theory" in talk of literature as opposed to "theory" in talk of science—see P. Livingston's analysis in his *Literary Knowledge* (Ithaca, 1988), 9–31.

Chapter Seven

Brentano and
Descriptive Intentionalism

Every mental phenomenon is characterized by what the scholastics of the Middle Ages called the intentional (and also mental) inexistence of an object.

—Franz Brentano

Every object of judgment enters into consciousness in two ways, as an object of presentation and as an object of affirmation or denial.

—Franz Brentano

IN THIS chapter I investigate more carefully one of the central elements in the ideas of aesthetic experience that Dilthey elaborated in his critical encounters with Kantian philosophy.[1] Defining the nature of the literary artwork in terms of aesthetic experience proved unsatisfactory largely because of the vague character of this notion. Consequently, the controlling idea here is that we may find a satisfactory way of defining the literary artwork by working out one of the central components that make up the too general notion of aesthetic experience. In particular, the question is whether we can define the nature of the literary artwork by appealing, if not to aesthetic experience, then perhaps to aesthetic intentions. I show that before we can attempt to answer this question directly, a number of precisions must be introduced.

In the first section of this chapter I try to specify the most influential understanding of intentions in one of the central figures in the realist backgrounds to modern philosophy, Franz Brentano.

[1]See the discussion in chapter 6.

Next I take up a critical examination of kinds of intentionalist theories used in the examination of artworks and isolate a weak version of intentionalist criticism that I first criticize and then amend. Finally, I draw on the initial analysis of intentionality in Brentano to construct a strong version of descriptive intentionalism only. This final move should open up the possibility of a more thorough critical examination of the strong version in the next chapter, where I pursue some further elements of the realist tradition in the work of Husserl.

Intentions

A great deal has been written about Brentano's doctrine of intentionality.[2] Unfortunately, there is still much to say. Understanding Brentano's major statement of his view in the first chapter of book 2 of his *Psychologie vom empirischen Standpunkt* has proved difficult.[3] Moreover, Brentano changed his own views on this matter—for example, in the later volumes of the *Psychologie*, in other later works, and in the unpublished manuscripts.[4] And in

[2]For more recent views see S. F. Barker, "Intensionality and Intentionality," *Philosophy Research Archives* 8(1982); 95–111; and P. Geach, "Intentionality of Thought versus Intentionality of Desire," *Die Philososphie Franz Brentanos*, ed. R. M. Chisholm and R. Haller (Amsterdam, 1978), pp. 131–38 (hereafter *DPFB*). For comparative studies in this area see Chandana Chakrabarti, "Intentionality: Brentano and Moore V. James," in *Logic, Ontology and Action*, ed. K. K. Banerjee 263–69 (Atlantic Highlands, N.J., 1982); and W. P. Bechtel, "Indeterminacy and Intentionality: Quine's Purported Elimination of Propositions," in *La doctrina de la intendionalidad en Bretano*, ed. S. Alvarez-Aquilina (Barcelona, 1961); R. M. Chisholm, "Brentano's Descriptive Psychology and the Intentional," in *Phenomenology and Existentialism*, ed. M. H. Mandelbaum and E. L. Lee (Baltimore, 1967); and R. M. Chisholm and W. Sellars, "Intentionality and the Mental," in *Concepts, Theories, and the Mind-Body Problem*, ed. H. Feigl, M. Scriven, and G. Maxwell, *Minnesota Studies in the Philosophy of Science* (Minneapolis, 1958); A. Gurwitsch, "Toward a Theory of Intentionality," *Philosophy and Phenomenological Research* 30(1970): 354–67; J. Kim, "Materialism and the Criteria of the Mental," *Synthèse* 22(1971): 328–45.

[3]Brentano, *Psychologie vom empirischen Standpunkt*, vol. 1 (Leipzig, 1874). Note that Brentano uses "intention" in a distinctive way. As an anonymous Cornell referee writes: "The phenomenological use of intention need not be psychological or even 'mental' in the sense that say Anscombe's analysis of intentions is." We need to keep these different uses of "intention" in sight throughout the following discussion.

[4]For later versions see Brentano, *Psychologie vom empirischen Standpunkt*, 2d ed., vol. 1, ed. O. Kraus (Leipzig, 1924), and *Psychologie vom empirischen Standpunkt*, vol. 3, *Vom sinnlichen und noetischen Bewusstsein*, 2d ed., ed. F. Mayer-Hillebrand (Hamburg, 1974). For the English translation see Brentano, *Psychology from an Empirical Standpoint*, trans. A. C. Rancurello, D. B. Terrell, and L. L. McAlister, of

the writings Brentano dedicated to aesthetics, published only posthumously under the somewhat misleading title *Grundzüge der Ästhetik*, he used the term "intentionality" in confusing ways.[5] Given this perplexing context, I shall confine my discussion of Brentano's view to the major and most influential of its statements, that of the *Psychologie* of 1874.

We need to understand just how Brentano distinguishes between the mental and the physical.[6] The initial problem is understanding what he means by the word *Realität*. If we follow Chisholm here, as I think we should, this word must be translated not as "reality" but as "thing."[7] Such a translation accurately represents Brentano's usual understanding of the term *Realität* during this period of his philosophical work. Consequently the distinction Brentano is urging here is not between what exists and what is real, but between what exists and what does not exist.

This point has been neatly summarized by Linda McAlister, one of the English translators of Brentano's *Psychologie*, in the second and more reliable of her two articles on intentionality in Brentano.[8] Here and in what follows, I rely on her analysis: "For Brentano," she writes, "a *reales* or a *Realität* is a particular individual thing, while an *irreales* is a non-thing, as, for example, a universal, a species, a genus, a state of affairs or values. Brentano maintained that something could be a *Realität*, i.e. an individual, a thing, even

---

the second edition of vols. 1 and 2 of *Psychologie vom empirischen Standpunkt* (1924) (London, 1973). For the unpublished manuscripts see J. C. M. Brentano, "The Manuscripts of Franz Brentano," *Revue Internationale de Philosophie* 20(1966): 477–84, and F. Mayer-Hillebrand, "Franz Brentanos wissenschaftlicher Nachlass," *Zeitschrift für Philosophische Forschung* 13(1959): 321–32. See also the material on psychology from the Nachlass, *Deskriptive Psychologie*, ed. R. M. Chisholm (Hamburg, 1982).

[5]Brentano, *Grundzüge der Ästhetik*, ed. F. Mayer-Hillebrand (Bern, 1959). See the second edition (Hamburg, 1988).

[6]Recent studies include O. T. Kent, "Brentano and the Relational View of Consciousness," *Man and World* 17(1984): 19–52; Tai Kim Ching, "Brentano on the Unity of Mental Phenomena," *Philosophy and Phenomenological Research* 39(1978): 199–207; H. M. Field, "Mental Representation," *Journal of Philosophy* 75(1978): 649–61. For more background see the essays by Chisholm and Sellars, and by Kim in ed. H. Feigl, M. Scriven, and G. Maxwell cited in note 2; and R. M. Chisholm, ed., *Realism and the Background of Phenomenology* (New York, 1960).

[7]See R. M. Chisholm, "Intentional Inexistence," in *Perceiving: A Philosophical Study* 168–85 (Ithaca, 1957), esp. 168–69.

[8]The first is L. L. McAlister, "Franz Brentano and Intentional Inexistence," *Journal of the History of Philosophy* 8(1970): 423–30, and the second is her "Chisholm and Brentano on Intentionality," *Review of Metaphysics* 28(1974): 328–38, reprinted *The Philosophy of Brentano*, ed. L. L. McAlister, 151–59 (London, 1976). Hereafter I give the pagination of the reprint, cited as McAlister.

if it did not exist. A unicorn or a hippogriff, for example, would be particular individual things, and hence *realia*, even though they do not exist. So *"eine Realität"* does not mean "something that exists."[9]

The next term that requires clarification is *physisches Phänomen*. Here McAlister has been able to correct Chisholm's interpretation by showing from other passages in the *Psychologie* that this phrase does not refer, as Chisholm thought, to physical activities, but applies to sensible qualities and indeed to sensible qualities of one peculiar kind.

For Brentano the word *Phänomen*, again in this period of his development, means whatever is the object of what are for him the two exclusive kinds of perception. The first of these two kinds is external perception, the second is direct inner perception. Both necessarily involve acts of existential judgment, that is, acts of affirmation or acts of denial that a putative object exists or does not exist.[10] But the first act, external perception, is a fallible judgment, whereas the second, direct inner perception, is a self-evidently true judgment. Now, among the objects of these two kinds of acts of perception are some that are ultimate in the sense of being simple, that is, indivisible objects.

Brentano uses the word *Phänomen* to refer to those simple ultimate objects of both inner and outer perception. The basic objects of direct inner perception are just those mental objects that appear to us on introspection, that is, on awareness of our own mental acts while attention is focused on something else.[11] Of these simple mental objects there can be for Brentano only three kinds: objects of presentation, objects of judgments, and objects of

[9]McAlister, 154. McAlister does not pursue how Brentano distinguishes between a particular individual and a thing. As a referee remarks: "It is one thing to say that *a* hippogriff is a thing; it is much more difficult to know what a claim about *this* hippogriff would mean since it does not exist and cannot be singled out."

[10]On Brentano's doctrine of judgments see Brentano, *Wahrheit und Evidenz*, ed. O. Kraus (Leipzig, 1930); Brentano, *Die Lehre vom richtigen Urteil*, ed. F. Mayer-Hillebrand (Bern, 1956); and Brentano, *Versuch über die Erkenntnis*, 2d enlarged ed. (Hamburg, 1970). See also Brentano, *The Theory of Categories*, trans. N. Guterman and R. M. Chisholm (Boston, 1981), and his *Sensory and Noetic Consciousness*, ed. O. Kraus and L. McAlister (London, 1981). A related article of special interest is R. Kamitz, "Das Problem der Objektivität der Wahrheit im Lichte der Evidenztheorie: Eine logische Analyse eines Arguments von Franz Brentano," *Conceptus* 11(1977): 87–91.

[11]Introspection is ambiguous. Brentano believes that attention focused on one's own mental acts is impossible, whereas attention focused on anything but one's own mental acts can include the awareness of one's own mental acts. See McAlister, 156, note 12.

volitions and emotions (a somewhat different classification than we have seen earlier in our reading of Dilthey). And the basic objects of external perception are simple sensible qualities only.[12] Thus Brentano's crucial distinction between the mental and the physical is to be understood as the distinction between mental acts and simple sensible qualities: the former, not the latter, are directed toward objects.[13]

It remains only to sharpen this distinction with several negations. A useful account is McAlister's correction of her own earlier article and summary of her present research. Brentano meant his thesis about intentionality

not primarily as a thesis about objects of mental phenomena, but about the fact that mental phenomena are by their very nature relational while physical phenomena are not. It is not, however, simply that mental phenomena are relational while physical phenomena, i.e. sensible qualities, are not. That would, at any rate, be false. For, as a matter of fact, physical phenomena are capable of standing and do stand in all sorts of relations.... Nor does the difference... consist in the fact that the former are necessarily relational while the latter are only contingently so.... the crucial difference... is that the former enter necessarily into a *particular kind of relation* which is wholly foreign to the realm of physical phenomena.... relations to something *as object*, and this is a kind of relation which a sensible quality could not possibly enter into, except as the object term. It could never be the subject term.[14]

In short, intentionality in Brentano's view is a necessary relation between one of the three basic kinds of mental acts and something that stands to this act as its object. As such, intentionality is the basic characteristic of the mental as opposed to the physical.

[12]See Brentano's late papers, *Die Abkehr von Nichtrealen*, ed. F. Mayer-Hillebrand (Hamburg, 1966). For commentary on Brentano's theories of objects see G. Bergmann's works, *Realism: A Critique of Brentano and Meinong* (Madison, 1967), *Brentano and Intrinsic Value* (New York, 1986), and *Brentano and Meinong Studies* (Atlantic Highlands, N.J., 1982); R. M. Chisholm, "Objectives and Intrinsic Value," in *Jenseits von Sein und Nichtsein*, ed. Rudolf Haller (Graz, 1972); and R. Grossman, "Non-existent Objects: Recent Work on Brentano and Meinong," *American Philosophical Quarterly* (1969): 17–32.

[13]See Brentano, *Untersuchungen zur Sinnespsychologie*, 2d ed., ed. R. M. Chisholm and R. Fabian (Hamburg, 1979). On mental acts see R. B. Grossmann, "Acts and Relations in Brentano," *Analysis* 21(1960): 1–5; R. Kamitz, "Acts and Relations in Brentano," *Analysis* 22(1962): 73–78.

[14]McAlister, 158.

Kinds of Intentionalist Theories

To see clearly the relevance of some kind of intentionalism to literary artworks, it will be useful to have an example before us. Here then is a poem, a dramatic monologue by Posthumus from act 2 of Shakespeare's *Cymbeline*.

> Is there no way for men to be, but women
> Must be half-workers? We are all bastards; all,
> And that most venerable man which I
> Did call my father was I know not where
> When I was stamp'd; some coiner with his tools
> Made me a counterfeit; yet my mother seem'd
> The Dian of that time; so doth my wife
> The nonpareil of this. O! vengeance, vengeance;
> Me of my lawful pleasure she restrain'd
> And pray's me oft forbearance; did it with
> A pudency so rosy the sweet view on't
> Might well have warm'd old Saturn; that I thought her
> As chaste as unsunn'd snow. O! all the devils![15]

Now, on reading such texts carefully we sometimes find ourselves asking different kinds of questions. But those I focus on here concern only semantic and evaluative elements. These are questions about how we are to determine the meaning and the value of complicated figurative utterances such as those sentences about jealousy, utterances that occur not just in our poets, but in our quarrels with our friends, our lovers, and even ourselves.

In many contemporary discussions, one central set of views that attempts to answer aesthetics about both the meaning and the evaluation of literary artworks is known, not unambiguously, as intentionalist criticism.[16] As regards the meaning of literary artworks,

---

[15]For some idea of the complexities in the understanding of this kind of text see G. Steiner, *After Babel: Aspects of Language and Translation* (New York, 1975), 1–8.

[16]G. Dickie, *Aesthetics: An Introduction* (New York, 1971), chap. 12, and R. G. Collingwood, *The Principles of Art* (London, 1958), 36–37, 139. Note that more sophisticated views abound. Hirsch, for example, as a referee points out, "would not privilege intention in an unqualified way but only in an authoritative way with respect to interpretation—i.e., one would not say that a work was good simply because it fulfilled an intention since the intention might itself be minor or bad, but one would say that, of competing interpretations, the one which corresponded to the author's intentions holds a privileged position vis-à-vis other interpretations. Evaluation follows similarly—one cannot credit an author with a fortunate accident because she did not intend it."

answers to such questions, according to this view, are to be sought in terms of just what the author intended the text to mean. Hence disputes about the meaning of ambiguous words or obscure lines (for example "counterfeit" in the phrase "some coiner with his tools / Made me a counterfeit") are resolved by privileging the author's intentions as opposed to just what the words of the text may be taken to assert, or just what the audience may succeed in grasping, or just what the critics may discover, or even just what aestheticians may postulate as theoretical entities. Intentionalist critics think it important to build into this idea of author's intentions not just those the author is consciously aware of but even those that may remain subconscious or unconscious. Moreover, the author's intentions are to be taken broadly as those intentions the author may develop in the process of completing the work or even on completion of the work, and not just those that accompany its beginning.

As regards the evaluation of literary artworks, again according to the intentionality views, answers to questions about whether an artwork is good or bad, successful or unsuccessful, promising or not (For example, is Posthumous's monologue a "dramatic flop," or does it "really work"?) are also to be sought in terms of the author's intentions. Thus a literary artwork is promising, successful, or just plain good to the degree that it incorporates the author's intentions. If the text falls short of incorporating those intentions, then the work is deficient; if it realizes those intentions to a great though not complete degree, then it is a successful artwork. This line of argument not only is applied to the problem of distinguishing between good and bad artworks, it is also used to distinguish relative degrees of perfection. Thus some good works are judged not only successful but indeed more or less successful than other good works. Hamlet's monologue "To be or not to be," for example, is generally taken to be superior to Posthumus's monologue. One way of effecting such graduations, this kind of intentionality criticism runs, is scaling a series of good artworks as a function of their relative success in incorporating the intentions of their authors. So intentions are called on both to distinguish between good and bad texts and to distinguish the relative merits among a series of good works.

Now such views, or some such set of views, have occasioned a fair amount of criticism. Without going into the obscurities of subconscious and unconscious versus conscious intentions or even into the intricate problems in the philosophy of mind that any talk of intentions seems to entail, I think we find problems enough. In what follows, if we begin by taking the term "intentions" quite roughly as, say, "a series of psychological states or events" in the author's mind (this is Beardsley's overly influential version),[17] and if we refer to versions of this view as "the intentionality view," then I think we can observe three general kinds of considerations that militate against finally appraising this view as an adequate one.

Arguments against Intentionalisms

The first argument against the intentionality view, which philosophers such as Beardsley and others like to use, makes the obvious point that such intentions cannot function as normative criteria for either the meaning or the evaluation of literary texts because they are often—and, most tellingly, for precisely the central cases of literary works of art—simply unavailable. It is true, of course, that we used to be able to consult Paul Celan about his intentions when he wrote some of his more obscure lines, and we can still consult Peter Weiss about his intentions in his plays and Peter Handke about his intentions as a novelist, whether they be honorable or otherwise. But the plain fact is that neither Homer nor Virgil nor Dante nor Shakespeare nor Goethe is among us any longer. Whatever intentions *they* had in writing particular texts are no longer accessible. To exaggerate the point, we might put it this way. However tingling with ambiguity and sparkling with metaphor his phrases are, we cannot ask Shakespeare just what he had in mind when he asked, "Is there no way for men to be, but women / Must be half-workers?"

A related consideration should be added just to show the force of this kind of argument. Even were we able to consult the masters as we can consult their epigones, this argument might continue, knowing the authors' intentions would provide no sufficient guarantee that *these* intentions and not some others were actually expressed in the text itself. Authors quite simply might not fulfill their primary intentions in their text at all. Again, the same conclusions must be drawn as in the main argument, but for a new reason. Authors' intentions cannot be normative criteria either for

[17]M. C. Beardsley, *Aesthetics: Problems in the Philosophy of Criticism* (New York, 1958), 18.

the meaning or for the evaluation of literary texts, not just because they most often are not available, but also because, even when available, they allow no adequate inferences to the meaning of the text itself.

A second argument against the intentionality position, which philosophers such as Dickie and others like to use,[18] turns not on the difficulty or even the impossibility of appeals to intentions but on the absurd consequences of such appeals in many cases. The critical move here involves focusing the intentionality claims particularly on questions about the evaluation of artworks as successful or unsuccessful. On the intentionalist view, it is argued, all literary works of art would be successful just in those cases where authors had minimal expectations of themselves—that is to say, very modest intentions.

Here, to take a simplistic case, is a short poem:

> The Easter Bunny comes at dawn.
> He scampers across your little lawn.
> When you awake he is gone.

Now, if my only intention as an eight-year-old boy trying to write this poem was to get the last words in all three lines to rhyme, then if the appeal to intentions is made to resolve the issue of the poem's success or failure as an artwork, clearly my poem was and remains a success. But surely this conclusion is controversial, even if my mother continues to think otherwise. Conversely, if the poet's intentions are at the other extreme—for example, if I intended to write another *Divine Comedy*—then once again the appeal to intentions will not do, since in this case virtually anything I write will turn out indisputably to be a failure. What makes such consequences absurd, of course, is that even in much less extreme cases we most often do judge literary works of art to be successes or failures on other grounds than such shaky appeals to authors' intentions, whether they be childishly minimal or simply megalomaniacal. So such appeals are not just wrongheaded, they are dispensable.

A final argument against the intentionalist view turns on the now familiar though still troublesome distinction in recent years between sentence meaning and speaker's meaning. The point of this distinction here can be seen by considering briefly any example

---

[18]See G. Dickie, *Art and the Aesthetic* (Ithaca, 1974).

we might wish to take of an ambiguous work or phrase in a literary text, say the word "counterfeit" in the monologue from *Cymbeline*. Intentionalist critics characteristically try to resolve such ambiguity by appealing to the author's intentions in such terms as "what Shakespeare meant to say by using the word 'counterfeit' here was such and such" or "study of other uses of 'counterfeit' in Shakespeare's dramatic works shows that here he intends the following." The additional difficulty here, besides the other ones we have already looked at, arises from our realization that no matter how these critics interpret the meaning of the ambiguity, the word or phrase remains ambiguous *in the sentence*. And the point is, of course, that different conditions govern the meaning of sentences than hold for utterances. Utterances can often be meaningful to the speaker so long as private intentions are fulfilled. Lear's mad speeches or Ophelia's songs are clear examples. But for sentences to be meaningful for others as well, certain public matters must be addressed. Nonlinguistic conditions such as context and the fact that one's audience belongs to a particular language community, and so on, must also be met if we are to have sentence meaning. Dickie formulates the consequences of this distinction as a critical principle: "If an author tells us what his poem means but it is possible to discuss that meaning in the poem independently of the author's statement, then it cannot be claimed that the poem means what its author claims it means."[19] More of course needs to be said, since the distinction this argument turns on raises some controversy in its own right. But for our purposes here the anti-intentionalist force of such an argument seems plain enough.

So much, then, for three kinds of arguments against what we might now with reason call "the weak version" of intentionalist criticism, the view—to repeat—that questions about meaning and evaluation are to be answered in terms of just what the author intended the text to mean.

We need to note, of course, that so far I have discussed intentionalist criticism only in the context of what we might call semantic intentionalism (meanings) and evaluative intentionalism (values). My major concern remains, however, descriptive intentionalism, the view that the nature of the text, whether artifact or artwork, can be decided by appealing in some way to intentions.

A second remark is also in order. We need to note that intentionalist criticism, as I have discussed it so far, refers exclusively to authorial

[19]Dickie 1971: 119.

intentions and not to the intentions of critics, readers, performers, translators, editors, and so on. There are, of course, related versions of intentionalism that would require distinctions were we to investigate each of them in turn. But however interesting such variants might be in their own right (consider philosophical formulations of such problems as plagiarism, forgery, influence, revision, and so on), each of these cases remains at a secondary level. The primary level is that of authorial intentions.

With the weak version of semantic and evaluative intentionalism (the author's intentions only) in hand, we will not need to delay over the illustration of a formulation of descriptive intentionalism. We can simply say, on the basis of the preceding discussion, that descriptive intentionalism is the view that it is the author's intentions that answer the question whether a putatively literary text is an artifact or an artwork.[20] Thus *Finnegans Wake*, Pynchon's *Gravity's Rainbow*, and Dos Passos's *1919* are literary artworks and not just verbal collages, because their authors intended them as such. Related views, of course, can be developed about genre questions (Goethe's *Werther* as a novel, not a poem). And this version of descriptive intentionalism will be properly characterizable, like semantic and evaluative intentionalism, as a "weak" version to the degree that it is vulnerable to the same three kinds of argument used against the previous views. The question now is how we can constructively move beyond the reach of these arguments precisely in the area of our inquiry, namely, the area of descriptive intentionalism. Is there any other version available—say, a "strong version" —of descriptive intentionalism? I believe there is.

A Strong Descriptive Intentionalism

Whatever their ilk, intentionalists are prone to retort on a number of points made against the rather vague set of claims held to constitute their views. Moreover, these retorts, though insufficient in themselves to constitute an independent view, can be

---

[20]Beardsley's view changed in some ways. Thus, as the same referee writes, "Beardsley gives a slightly different version of the descriptive thesis in the essay he wrote specifically for Dickie and Sclafani; there something is a literary work because the author intends an aesthetic effect (which is slightly different from intending the work as an artwork since it includes such non-artworks as political speeches in some cases). This view is compatible with the criticisms of semantic and evaluative intentionalism: Beardsley holds this view but is the classic critic of the others."

developed into such a view to the degree that we can reconstruct the vague idea of "intention" behind the weak version with the help of clearer ideas about intentions, such as those of Brentano. Here are some of the useful replies to criticisms of intentionalism. For our purposes I shall formulate these replies more narrowly than their usual purport in order to focus the discussion only on descriptive intentionalism. I will then reach back to our starting point with Brentano and try to construct an independent version of descriptive intentionalism that might merit characterization as a strong version.

As a rejoinder at least in part to these arguments and their like, intentionalist critics begin engagingly by agreeing to a number of points. They concede, for example, the shakiness of any distinction between conscious and unconscious intentions on the grounds that construing the terms of such a distinction satisfactorily is insistently problematic.[21] They concede, too, the obvious points that most of the literary artists in history cannot be consulted about their intentions, that an appeal to authorial intentions as regards the description of the putatively literary texts can have absurd consequences, and that the linguistic basis of literary works remains open for inspection regardless of whose intentions are inventoried.

But these critics quickly point out that much of this argument goes right past the essential feature of the literary work of art, which they are trying to get into focus. A one-sided insistence on the linguistic basis of the literary work of art, they insist, overlooks the peculiar character of literary works. Unlike many, but not all, other entities in the world—stones, trees, and animals, for example— literary works are artifacts. Moreover, they are artifacts of a particular kind. However they may have been recorded, reproduced, recited, performed, translated, or edited, they are composed, written texts. And it is a condition for the existence of such texts that their authors in some sense intended to produce them. Consequently, if anything can properly be referred to as an intentional object, a literary work of art must be such a thing, for an essential feature of its nature is to express the intentions the author wished to embody in this medium.

Moreover, these anti-intentionalist arguments are misleading. For it need not be a central feature of an intentionalist view that

---

[21]See P. Merlan, "Brentano and Freud," *Journal of the History of Ideas* 6(1945): 375–77, and "Brentano and Freud: A Sequel," *Journal of the History of Ideas* 10(1949): 451–52.

authors' unconscious intentions be taken into account, or that authors be consulted in person about their intentions, or that such intentions be normative for the description of literary artworks, or even that the controversial distinction between speakers' utterance and sentence meaning be overlooked.

The anti-intentionalist may of course reply that even if we concede that the text is an intentional object, no valid conclusion can be drawn about whether the nature of the text is to be determined by appeal to intentions. But this reply does not faze the intentionalists. They need only retort that the nature of the text is to be construed not as identical with the author's intentions but as loosely connected, in ways to be argued through by the critics, with only those authorial intentions that are in fact embodied in the text itself. Hence the text remains just as fundamental to the intentionalists as to their opponents.

The difference between the two now seems to be in just what the text is taken to be evidence for. To the anti-intentionalist, only the text is adequate evidence for its description, whereas to the intentionalist the text indeed provides evidence of its own description, but this evidence cannot count as adequate without its conjunction with precisely those authorial intentions that the text successfully embodies. To the degree that *these* intentions and no others are also accessible through the text, the meaning of sentences themselves sometimes must be supplemented with the author's intentions. Specifically, if we are to determine both the full basic text of the work itself and the correct reading of the full basic text, some appeal to the author's success, as Anthony Savile puts it, "in producing a text whose reading is just what its creator wants it to be"[22] is essential. Such an appeal inevitably involves relying on intentions.

It is important to be clear that this new set of intentionalist views is not identical with the weak version, because a number of features are not held in common. Moreover, this new set of views is not defeasible by the arguments against the weaker version, because either—as in the case of untenable distinctions between conscious and unconscious intentions—the cardinal points in these arguments are assimilated into the new view or—as in the case of speaker versus sentence meaning—these points are called into serious doubt. This new set of views we might refer to as an

[22]A. Savile, "The Place of Intentions in the Concept of Art," in *Aesthetics*, ed. H. Osborne, 168 (Oxford, 1972).

amended version of descriptive intentionalism, the view that the nature of a putatively literary text is to be determined by just those conscious intentions that the author succeeds in embodying in the linguistic structure of the work.

This amended version, however, still suffers from a basic difficulty— the initial because most influential account of intentions as "a series of psychological states or events" in the author's mind.[23] What makes this account deficient is its identification of the nature of the literary artwork with an undifferentiated sequence of purely mental events in the author's mind alone. No distinction is offered as to the ultimate components of such a sequence, nor is any account provided of the relation between this event in the author's mind and its reconstitution, at least in part, in the mind of the readers.

The second difficulty we shall have to consider in much greater detail in later chapters. But the first requires immediate attention precisely because Brentano has put at our disposal a much more sophisticated account of intentions than the one built into even the amended version of descriptive intentionalism. Thus Brentano's view enables us to decide just what kinds of mental events are in question when we refer to authorial intentions. And it also enables us to isolate two central ambiguities. But before detailing those features of Brentano's account, we need to specify just why the understanding of intention so far is gravely deficient. We can do this briefly by considering the following general argument against any strictly mentalistic account of intentions, whether Dilthey's, Croce's, Collingwood's, Richards's, or whoever's.

The mentalistic account, in fact, asserts that determining the nature of the putatively literary text involves no necessary reference to the text itself, but only a contingent one. Determining authorial mental states or events, in short, is sufficient for determining the controversial texts. Now someone may concede that there is a necessary psychological relation of dependence between mental entities and literary texts and yet deny that this dependency relation is logically necessary. And psychological necessity without logical necessity is insufficient to sustain the mentalist account. There can be no relation of logical necessity, because it is precisely this relation that the mentalist formulation rejects in affirming a contingent dependency. Thus on its own terms the mentalist

[23]G. Dickie's *Art and the Aesthetic* (Ithaca, N.Y., 1974).

account of intentions cannot be an adequate formulation of the central term in descriptive intentionalism.

Besides this inconsistency argument against mentalism, there is a second, more telling objection. We need only ask the following question to embarrass this theory inexorably. If there is no logical connection between authorial intentions and literary texts, then how can we recognize just which of the multiple events in the mind of the author are to count specifically as authorial mental events and not as some other peculiar kind? Moreover, assuming that we hit upon some set of mental events that seems not irrelevant to the production of literary texts—say, judgments as opposed to volitions (although these distinctions lie outside the superficial mentalist account we are dealing with here)—just which of these putative authorial judgments are relevant to determining the nature of the literary text as opposed to determining its meaning or its evaluation? In the first instance we are left with no way of identifying authorial intentions at all, whereas in the second, even if we hit upon such intentions by luck, we have at hand no criteria of descriptive relevance. A mentalistic theory of intentions, I conclude, just won't do.

What help do Brentano's account and the realist tradition provide? We might begin by recalling Brentano's understanding of intentions from the account we were able to work out previously. Intentions for Brentano are instances of intentionality, a necessary relation between one of three basic kinds of mental acts and its correlative object. Several features of this view require comment.

First, Brentano's account includes a distinction between basic kinds of mental acts and basic kinds of mental objects. The relation between each of these kinds and its relevant object is necessary in the sense that there can be no such act without its respective object. And the relation is reciprocal in the sense that whatever mental objects there may be, these objects are correlates of their respective mental acts.

Second, among the three kinds of basic mental acts and objects is one that is especially pertinent to the problem of determining the nature of putative literary texts. Such texts can be directly related neither to presentations nor to volitions, but only to judgments. This is to say that affirming or denying that something is true is directly relevant to characterizing the nature of problematic texts.

Third, this account involves no set of specific features that apply to texts of any kind whatever. Brentano's theory is presented, that is, as a general theory of basic mental entities. It thereby accommodates applications without incurring the difficulties that reconstructing any particular feature of this theory would inevitably involve. Hence, when we apply such a general theory to the problem at hand, we can build into the applied theory the required features without, as in the case of the too narrow mentalistic theory, risking inconsistency.

What would a strong version of descriptive intentionalism look like? I think, on the basis of the analysis and criticism so far, we need to formulate such a version along the following lines. Strong descriptive intentionalism is the view that determining the nature of putative literary texts necessarily involves reference to the reciprocal relations between those basic authorial entities that we now characterize not vaguely as intentions but specifically as authorial basic judgments and their correlative basic objects. Thus, those intentions of the author that are relevant to determining the nature of putative literary texts are precisely the author's basic judgments about such texts and the basic objects of those authorial judgments about such texts.

To the degree that it is stipulated as implying those retorts that make up the amended version, descriptive intentionalism on this formulation is impervious to the kinds of arguments most often directed against the weak version. This formulation, moreover, counts as a strong version and not just as an amended one, because it includes a reconstructed account of the cardinal concept of intentions. Reference to descriptive intentions, then, needs to be understood as reference to the strong version of descriptive intentionalism.

We have managed to distinguish between two kinds of intentionalism, a weak version and a strong version. Moreover, we have been able to focus this account, with the help of a number of distinctions, precisely on weak and strong versions of descriptive intentionalism. And, with the help of other distinctions we have restricted descriptive intentionalism to the problem of a carefully analyzed account of authorial intentions.[24] Finally, and above all with the help of Brentano's theory of intentionality, we have been able to construe the nature of those intentions very generally indeed as mental events that (1) consist of necessarily reciprocal relations between basic mental acts and basic mental objects and

[24]For an outstanding collection of papers on intentionalism see N. de Molina, ed., *On Literary Intentions* (Edinburgh, 1976).

that (2) have not a contingent but a necessary connection to whatever putative literary texts may be in question at any time.[25]

The question we now need to examine further is this: How adequate is descriptive intentionalism itself? I turn to this issue in the next chapter on aesthetic psychologism, where once again I draw on still other resources of a tradition in aesthetics that is neither analytic nor hermeneutic, one that derives from Bolzano's critique both of the details of Kant's aesthetics and of its place in eighteenth-century thought.

Appendix 7: Things and Objects

We need to have Brentano's exact 1874 formulation clearly in mind to understand with sufficient precision the distinction he attempts there between mental and physical phenomena. Here is the central passage, including Brentano's important footnotes.

Jedes psychische Phänomen ist durch das charakterisiert, was die Scholastiker des Mittelalters die intentionale (auch wohl mentale) [B1] Inexistenz eines Gegenstandes genannt haben, und was wir, obwohl mit nicht ganz unzweideutigen Ausdrücken, die Beziehung auf einen Inhalt, die Richtung auf ein Objekt (worunter hier nicht eine Realität zu verstehen ist) oder die immanente Gegenständlichkeit nennen würden. Jedes enthält etwas als Objekt in sich, obwohl nicht jedes in gleicher Weise. In der Vorstellung ist etwas vorgestellt, in dem Urteil ist etwas anerkannt oder verworfen, in der Liebe geliebt, Hasse gehasst, in dem Begehren begehrt usw. [B2]

Diese intentionale Inexistenz ist den psychischen Phänomenen ausschliesslich eigentümlich. Kein physisches Phänomen zeigt etwas ähnliches. Und somit können wir die psychischen Phänomene definieren, indem wir sagen, sie seien solche Phänomene, welche intentional einen Gegenstand in sich enthalten.

Every mental phenomenon is characterized by what the Scholastics of the Middle Ages called the intentional (or mental) inexistence of an object, and what we might call, though not wholly unambiguously, reference to a content, direction toward an object (which is not to be

[25]For related work of special interest see P. B. Simons's two articles, "Brentano's Reform of Logic," *Topoi* 6(1987): 25–38, and "A Brentanian Basis for Lesniewskian Logic," *Basis Logic et Analyse* 308(1984): 27–297; R. M. Chisholm, "Brentano's Conception of *Substance and Accident*," DPFB, 183–97; B. Terrell, "Quantification and Brentano's Logic," DPFB, 45–66; and S. Körner, "On the Logic of Relations," *Proceedings of the Aristotelian Society* 77(1976): 149–63.

understood here as meaning a thing), or immanent objectivity. Every mental phenomenon includes something as object within itself, although they do not all do so in the same way. In presentation something is presented, in judgment something is affirmed or denied, in love loved, in hate hated, in desire desired and so on.

This intentional in-existence is characteristic exclusively of mental phenomena. No physical phenomenon exhibits anything like it. We can, therefore, define mental phenomena by saying that they are those phenomena which contain an object intentionally within themselves.

The two footnotes that complete this text, which I have labeled B1 and B2, must now be added.

[B1] Sie gebrauchen auch den Ausdruck "gegenständlich (objektiv) in etwas sein," der, wenn man sich jetzt seiner bedienen wollte, umgekehrt als Bezeichnung einer wirklichen Existenz ausserhalb des Geistes genommen werden dürfte. Doch erinnert daran der Ausdruck "immanent gegenständlich sein," den man zuweilen in ähnlichem Sinne gebraucht, und bei welchem offenbar das "immanent" das zu fürchtende Missverständnis ausschliessen soll.

[B2] Schon Aristoteles hat von dieser psychischen Einwohnung gesprochen. In seinen Büchern von der Seele sagt er, das Empfundene als Empfundenes sei in dem Empfindenden, der Sinn nehme das Empfundene ohne die Materie auf, das Gedachte sei in dem denkenden Verstande. Bei Philosophen finden wir ebenfalls die Lehre von der mentalen Existenz und Inexistenz. Idem er über diese mit der Existenz im eigentlichen Sinne confundiert, kommt er zur widerspruchsvollen Logos- und Ideenlehre. Ähnliches gilt von den Neuplatonikern, Augustinus in seiner Lehre vom *Verbum mentis* und dessen innerlichem Ausgange berührt dieselbe Tatsache. Anselm tut es in seinem berühmten ontologischen Argumente; und da er die mentale wie eine wirkliche Existenz betrachtet, wurde von manchen als Grundlage seines Paralogismus hervorgehoben (vgl. Überweg, *Geschichte der Philosophie*, II). Thomas von Aquin lehrt, das Gedachte sei intentional in dem Denkenden, der Gegenstand der Liebe in dem Liebenden, das Begehrte in dem Begehrendem, und benützt dies zu theologischen Zwecken. Wenn die Schrift von einer Einwohnung des heiligen Geistes spricht, so erklärt er diese als eine intentionale Einwohnung durch die Liebe. Und in der intentionalen Inexistenz beim Denken und Lieben sucht er auch für das Geheimnis der Trinität und den Hervorgang des Wortes und Geistes *ad intra* eine gewisse Analogie zu finden.[26]

[B1] They also use the expression "to exist as an object (objectively) in something," which, if we wanted to use it at the present time, would

[26]*Psychologie* (1874), 124–25, transl. McAlister, 88–89.

be considered, on the contrary, as a designation of a real existence outside the mind. At least this is what is suggested by the expression "to exist immanently as an object," which is occasionally used in a similar sense, and in which the term "immanent" should obviously rule out the misunderstanding which is to be feared.

[B2] Aristotle himself spoke of this mental in-existence. In his books on the soul he says that the sensed object, as such, is in the sensing subject; that the sense contains the sensed object without its matter; that the object which is thought is in the thinking intellect. In Philo, likewise, we find the doctrine of mental existence and in-existence. However, since he confuses them with existence in the proper sense of the word, he reaches his contradictory doctrine of the *logos* and Ideas. The same is true of the Neoplatonists. St. Augustine in his doctrine of the *Verbum mentis* and of its inner origin touches upon the same fact. St. Anselm does the same in his famous ontological argument; many people have observed that his consideration of mental existence as a true existence is at the basis of his paralogism (cp. Überweg, *Geschichte der Philosophie*, II). St. Thomas Aquinas teaches that the object which is thought is intentionally in the thinking subject, the object which is loved in the person who loves, the object which is desired in the person desiring, and he uses this for theological purposes. When the Scriptures speak of an indwelling of the Holy Ghost, St. Thomas explains it as an intentional indwelling through love. In addition, he attempted to find, through the intentional in-existence in the acts of thinking and loving, a certain analogy for the mystery of the Trinity and the procession *ad intra* of the Word and the Spirit.

Chapter Eight

Husserl and
Aesthetic Psychologism

Everything "purely" logical is "in itself" an "ideal" which includes in this "in itself"—in its proper essential content—nothing "mental," nothing of acts, of subjects, or even of empirically factual persons or actual reality.

—Edmund Husserl

No theory can eliminate what is the ultimate standard for all theory: that which is given in plain seeing and is, therefore, original.

—Edmund Husserl

PROBLEMS ABOUT intentions and works of art are difficult. On the one hand, a series of arguments is available purporting to show that appeal to intentions in the critical discussion of questions about the description, meaning, and evaluation of artworks is unreasonable. On the other hand, arguments abound that purport to show the central place of intentions in the concept of art itself. The tension between these two poles is extensive because often what is at issue is not just the validity and soundness of particular arguments but the intelligibility and the persuasiveness of radically different paradigms for doing philosophy. Thus, analytic philosophers characteristically treat those problems differently than hermeneutic philosophers do.

Moreover, the matter here is a thorny one just because it centers on how we are to accommodate two essential features of literary works of art—the linguistic fact and the fact that several features of linguistic entities like meanings are in some sense intentional. Even if we exclude questions about meaning and evaluation, we are

still stuck with questions about description. These questions center on the nature of literary works of art, and it is at least arguable
that any adequate account of the former issues about meanings and
evaluations must centrally include an account of the latter. In this
chapter I reexamine critically the role of aesthetic intentions, once
again trying to put on exhibit some of the neglected resources in
the realist backgrounds of modern aesthetics, a different tradition
than either the analytic or the hermeneutic readings of Kant and
eighteenth-century aesthetics have led to today.[1]

I begin with hopes of sharpening the idea of descriptive
intentionalism by examining the provenance of this doctrine's
central concept, Brentano's concept of intentionality, and by
making specific use of Husserl's critical comments about this
concept in his Fifth Logical Investigation. This inquiry suggests
that descriptive intentionalism, even when a number of distinctions have been taken account of, is in fact aesthetic psychologism.
I then begin the search for arguments against such a strong theory
by recalling an analogous doctrine in the different area of the
philosophy of logic—namely, logical psychologism—and the kinds
of arguments Husserl developed against this view. My aim here is
to find in Husserl's arguments against strong versions of logical
psychologism resources for dealing decisively with the insistent
rebuttals that intentionalist critics continue to direct against their
opponents. In the third section I transpose Husserl's arguments
against logical psychologism into arguments against the strong
form of aesthetic psychologism called descriptive intentionalism.
I conclude that these arguments are valid and consequently that
descriptive intentionalism, however strongly formulated, cannot

---

[1]Despite Gadamer's apparent connections to Husserl, his work is finally to be
understood in terms of Heidegger's rejection of Husserl. For Husserl and realism see
K. Ameriks, "Husserl's Realism," Philosophical Review 86(1979): 498–519; H. Hall,
"Was Husserl a Realist?" in Husserl, Intentionality, and Cognitive Science (Cam-
bridge, Mass., 1982); and the rejoinder of H. Pietersma, "A Critique of Two Recent
Husserl Interpretations," Dialogue 26(1987): 695–703. For intentions and literary
artworks see, for example, A. J. Ellis, "Intention and Interpretation in Literature,"
British Journal of Aesthetics 14 (1974): 315–26; P. D. Juhl, "Intention and Literary
Interpretation," Deutsche Vierteljahresschrift für Literaturwissenschaft und
Geistesgeschichte 45(1971): 1–23; A. Marras, ed., Intentionality, Mind and Language
(Urbana, Ill., 1972). For recent analyses of Brentano see K. Hedwig, "Brentano's
Hermeneutics," Topoi 6(1987): 3–10; B. Terrell, "Brentano's Philosophy of the
Mind," in Contemporary Philosophy: A New Survey, ed. G. Fløistad (The Hague,
1983), 223–47; R. M. Chisholm, "Brentano als analytischer Metaphysiker," Conceptus
11(1977): 77–82; as well as Die Philosophie Franz Brentanos, ed. R. M. Chisholm
(Amsterdam, 1978). For general accounts of Brentano's philosophy see also L.
Gilston, Méthode et métaphysique selon Franz Brentano (Paris, 1955).

adequately account either for the nature of literary artworks or for the nature of aesthetic intentions themselves.

Intentionalism and Its History

The concept of intentionality, which Brentano[2] made the hinge of his distinction between the mental and the physical, needs to be seen in terms of its provenance and its influence. The former is Scholastic, in particular Thomistic, while the latter is phenomenological, in particular Husserlian. If we are to assess critically the satisfactoriness of descriptive intentionalism, we will need to look critically at its central concept of intentionality. One way to do so is to situate this concept at the juncture of this double perspective. The strategy is to identify any possible critical weaknesses in descriptive intentionalism by scrutinizing both the origin and the reception of its cardinal concept.

Brentano's concept of intentionality owed a good deal to the history of philosophy.[3] Brentano amply acknowledges this himself in the long footnotes that are almost always omitted in citing his account of intentionality in his book *Psychology from an Empirical Standpoint*.[4] The major influence was, of course, Aquinas.[5] Brentano

[2]For Brentano's work see R. M. Chisholm, "Bibliography of Public Writings of Franz Brentano," in *The Philosophy of Brentano*, ed. L. L. McAlister, 240–54 (London, 1976). (Hereafter cited as McAlister.)

[3]For recent work see K. Obstfeld, "The Conflict between Intentionality and Inner Observation," *Philosophy and Phenomenological Research* 44(1983): 271–78; K. Hedwig, "Intentions: Outline for the History of a Phenomenological Concept," *Philosophy and Phenomenological Research* 39(1979): 326–40; and K. Lambert, "The Place of the Intentional in the Explanation of Behaviour: A Brief Survey," *Grazer Philosophische Studien* 6(1978): 75–84. For Brentano's doctrine see especially R. M. Chisholm, "Brentano's Descriptive Psychology and the Intentional," in *Phenomenology and Existentialism*, ed. M. H. Mandelbaum and E. N. Lee (Baltimore, 1967); R. M. Chisholm, "Franz Brentano," in *Encyclopedia of Philosophy*, ed. Paul Edwards (New York, 1967); R. M. Chisholm and W. Sellers, "Intentionality and the Mental," in *Concepts, Theories and the Mind-Body Problem*, ed. H. Feigl, M. Scriven, and G. Maxwell (Minneapolis, 1958); A. Gurwitsch, "Toward a Theory of Intentionality," *Philosophy and Phenomenological Research* 30(1970): 354–67; W. Lycan, "On Intentionality and the Psychological," *American Philosophical Quarterly* 6(1969): 305–11; and J. C. Morrison, "Husserl and Brentano on Intentionality," *Philosophy and Phenomenological Research* 31(September 1970): 27–46.

[4]See *Psychology from an Empirical Standpoint* (London, 1973), trans. A. C. Rancurello, D. B. Terrell, and L. L. McAlister from the second edition of vols. 1 and 2 of *Psychologie vom empirischen Standpunkt* (1924).

[5]See Brentano, *Geschichte der mittelalterlichen Philosophie im christlichen Abendland* (Hamburg, 1980), and A. Marras, "Scholastic Roots of Brentano's Conception of Intentionality," in McAlister 1976: 128–39. Brentano's detailed and extensive work on Aristotle is also very important. Besides his 1911 book, *Aristoteles und*

clearly owed to Aquinas the first of the two notions that make up his concept of intentionality, the notion of "intentional (mental) inexistence." As for the second major component in his concept of intentionality, the notion of "reference to a content, direction toward an object... immanent objectivity," the matter is controversial. Herbert Spiegelberg has claimed, in his history of the phenomenological movement, that the notion of reference to an object was an original contribution by Brentano. Against this view A. Marras has argued persuasively that this notion is not original since, "not only is [it] not incompatible with the scholastic idea of intentional inexistence, but [it] is in fact *constitutive* of that very idea."[6] Without repeating the details of this controversy here, I think that on the evidence and the arguments presented so far, we need to conclude provisionally that both and not just one of the two central elements in Brentano's theory are of Scholastic origin, rather than of Brentano's own making.

This discussion of the provenance of Brentano's doctrine is not irrelevant to our immediate concern with taking the critical measure of a strong version of descriptive intentionalism. For it focuses on one of the most important questions we can raise about the satisfactoriness of Brentano's concept of intentionality. The question, as Marras shows neatly, is whether the notion of intentional inexistence entails the existential dependence of any object that is known. In short, the issue is whether this notion implies an immanent as opposed to a realistic epistemology. If the answer is yes, as Spiegelberg thinks, then whatever other interests there may be in Brentano's concept of intentionality, this concept cannot be effectively put to work on the reconstruction of descriptive intentionalism,[7] for the independent existence of the artifact would be fatally compromised. On the basis of an extremely thorough critical analysis of the Scholastic texts that Brentano refers to, and others besides, Marras concludes that Spiegelberg is wrong on this issue. Holding the doctrine of intentional inexistence does not

---

seine Weltanschauung (Hamburg, 1977) and his *Aristoteles Lehre vom Ursprung des menschlichen Geistes*, 2d ed. (Hamburg, 1980), see his papers in *Über Aristoteles* (Hamburg, 1986).

[6]Marras 1976: 129.

[7]See H. B. Spiegelberg, " 'Intention' and 'Intentionality' in the Scholastics, Brentano, and Husserl," in McAlister 1976: 108–27, and H. B. Spiegelberg, *The Phenomenological Movement*, 3d ed. (The Hague, 1975). See also D. W. Smith and R. MacIntyre, *Husserl and Intentionality: A Study of Mind, Meaning and Language* (Boston, 1982); S. F. Barker, "Intentionality and Intentionality," *Philosophy Research Archives* 8(1982): 95–111; B. Mijuskovic, "Brentano's Theory of Consciousness," *Philosophy and Phenomenological Research* 38(1977): 315–24.

preclude providing a consequential account of the independent existence of nonmental objects; such a position commits one merely to holding for the existence of a representation (whether species or form) of the object. And this representation, "the *species* or *intentio,* is not that which (*id quod*) is directly or primarily known by the understanding (as is the 'impression' or 'idea' of classical empiricism), but is instead that by means of which (*id quo*) the extramental object is known. That is, the species is the *vehicle* which carries the reference to the extramental, non immanent object, which alone is known primarily."[8] The basic text behind this persuasive interpretation of intentional inexistence is that of Aquinas: "Species intelligibilis," Aquinas writes, "non est quod intelligitur, sed id quo intelligit intellectus."[9]

Whatever the actual terms Brentano took in his later philosophy (the so-called *Immanenzkrisis* of 1905, when Brentano rejected his previous belief in mind-dependent objects, i.e., ideal entities as the only referents to mental acts, in favor of his so-called reistic belief in mind-independent objects, i.e., real entities as those referents), it is clear that his concept of intentionality as we have used it is not incompatible with holding for the existence of real entities as referents for mental acts. Thus any charge against descriptive intentionalism that makes use of Brentano's concept of intentionality as immanentist must be rejected. If descriptive intentionalism has a central weakness, this weakness must be sought in some direction other than in its ultimately Scholastic provenance.

Perhaps a closer look at the transmission of this concept from Brentano to Husserl will prove constructive.[10] The major text here is Husserl's discussion of Brentano's doctrine in the early section of chapter 2 of the Fifth Logical Investigation.[11] Again, however, just

---

[8]Marras 1976: 138.

[9]*Summa Theologica* 1.85.2; cited in Marras 1976:138, note 34. For some of Brentano's views on Aquinas see "Thomas von Aquin," review of Johannes Delitzsch, *Die Gotteslehre des Thomas von Aquino, Theologisches Literaturblatt* (Bonn) 5 (1870): 459–63; *Die vier Phasen der Philosophie und ihr augenblicklicher Stand* (Stuttgart, 1895); and H. Windischer, *Franz Brentano und die Scholastik* (Innsbruck, 1936).

[10]See H. B. Spiegelberg's two articles, "Zwei Briefe von Edmund Husserl und Franz Brentano über Logik," *Grazer Philosophische Studien* 6(1978): 1–12; and "On the Significance of the Correspondence between Brentano/Husserl," *Die Philosophie Franz Brentanos,* ed. R. M. Chisholm and R. Haller (Amsterdam, 1978), 95–116 (hereafter *DPFB*). In general, see M. Brück, *Über das Verhältnis Edmund Husserls zu Franz Brentano, vornehmlich mit Rücksicht auf Brentanos Psychologie* (Würzburg, 1933).

[11]Translated by J. N. Findlay (New York, 1970). For the necessary background see R. Bernet, I. Kern, and E. Marbach, *Edmund Husserl: Darstellung seines Denkens*

as in our interpretation of Brentano and the Scholastics, we need to be careful about what is actually being said.[12]

What, then, is the gist of Husserl's reading of Brentano on intentionality? On Spiegelberg's account, the essential is Husserl's warning of two possible misunderstandings of Brentano's doctrine and some specifications of Husserl's own doctrine. According to Spiegelberg, Husserl took over from Brentano the idea of intentionality as relatedness or directedness to an object while leaving aside Brentano's notion of intentional inexistence. This relatedness, however, must not be construed, Husserl warns us first, as an actual relatedness of experiences, which in turn would imply "a real relation between the ego and the object known."[13] Such a real relation, in the period of Husserl's development after the breakthrough of 1905 to 1907, would of course be unacceptable to Husserl. And the object of this relatedness or directedness, Husserl next warns, must be construed not as "immanent" in the way sense data and appearances are said to be immanent, but as "transcendent" in a sense yet to be shown.[14] Besides these cautions, Spiegelberg notes in Husserl's account a stress on "intentional

---

(Hamburg, 1988), and R. Sokolowski, ed., *E. Husserl and the Phenomenological Tradition* (Washington, D.C., 1988). See also the essays of D. Carr in his *Interpreting Husserl* (Dordrecht, 1987).

[12]This is difficult to determine for two reasons. First, more than fifty years ago Spiegelberg wrote a very influential discussion of this matter under the title "Der Begriff der Intentionalität in der Scholastik bei Brentano und bei Husserl," in *Philosophische Hefte* 5(1936), reprinted in McAlister, 108–27. This text was reprinted in German in *Studia Philosophica*, then translated into English in 1976 with very few changes (see note 7). But despite the importance of this article, we need to be very particularly wary in accepting Spiegelberg's view of this matter without independent examination of the text. For we have already seen that his interpretation of both the provenance and the sense of the doctrine of intentional inexistence in his history of the phenomenological movement is faulty.

Second, returning to the texts involves problems of its own. Husserl's Fifth Logical Investigation has itself gone through six editions from the first edition of 1901 through the revised edition of 1913 into the unchanged reprintings of the 1913 edition in 1922, 1928, and 1968 and finally the restoration of the original 1901 text in the sixth edition of 1975. But a seventh edition is in preparation as part of the critical edition of the *Logical Investigations* in the Husserliana series. A further difficulty involves examining Husserl's remarks about Brentano in the Fifth Logical Investigation with a further set of remarks on similar themes under the title "Äussere und innere Wahrnehmung: Physische und psychische Phänomene," which Husserl added at the end of the even more textually complicated Sixth Logical Investigation. In the light of the research done so far on these matters, however, I think we are obliged to examine carefully only the 1901 and 1913 version of Husserl's comments on Brentano. Since the appendix to the Sixth Logical Investigation covers almost entirely the same ground already mapped out in the 1901 and 1913 texts, I think we are justified in ignoring that appendix for our purposes here.

[13]Spiegelberg 1975: 123.
[14]Spiegelberg 1975: 123.

experiences" rather than on "intentional objects," that is, "certain classes of objects which relate to experiences" (Husserl, Fifth Logical Investigation, section 13); an emphasis in Husserl and not in Brentano on linguistic expressions as bearers of intentionality and not just mental acts; and a more specific sense in Husserl than in Brentano for the term "intention" as applied to object, the "intentional" (versus *reell*, contained in experience) referring "to everything which lies beyond the realm of experiences and their 'components' but which is still actually meant or intended by the acts as 'correlates.' " Finally, Husserl moves the sense of intentionality closer to idealism by using it with respect to objects to mean "the mode of being of such objects, which only exist thanks to consciousness, as opposed to the mode of being of reality," a use that led Husserl to confuse intentionality as directedness to an object with intentionality as the constitution of the object.[15]

To summarize: Spiegelberg takes Husserl to be correcting Brentano's notion of intentionality by stressing the constitutive character of the act of intentionality and the immanent character of its object. But if this is the gist of Husserl's reading of Brentano, I think we must conclude that Husserl's corrections are in fact errors. For the stress on the nonimmanent character of the object of intentionality is simply a misunderstanding of Brentano's Scholastic doctrine of *intentio* as, in Marras's reminder, "an *ens rationis*, a universal and thus an attribute . . . [having] unlike *particulars* a dependent mode of existence" but not precluding a relation between its content and independently existing objects.[16] And the stress of intentionality as constitutive in Husserl's own misguided doctrine, not Brentano's at all. Perhaps if we scrutinize Husserl's texts anew, however, we may find more to his account of Brentano than those features Spiegelberg has underlined.

A preliminary question is which of the two editions we can take as normative. A comparison of the important passages where Husserl analyzes Brentano's doctrines show three differences, of which one is relatively unimportant, being the addition of a footnote to Husserl's discussion of *meinen* in chapter 2, paragraph 11. Of the two remaining, one change is in the title of chapter 2 itself. The original title, "Bewusstsein als psychischer Akt," in the 1901 edition becomes "Bewusstsein als intentionales Erlebnis" in the 1913 edition. This change is in line with the emphasis Spiegelberg

---

[15]Spiegelberg 1975: 124.
[16]Marras 1976: 139.

noted on Husserl's discussion of intentionality in terms of experiences rather than acts. But given the importance of Husserl's move toward idealism at the same period when the second edition appeared (see especially *Ideen I* and the 1913 *Draft of a Preface to the Logical Investigations*), we need to stress the importance of the first title in the context of Husserl's discussion of Brentano. Thus intentionality in Brentano is seen as a psychological reality.

The final change is the most important. It occurs in paragraph 10, where a very long sentence and a long note are inserted, presumably to clarify the sense of Husserl's comment on Brentano's definition of "psychical phenomena." Husserl goes on to reject this phrase in paragraph 11 because he finds each of its terms to be seriously misleading. But these interpellations are also idealistic in their appeal to concepts such as *"rein phänomenologische Gattungsidee"* (my italics), "intentionales Erlebnis," "Apperzeption," and "reine Begriffe der Erlebnisse."[17] Consequently, here too I think we are best advised to remain with the statement of Husserl's views as they appear in the first edition of 1901. I conclude that for our purposes the first edition alone may be taken as the normative text for Husserl's reading of Brentano on intentionality.

The next question is just what features of Husserl's account of Brentano on intentionality are pertinent to our critical concern with descriptive intentionalism. Husserl begins his chapter "Consciousness as Psychical Act" by praising, in section 9, the seminal importance of Brentano's 1874 *Psychologie*. He then takes up in section 10 "the descriptive character of the act as 'intentional' experience." It is important to note that Husserl uses the term *psychische* here to stand for what we earlier discussed as "mental" in the context of Brentano's distinction between the mental and the physical. The sequence goes like this. The essence of consciousness is the mental, and the essence of the mental is intentionality. After focusing his discussion on the intentional character of the mental only, Husserl goes on to cite Brentano's *Psychology* at length (without the notes that included the important references to the Scholastics). And the specific item in Brentano's text that elicits his comment is the notion of *Weise*, the mode of the relation between the intentional act and its object.

What strikes Husserl is that Brentano's talk of modes suggests that specifically different kinds of relations hold between intentional acts and their objects. And these relational differences can be

---

[17] *Logische Untersuchungen* (1913), 369.

characterized otherwise than by appealing merely to the differences in intentional objects. Thus what distinguishes the relation itself in such different intentional acts as representing or judging or loving (to take instances from each of Brentano's three basic classes, which Husserl takes over without revision) is not necessarily the represented object or the judged object or the loved object, but the way the act-object relation is structured. "Die Weise," Husserl writes, "in der eine blosse Vorstellung eines Sachverhalts dessen ihren 'Gegenstand' meint, ist eine andere als die Weise des Urteils, das diesen Sachverhalt für wahr oder falsch hält" ["The manner in which a 'mere presentation' refers to its object differs from the manner of a judgment, which treats the same state of affairs as true or false."].[18] Even though many intentional acts are complex ones that include more than one of the three basic kinds of mental acts (Husserl's example is a mental act of emotion such as loving or hating), nonetheless for Husserl this complexity is reducible to "primitive intentional Charactere," which are not properly describable by reference beyond themselves to other mental experiences. The unity of such complex mental acts is to be found in the essence of their primitive intentional character. And this essential unity itself of one of the three particular basic kinds of mental acts cannot be accounted for by reference to some features of the remaining kinds.

Husserl then provides an important example that it will prove useful to have in hand.

So ist z. B. die ästhetische Billigung oder Misbilligung eine Weise intentionaler Beziehung, die sich als evident eigenartig erweist gegenüber dem blossen Vorstellen oder theoretischen Beurteilen des ästhetischen Objekts. Die ästhetische Billigung kann zwar ausgesagt werden, und die Aussage ist ein Urteil und schliesst solche Vorstellungen ein. Aber dann ist die ästhetische Intention, ebenso wie ihr Objekt, Gegenstand von Vorstellungen und Urteilen; sie selbst bleibt von diesen theoretischen Akten wesentlich verschieden.[19]

Aesthetic approval or disapproval, e.g., is evidently and essentially a peculiar mode of intentional relation as opposed to the mere presentation or theoretical assessment of the aesthetic object. Aesthetic approval and aesthetic predicates may be asserted, and their assertion is a judgement, and as such includes presentations. But the aesthetic

---

[18]*Logische Untersuchungen* (1901), 27. Cited hereafter as *LU*; trans. Findlay, 554.
[19]*LU*, 28; trans. Findlay, p. 555.

intention and its objects are then *objects* of presentations and judgements: it remains essentially distinct from these theoretical acts.

In short, there are at least three basic kinds of intentionality.

Finally, Husserl finishes this section of his account by distinguishing between the nature of the content of an intentional object and the content of a perceptual object. Only the first and not the second is intended as a whole.[20] There is no talk, pace Spiegelberg, of dependent or independent existence in either case. Husserl is content to draw the distinction by relying completely on the references to parts and wholes and implicitly on the detailed examination of parts and wholes that is the subject of the Third Logical Investigation.[21]

We need then to ask, finally, just which of these features in Husserl's own account as opposed to Spiegelberg's influential reading are consequential for our purposes. Whatever the direction of Husserl's own later thought, suggested to him when he reworked these passages in 1913, it is already clear in this text from 1901 that he has interpreted Brentano's notion of directedness to an object in a mind-dependent way. The only object the intentional relation implies, whether this relation is in the representational, judgmental, or emotional mode, is a mental object only. Indeed, this mental object—as in the case of a perceptual object, but not in the case of, say, my representation of Jupiter (to use Husserl's example in section 11)—can in addition have a relation to a non-mentally-dependent object in the world. But this second relation is only contingent, not necessary. Thus the doctrine of intentionality is a psychological doctrine in the sense that whatever objects are in question are either necessarily related as correlates only to the existence of mental acts or are only contingently related to the possible existence of physical objects in the world. In either case, whatever may or may not exist in the world has no necessary connection with mind. Perhaps this is indeed the weakness Brentano himself came to see about this doctrine of intentionality, when about 1905 he reoriented his own epistemology in the direc-

---

[20]*LU*, 20.

[21]On several technical matters here see D. Føllesdal, "Brentano and Husserl on Intentional Objects and Perceptions," *DPFB*, 83–94; Q. Smith, "Husserl's Early Conception of the Tragic Structure of the Intentional Act," *Philosophy Today* 25(1981): 81–91: R. E. Acquila, "The Status of Intentional Objects," *New Scholasticism* 45(Summer 1971); and R. B. Arnaud, "Brentanist Relations," in *Analysis and Metaphysics*, ed. K. Lehrer (Dordrecht, 1975): 189–203.

tion Kotarbinski's reism was to take. It is somewhat ironic to note that not much later Husserl was engaged in reorienting his own epistemology in the opposite direction in *Ideen I* (1913).

The examination of the Thomistic provenance of Brentano's theory of intentionality, we might say in summary form, shows a realistic bias in the sense that it in no way precludes relation between intentional objects of whatever kind and physical objects existing in the world. The examination of the Husserlian reception of Brentano's theory, however, shows an idealistic bias in the sense that it allows no necessary relation at all between even that class of intentional objects we call perceptions and physical objects existing in the world.

The basic difficulty once again has to do with the overgenerality of the theory in question. Because Brentano himself wavers about the kinds of objects that can properly stand in relation to intentional acts and about the kinds of relations these objects can accommodate not with respect to consciousness but with respect to the physical world, his theory of intentionality remains too vague. In other words, the two notions that make up Brentano's theory of intentionality—intentional inexistence and directedness to an object—are insufficiently detailed, since neither the natures of these objects nor the specific kinds of relations they can enter into are explicated. I conclude that the different perspectives opened up by an examination of both the provenance and the reception of Brentano's theory are to be explained quite simply: the cardinal concept of Brentano's theory is ambiguous. It follows that the strong version of descriptive intentionalism must also be ambiguous.

We need to note an even more important conclusion, however, for the ambiguous character of Brentano's theory conceals another of its basic features. To the degree that this ambiguous character is an essential feature of the theory, we are in fact dealing with a psychologism. Yet the ambiguity derives precisely from the notion of reference to an unspecified object. And this notion in turn, as Marras has argued, implies the only other notion in the concept, that of intentional inexistence. To remove the ambiguity from the concept of intentionality as Brentano presents it would involve doing away with the overgeneral notion of reference to an object. But to do this is to dissolve the concept itself. Thus the ambiguity in Brentano's concept is inexorable.

I conclude further that descriptive intentionalism not only is ambiguous, it is essentially ambiguous in entailing precisely the primacy of the mental. As such, descriptive intentionalism is a species of psychologism that, since descriptive intentionalism is concerned with describing the nature of artworks, we might term descriptive aesthetic psychologism. Thus we may take descriptive aesthetic psychologism as the view that the nature of putative literary artworks is to be determined preeminently by reference to those mental acts and mental objects of the author that we characterize as aesthetic intentions. On this account, describing the nature of literary artworks comes down to describing the nature of aesthetic intentions.

Intentionalism and Psychologism

Husserl discusses logical psychologism in great detail in chapter 3 of the Prolegomena to the *Logical Investigations*.

> The reader of the Prolegomena is made a participant in a conflict between two motifs within the logical sphere which are contrasted in radical sharpness: the one is the psychological, the other the purely logical. [By "pure logic" Husserl means here most generally *mathesis universalis*, "the sum total of the formal a priori." This idea, he continues, "is directed towards the entirety of the 'categories of meaning' and toward the formal categories for objects correlated to them or, alternatively, the a priori laws based upon them."[22]] The two do not come together by accident as the thought-act on the one side and the thought-meaning and the object of thought on the other. Somehow they necessarily belong together. But they are to be distinguished, namely in this manner: everything "purely" logical is "in itself" and "ideal" which includes in this "in itself"—in its proper essential content— nothing "mental," nothing of acts, of subjects, or even of empirically factual persons of actual reality.[23]

One convenient way of summarizing this *different* discussion of logical psychologism is to isolate a series of different formulations of this doctrine in the positions Husserl discusses from Mill, Lipps, Wundt, Sigwart, and others. With these formulations in hand we can then reduce the various formulations to two basic theses, each with a corollary, one being a stronger version than the other. This in fact is the strategy worked out in Michael Sukale's important

---

[22]Husserl, *Introduction to the Logical Investigations: A Draft of a Preface to the Logical Investigations* (1913), trans. P. J. Bossert and C. H. Peters (The Hague, 1975), 28. Cited hereafter as *Draft*.
[23]*Draft*, 20.

work on psychologism.[24] Here is a slightly amended version of the results: "*Strong logical psychologism*: Psychological investigations of actual human thought processes are the necessary and sufficient conditions of logical investigations. (Corollary: the analysis of logical laws is equivalent to the analysis of particular human thought processes.)"[25] This strong formulation is easily weakened to accommodate more nuanced views by omitting the phrase "and sufficient" in the thesis statement and substituting "consists partly of" for "is equivalent to" in the corollary statement. An example of this thesis is to be found in Husserl's discussion of Mill. Mill subscribes to logical psychologism when he interprets the principle of contradiction as consisting of the view that no two contradictory statements can both be *judged* true at the same time. The nonpsychologistic formulation would be that no two contradictory statements can both *be* true at the same time. On the first view, logical contradictories are two statements that cannot both be believed to be true at the same time: on the second, logical contradictories are two statements that cannot both be true at the same time.

Two basic arguments are usually used to support logical psychologism in the versions Husserl discusses.[26] Other arguments also appear, but these two seem most representative. The first argument calls attention to the fact that logic must deal with mental activities just because it deals with judging, inferring, proving, and so on. The second argument reminds us that nothing, not even logical laws, can be dealt with independent of thinking. Nothing, the claim is, can be an object without at the same time already being dependent on mind. The first argument is properly psychologistic, whereas the second is more generally idealistic. Of the two, as we would expect, the general argument is the more powerful. To see

---

[24]M. Sukale, *Comparative Studies in Phenomenology* (The Hague, 1976), 23–49.
[25]Sukale 1976: 24.
[26]On the topic of psychologism see especially J. W. Meiland, "Psychology in Logic: Husserl's Critique," *Inquiry* 19(1976): 325–39; W. Schupe, "Zum Psychologismus und Normcharakter der Logik: Eine Ergänzung zu Husserls *Logische Untersuchungen*," in *Husserl*, ed. H. Noack, 16–34 (Darmstadt, 1973); and D. Willard, "Concerning Husserl's View of Number," *Southwestern Journal of Philosophy* 5(1974): 97–109. For a more general perspective in this area see "Intentionalität und Sprache: Psychologische oder sprachliche Charakterisierung der intentionalen Beziehung," (1983); Elizabeth Anscombe, "Will and Emotion," *DPFB*, 139–48; and R. M. Chisholm and R. Grossman, "Structure versus Sets: The Philosophical Background of Gestalt Psychology," *Critica* 9(1977): 3–21.

this point we need only make use of a dilemma. "If, for example, we want to compare what we think of an object with that object itself, we will run into a dilemma: how can we compare our thought of the object with the object without thinking once more about the object? But if we do so then what we really compare are two thoughts of ours and not an object with a thought. If, on the other hand, we refrain from thinking about the object, how can we ever compare our thought of the object with the unthought object?"[27]

The point at issue is whether there are indeed objects or simply things we take to be objects. More basically, the issue is one of truth. Are there truths, or are there no more than what we take to be truths? This is the formulation Frege settles for in his preface to *The Basic Laws of Arithmetic* (1893). "All I have to say to this," he writes there, "is being true is different from behind taken to be true, whether by one or many or everybody, and in no case is to be reduced to it. There is no contradiction in some things being true which everybody takes to be false. I understand by 'laws of logic' not psychological laws of takings to be true but laws of truth."[28] This position, of course, once the errors in this first volume of *The Philosophy of Arithmetic* (1891) are grasped, becomes Husserl's as well. But both Frege and Husserl themselves are aware that such a position cannot itself be defended with the help of the laws of logic. In short, whether a law of logic is acknowledged to be true comes down to nothing more than opinion[29]—whence both the force of the strong psychologistic position and its continued recurrence especially in Husserl's thought. Although Frege remained with this view, Husserl came to believe by the time of the first edition of the *Logical Investigations* in 1900 to 1901 that the psychologistic position could be refuted. Whether his arguments were sufficient to refute as well the strong or idealistic position that troubled Frege so deeply still remains controversial.[30]

---

[27]Sukale 1976: 25.

[28]Frege, *The Basic Laws of Arithmetic* (Oxford, 1950), p. 13, cited by Sukale 1976: 28. For Frege's work and critical discussions see W. Mayer, "Bibliographie," in *Studien zu Frege III*, ed. M. Shirn (Stuttgart, 1976), 157–97.

[29]See Frege 13.

[30]On Husserl and Frege see J. N. Mohanty, "The Frege-Husserl Correspondence," *Southwestern Journal of Philosophy* 5(1974): 83–96, and "Husserl and Frege: A New Look at Their Relationship," *Research in Phenomenology*, 4(1974): 51–62; H. Pietersma, "Husserl and Frege," *Archiv für Geschichte der Philosophie* 49(1967): 298–323; and R. C. Solomon, "Sense and Essence: Frege and Husserl," *International Philosophical Quarterly* 10(1970): 379–401.

If Husserl stops short of a refutation of idealism,[31] what are the central lines of force in his refutation of psychologism in the Prolegomena? Husserl's refutation, which is the substance of almost 150 pages in the Prolegomena, consists of trying to disprove three assumptions behind the psychologistic view and providing three sets of arguments against the correctness of the psychologistic view. A number of authors have gone through this material thoroughly, with somewhat different results. For our purposes it is convenient to remain for the moment with Sukale's reading. Sukale thinks Husserl succeeds in discrediting only one of the three assumptions, and I agree; he thinks further that all three sets of Husserl's counterarguments fail, with the possible exception of the second set—and here I disagree. On my view the first set of arguments, when sufficient distinctions are taken into account, are not question begging. Consequently, in what follows I construe Husserl's refutation of psychologism in only those terms in which I think it actually succeeds. Thus I will adopt his criticism of the normative/theoretical distinction and adapt his arguments against the empiricist consequences of psychologism. All of Husserl's other criticisms and counterarguments I shall leave aside as of dubious value.

The view I have been characterizing as logical psychologism makes a central assumption—that the acquisition of knowledge is based upon the laws of logic, and that these laws are normative. Since the acquisition of knowledge implies a sequence of mental acts, it is argued that the laws of logic that govern such an acquisition also imply a sequence of mental acts. Hence determining the nature of logical laws requires determining the nature of the mental acts these laws imply.

Husserl criticizes this view for overlooking a central distinction between the content of logical laws and the use of logical laws. Here is Sukale's convenient summary.

Husserl concedes that logical laws can be used for the construction of a system of methodological rule which anybody would have to follow who wanted to think correctly. But that we can use logical laws for these normative purposes does not imply that the logical laws are in

31Later Husserl goes further. See T. W. Adorno, "Husserl and the Problem of Idealism," *Journal of Philosophy* 37(1940): 5–18; T. De Boer, "The Meaning of Husserl's Idealism in the Light of His Development," *Analecta Husserliana* 2(1972): 322–32; R. Ingarden, *On the Motives Which Led Husserl to Transcendental Idealism*, trans. A. Hannibalsson (The Hague, 1975); R. H. Holmes, "Is Transcendental Phenomenology Committed to Idealism?" *Monist* 59(1975): 98–114; and K. Ameriks, "Husserl's Realism," *Philosophical Review* 86(1977): 498–519.

themselves of normative content. "We can imply our proposition for normative purposes (Husserl writes on p. 168 of the *Prolegomena*), but it is not therefore a norm." What logical laws assert is not normative and has no reference to psychic process.[32]

Without this distinction or one quite like it, if we wish (as Husserl himself did later on) to modify our talk of content and uses, we cannot talk of truth in any mind-dependent—that is, objective—way at all.

Making such a distinction, however, is in itself no adequate rejection of logical psychologism. The claim still stands that logical laws, to be objects at all, must be objects for thinking. Hence in this respect at least, even if not in terms of sequences of mental acts, logical laws are essentially mind dependent.

Husserl thus develops a series of arguments against psychologism. The one I retain here turns on the essential difference between the character of psychological laws and that of logical laws. In short, Husserl argues that if logical laws were based upon psychology, then absurd consequences would follow—that agreed-upon features of logical laws would no longer be recognizable as such.

Husserl begins with the controlling idea that psychology is an empirical science. The laws of psychology thus are in their essential features just like the laws of any other empirical science. That is to say, psychological laws are generalizations about experience that hold true only to the degree that certain other conditions about the empirical world remain steady (the "ceteris paribus" clause). Moreover, psychological laws are not certain truths but are only probable truths, because their justification cannot be achieved through deductive procedures but comes only through inductive procedures. Finally, the content of psychological laws is strictly empirical in the precise sense that this content necessarily implies the existence of concrete, discrete states of affairs, in this case mental events.

If logical laws were ultimately based upon psychological ones, then logical laws themselves would have to manifest at least these three general features of any set of empirical laws. But when we analyze such logical laws as the principle of contradiction or *modus ponens*, we find the highest form of exactness instead of vague generality, certain truths instead of only probabilities, and no

[32]Sukale 1976: 39.

relations of necessary implication whatever between the contents of these laws and the existence of independent states of affairs. Since logical laws do not manifest any of the features of empirical laws, they cannot be based upon psychological laws, which are empirical. Husserl concludes that logical psychologism is mistaken not just because it overlooks a distinction between the content and the use of a law, but most fundamentally because it cannot account for the defining features of logical laws themselves.

Logical and Aesthetic Psychologism

If we are to apply this discussion critically, we will need first to restate the doctrine of aesthetic psychologism in a way analogous to the doctrine of logical psychologism. We will then need to transpose the arguments against logical psychologism into those against aesthetic psychologism. Finally, in light of this transposition we must formulate a critical judgment on the adequacy of descriptive intentionalism as an account of the nature of the literary artwork.

Suppose we begin by reminding ourselves what psychologism is. We can then restate descriptive intentionalism as an aesthetic psychologism by using the model of logical psychologism operative in Husserl's Prolegomena. And again in the light of our particular interests we will restrict the statements of aesthetic psychologism in such a way as to exclude questions about the meaning of literary texts and the evaluation of these texts and to include only questions about the nature of the text.

For a statement of the doctrine of psychologism we may turn to a cogent and succinct account Husserl gave in a summary of a University of Halle paper, "On the Psychological Grounding of Logic," discovered and published in 1959.[33] "The following thesis," Husserl writes there, "characterizes psychologism: the theoretical foundations of logic lie in psychology. For it is unquestionable, so

---

[33]Husserl, "Über psychologische Begründung der Logik," *Zeitschrift für Philosophische Forschung* 13(1959): 436–48. Note that we need to keep in mind throughout the distinctions between logical systems and aesthetic texts. As an anonymous Cornell referee comments, these two "are not self-evidently analogous because while a logical system can be presented axiomatically, a literary text cannot. . . . Even if the problem is restricted to identifying literary texts, the object of the intentions can be various—it may be the text itself, it may be an aesthetic experience, it may be some type of the text, etc."

the argument goes, that the rules of knowledge, as a psychological function, are to be grounded only through the psychology of knowledge." Descriptive aesthetic psychologism becomes the view that psychological investigation of actual human thought processes, whether by introspection or by other means, are the necessary and sufficient condition of descriptive investigations into the nature of putative literary texts. And the corollary reads: the analysis of the nature of putative literary texts is equivalent to the analysis of particular human thought processes. This thesis comes to the view that a literary text is whatever its author can judge to be a literary text. In short, what distinguishes a text precisely as literary are the intentions of its author, where the cardinal term "intentions" is understood with the successive qualifications we have had to introduce so far in order to render it impervious to the usual arguments both against intentionalist criticism and against those who pay insufficient attention to the relational character of intentionality.

Before we can consider transforming Husserl's arguments against logical psychologism into arguments against his thesis, a number of precisions are in order. For logical psychologism and aesthetic psychologism, even if analogous doctrines, are certainly not identical ones. We are thus required to take account not just of the similarities but also of the differences.

The major contrast between these related doctrines turns on the difference between the kind of entity at issue in each. If we argue that literary artworks as opposed to literary texts are ideal entities, though of a different kind than logical laws, we can use Husserlian types of argument to defeat descriptive aesthetic psychologism. If, on the other hand, we argue that whatever kind of entity literary artworks turn out to be, in no coherent way can they be reasonably construed as any kind of ideal entities, then these Husserlian arguments will not work.

This contrast turns out to be of extraordinary importance, for it focuses our attention on another element in the intentionality thesis that we have so far been content to leave on the margins of our account. We have indeed analyzed the relational character of intentionality as well as the kinds of relations that may subsist between mental objects and their ideal, mind-dependent referents as opposed to those subsisting between mental objects and real, non-mind-dependent referents. What we have not investigated, this contrast suggests, is the ontological states of precisely those different kinds of mental objects that can accommodate the intentionality relation. In our present context we can specify this issue more particularly. The controversial ontological status of the different kinds of entities at issue in logical and aesthetic psychologism requires further analysis of the kind of entity that is the correlate of specific aesthetic intention. Thus the new question concerns that species of mental objects we usually refer to under the heading "aesthetic objects." And the question can be put quite simply as just whether there are any such distinctive entities as aesthetic objects at all.

Whatever the outcome of that discussion, we still are faced with the problem of how to interpret literary artworks in the present context. Since many theorists insistently hold the view that literary artworks are precisely those ideal entities we call aesthetic objects, and since this has been the strongly argued view of the finest theorist on these matters, Roman Ingarden, for now I shall adopt the convenience of following suit. My view here will be that logical psychologism and aesthetic psychologism both deal with ideal entities, but presumably ideal entities of different kinds. In the first case the ideal entities are logical truths, whereas in the second they are aesthetic objects. The thesis of descriptive aesthetic psychologism thus becomes the view that a particular verbal text is a literary artwork just in that case where the author's intentions are to be construed as an aesthetic intention directed upon an aesthetic object for which the existing artifact is the real referent. Whatever written text of mine I intend aesthetically as an aesthetic object becomes by that fact an artwork.

Before we examine the force of Husserl's arguments against this kind of view, it is useful to point up its surprising plausibility. For it does indeed seem to be true that authors can direct their attention to certain features of almost any of their written texts and find in the object contemplated a unity, simplicity, and harmony that could be adduced as evidence for their at first startling claim that any of their written texts are literary artworks. We may wish to argue any particular claim such authors would make by referring presumably to other features of their texts that they may have conveniently left quite out of their ken. But that would still leave open an argumentative avenue for the authors to pursue. For they could easily enough retort by beginning to make an indefinite series of distinctions between parts and wholes of the text in question. The unity that they assert, they might go on to claim, is that of certain part but not even of all individual parts and not that of the whole. And so the dispute would continue, with the authors insisting on the ultimate authority of their particular aesthetic intentions to decide the nature of questionable concrete instances of literary artworks, and the critics insisting just as stubbornly on the manifest arbitrariness of the authors' aesthetic intentions' being the single normative authority in such disagreements.

Against Aesthetic Psychologism

But we need not follow the tortuous paths of that kind of dispute here. For there is already available another way of dealing with authorial claims such as those about the normative status of aesthetic intentions. In other words, we need only follow a Husserlian strategy.

Thus we first need to distinguish between the content of the aesthetic object of this intention and the particular use it is being put to. Authors are surely free to make whatever use they see fit of the specific ideas they have in mind at a particular time about any of their written texts. And if one of those ideas comes to the thought that a particular text is a literary artwork, well enough and good for them. For the critic, however, it is still an open question just what the idea of this text as a literary artwork could really come to. For it is arguably the case that an author's putative idea of an artwork is no more than the empty wish that at some future time the text in question might take on a finally—that is to say, more than just subjectively—suitable form. Until there is evidence for that suitability in the text itself and not just as subjectively reported in the author's mind, the critic can plausibly argue that the author's aesthetic intentions by themselves are not sufficient to define this particular verbal artifact as a literary artwork.

More interesting, however, is the argument the critic might then turn to, going on to suggest that if the nature of the verbal artifact in question were in fact to be determined on the basis of an investigation of the author's aesthetic intentions alone, it would quickly appear that such an investigation would be impossible. For the object of the aesthetic intention as precisely an ideal entity is exactly characterizable a priori in its certainty and is noncontingent in the analogous way that the truth of a logical law is exactly characterizable, a priori, and noncontingent. But whatever series of mental acts or objects would be laid bare by the appropriate investigations in the psychology of creation could be only hypothetical entities, and thus vague generalizations whose certainty was only a posteriori and whose basic character was contingent. Aesthetic descriptive intentions alone could not adequately define a verbal artifact as a literary artwork, because the nature of those intentions are necessarily incommensurate with the results of any possible empirical inquiry. Whatever intentions, aesthetic or otherwise, authors may have are surely for them to say. But on no analysis can such intentions alone be propounded as both necessary and sufficient conditions for the definition of verbal artifacts as literary artworks just because the ultimate nature of these intentions and their mental objects is available for no other inspection than the authors' own. In short, descriptive aesthetic psychologism is as radically subjective as logical psychologism. And the consequence in both cases comes to the same impasse—critical solipsism.

To conclude, I recall the main lines of this investigation of the role of aesthetic intentions in the definition of the nature of verbal artifacts. We began with an inquiry into the provenance and the reception of Brentano's doctrine of intentionality. This inquiry led to conflicting results, and we interpreted the conflict as an indication that the doctrine of intentionality might in fact be ambiguous. The basis, in turn, of this ambiguity was a psychologism.

We then turned to an investigation of Husserl's dealing with logical psychologism in the Prolegomena of the *Logical Investigations*. There we are able to formulate carefully a general version of logical psychologism. In addition we took over just those arguments of Husserl against logical psychologism that remained telling ones after critical examination.

Finally, we returned to the role of aesthetic intentions in the definition of the nature of verbal artifacts. We first used the contrast between logical and aesthetic psychologism as a heuristic to uncover the role of aesthetic objects, then we transformed Husserl's arguments against logical psychologism into arguments against its counterpart in aesthetics. This examination showed the inexorable weakness of any intentionalist account by itself.

Consequently, at least this appeal to aesthetic intentions to define the nature of verbal artifacts is a failure. What remains to be seen is whether, having lost this game, the intentionalists can go on to win the match by shifting the discussion into the realm of aesthetic objects. This move would come down to the claim that the nature of verbal artifacts is definable not by reference to aesthetic intentions alone but only by reference to aesthetic objects. But that is another story, one I take up in the next chapters as still another attempt to retrieve for contemporary discussion still other conceptual resources of the realist backgrounds of modern aesthetics.

Appendix 8: Logical Laws and Intuitionism

Several objections to this argument need brief attention. The first is Husserl's own: the second is Sukale's (with some inspiration from Føllesdal, which I neglect here).[34]

Husserl is willing to concede that some empirical laws, for example, those in the natural sciences as opposed to those in the social sciences, are formulated like Newton's law of gravitation without a ceteris paribus clause (therefore exact, not vague) and without factual content (therefore with no entailment relation to an existing state of affairs). He is unwilling to accept, however, the further step that those psychological laws that are supposed to obtain at the foundations of logic are like natural scientific laws rather than like social scientific laws. Instead, he claims that even natural scientific laws such as the law of gravity do not fulfill the third criterion (certainty rather than probability, however high). Moreover, the kind of evidence that the truth of natural scientific laws is based upon regardless of how those laws are actually situated is "hypothetical, a posteriori, and factual" and therefore not conformable with the apodictic, a priori, and nonfactual character of the evidence for the truth of logical laws.[35] So trying to exploit the difference between the laws of a social science and those of a natural science will not ultimately work in favor of the psychologistic thesis.

The second objection is simply this: Husserl's refutation of psychologism comes to a petitio principii.

If we go through Husserl's discussion of the empiricist consequences of psychologism, we find that he assumes already a fixed meaning of the laws of logic which, though plausible, is not demonstrated by him. In this he is not better off than Frege. Both thinkers just stipulate that logical laws are eternal, a priori true and refer to timeless entities. The next task is, of course, to show that this is the proper meaning of logical laws and can therefore not be changed by the psychologicians.

[34]D. Føllesdal, *Husserl and Frege* (Oslo, 1958).
[35]Sukale 1976: 33.

In order to show this we would have to leave the question of what logical laws mean at first open and begin the argument from some other point.[36]

In short, Husserl is accused of assuming something he has the responsibility for proving.

But if we go through Husserl's discussion again, we find that he does try to show not just that the exact, a priori, and nonfactual character of logical laws is a stipulated meaning, but that this agreed-upon and on Sukale's own admission plausible account is indeed the proper one. For Husserl argues further that trying to account for the principle that justifies the truth of logical laws must end, if both vicious circles and infinite regresses are to be avoided, in the recognition that these principles are immediately evident and that the evidence for them is apodictic. In other words, Husserl gets around the charge of petitio principii by relying on a species of intuitionism.

I think we must reply to this charge with a simple denial. Husserl is not begging the question, because he is not assuming that logical laws are ideal entities as such. This would in effect make his own position here subject to the strong criticisms Wundt[37] makes of Husserl's view in his article "Psychologismus und Logismus" from the *Kleine Schriften I* of 1910 (Husserl calls it "a great and really brilliant essay"; *Draft*, 52). And these criticisms of logicism, the entities of psychologism, are explicitly rejected by Husserl in the *Draft of a Preface to the Logical Investigations* from 1913.[38] Husserl, rather, is claiming that the ideality of logical laws is the result not of stipulation but of the way logical laws present themselves to intuition. He emphasizes that he does not start from a Platonist position about the ontological status of these entities; instead, he asserts that intuitive experience leads on ultimately to "original givens."[39] In short, he is attempting "to attain in pure intuition [*reiner Anschauung*] and faithful description a truly stable basis for discoveries which could seriously be called 'scientific.' "[40] Husserl discusses in great detail the kind of ideality at issue here in the first chapter of the Second Logical Investigation, which is devoted to an analysis of what he calls in his account of volume 2

---

[36]Sukale 1976: 46.
[37]For Wundt's definition of "logicism" see *Draft*, 53, 55.
[38]See especially *Draft*, 52–61.
[39]*Draft*, 25.
[40]*Draft*, 16.

of the *Logical Investigations* "the general question of the ideality of species (of 'general objects')," namely, universals.[41] The analyses show further that Husserl is not stipulating the meaning of logical laws. "One cannot philosophize away," he writes in the *Draft*, "anything thus intuitively seen."[42] Rather, he is trying to describe "the ideal as something given prior to all theories."[43] He does not champion the ideal over the real in their traditional senses but looks for some middle ground. Hence his talk, in the *Draft* and in the Second Logical Investigation, of intentionality, fulfillment, acts, lived experience, and so on. He is insisting on what he calls "the simple minor acceptance of something that is manifestly given."[44]

Now it may be that intuitionism precisely here has its own difficulties. Indeed, others have argued many cases against various forms of intuitionism in Husserl.[45] These quarrels are difficult to pick with Husserl, since he was engaged in trying to move his analysis into an area where, as he often complains, historical prejudices about so-called Platonism had kept philosophers from entering. Describing this unexplored region often led him into terminological difficulties that in turn became easy starting points for critical disagreement. Thus he claims that the ultimate sources of knowledge are directly seen principles that, because they are clearly seen prior to all theorizing, are called original principles.[46] Or he speaks of prejudgmental experiences, what he calls "originally presenting intuitive experience" (*originär gebende Anschauung*).[47] Or again he writes: "All phenomenological analyses...have the character of a priori analyses in the only valuable sense of analyses that subject ideas given in pure intuition [i.e., self-given in genuine

---

[41]Husserl, "Notice of *Logische Untersuchungen: Untersuchungen zur Phänomenologie und Theorie der Erkenntnis*," *VFWP* 25(1901): 260. Translated by P. J. Bossert and C. H. Peters in *Introduction to the Logical Investigations* (The Hague, 1975), 5–8. For technical issues here see essays in J. N. Mohanty, ed., *Readings on E. Husserl's Logical Investigations* (The Hague, 1977).

[42]*Draft*, 27.

[43]*Draft*, 22.

[44]*Draft*, 39.

[45]See E. Levinas, *The Theory of Intuition in Husserl's Phenomenology*, trans. A. Orianne (Evanston, Ill., 1973); S. Strasser, "Intuition und Dialektik in der Philosophie Edmund Husserl," in *Edmund Husserl, 1859–1959* (The Hague, 1959), 148–53; and D. Sinha, "Phenomenology: A Break-through to a New Intuitionism," in *Phänomenologie Heute: Festschrift für Ludwig Landgrebe*, 27–48 (The Hague, 1972). Cf. S. Kanata, "Die Imagination als komplizierte Struktur: Über das Bildbewusstsein bei E. Husserl," *Aesthetics* 2(1986): 69–87.

[46]*Draft*, 24.

[47]*Draft*, 23.

original intuitive experience] to a pure description of their essential content."[48]

All these matters touching on intuitive experience Husserl acknowledged as being very difficult. One of his most important statements in the *Draft* concerns just this difficulty:

> The deepest philosophical problems are attached to the givenness [Gegebenheit] and to the "being" to be given [zu gebendes "Sein"] and, of course, these problems differentiate themselves according to the basic types of givenness and their correlative basic types of objects. But what precedes this problematic and what specifies its sense is that one just looks at the types of being and givenness, accepts them from the beginning simply as observables, and brings to mind the realization that no theory can eliminate what is the ultimate standard for all theory: that which is given in plain seeing and is, therefore, original.[49]

But the difficulties of intuitive experience are entirely another matter than is begging the question. To sustain the charge of question begging it is not enough for Sukale to defend the psychological empiricist against Husserl by allowing him to claim that the rules of inference are immediately evident not as eternal laws but as "the normal, factual practice of scientists."[50] For this move entails changing the meaning not of "logical laws" but of the familiar enough phrase "immediately evident." And *that* move cannot be made without further and indeed quite difficult argument of its own.

If Husserl's refutation of psychologism is faulty, it is not because of question begging, and in the absence of a valid and persuasive argument against Husserl's intuitionism, I conclude that his refutation, at least in the sharply limited form I have given it, still holds. We now need to see the consequences of this discussion in the context of our dealings with descriptive aesthetic psychologism.

[48]*Draft*, 52.
[49]*Draft*, 26–27.
[50]Sukale 1976: 46.

Chapter Nine

Twardowski and Aesthetic Contents

> The constituents of the object of a presentation are to be contrasted
> with the constituents of the corresponding content; the parts of the
> object with the parts of the content.
> —Kazimierz Twardowski

> The number of formal constituents of an object is determined by
> the number of its material constituents.
> —Kazimierz Twardowski

So far we have been exploring different aspects of the notion
of the aesthetic in both Dilthey's discussions of aesthetic experience and Brentano's and Husserl's analyses of aesthetic intentions.
Another side of aesthetic intentions now needs examination. One
recurring problem, at least in literary aesthetics, is the persistent
puzzle that arises when some intentional objects like characters
and situations in a novel are understood as having no real reference.
In this chapter I look more closely at this problem area and
examine the contribution of Brentano's less well-known student,
Kazimierz Twardowski (1866–1938). Not only was Twardowski's
work the beginning of modern philosophy in Poland, the so-called
Lwów school, his reflection also was a seminal influence on Meinong,
Husserl, Ingarden, Moore, and Russell.[1] His work intersects in

---

[1] For background on Twardowski's work see R. Haller, "Österreichische Philosophie,"
Conceptus 8(1977): 57–66; H. Buczynska-Garewicz, "Semiotics in Poland and Its
Historical Roots," *American Journal of Semiotics* 1(1981): 213–22; T. Czezowski,
"Kazimierz Twardowski as Teacher," *Studia Philosophica* (Posnan) 3(1948): 13–17;
R. Ingarden, "The Scientific Activity of Kazimierz Twardowski," *Studia Philosophica*
(Posnan) 3(1948): 17–30; and R. Ingarden, "Kazimierz Twardowski," in *Z badán nad
filozofia wspoczesna*, 251–65 Studies in Contemporary Philosophy (Warsaw, 1963).

important and still unnoticed ways with Frege's concerns and some of the issues Wittgenstein belabors in the *Tractatus*. Twardowski thus stands at the point where two of the major streams in philosophy today first divided.[2] More important than this historical fact, however, is the series of reflections Twardowski presented on the problem of specifying the nature of the intentional objects we find under discussion in literary aesthetics. Since most of his central reflection on this topic is available in his 1894 work *Zur Lehre vom Inhalt und Gegenstand der Vorstellungen*, in what follows I shall rely largely though not exclusively on the account Twardowski offers there.[3] My concern will be not so much to solve puzzles about the putative contents of intentional objects and states of affairs as to articulate, with Twardowski's help, at least one of the perduring questions here. And once again my general aim, like that in the other chapters of part 2, is to call attention to the richness of certain conceptual analyses in the realist backgrounds of modern aesthetics that derive from Bolzano's distinctive reading of Kant.

Acts, Contents, and Objects

If we are to come to critical grips with Twardowski's contribution, it is important to grasp at the outset the main features of his terminology.[4] We need to note especially that the relation that

---

[2]See H. Skolimowski, "Kazimierz Twardowski and the Rise of the Analytical Movement in England," in his *Polish Analytical Philosophy*, 24–56 (London, 1967). See especially the very important recent papers collected in *The Vienna Circle and the Lvov-Warsaw School*, ed. K. Szaniawski (The Hague, 1988), and a series of essays on A. Reinach (1883–1917), an important figure who shares some of Twardowski's central concerns, in K. Mulligan, ed., *Speech Act and Sachverhalt: Reinach and the Foundations of Realist Phenomenology* (The Hague, 1987). Reinach's works are now available again in *Sämtliche Werke*, 2 vols. (Munich, 1989). A different perspective is found in J. Proust's excellent book *Questions de forme* (Paris, 1986).

[3]The standard bibliography is that of D. Gromska, "Bibliografia prac Kazimierza Twardowskiego," in *Wybrane pisma filozoficzne* [Selected philosophical papers] by Kazimierz Twardowski, xiii–xxxvi (Warsaw, 1965). Another important figure here is C. von Ehrenfels. See his *Philosophische Schriften*, 4 vols. (Munich, 1983–89), especially vol. 2, *Aesthetik* (Munich, 1986).

[4]For further background here see Z. A. Jordan's discussion in his *Philosophy and Ideology* (Dordrecht, 1963). And on the important related question of meaning see H. Buczynska-Garewicz, "Twardowskis Bedeutungslehre," *Semiosis* 2(1977): 55–66. The terminology may need to change according to the kind of artwork at issue. See, for example, S. Shono, "Artworks, Aesthetic Processes, and Situations in Music," in *The Reasons of Art*, ed. P. McCormick, 51–56 (Ottawa, 1985).

Brentano and Husserl refer to as intentionality, Twardowski analyzes into three components. These elements Twardowski calls act, content, and object. All three make up the basic kinds of mental acts that are—if we follow Brentano, as Twardowski did—presentations, judgments, and feelings. We should also note that Twardowski admits of only these three basic kinds of mental acts, allowing no intermediate kinds:[5] "There are no transitional stages between the two kinds of intentional relation [presentations and judgments], neither continuous nor discontinuous."[6] In the interests of simplicity, I will deal here only with the first two kinds of mental acts. The last, of course, is the subject of Meinong's brilliant work, *On Emotional Presentation*,[7] which I will look at in detail in chapter 10.

Presentations (*Vorstellungen*) thus may be analyzed into presentational acts, presentational contents, and presentational objects. The first is the intentional act, the second the intentional object, and the third the referent of the intentional object (whether existing in the real world of space-time or not). The act is what accounts for the kind of presentation in question (presentation, judgment, or volition), whereas the content determines the kind of mental entity at issue. The object (when there is one) is the nonmental counterpart of the content. Note here the distinction Twardowski takes over from Höfler and Meinong. "The words 'thing' and 'object' are used in two senses," Twardowski quotes: "on the one hand for that independently existing entity... at which our presentation and judgment aim, at it were; on the other hand for the mental, more or less approximate 'picture' of that real entity which exists in us."[8]

---

[5]In his influential *Logik* (Halle, 1892), B. Erdmann did allow for intermediate kinds of mental acts. For a good discussion of a difficulty here see E. Paczkowska-Lagowska, "Twardowski's Refutation of Psychologism," *Prace Filozoficzne* (Cracow) 6(1976): 29–43.

[6]Twardowski, *On the Doctrine of the Content and Object of Representations*, trans. R. Grossmann (The Hague, 1977), 3. A reprint of the 1894 Vienna edition, *Zur Lehre von Inhalt und Gegenstand der Vorstellungen*, has been published by Philosophia Verlag (Munich, 1983). It is cited hereafter as *Zur Lehre*. For further materials on topics treated in this extraordinary book from roughly the same period of Twardowski's development, see *Idee und Perzeption* (Vienna, 1892), *Wyobrazenia i pojecia* [Images and concepts] (Lwów, 1898), and a shorter and reworked version of the same text, "Über begriffliche Vorstellungen," in *Beilage zum XVI Jahresbericht der philosophischen Gesellschaft a. d. Universität zu Wien*, S. 3–28 (Leipzig, 1903).

[7](Vienna, 1917).

[8]Cited (Vienna, 1890), para. 6 in *Zur Lehre*, 2. Note that for Twardowski, as for Meinong, the object is *Daseinsfrei*; it may exist or it may not. In any case, an object for Twardowski is not necessarily a real spatiotemporal thing. I owe this point to H. B. Garewicz.

Twardowski goes on to distinguish between individual contents and general contents. The first are individual ideas (Kant's "intuitions"), while the second are general ideas (Kant's "concepts"). An individual idea thus is an idea of an individual thing, something Twardowski construes as a complex of properties. A general idea or a concept is a group of individual things, something Twardowski construes as a group of complexes of particular properties or, more simply, as a group of instances. So far, then, we have individual ideas and individual things, on the one hand, and on the other hand concepts and groups of instances.

The question now arises whether for Twardowski individual things are objects, and whether groups of instances are groups of objects. So long as we restrict the word "object" to spatiotemporal entities and the word "content" to mental entities, we still require a word to refer to those entities like "the present king of England" whose kind—idea or judgment?—is left undetermined. To do this job the word "intention" has been suggested. Thus we may read Twardowski as holding that "the intentions of individual ideas are objects, while the intentions of concepts are groups of objects."[9]

Twardowski modifies this theory of mental acts when he applies it to judgments. In both theories we do have a triple distinction between act, content, and object. And in both we also have a similar account of the act component. Thus, just as there is the act of presentation or having an idea, so there is the act of judgment or making a judgment. Twardowski puts the matter this way. "The analogy with the situation which obtains in the area of presentations is a perfect one."

Here, as there, one has a mental act; here the judging, there the presentation. The former, just like the latter, relates to an object that is presumed to be independent of thinking. When the object is presented and when it is judged in both cases, there occurs a third thing, besides the mental act and its object, that is, as it were, a sign of the object: "its mental picture when it is presented, and its existence when it is judged."[10]

This citation shows that the analogy is not, as Twardowski says, a perfect one. It is not the case that just as there is the mental counterpart (idea) of an object so to there is the mental counterpart

---

[9]R. Grossman in his excellent introduction to his translation of *Zur Lehre*, ix. H. B. Garewicz, by contrast, prefers to use the word "intention" in the sense of intentional *act*. For other views see S. T. Sommerville, "Believing in Intensional Logics," *Philosophical Papers* 11(1982): 39–49; and W. Chudy, "La question de la présentification des actes de connaissance," *Roczniki Filozoficzne* 29(1981): 165–232.

[10]*Zur Lehre*, 7.

(judgment) of an object that is judged. For instead of a parallel account, Twardowski follows Brentano's early theory of judgment in *Psychologie vom empirischen Standpunkt*.[11]

This is the "ideogenetic theory," which "sees the nature of the judgment in the affirmation or denial of an object."[12] According to this view, every judgment is either an affirmation or a denial of the existence or subsistence of an object. Consequently, the content of the judgment is not a mental counterpart of anything at all but is the content of the underlying presentation.[13] Unlike Brentano, Twardowski identifies this content with the subsistence itself of whatever object is affirmed or denied. The result is that, while presentations have special contents or intentions, judgments do not.

Twardowski provides a summary of his view in a letter of 11 July 1877 to Meinong. After describing his present work on a long-planned theory of judgment on the basis of work by Brentano, Meinong, and Alois Höfler, Twardowski writes: "Hauptgedanke meines Ansichts ist: in jedem Urteil ist zu unterscheiden 1. Act (Bejahung oder Verneinung); 2. Inhalt: Das Existieren, Vorhandensein, Bestehen; 3. Gegenstand (der beurteilte Sachverhalt: entweder ein absolutes Datum oder eine Beziehung oder beides zusammen). Beispiel: 'Gott existiert': Gegenstand: Gott; Inhalt: Existenz; Act: Beziehung. Oder 'Zweimal Zwei ist Vier': Gegenstand: Gleichheit zwischen dem Product aus Zweimal Zwei und Vier; Inhalt: das Existieren (Bestehen) dieser Gleichheit; Act: Beziehung [The main line of thinking in my view is this: we need to distinguish in every judgment between (1) the act (affirming or denying); (2) the content; existing, being present to hand, subsisting; (3) the object (the judged state of affairs: either an absolute *datum* or a relation or both together). Example: "God exists": object: God; content: existence; act: relation. Or "Two times two is four": object: equality between the product of two times two and four; content: the existing (subsisting) or this equality; act: relation.]"[14] Further reference to the content of judgments as existence or subsistence is to be found in another of Twardowski's letters to Meinong several weeks later, 25 July 1877.[15] This point is put even more explicitly

---

[11]See volume 2 (Leipzig, 1924), chap. 7.

[12]*Zur Lehre*, 25.

[13]See Husserl's analysis of Brentano's doctrine in the Fifth Logical Investigation.

[14]"Briefen an Meinong," in *Philosophenbriefe: Aus der wissenschaftlichen Korrespondenz von Alexius Meinong*, S. 143–44 (Graz, 1965). The letters from Twardowski are from 11.7 (1987); 25.7 (1897); 13.5 (1898); 14.11 (1899).

[15]*Philosophenbriefe*, S. 146.

in the *Zur Lehre* (1894) when Twardowski writes: "The content of a judgment is thus the existence of an object, with which judgment is concerned; for, whoever makes a judgment, asserts something about the existence of an object. In affirming or denying the object, he also affirms or denies its existence. What is judged in the real sense is the object itself; and in being judged, there is judged also, but in another sense, its existence."[16]

Twardowski's attempt to fit Brentano's early theory of judgment into his own general theory is misguided, however. For Twardowski's theory entails that some objects (ideas) have as their mental counterparts one kind of intention (presentational contents), while other objects (things judged) have as their mental counterparts a different kind of intention (existence or subsistence). But on such an account it remains obscure just how such different kinds of beings as both presentational contents and something called existence or subsistence could properly be said to be intentions at all. The first, a presentational content, is both a kind of mental picture and a mental counterpart to an object; it therefore merits the description "intention." The second, existence or subsistence, however, is neither a mental picture nor a mental counterpart; it therefore is described improperly as "intention."

But when Twardowski's doctrine is amended and the category of "state of affairs" is taken over from Husserl and Meinong, a parallel is then reinstated between the theory of presentations and the theory of judgments. For now we can say that just as acts of presentation have mental counterparts of objects as their intentions, so acts of judgment have states of affairs of things judged as their intentions. But appeal to states of affairs raises a fundamental problem—how to account for those kinds of judgments we call beliefs in nonexistent states of affairs and those kinds of ideas we call ideas of nonexistent objects.

Nonexistent Objects and States of Affairs

Twardowski holds that having an idea or making a judgment always entails an intentional relation between the act and its content. Whatever the kind of act in question, there is always a mental correlate. Here is Twardowski's comment at the end of his chapter on so-called objectless presentation:

[16]*Zur Lehre*, 7; see also 24.

The relation between the act of presentation and the corresponding object is independent of the question of whether or not this object exists. Hence nothing stands in the way of asserting that to every presentation there corresponds an object, whether the object exists or not. The expression "objectless presentation" is such that it contains a contradiction: for, there is no presentation which does not present something as an object; there can be no such presentation. But there are many presentations whose objects do not exist, either because the objects combine contradictory determinations and hence cannot exist, or because they simply do not in fact exist. And in all such cases an object is presented, so that one may speak of presentations whose objects do not exist, but not of presentations which are objectless, a presentation to which no object corresponds.[17]

Thus, having the idea of a golden mountain and believing that Dr. Zhivago is a historical personage entail the subsistence of the mental entities "golden mountain" and the state of affairs "that Dr. Zhivago is a historical personage." Whether such mental correlates of these different acts also have nonmental counterparts in the world of space-time is a separate question. In this case, since there are no golden mountains and since it is not a fact that Dr. Zhivago is a historical personage, those subsisting mental correlates do not stand in any relation to existing nonmental counterparts, just because no such real objects (individual things) and no such real states of affairs (facts) exist.

The nonexistence of an individual thing and the nonexistence of a fact, Twardowski holds, must not be confused with the nonexistence of a mental content and the nonexistence of a mental state of affairs. Whenever we have an idea or make a judgment, there necessarily exists for each of these acts its respective mental correlate; but there do not necessarily exist real counterparts for these mental correlates. In short, all mental acts have contents, but not all contents have being. Thus, when I make the judgment that there are no round squares there is an idea before the mind, the idea that there are round squares because the properties of mental contents, their characteristics, need not be compatible; but there is no idea of a round square, because there is no fact that is the counterpart of such an idea, since the properties of a fact cannot be incompatible.

The matter at issue here is more complex than my summary indicates, for Twardowski argues his case against Bolzano's opposed

[17]*Zur Lehre*, 26. Cf. B. Hale, *Abstract Objects* (Oxford, 1982).

view in the *Wissenschaftslehre*.[18] The unabridged argument requires distinguishing among three kinds of presentations: presentations of the negation of something (nothing); presentations whose contents involve incompatibles (round square); and presentations of possible empirical objects of which till now there are no real instances (tenth-generation computers). But we need not go into the details of this discussion here, for Twardowski's general position is already clear enough. "The confusion of the proponents of objectless presentations like Bolzano," Twardowski summarizes, "consists in that they mistook the non-existence of an object for its not being presented."[19]

We need, however, not just to reconstruct Twardowski's account of judgment on a different basis than Brentano's early theory; we also must avoid Twardowski's own confusion between complex individual things and complex properties of individual things. To understand this confusion, we must examine more closely how Twardowski thinks that nonexistent intentions, whether contents or states of affairs, can be said to have properties at all.

Ordinary objects of perceptions for Twardowski—say, a fountain pen—are complex objects that have properties. Now the properties themselves of complex objects are instances of the same properties exhibited by perceptual objects of the same kind. And what individuates these instances of properties are spatial and temporal circumstances. Thus, having a fountain pen is not just a property but an instance of a property, while having a particular pen in a certain place at a certain time is an individuated instance of a property. Properties of objects, then, are both instantiated and individuated. For Twardowski, moreover, properties of individual objects are not exemplifications of something further in the objects or participations in the objects; they are, rather, parts of that whole we call the object. In other words, the relation between properties and their object is that of part and whole, not that of exemplification or of participation. "Just as the whole object is presented through a presentation," Twardowski writes, "so the single parts of the object are presented through corresponding parts of the presentation. Now, the parts of the object of a presentation are again objects of presentation, and the latter in turn are parts of the whole presentation. Parts of the content of a presentation are contents, just as parts of an object are objects. In analogy to the way in which

[18](Sulzbach, 1839), para. 67.
[19]*Zur Lehre*, 22.

parts of an object form the whole uniform object, parts of a content form the complete content."[20]

If we then try to account for the properties of nonexistent objects, say a golden mountain, several changes must immediately be introduced. To begin with, we are no longer dealing with an individuated object but are dealing specifically with a nonexistent individual object. Consequently, no individuating features exist either, for spatial and temporal parameters do not hold literally for nonexistent objects. Moreover, since a fortiori there are no other golden mountains either, the properties of the golden mountain in question, though complex, cannot be instances. Twardowski accordingly holds that a nonexistent object is a complex of properties, whereas a real object is a complex of instances of properties.

Twardowski's view arises from his elaborate discussion of characteristics. In chapter 8 he argues that the parts of objects and the parts of contents cannot be the same, because objects and contents are not the same. Hence use of the term "characteristic" in connection with both object and content is abusive. For his own view he cites Bolzano and Überweg[21] in support. And he summarizes his view as follows: "The constituents of the object of a presentation are to be contrasted with the constituents of the corresponding content; the parts of the object with the parts of the content; they must be as little confused with each other as the content of a presentation with its object."[22] Although Twardowski discusses in enormous detail in the following chapters the nature and kinds of these different constituents, he nevertheless overlooks a confusion.

The difficulty is that there are two complexes that must be kept distinct. On the one hand, there is a complex entity, a golden mountain, and on the other there is a complex property, being golden and a mountain. Twardowski's theory does not allow us to distinguish between the two, since according to that theory the complex unity (golden mountain) and the complex property (being golden and a mountain) are both construed as wholes having exactly the same parts. For all the subtleties of his analysis of constituents, these constituents are unfailingly viewed in the context of part-whole relations.

What generates the difficulty? If we go back to Twardowski's account of what properties are, we find an answer. For when we set

---

[20]*Zur Lehre*, 39.
[21]*System der Logik* (Bonn, 1882).
[22]*Zur Lehre*, 44.

aside the construal of properties as parts of wholes and substitute, at least for the moment, a traditional construal of parts as exemplifications, then at least this difficulty disappears. On the traditional construal of property we can distinguish between a complex entity and a complex property. We need only hold that whereas the complex entity exemplifies its properties, the complex property consists of its properties. The traditional view of exemplification, of course, as Grossmann correctly points out, has its own problems, particularly in dealing adequately with classical distinctions between substance and nature. But whatever these difficulties come down to, they are beside the relevant point here—that the part-whole construal of properties does not allow of a central distinction between complex entity and complex property and the exemplification construal does. The conclusion such a distinction allows is clear: a golden mountain consists of the properties of being golden and being a mountain, but since no golden mountains exist, a golden mountain does not exemplify such properties. More simply we can say, when I have an idea of a golden mountain the content of that idea is a complex property that consists of that content. The content itself, however, has no real counterpart in the precise sense that there exist no real complex individual objects properly called golden mountains.

We need simply to apply this account analogously to judgments about nonexistent states of affairs. Thus, when I make a judgment that there are no golden mountains, the act of judgment has a mental correlate whose content is constituted by the complex property being golden and a mountain. But this correlate itself has no real counterpart in the precise sense that there exist no real states of affairs (facts) properly called golden mountains.

In summary, we need to distinguish, as Twardowski himself did not always do, between complex contents, complex individuals, and their complex properties, as well as between complex states of affairs, complex facts, and their complex properties. Otherwise we cannot adequately account for nonexistent intentions, whether they are contents or states of affairs.

Imaginary Contents

We have now looked in some detail at the main features of Twardowski's theory. Since our concern is with the literary work of art, it will now be useful to focus this theory on the particular question of the nature of imaginary contents and imaginary states of affairs. In what follows I will assume that imagining is an act of presentation that necessarily has a content but does not necessarily have an object. The major concern will be to describe more fully just how the structure of this content differs from the structure of its occasional objective counterpart.

To begin with, we need to recall that imaginary contents are related to the three basic kinds of contents, which in the case I am discussing have no objects. Imaginary contents thus may be particularized as imaginations of negations, imaginations of contradictions, and imaginations of objects that do not yet have instances in the empirical world. Although each of these kinds allows critical discussion, I limit analysis here to the most basic kind of imaginations, namely, those positive noncontradictory but nonempirical imaginations that make up the third kind. And since "imagination" is an ungainly term to describe the contents of this particular kind of imaginative presentation, when referring to these contents in what follows I will speak instead of "the third kind of imagination" —quite simply of "fictions." In short, fictions are construed here narrowly as those positive, noncontradictory, and nonempirically instantiated contents of acts of imaginative presentation that do not necessarily have spatiotemporal objective counterparts.

A second preliminary is also in order. Thus we need to recall that there are two kinds of fictions. Both are generally describable as intentions. The first kind of fiction comprises fictional entities, that is, that class of imaginative intentions to which nonexistent individual things would stand as spatiotemporal counterparts. The second kind of fiction comprises fictional states of affairs, that is, that class of imaginative intentions to which nonexistent facts would stand as spatiotemporal counterparts.

A final preliminary. Since we are centrally concerned with fictional states of affairs, we need to notice that such a matter constitutes the contents of a mixed rather than a pure mental act. For insofar as we are speaking of fictional contents rather than real ones (i.e., those contents that have spatiotemporal contents), we are concerned with just that kind of mental act called imaginative presentation. But insofar as we are also speaking of states of affairs rather than mental objects, we are also concerned with that kind of mental act called judgment. Hence the mental act in question, when we deal with fictional states of affairs, is both presentational and judgmental. These mixed or, we may say, composite kinds of mental acts are allowed by both Twardowski and Husserl, although, as we have noted, Twardowski argues against Erdmann's views[23] that there are no intermediate kinds of mental acts between presentation and judgment. The mental act at issue here is a composite act, however, not a transitional one. Thus only one mental correlate is at issue—fictional states of affairs—not a series of at least two mental correlates, first a fictional content and then a state of affairs.

To summarize these three preliminaries, we may say that talk about literary artworks, as I will be construing it, is centrally talk about fictional states of affairs as intentions of composite mental acts of imaginative presentation and judgment.

What, then, is the structure of fictions? We can, once again with help from Twardowski, divide the structure of fictions into material and formal constituents. The material set is the totality of the parts of a complex content, while the formal set is the totality of the relations that obtain among the parts of a complex content. Here, however, especially in light of our earlier criticism of the part/whole schema in Twardowski's thought, we need to be more specific. Let us say with Twardowski that "the word 'part'...has to be taken in its widest sense. Not only what the ordinary language of the mathematician calls a part is meant by the word, but generally everything that can be distinguished in or about the object i.e. mental object, namely content of a presentation irrespective of whether one can speak of a real analysis into the distinguishable parts or merely of an analysis in thought."[24]

Material and Formal Constituents

Consider first the material constituents of fictional entities. Since fictional entities do not by definition require spatiotemporal counterparts, not all material constituents of objects are also by that fact alone material constituents of fictional entities. Although these counterparts are not required, however, they are nonetheless allowed. Hence some material constituents of objects are also material constituents of fictional entities. We may proceed, then, as follows. We may first critically adopt Twardowski's account of the material constituents of objects and then by elimination retain only those elements that are consistent with the nature of fictional

---

[23]In B. Erdmann, *Logik* (Halle, 1892).
[24]*Zur Lehre*, 46–47.

entities as the imaginable material constituents of those entities.

Twardowski takes up our first question in chapter 9. One of the merits of his treatment there is immediately evident. Twardowski does not attempt to provide any complete classification of material constituents or a genetic account of how such complexes arise, tasks that may well be handed over to the empirical sciences. Instead, he sketches a general account of "what is common to all kinds of parts and to all forms of composition of parts."[25] The initial distinctions such a general account involves are (1) that between simple and complex parts; among the latter, (2) that between closer and more distant complex parts; and where more precision is required, (3) that between first, second, . . . , and n^{th}-order parts. An adaptation of Twardowski's example is helpful. Thus in the case of a book we may distinguish (1) between cover and pages; further, (2) between the front and the back cover; and still further, (3) between the front and back of the front cover and the color and size of the pages; and so on. Distinctions among orders are relative, however, a point Twardowski's own example brings out well. Thus he writes: "If one now distinguishes between the color and the size of the pages, on the one hand, and the front and back of the cover on the other, then these are parts of the second order of the book, but parts of the first order of the pages and the cover, respectively."[26] Further kinds of relativity may also be noticed, but we need not go so far here.

Besides this initial division of material constituents into simple and complex and then into complex of the same or of different orders, two further divisions require mention. Thus we can also distinguish natural constituents into those that function in only one way as parts of a whole (extension in one, two, etc., dimensions or time) and those that may function in more than one way (red). The latter functions differently as a constituent of all mixed colors, and of a spectrum, and of a red ball; the former functions in this same way as a constituent of any kind of material object. And third, we can distinguish material constituents into those that can exist independent of wholes, those that cannot, and those that exist only mentally with their wholes.

If these are three ways of dividing material constituents of spatiotemporal objects, which divisions do not apply to those mental contents we are calling fictional entities? Clearly the third

[25]*Zur Lehre*, 46.
[26]*Zur Lehre*, 47.

division must be excluded, for talk of fictional entities deliberately excludes talk of the existence of such entities. Like both Twardowski and Husserl, when we talk of this class of mental entities we disregard any consideration whatever of their being spatiotemporal counterparts of such fictional entities. No such problem affects the first two divisions. More specifically, as regards the second division, single or multiple functions of the material constituents are not incompatible with either simple or complex parts of imagined fictional entities. And as regards the first division, relative closeness or distance of the parts of the whole is also not incompatible with either single or complex parts of imagined fictional entities. We can conclude, then, that the imagined material constituents of fictional entities may be (1) simple or complex, or among the complex, (2) of one order or another, or (3) single or multiple.

Consider next the formal constituents of fictional entities and proceed in a similar way, that is, by description of the formal constituents of spatiotemporal objects and then, by elimination, to those of fictional entities.

Twardowski holds that there are two kinds of formal constituents. The primary ones are those relations that obtain between the object and its constituents, the secondary ones those that obtain between the constituents themselves.[27] The difference between the secondary and the primary is that only parts of the whole and never the whole as such occur among the "terms" of secondary formal constituents.[28] Primary formal constituents, moreover, may be primary either in a strict or in an extended sense. In the strict sense, these relations are those that make up the unity of the complex in such a way that the whole is said "to have" those parts and the parts are said "to form" this whole. In the extended sense there are also relations (e.g., succession, similarity) that hold between whole and part in addition to that between the whole as such and the part as such. Since there can also be relations between relations when the terms are relations themselves and no parts and wholes, we can speak further of relations of degree. Thus relations between relations are relations of the second degree, and so on.

Without going into further detail here, we can immediately move to Twardowski's summary formulations. "The number of formal constituents of an object," he writes, "is determined by the number of its material constituents."[29] We may add to this a second

[27]Zur Lehre, 50.
[28]Zur Lehre, 56.
[29]Zur Lehre, 57; cf. 59.

principle: the kind of formal constituents of an object is also determined by the kind of its material constituents. When we then apply these two principles to the question at hand, we can conclude simply as follows. Fictional entities have just that number and kind of formal constituents that can hold between imagined material constituents of fictional entities. If we recall our earlier conclusion here, we can say that the formal constituents of fictional entities are whatever relations, whether property relations or secondary relations between wholes and all kinds of parts, that can hold between simple or complex (of one order or another) imagined material constituents or between single or multiple fictional material constituents.

The question now remaining is this: If we construe the structure of fictional entities along the lines suggested by a critical reading of Twardowski, to what degree can we pursue a similar course in dealing with the structure of fictional states of affairs? Recall that we need to be careful here, for the major weakness in Twardowski's theory of those mental acts we call judgments was the lack of a strict parallel between his treatments of the contents of presentations and those of judgments. The first and not the second could be construed metaphorically as a kind of mental picture, because the first and not the second was a species of mental object. In the case of judgmental contents Twardowski, we remember, substituted the notion of existence or subsistence. The consequence was his claim that judgmental acts have no contents whatever.

This consequence, however, is inconsistent with Twardowski's general principle, against Bolzano, that all mental acts, and therefore judgments too, have contents or mental objects. To reconcile Twardowski's views, we need not go as far as I indicated earlier, reconstructing his part/whole account in terms of an exemplification theory, which has its own difficulties. We need only retain Twardowski's commonsense view that mental acts of judging intend something about the existence or subsistence of things judged, while rejecting the argument that judgmental acts have no contents just because existence is not a mental picture. Talk of mental pictures is after all inexact.[30] Let us say, then, that acts of judging do have contents, but that in the case of such judging acts, and not in all other cases of mental acts, these contents constitute situations—

[30]Note the instructive comment here of an anonymous Cornell referee: "Talk of mental pictures takes us back to psychologism, but it also suggests a common misunderstanding of 'picture theories' of meaning. It is important to note that 'picture' can be used in a non-psychological sense. (Wittgenstein in the *Tractatus* for example.)"

affirmations or negations that something is the case. Further, these situations may or may not have spatiotemporal counterparts. Where there are such counterparts, we may speak of acts of judging, the contents of acts of judging, and facts—that is, things judged that exist in the spatiotemporal world. Where there are no such counterparts we may speak more economically of acts of judging and of situations. Thus the expression "situations" is used to refer to just those intentions of acts of judging that do not have spatiotemporal counterparts.

Now some situations are impossible beliefs, for example, the contents of my lyrical belief that some bachelors are not unmarried males. Other situations are false beliefs, for example, the contents of my belief that the Americans were the first in space. Still others are mistaken beliefs, for example, the contents of my belief that Antarctica was explored by Americans. The belief here is mistaken in the sense of being incomplete: the Russians and many others have also explored Antarctica. Further kinds of mistaken beliefs, of course, can be elaborated. Finally, some situations are imagined, for example, the contents of my belief that Zhivago loved Lara. It is only the structure of this last kind of situation that is in question, the structure of imagined situations. These situations I want to call "fictional states of affairs." When on reading Boris Pasternak's work *Dr. Zhivago* I judge that Zhivago loves Lara, what is the structure of the fictional situation that is the content of my mental act of judging?

Since this fictional situation consists in part of the fictional entities "Zhivago" and "Lara," it is clear that its structure may include any one or a combination or all of the imaginary material and imaginary formal constituents of fictional entities. Our question thus comes down to the issue whether, and if so in just what sense, is affirming the existence of a fictional situation an intelligible operation? In short, granted that we do make genuine judgments about that class of nonexistent facts we call fictional situations, how do we manage to?

Without trying to pursue this particular issue any further here, I turn to a related set of questions in the still-neglected work of another Brentano pupil, Alexius Meinong, as one more attempt to call attention to the conceptual resources still on insufficient view within the realist background of modern aesthetics.

Appendix 9: Degrees, Ranks, and Orders

We are not in a position to introduce a further distinction. And here it is best to rely on Twardowski's own account. When we take the frequent case of an object whose primary *material* constituents are complex,

> then one can discern in them, insofar as they in turn are considered as objects, all the earlier mentioned primary *formal* constituents [my emphasis]. For the material constituents of the second order, too, stand to the material constituents of first order...in the relation of being a part of a whole (primary formal constituents in the strict sense); but there exist, furthermore, relations between the just mentioned material constituents which are different from the relation between the whole and its parts as such (primary formal constituents in the extended sense). Thus we have, in analogy to the material constituents of first, second,...order, primary formal constituents of first, second ...rank, namely those in the strict sense as well as those in the extended sense.[31]

It is important to note that Twardowski speaks of formal constituents in terms of rank and not, as he does with material constituents, in terms of order. This peculiarity is deliberate. For Twardowski reserves talk of order to describe a final distinction, the one between primary formal constituents that are closer or more distant. Thus in strict parallel to the earlier treatment, closer formal constituents are analyzable into more distant formal constituents. In such cases the relation between the latter and the former are said to be those of the second order, of the third order, and so on.

To summarize so far, we have primary and secondary formal constituents. The former can be called primary in either a strict or an extended sense. Primary formal constituents in the extended sense can be of different degrees (when the terms are relations themselves—consider a relation between similarity and identity), of different ranks (depending on whether the relation is taken as a whole or a part—consider the causal relation where only one but not both terms is analyzed as a part), and of different orders (depending on whether a relation is analyzable into still another relations—consider a relation of similarity that is analyzable into one of relative identity).

Since material constituents differ greatly, primary formal constit-

[31] *Zur Lehre*, 51.

uents from these wholes are also properties of these wholes in very different ways. But in whatever case we take, we are always dealing with a synthesis between wholes and parts, even though the relation within that synthesis varies enormously. This allows us to hold that, despite the variety, all complexes can be viewed in some way as functions of their parts. For this reason Twardowski adopts a formula from Lotze[32] and Zimmerman[33] to characterize this synthesis. A complex object thus is treated as follows:

$O = f(P_1, P_2, \ldots P_3)$, where the P_n are its parts, namely, the material constituents of the first order. Depending on the category of object under study and the kind of material constituents, the way in which the constituents are contained in the whole will be different and, hence, will be designated as f, f', F, F', , ', etc. For, the sign for the function is the sign for the containment of the parts in the whole. . . . If the object can be analyzed into more distant material constituents, that is, if P_1, P_2, , , , P_n are in turn complex objects, then the first formula must be elucidated by additional formula of the kind: $O_1 = P_1 = f_1 (p_1 p_2, \ldots P_n) O_2 = P_2 = f_2(\pi_1 \pi_2, \ldots \pi_n)$, etc.[34]

Twardowski now moves to simplify his account. Thus he proposes that the primary formal constituents of an object be referred to most generally as "properties." This word, he notes, can refer either to a relation or to one term of the relation. Hence Twardowski specifies that the primary formal constituents of an object are properties in the sense of the relation itself between part and whole, no matter of what kind. More explicitly, he speaks of primary formal constituents as "property relations."[35]

This is the gist of Twardowski's account of primary formal constituents. But what are the kinds of secondary formal constituents, that is, those relations whose terms are always parts of wholes and never wholes as such? The most important are those relations, like that of causal dependency, among the primary formal constituents or property relations. The essence of an object, Twardowski adds, may be construed as "the totality of property relations from which one can derive, because of causal dependency, all other property relations of an object."[36] A second group of relations is

[32]Logik (Leipzig, 1881).
[33]Philosophische Propaedeutik (Vienna, 1897).
[34]Zur Lehre, 53.
[35]Zur Lehre, 56.
[36]Zur Lehre, 57.

that among the material constituents, either those that belong to the parts just insofar as they are parts ("the relative position of the three sides of a triangle") or those that belong to the parts even in those cases where the parts can also be construed as wholes ("the relationship of equality among the three sides of a triangle"). Each of these two groups, moreover, may be further discussed by analogy with the way the primary formal constituents were discussed. But we need not go so far here.

Chapter Ten

Meinong and
Aesthetic Feelings

When I say, "the sky is blue," and then say, "the sky is beautiful,"
a property is attributed to the sky in either case. In the second case
a feeling participates in the apprehension of the property, as, in the
first case, an idea does. And it is natural to let the feeling be the
presentative factor in the second case, as an idea is always taken to
be in the first case.

—Alexius Meinong

The predicate in "the flower is red" is analogous to the predicate in
"the flower is pretty" and exhibits an object that can only be
presented by a feeling.

—Alexius Meinong

At the conclusion of his important paper "On So-Called
Truth in Literature" Roman Ingarden writes: "If someone wants to
accept the existence of 'realistic' works and attaches a special value
to their realism, he must abandon the view that literary works
contain logically true sentences and if he nevertheless wishes to
ascribe truth to such works, he must do so in a new sense
compatible with the quasi-assertive character of predicating sentences in literature."[1]

Regardless of either Ingarden's or our own interest in realism and
the realist backgrounds of modern aesthetics, the importance of
accounting for the status of aesthetic or literary truths in some
terms other than those of logically true sentences is rather widely

---

[1]Trans. A Czerniawski in *Aesthetics in Twentieth Century Poland*, ed. J. G.
Harrell (Lewisburg, Pa., 1973), 203. Cited hereafter as "TIL."

252

acknowledged today. Less noticed, however, is the problematic relationship between what literary truths are and just how these putative truths are presented in literary works. Of these two questions I look in some detail only at the second one, as a further attempt to explore the problematic notion of the aesthetic. And in doing so I pursue particularly a distinction Ingarden suggests between what literary works say and what they show. "The poetic work," Ingarden has written, "Shows, reveals, and uncovers the palpable *Gestalt* of qualities with which it affects the reader directly. A theoretical account describes, names, and judges what is being named only in a conceptual way, so that our emotional response too is different in both the situations."[2] The task here, of course, is to say what "showing" is in literary artworks. And I will point out in this regard the interest to be found in a rather neglected side of Meinong's work.

I begin with a recent attempt to exhibit a distinction between saying and showing and try with the help of this example both to make concrete the problem of how literary truths are presented and to indicate several general questions as guidelines for the subsequent inquiry. Against this background I then call attention to the complicated yet very suggestive reflections of Alexius Meinong. After sketching the context of his work and providing a brief overview of the relevant topics, I look in some detail at his account of what emotional presentation is and what its contents are. With this material in hand, I then return to the initial guideline questions and offer several brief observations on the cognitive character of showing in literary works of art as part of the more general issue of the cognitive and the aesthetic.

Sayings and Showings

One way to get on with formulating the issues here is to consider a statement about literary works of art by a philosopher working outside aesthetics. Paul Feyerabend calls attention to how one kind of literature can show us something more than it says.[3]

---

[2]"TIL," 191; see also 203. The ontology here is very important, as we will see in chapter 11. A helpful overview of most of the key issues that will be important to both Meinong and Ingarden can be found in J. Fizer, "Ingarden's and Mukařovsky's Binomial Definition of the Literary Work of Art: A Comparative View of Their Ontologies," ed. B. Dziemidok and P. McCormick, 159–87 in *On the Aesthetics of Roman Ingarden* (Boston, 1989).

[3]P. Feyerabend, "Let's Make More Movies," in *Owl of Minerva*, ed. C. J. Bontempo, 201–14 (New York, 1975).

He takes his example from Bertolt Brecht's play *The Life of Galileo*, scenes 7 and 9, where Galileo explains himself first to a boy about the relativity of motion and then to a cardinal of the Roman Catholic church about weaknesses in Aristotle's cosmology. The point of the examples is to show that argument has more than just a logical structure; it has in its dramatic forms a particular physical instantiation. What this drama does in an exemplary way is to set the second feature of argument as a commentary on the first by way of dramatizing the contrast between the physical appearances of a bare-chested fat man gesticulating flamboyantly and the relative lack of information communicated by the words alone. This contrast Feyerabend, of course, puts at the service of more general points than distinguishing between what is said and what is shown. Our purposes, however, do not entail following him that far. Rather, we need to look more closely at just how he puts the matter of showing.

Here is the key section of Feyerabend's discussion of the example:

> The problem that appears in the play is one of the most important *philosophical problems*. It is the problem of the role of reason in society and in our private lives, and of the changes which reason undergoes in the course of history.... On the stage the problem is not dealt with in a purely conceptual manner. It is *shown* as much as it is *explained*. This is anything but a disadvantage. Philosophical discussion has often been criticized for being too abstract, and one has demanded that the analysis of such concepts as reason, thought, knowledge, etc., be tied to concrete examples. Now concrete examples are circumstances which guide the application of a term and give content to the corresponding concept. The theater not only provides such circumstances, it also arranges them in a way that *inhibits* the facile progression of abstractions and forces us to reconsider the most familiar conceptual connections. Also the business of speculation which occasionally seems to swallow everything else is here set off from a rich and changing visual background that reveals its limitations and helps us to judge it as a whole.... It is of course possible to present the additional elements in words, but only at the expense of regarding our problem as solved before we have started examining it. For we now simply assume that everything can be translated into the medium of ideas. We have to conclude, then, that there are better ways of dealing with philosophical problems than verbal exchange, written discourse, and, *a fortiori*, scholarly research.[4]

[4]Feyerabend 1975: 204–5; emphases omitted.

Now, without necessarily accepting the conclusion here, there are several items that should be emphasized. I shall point out three.

The first is the stress Feyerabend puts on the importance of the problem this particular case is concerned with. What strikes him in the Brecht play is not just that drama has taken up a philosophical problem, but that the philosophical problem dramatized is an important one. Feyerabend corroborates this idea when he points out other important philosophical problems that require the control of concrete examples for their proper understanding. It could be, of course, that particular detailed problems in philosophy could be exhibited helpfully in literary texts. But the point here is that an important philosophical problem, indeed a very general one, is what makes this dramatization the interesting case.

The second feature of this reflection that calls for attention is Feyerabend's distinction between explaining a problem and showing it. What strikes him is that the general problem at issue here—how to understand the role of reason in life and society—is not explained in the way one would explain, say, an engineering problem to a team trying to get some part of a Mars landing module to function correctly. Rather, the sense of the problem is displayed instead of the elements being analyzed. Thus Galileo's accounts of particular problems are presented in puzzling contexts—the boy made a mimic the libertine, the scientist made to explain himself to a cardinal—that themselves make the larger aspects of the problem apparent. Reason is to be understood not just on the model of a problem in mechanics, but in the context of hero worship, the education of the young, threats of censure, political strands, even sexual roles among men and boys.

Feyerabend is at some pains to put this point precisely, since it is difficult to state clearly why some matters should sometimes not be stated clearly at all. His basic idea, however, does come through. Thus he holds that the spectacle of the dramatic presentation, especially in the full and very complex features of the visual components, suggests by its richness a peculiar poverty to the chains of arguments Galileo strings together with his concepts. The contrast, then, is between the little that these arguments succeed in stating unequivocally and the great deal that the context of these arguments suggests without any verbal formulation at all.

The final point involves Feyerabend's remarks on how examples function here. The general and vague term "reason," Feyerabend thinks, is selectively applied by the spectators at such a dramatic presentation of the problem because of the examples of reason they are provided with. But notice that these examples fall into two groupings. Some are to be found in Galileo's verbal explanations of his theories, while others are to be gathered by suggestion from the different ways Galileo expresses these views and the different circumstances that condition his expressions. Again, Feyerabend finds a tension here between these two kinds of examples. The first set, if successful, clarifies our conceptual understanding of Galileo's abstract points about whatever matter may be under discussion. But the second exhibits certain limits to that conceptual understanding by inserting these abstractions back into the complex give and take of multiple nonverbal circumstances.

We might put these three emphases together now in some such form as this. Some works of art and in particular literary works of art on occasion deal in an illuminating way with important philosophical problems. They present situations in which the explicitness of abstract conceptual formulations is counterpointed by the suggestiveness of concrete nonconceptual circumstances. This counterpoint between abstraction and concreteness, between the conceptual and, say, the material, can be noticed particularly in the different ways two kinds of examples operate. Examples of abstract points clarify those issues when successful, whereas physical manifestations of similar abstract points often suggest doubts about the usefulness and indeed the adequacy of the clarity that language alone allows. In short, literary texts not only describe but often show the familiar truth that our lives are richer than our theories.

If the general point that literary works do on occasion exhibit some kinds of truths is reasonably plain, the particular point of just how such works accomplish this exhibition remains to be clarified. One way to effect such a clarification, I think, is to recall and to criticize sympathetically some theories first proposed by Meinong in the interest of pursuing one step further our inquiries into part of the still-controversial legacy of eighteenth-century aesthetics—the problematic notion of the aesthetic itself.

Emotional Presentations

Meinong's work on "emotional presentation" and on other topics as well has been largely obscured in Anglo-American circles by the inordinate prominence of his much-criticized theory of objects. This prominence is largely the result of the lack of translations of Meinong's work and the importance both of Bertrand Russell's early article in *Mind* and of J. N. Findlay's study of Meinong, which first appeared in the thirties.[5] Recently, however, renewed attention to other areas of Meinong's philosophy, together with the completion of the publication of Meinong's collected works, has begun to enlarge our appreciation of this many-sided philosopher.[6]

A useful general orientation of Meinong's work that sets the context for our own more narrow interests there can be found in the memoir of his life and works that Meinong himself wrote in 1914.[7] In Meinong's own view, his most important academic contributions included the establishment of the first experimental psychology laboratory in Austria (at Graz, in 1894), and especially the development of the Philosophy Department at Graz, which included among others Vittorio Benussi, Alois Höfler, Ernst Mally, and Stephan Witasek.[8] Meinong's major fields of research were epistemology, psychology, and ethics. Each of these areas was in some way already marked by the influence of his teacher Franz Brentano, who first steered Meinong to the works of Hume. In his *Hume Studies I* and *Hume Studies II* Meinong concerned himself particularly with the theory of abstraction, the theory of concepts,

[5]B. Russell, "Meinong's Theory of Complexes and Assumptions," *Mind* 8(1904): 204–19, 336–54; J. N. Findlay, *Meinong's Theory of Objects* (Oxford, 1933; 2d ed., 1963). See R. Grossmann's defense of Russell, "Non-existent Objects versus Definite Descriptions," *Australasian Journal of Philosophy* 62(1984): 363–77. The background can be found in D. J. Marti-Huong, *Die Gegenstandstheorie von A. Meinong* (Stuttgart, 1984).

[6]A. Meinong, *Gesamtausgabe*, ed. R. Haller and R. Kindinger, 7 vols. (Graz, 1968–75). For early bibliography see M. Lenoci, "Bibliografia degli studi su A. Meinong," *Rivista di Filosofia Neo-Scolastica* 62(1970): 437–73, and the annotated bibliography in her excellent book, *La theoria della cognoscenza in A. Meinong* (Milan, 1972), 305–69. More recent work is cited in M. L. Schubert-Kalsi's *Meinong's Theory of Knowledge* (Dordrecht, 1987).

[7]See appendix 2 in R. Grossmann, *Meinong* (London, 1974), 230–35, hereafter cited as "Memoir." Meinong summarized his work in much greater detail in R. Schwundt, ed., *Die deutsche Philosophie der Gegenwart in Selbstdarstellungen*, vol. 1 (Leipzig, 1921), 91–150.

[8]For the background of Meinong's work see J. C. Nyiri, ed., *Austrian Philosophy: Studies and Texts* (Munich, 1981), and W. M. Johnston, *The Austrian Mind* (Berkeley, 1972), 290–308, hereafter cited as Johnston 1972. For Meinong's students see K. Wolf, "Die Grazer Schule: Gegendstandstheorie und Wertlehre," *Wissenschaft und Weltbild* 21(1968): 31–56. An important recent work on a key topic is K. Lambert's *Meinong and the Principle of Independence* (Cambridge, 1983). R. M. Chisholm's essays are helpful: *Brentano and Meinong Studies* (Atlantic Highlands, N. J., 1982). Good essays can be found in R. Haller, ed., *Jenseits von Sein und Nichtsein: Beiträge zur Meinong Forschung* (Graz, 1972), hereafter cited as Haller 1972.

and the theory of relations, work that still requires examination in the light of Hume's aesthetics.[9] Later these studies were to be pursued in the three fields already mentioned.

One topic first touched on at this time, however, which was to be of particular importance for his work on emotional presentations, was the notion of surmises. This topic, Meinong claimed, "had been completely neglected by the tradition in logic and epistemology."[10] Somewhat later, in his book *Über Annahmen*,[11] a further idea became clear that stands behind the work on emotional presentation. Among other things, Meinong tried to indicate in the 1902 work "an additional kind of experience which, as it were, lies between presentation and judgment, which has an analogue in the presentations of imagination, and which, in turn, points to analogous cases in the area of emotions and desires, thus suggesting an extension of the concept of imagination from the intellectual area to the emotional one, and hence to all the basic classes of inner experiences."[12] In his later work *On Emotional Presentation*,[13] Meinong thought he had successfully overcome the psychologistic orientations in the earlier publications on what he thought of most fundamentally as value theory. It was in this area that perhaps his most famous student from his period as privatdocent in Vienna (1878–82), Christian von Ehrenfels, was to center most of his own important work.

One of Meinong's modern admirers, R. M. Chisholm, has provided a helpful brief overview of the content of Meinong's 1917 work that will prove useful to have on hand for general orientation when we come shortly to look at some of the details. "There is an analogy," Chisholm writes, "between the way in which we come to know, say, that the temperature is high and the way in which we come to know that the temperature is agreeable. . . . If it is by means of a subjective feeling that we perceive the temperature to be agreeable, it is also by means of a subjective sensation that we

---

[9]See K. F. Barber, *Meinong's Hume Studies: Translation and Commentary* (Ann Arbor, 1967, microfilm); and his articles, "Meinong's Hume Studies: Part I: Meinong's Nominalism," *Philosophy and Phenomenological Research* 30(1969): 550–67, and "Meinong's Hume Studies: Part II: Meinong's Analysis of Relations," *Philosophy and Phenomenological Research* 31(1970): 564–84.

[10]"Memoir," 233.

[11](Leipzig, 1902; revised and expanded, 1910); translated J. Hean (London, 1977); see L. D. Broad's important early review in *Mind* 22(1913): 90–102.

[12]"Memoir," 234. Cf. the related but importantly different distinction between presentation and representation in A. Amagasaki, "The Function of the Subject Complex in *Tanka*," *Aesthetics* 3(1988): 91–101.

[13]First published 1917 and now in the *Gesamtausgabe*, vol. 3.

perceive the temperature to be high. In neither case is the subjective experience the object of the presentation; in neither case is our apprehension a matter of inference or of reasoning from effect to cause."[14] But this basic idea must be situated in a somewhat fuller sketch of the contents of Meinong's *On Emotional Presentation*.

Meinong's 1917 book, Findlay writes in his foreword to the 1972 English translation, "is one of the most magnificently thorough of his works and perhaps the only fully lucid and intelligible theory of the possibility of there being values at once given in and through emotion and yet also ontologically independent of emotion or of any subjective attitude."[15]

This work, however, is difficult despite its relative brevity, and the short account we do have is filled with elliptical sections that are only partly filled out with the help of the related materials found in the *Nachlass* and finally available in the collected works. Nonetheless, the basic ideas in this work can be set out briefly without, perhaps, excessive distortion if we keep in mind Chisholm's general summary and, in addition, an elaboration of that point. Both indicate the major theme here for our own purposes. The elaboration runs as follows: "How we feel toward things and what we demand of things 'raises ... a new creation'; objects come before us in a new light as precious or base, lovely or unlovely, authentically true or spuriously false, or as simply attractive or unattractive.... And where there can be this sort of objectivity, there can also be evident knowledge; and we reach the ultimate paradox that love and faith with their strong element of feeling and wish, may nonetheless be revealers of the nature of things."[16]

This passage is related, Findlay points out, to Husserl's position in *Ideen I*, sections 116, 117, and 152, although despite *Ideen I*'s being published in 1913 there seems to be no direct influence.

---

[14]"Meinong, Alexius," in *The Encylopedia of Philosophy*, ed. P. Edwards (New York, 1968), 6:262–63. See Chisholm's influential anthology *Realism and the Background of Phenomenology*, 2d ed. (New York, 1967), and his articles "Beyond Being and Non-being," *Philosophical Studies* 24(1973): 245–55, and "Homeless Objects," *Revue Internationale de Philosophie* 17(1973): 207 ff.

[15]Translated by M. L. Schubert-Kalsi (Evanston, Ill., 1972), xi. The translation is cited hereafter as *EP*. In the following summary I rely on Findlay's excellent account. See also his earlier remark about Meinong's work as "what is probably the most brilliantly elaborated of all theories of the possibility of what may be called 'emotional knowledge'" (*Axiological Ethics* [London, 1970], 24). See two of his other pieces on Meinong, "Einige Hauptpunkte in Meinongs philosophischer Psychologie," in Haller 1972: 15–24; and "Meinong the Phenomenologist," *Revue Internationale de Philosophie* 27(1973): 161–77.

[16]Findlay's foreword to *EP*, xvi.

Meinong's own position, Findlay continues, was already stated in his article, "Für die Psychologie und gegen den Psychologismus in der allgemeinen Werttheorie."[17] Further similarities between Meinong and Husserl include their interest in a nonempirical psychology, the concept of intentionality, Brentano's tripartite division of mental acts into representations or ideas, judgments, and volitions (included here are feelings, emotions, desires, and volitions, the set of which Meinong called "assumptions"), and the notion of an immanent element in experience (Twardowski's notion of content). These similarities, however, should not lead us to overlook the distinctive emphasis in Meinong's doctrine, not on the parallels between truths and values, but on the range of objective modalities that judgmental acts about these truths and values can project onto the states of affairs (Husserl's *Sachverhalte*) or "objectives" (Meinong) correlated with them.[18] Now, however, we need to look at the context of this doctrine in more detail.

By "presentation" Meinong understands an idea's bringing something before consciousness, whether some aspects of our own inner experience (self-presentation—a very obscure notion in Meinong)[19] or the presentation of something else (other-presentation). In either case Meinong holds that presentation is not effected at the level of mere acquaintance with something, but occurs only at the level of judgment.[20] For he had argued in *Über Annahmen* that something can be taken as existing or as of a particular character only at the level of judgment. Besides these two basic kinds of presentation, there are many others including both total- and partial-presentation, which Meinong takes obscurely to overlap with self- and other-presentation. Thus other permutations appear. One possibility is Findlay's "I manage to refer to the anguished discovery of the dead Romeo by Juliet by counterfeit states of belief and dismay in myself. In such a case we have my *whole* unserious state of mind, helping to present *another* whole serious state of mind, and we

[17]*Logos* 3(1912): 13 ff.

[18]See A. Süssbauer, "Propositionen und Sachverhalte in der österreichischen Philosophie von Bolzano bis Poper," *Philosophia Naturalis* 24(1984): 479–99. Husserl's *Sachverhalten* and Meinong's *Annahmen* have an interesting history. "The notion of the circumstance or state of affairs as a unique kind of object of conscious reference," Findlay writes, "was anticipated by the Stoic doctrine of *lekta* and by Bolzano's doctrine of propositions-in-themselves (*Sätze an sich*)" (*Axiological Ethics*, 28).

[19]See Schubert-Kalsi's introduction to *EP*, xlvii–li.

[20]See, however, J. Hintikka, "Knowledge by Acquaintance and Individuation by Acquaintance," in Haller 1972: 205–22.

have therefore a case of *total-presentation* which is also a case of *other-presentation*."[21]

Among these variations is the idea of a partial-presentation that is also a case of other-presentation, as in the case of some things' being for Meinong at least as objectively boring or ridiculous as other things are objectively crooked or slow. But here we have moved from the realm of representations or ideas to that of feelings, the second in Brentano's triad.[22] Thus I have a feeling about something and this feeling presents itself to me in its act-aspect, as Husserl would say. But in addition, the suggestion here is, the same feeling in its content-aspect may project onto the object some kind of nonfeeling content. The problem, of course, is finding a satisfactory account of what Meinong is calling "content," the "experiential element which connects the experience with one appropriate object."[23] And what is problematic is determining, as Findlay notes, what the status of this "element" is, whether something merely postulated or something claimed as intuited. This difficulty becomes a cardinal one, as we shall see when Meinong turns to discuss aesthetic feelings.

After proposing and sorting through a series of distinctions about acts and contexts in all three of the Brentanist realms, Meinong settles on a comprehensive distinction among "four distinct objects of feeling-presentation: (1) the agreeable (disagreeable), projected by idea-act-feelings, though not involving feelings as part of their meaning; (2) the beautiful (ugly), projected by idea- and assumption-content-feelings, . . . ; (3) the true and probably true (false and doubtful), in a special axiological sense, which are projected by judgment-act-feelings; and finally (4) the valuable or good (disvaluable or bad), projected by judgment-content-feelings."[24] This catalog of course immediately raises fears once again of an overgrown theory of objects.[25] But despite the proliferation of objects of various orders, we must not overlook the suggestiveness especially of the third item for our purposes. The account of the true and the probably true is particularly useful in that the indication here of the act-aspect of feelings at the level of judgment provides us with

[21]Foreword to *EP*, xix.
[22]See G. Bergmann, *Realism: A Critique of Brentano and Meinong* (Madison, Wis., 1967).
[23]Foreword to *EP*, xx.
[24]Foreword to *EP*, xxiii.
[25]See R. Campbell, "Did Meinong Plant a Jungle?" *Philosophical Papers* 1(1972): 89–102, and R. Routley, *Meinong's Overgrown Jungle* (Canberra, 1979).

a nonsentential glass on Ingarden's notion of literary truths as quasi-judgments. Thus the inadequacies of Ingarden's discussion of quasi-judgments are not in principle objections, since that account may be revisable in terms of Husserl's act/content distinction plus Meinong's notion of projection.[26] Before we can see the point of Meinong's own description, however, we require still further precision.

Meinong is concerned, as we have noticed, not just with intellectual presentations but especially with "emotional" ones—that is, with all those mental experiences that involve the presentation to consciousness of attributes of the pleasant, the beautiful, the valuable, and the obligatory. All these attributes are mental objects of different sorts. Each may be described, Meinong thought, by analyzing the kind of mental experience that involves their presentation to consciousness. But Meinong hoped to be able to describe the mental objects independently of such mental experiences. This is one of the major reasons he continued to polemicize against psychologisms of different sorts.

In the famous passage quoted in the epigraph, Meinong writes: "When I say, 'The sky is blue,' and then say, 'The sky is beautiful,' a property is attributed to the sky in either case. In the second case a feeling participates in the apprehension of the property, as, in the first case, an idea does. And it is natural to let the feeling be the presentative factor in the second case, as an idea is always taken to be in the first case."[27] The major point of this passage I adumbrated earlier in saying that feelings not only may present to consciousness the quality of an inner experience, they may also characterize external objects in particular ways. In this sense Meinong spoke of something as being ugly in itself, not just in my consciousness of it. To put this point another way, consider Schubert-Kalsi's comment on this passage. "In analogy to ideas, feelings function as 'content-presentatives of objects.' In the same way as ideas are called content-presentations or partial presentations and passive experiences, so feelings are called content-presentations, partial presentations, and passive experiences."[28]

---

[26]I discuss Ingarden's view on quasi-judgments in *Fictions, Philosophies, and the Problems of Poetics* (Ithaca, 1988), 93–97. Husserl's views on Meinong, however, have subtle nuances. See, for example, his "Meinongs Unterscheidung in distribuierte und indistribuierte Gegenstände," in his *Zur Phänomenologie des inneren Zeitbewusstseins* (The Hague, 1966), 216–28. See also H. Shermann, "Meinong und Husserl," Ph.D. diss. (Louvain, 1970).

[27]*EP*, 28.

[28]Schubert-Kalsi's introduction to *EP*, lx.

Finally, the feelings that present values are not true or false but are what Meinong calls justified or not justified. But these justifications, since they concern higher-order entities (values that depend upon objectives), themselves depend on the justification of judgments about values. Thus some feelings may be unjustified to the degree that they depend upon value judgments that are either intellectually erroneous (a sugar pill valued for its healing power) or counterconsensual (the Venus de Milo is not valued as a great work of sculpture). This concern for justification must be kept in mind when we consider Meinong's talk about feelings, attributing certain characteristics to nonmental objects. We must recall too that the entities to which feeling directs its attention need not always be extramental. Thus, feelings can be taken as attributing characteristics to individuals as well as to fictions.

Contents and Objects

After this general overview of Meinong's *On Emotional Presentation*, I now look more carefully and more critically at some of the details in his treatment of the presentation of values through feeling. This more specific investigation will involve a closer look at the notion of presentation, the notion of content, and the way feelings present their objects to consciousness. The point of going into such detail will be to suggest the fruitfulness of Meinong's views for our understanding of aesthetic feelings.

Presentation, as we have already seen in general, is a complicated notion that Meinong treated in a variety of places.[29] Part of the complication involves the distinction between presentation and idea. This distinction turns mainly on Meinong's claim that "there are objects, i.e., *objectives*, which can be apprehended even though we cannot have ideas of them."[30] A supporting reason for the distinction is the observation that some ideas enable us to apprehend a mental object, even in its specific character, although apprehension remains incomplete.[31] Since for Meinong it is not the form but the content of a particular thought that allows us to

---

[29]See Meinong's references in his note 1 in *EP*, 3.

[30]*EP*, 4. See C. J. Kelly, "On Things That Do Not Now Exist and Never Have Existed," *Proceedings of the American Catholic Philosophical Association* 61(1987): 181–90.

[31]*EP*, 3.

apprehend the mental object of that thought, Meinong wants to say that "the content presents the object to thought," and in this respect the content might be called the "presentative." Meinong here, as elsewhere, seems to be relying not just on these considerations but also on experimental work carried out at Graz by Alois Höfler and Stephan Witasek.[32] But the cardinal notion of presentation as in some sense the function of the content of an idea is Meinong's, as is the related notion that every presentation presupposes an idea as its mental object, or what Meinong calls its "presuppositional object" (Voraussetzungsgegendstand).[33]

This notion of presentation is common to both intellectual presentation of ideas and emotional presentation of values. In the first case the presentatives are the contents of ideas, whereas in the second they are the contents of what Meinong calls, in the larger sense, thoughts—that is, judgments and assumptions. In the Nachlass under the heading "On the Concept and Term 'Emotional Presentation,'" Meinong adds several further notes to this description.[34] Thus he speaks of what the presentative presents as the "presentation." This notion enables him to describe intellectual presentation in terms of three steps: (1) The presentative usually comes first in time; (2) the presentative conditions the direction of thought to the object in question; (3) the presentative is in its nature so closely related to the object to be apprehended that the object, the presentation, will change whenever the presentative changes.[35] The final point that has to do with the modification of the object is especially important for our concerns. We already note, however, the incipient ambiguity in Meinong's talk of "object," since we know from our general survey that he is ultimately interested in claiming modifications not just in the mental object but in the actual object as well.

When this description is applied to emotional presentation—that is, to those situations in which thoughts (judgments and assumptions) and not ideas apprehend certain mental objects—Meinong introduces several changes. There is no temporal priority of the emotional presentative over the presentation. Moreover, the emo-

---

[32]EP, 3, n. 2. Cf. the papers in B. Smith, ed., Foundations of Gestalt Theory (Munich, 1988).

[33]EP, 9. See G. Küng's helpful article, "The Intentional and the Real Object," Dialectica 38(1984): 143–56.

[34]Selections from Nachlass that I am relying on here are in the appendix to EP, cited hereafter as Nachlass.

[35]Nachlass, 160.

tional presentative is not external to the recipient (the recipient being that to which something is presented) but internal "whether or not the whole thought-experience or merely the act-aspect is treated as recipient."[36] Thus Meinong speaks of outer and inner presentation. In the first case the presentative is an idea; in the second it is a content.

Besides these descriptions of presentation in general, we recall that for Meinong in every case of intellectual and emotional presentation we need to ask whether the presentation is self-presentation or other-presentation. As I noted already, the notion of self-presentation as such is opaque. Meinong calls it only "presentation of the subject's own simultaneous experiences."[37] But he glosses this distinction with another between content-presentation (the presentative is the contents of the idea or thought) and act-presentation (the presentative is the act of the idea of thought). Since in act-presentation the act is not the only presentative factor, however, we may speak of act-presentation as partial presentation. Thus the original distinction between self- and other-presentation is first transmuted into a distinction between act- and content-presentation and finally into one between partial and whole presentation. But this account is somewhat misleading, since Meinong holds that there are two kinds of other-presentation, one partial and the other whole. Thus the terms of the distinctions must not be placed in parallel but need to be construed as allowing some overlap.

We can make this account clearer if we now try to distinguish more sharply, within the realm of emotional presentation only, between total other-presentation and partial other-presentation.

If we grant Meinong that we may have a feeling without necessarily having an idea of a feeling, and that consequently the notion of *emotional* (if not intellectual) self-presentation makes sense, then the question arises with regard to emotional *other*-presentation as to just what the presentative is. And of course the answer depends on just which kind of thought we wish to consider, whether judgments (serious thoughts) or assumptions (say, imaginative thoughts). Arguing by analogy with the case of both perceptual ideas and serious thoughts leaving dispositional traces, Meinong claims that imaginative thoughts depend on the dispositional traces of serious thoughts.[38] Thus when I feel myself imaginatively into a

---

[36]*Nachlass*, 160.
[37]*EP*, 39.
[38]See *EP*, 40. Cf. my discussion, "Feelings and Fictions," *Journal of Aesthetics and Art Criticism* 43(1985): 375–83.

particular situation, say, in finding myself moved emotionally when reading a novel, even though my imaginative feelings are not "serious" they depend upon the dispositional traces of serious thoughts. "In such imaginative experiences," Meinong writes, "the means are clearly given by which to apprehend in memory past emotional experiences without having to depend upon presenting ideas."[39] Here we have a case of emotional total other-presentation.

Emotional partial other-presentation, Meinong holds, is more difficult to work out. The problem is with the existence of *partial* presentations. For both psychological experiments and linguistic analyses raise doubts here. In the first case Meinong adduces the fact that most persons confound gustatory smelling with tasting, and in the second "language seems to be clearer concerning the objects of those primarily expressed experiences such as the judgment (A is B) than in the case of secondarily expressed experiences" such as "I feel pain."[40] Nonetheless, other data are available that point us in the direction of partial presentations. Meinong's examples, again from the *Nachlass*, include sentences like "the flower is pretty," "this or that should be the case," or "in order for A to be, B is." Thus he writes, "The predicate in 'the flower is red' is analogous to the predicate in 'the flower is pretty' and exhibits an object that can only be presented by a feeling."[41]

The issue comes down to whether in the case of emotional presentation we can differentiate between act and contents as presentatives. And Meinong's central strategy is to qualify the sense in which something is the content of a feeling. If we take the cases of someone's liking the color red, for example, and someone else's having the idea of red, both persons' presentations have a content. In the second case the content is that of the idea. In the first case, however, the content is not so much that of the feeling as of what Meinong calls "the experience which constitutes the psychological presupposition of the feeling... , the presuppositional content of the feeling."[42] And the presuppositional content of emotional presentations Meinong ascribes to the act component. But since the distinction between partial and total presentation is made largely but not exclusively in terms of act and contents, cases of presuppositional contents provide us with instances of partial other emotional presentations. With the notion of emotional pre-

[39]*EP*, 25.
[40]*Nachlass*, 162.
[41]*Nachlass*, 163.
[42]*EP*, 27.

sentation now sketched more fully, I turn to the closely related theme of content.

Content for Meinong is correlative with act. But this correlation is a peculiar one in that neither one term nor the other may be abstracted from the correlation. Yet content, "while it cannot by some process of abstraction be separated from the act,...can, in relation to the act, be, as it were, pushed into the foreground."[43] Here again the gestalt experiments, especially those of Höfler and Ehrenfels, are part of Meinong's context. Granted that some kind of rational distinction can be made between act and content, however, Meinong takes another step in distinguishing between the object that belongs to the content and the content itself.[44] This tenuous distinction, it is conceded, is hard to discern in the case of emotional presentation. When the act is the presentative in the case of other-presentation, we have total presentation; otherwise presentation is partial only—that is, either when the content is the presentative or when we have the case of self-presentation.

Now total presentations in the form of act-presentations are, says Meinong, "normally accomplished by imaginative experiences," emotional, therefore, and not intellectual presentations.[45] And these experiences fall into two basic kinds, either quasi-serious experiences or what Meinong calls shadowy experiences. The first kind is characterized by the presence of intuitive ideas that have a close affinity with the serious ideas of perception, whereas the second lacks these ideas and consequently is a much more fugitive and elusive experience. We may, that is, imagine the misery of men at war and also empathize with these men in the sense of feeling our way imaginatively into their situations. In both cases we are dealing with imaginative experiences, but only the first is marked with the presence of quasi-serious perceptual ideas. The quasi-serious imaginative experiences are construed as aids in intellectual presentation of serious experiences themselves, whereas the shadowy imaginative experiences are construed as aids in the emotional presentation of values.

We need to note that Meinong is not insensitive to the metaphorical character of all his talk about "content," an expression he uses over an almost twenty-year period.[46] His own usage varies

---

[43]EP, 39.
[44]See EP, 40.
[45]EP, 24.
[46]See EP, 48. For the general background here see K. Wolf, "Der Bedeutungswandel von 'Gegenstand' in der Schule Meinongs," in Haller 1972: 63–68.

considerably during this period, largely because of his sympathetically critical reaction to similar usages in Twardowski's great work of 1894, Husserl's five senses of the term in his *Logical Investigation* of 1900, and the work of Theodore Lipps. A first precision in his use of the term in *On Emotional Presentation* derives from perception. "When I observe the blue of the sky or the green of a meadow," Meinong writes, "the two objects blue and green are naturally not apprehended by two utterly similar experiences, though they are similar in some respects, especially in the circumstance that they are both ideas, or perhaps even perceptual ideas. Now that in which the two ideas must differ in order to be such as to apprehend different objects I called the 'content' of these ideas."[47]

A second precision results from the strategy of trying to distinguish those elements of an object that change from those that do not. Once we understand Meinong's peculiar use of "act" as meaning something other than activity and hence the act-aspect of ideas as passive experiences, we can make sense of his subsequent claim that "ideas as acts can change, and that the change does not concern their content is shown by the fact that the object to be apprehended by the ideas remains unaffected by the change."[48] Thus content is what remains unchanged despite modifications in the act-aspect.[49]

Further precisions are harder to come by. For example, distinctions between content and object are often to be found in the literature, but the distinction remains, at least for Meinong, very difficult to maintain. "Usually," he writes, "it seems what is called 'content' is itself an object, by preference an object of apprehension, and a more immediate rather than a remoter object."[50] But as his own metaphors show, these reflections are not without their own obscurities. Similar obscurities cloud most attempts to explicate the notion of content by appealing to a distinction between immanent and transcendent features. All these difficulties are magnified when we turn from the contents of ideas that Meinong calls "objects" to those of judgments and assumptions he calls "objectives."

Without extending his treatment further, Meinong is satisfied to summarize his notion of content in terms of partial presentations. The presentative in all such experiences is the content either by itself, in which case no process of abstraction takes place, or as the

[47]*EP*, 50.
[48]*EP*, 50.
[49]Note the apparent inconsistency between this passage and the *Nachlass*, 167.
[50]*EP*, 52.

main element in conjunction with a subordinate role played by the act-aspect. With this qualification, then, Meinong concludes: "The content is that part of an experience which is so coordinated with the object to be apprehended by the experience, and immediately presented by the latter, that it varies or remains constant with, and in dependence upon, the object. The act is that part of an experience which is independently variable in respect to its object."[51]

So much for fuller detail on the notion of content.

Showing and Cognitivity

In light of Meinong's discussion of emotional presentation, I now return to the different senses of showing and bring at least some of these recalcitrant materials into a kind of order.

Besides the suggestions from Feyerabend we have already seen in this chapter, some helpful contrasts are to be found in work on the imagination that can give us some of the distance we now require on Meinong's detailed reflections. Ronald W. Hepburn's aim, to take only one example, is to investigate various related problems that center on the difficulties of appraising one use of poetic discourse.[52] The use in question is what Mary Warnock has called "concrete imagination."[53] Although Hepburn thinks that concrete imagination can allow poetic discourse to make cognitive claims, his emphasis on appraising such claims rather than on describing just how these claims are made is somewhat beside the point of our concern with the presentation of aesthetic feelings and the showing of aesthetic truths. Nonetheless, before entering on the major part of his investigation Hepburn does touch on several descriptive issues in a suggestive way.

To begin with, we need to notice here that the guiding assumption construes literary discourse as capable of making truth claims. In his own terms, Hepburn presupposes "that a poem *can* be concerned with truth, and with truth-to-how-the-world-is outside

---

[51]*EP*, 55. See also R. Routley, "Rehabilitating Meinong's Theory of Objects," *Revue Internationale de Philosophie* 27(1973): 224–54.

[52]See R. W. Hepburn, "Poetry and 'Concrete Imagination': Problems of Truth and Illusion," *British Journal of Aesthetics* 12(1972): 3–18.

[53]"The Concrete Imagination," *Journal of the British Society for Phenomenology* 1(1970): 6–12. See also her related paper, "Imagination in Sartre," *British Journal of Aesthetics* 10(1970): 322–36. Contrast her book *Imagination* (Berkeley, 1976) with the very different approach in E. Casey, *Imagination* (Evanston, Ill., 1979).

the poem."[54] Hepburn is aware of other theories that deny his own presupposition. But he holds that such theories "exaggerate and distort when they deny that a poem can also make a statement about the extra-poetic world."[55]

Further, he rightly points out that attentiveness to putative truth claims that might seem to be part of some literary artworks need not deflect attention from the internal coherence of the work itself. Hepburn goes on to formulate a position that governs his subsequent reflections on the appraisal issue. "In a word," he writes, "I want to say that a poetic statement can be appraised as true or false without our having to deny that the poem has been creative, and without having to say that its truth or falsity are matters of the internal relations of its elements."[56]

Finally, and most interesting from our perspective, is a brief description of four ways literary discourse can be concerned with truth. First, a literary work such as Lucretius's *De rerum natura* or Pope's *Essay on Man* "may make a direct statement on any subject whatever" and make "truth claims directly." Second, a literary work "may seek to be 'true-to'...its subject matter." Third, a literary work may disclose the obstacles to successful communication. And last, a literary work may make truth claims by presenting "a *concrete* description or image of some phenomenon which points beyond itself and reveals the way things are."[57] This fourth way some literary works are taken as cognitive is then illustrated, especially with the help of several Sartrean descriptions such as that of the viscous in *La nausée*. These illustrations provide the final gloss on how literary works can refer beyond themselves. "Perhaps the strongest reasonable claim here," Hepburn concludes, "is that *if* you organize your view of the whole round a certain image—decay, fecundity, viscosity, struggle—you will find that a greater coherence is given to it than by any alternative image."[58]

Now whatever judgment we ultimately want to make about whether this pointing beyond itself can be appraised, especially in the light of Ingarden's similar investigations with which we began, we should already be clear that the cognitive status of such con-

[54]Hepburn's emphasis, 1972: 3.

[55]Hepburn cites R. K. Elliott, "Poetry and Truth," *Analysis* 27(1967): 77–85.

[56]Hepburn 1972: 4. Some of this can be transposed into the context of the aesthetics of theater. See, for example, K. Sasaki, "Expérience de l'espace au théâtre: Projet d'une autre essence du théâtre," *Journal of the Faculty of Letters* (Tokyo) 12(1987): 55–65.

[57]Hepburn 1972: 4–9.

[58]Hepburn 1972: 6–7.

crete description is not uncontroversial. The immediate issue is just how we are to interpret these concrete descriptions. We should set aside for our present discussion, I think, at least three possible interpretations. We need not, that is, construe concrete description as functioning in terms of some kind of inference once we recall the difficulties of parsing such a term in literary contexts. Nor do we need to interpret these descriptions that point beyond themselves by appealing to some counterfactual explication, because such explications introduce too many difficulties of their own. Rather, we need to recall Meinong's discussion of emotional presentation.

At the outset of this chapter I suggested that we have little difficulty attaching general sense to the idea that some literary works may exhibit very general kinds of truths. One example of such a truth seemed evident in Feyerabend's reflections on Brecht's Galileo play—our lives are often richer than our theories. Moreover, in working our way through some of the complexities in Meinong's laminated doctrine of kinds of mental objects and species of emotional presentations, we came upon the distinction between "quasi-serious imaginative experience" and "shadowy imaginative experiences." I suggest now that, however speculative, such a distinction allows us to attach some general sense also to the idea that some works of art and especially some literary works may exhibit more particular kinds of truths. An example of such a truth would be, on reading imaginatively Tolstoy's description of the Battle of Borodino, that Napoléon was uncharacteristically miserable at the plight of his soldiers going down to defeat. Here, of course, the emphasis would be on the first and not on the second pole of Meinong's distinction, since what is at issue is not so much the presence or absence of empathic feelings in the reader for either Napoléon or his soldiers but the presence of what Meinong calls an intuitive idea.

In both cases—that of general truths about, say, the irreducible richness of human experience and that of particular truths about, say, the state of mind of a historical personage in a historical novel—some may choose to describe this matter further by claiming that we have genuine instances of how some literary works can point beyond themselves. In short, some may wish to claim that literary artworks may indeed show or exhibit truths in this way. Hence the conclusion might be drawn that some literary artworks are cognitive in the precise sense that they are sources of knowing that something or other is the case. In other words, there may indeed be good and sufficient reasons for holding that literary artworks cannot properly speaking say anything true or false, although they may more loosely speaking show something as true or false. Part of trying to account for such a showing, and perhaps more generally for the cognitive aspects of the aesthetic, requires looking anew at Meinong's theory of emotional presentation as a key element in the realist backgrounds of modern aesthetics.

Appendix 10: The Presentations of Feeling and Desire

The mental objects of intellectual presentation Meinong called "objects" and "objectives," whereas those of emotional presentation he termed "dignitatives" and "desideratives." The first pair is somewhat beside our concern here, so I will be content to discuss only the second.[59] We should note several points in passing, however. "Objects" for Meinong include individuals, most relations, and most properties (except aesthetic and moral relations and properties), whereas "objectives" include complex "objects," the being of "objects" (their existence, subsistence, or what Meinong calls their *Aussersein*), and *the facts that* "objects" have certain ways of being or properties. Ideas present "objects," whereas judgments and "assumptions" present "objectives," the former by the emphatic acceptance or rejection in its act-aspect and the latter by, again in its act-aspect, its mere entertaining of a mental object without any acceptance or rejection at all. Emotional presentations are act-presentations and total ones for Meinong, whereas idea presentations are content-presentations and partial ones.[60]

When we turn to the mental objects of emotional presentation, dignitatives and desideratives, we need to keep in mind Meinong's interest in determining whether there are distinctive mental entities called moral and aesthetic objects.

[59]See Schubert-Kalsi's introduction to her translation of *EP*, hereafter cited as "Schubert-Kalsi." Some of the issues here are very important for understanding so-called "fictional objects" in literary works of art. See T. Parsons, *Non-existent Objects* (New Haven, 1980), and D. Hunter's objections to Parsons precisely on the grounds that Parsons's formalization of Meinong's theory of objects leaves no room for fictional objects: "Reference and Meinongian Objects," *Grazer Philosophische Studien* 14(1981): 23–36.
[60]Some help here can be found in E. Morscher, "Von Bolzano zu Meinong: Zur Geschichte des logischen Realismus," in Haller 1972:69–102; M. S. Gram, "Ontology and the Theory of Descriptions," in *Essays on B. Russell*, ed. E. D. Klemke, 118–43 Urbana, Ill., 1970); and R. Haller, "Über Meinong," *Revue Internationale de Philosophie* 27(1973): 148–60.

Dignitatives include the beautiful, the good, the true, the pleasant, and their contraries. Moreover, each of these properties can be combined with another. These properties depend for their occurrence on other properties and hence are referred to as objects of a higher order, that is, entities that presuppose other entities as their bases.[61] In turn the second kind of objects of emotional presentation, desideratives, are objects of a still higher order in the sense that they depend for the occurrence on dignitatives. Obligations thus depend on the presupposition of their being values to begin with. Moreover, there are two kinds of dignitatives, "simple obligations" and "obligations of means." Instances of the first are entities where value is unconditional, like the value of a great artwork, whereas instances of the second are entities where value is conditional on some purpose, like the value of training in perspective for becoming a painter.

Dignitatives are presented, Meinong holds, through feelings, whereas desideratives are presented through desires. For Meinong feelings are closer to ideas, and they present values, whereas desires present obligations. The nature of the presentation here in each case is difficult to make out clearly because of Meinong's insistence that both objects and objectives are presuppositions for dignatives and that all those are presuppositions for desideratives. This means that describing the nature of those presentations that take place by means of feelings (dignitatives) and desires (desideratives) entails making final sense of both objects and objectives as well as of ideational and judgmental presentation—something neither Meinong himself nor his commentators so far have been able to do in a noncontroversial way. Nonetheless, if we leave aside the final category of desideratives and its presuppositions, we can still make some sense of how feelings present values.

[61]The notion of "order" here derives from Ehrenfels. "To clarify the problem of Non-Existent Objects," W. M. Johnston explains, "Meinong borrowed Ehrenfels's distinction between Gestalt qualities and their foundation (Fundament). This foundation Meinong rechristened a founding content (fundierender Inhalt) or object of a lower order (Inferiora). The Gestalt quality he called, after Ehrenfels, a founded content (fundierter Inhalt) or object of a higher order (Superiora). Objects of lower order can exist, Meinong held, by themselves, whereas objects of a higher order must have those of a lower object to accompany them" (Johnston 1972: 297).

Chapter Eleven

Ingarden and
Aesthetic Structures

The literary work of art is a purely intentional formation. But it is not a psychological phenomenon and it is transcendent to all experiences of consciousness.

—Roman Ingarden

Every work of art of whatever kind has that distinguishing feature that it is not the sort of thing which is completely determined in every respect by the primary level varieties of its qualities.... it contains within itself characteristic lacunae in definition, areas of indeterminateness: it is a schematic creation.

—Roman Ingarden

IN THIS final chapter I look at still another aspect of the problematic notion of the aesthetic and draw on still another figure in the realist backgrounds of modern aesthetics, in the interest of exploring further reflections on aesthetic objects.[1] In dealing with these complicated issues, as we have seen in the cases of Twardowski and Meinong, some unity has seemed especially requisite. Hence I have decided to treat the issues largely with the help of critical and argumentative contrasts. Although others who deal with these topics are also brought in when their views seem particularly rele-

---

[1] For more recent work see Michael Mitias, "Ingarden on the Aesthetic Object," *Philosophy and Phenomenological Research* 45(1985): 357–82. For earlier treatment of this issue see Gary Iseminger's article, "Roman Ingarden and the Aesthetic Object," *Philosophy and Phenomenological Research* 33(1973): 412–20, which I discuss in appendix II. Iseminger has returned to this cardinal issue in "Constituting the Aesthetic Object," in *Studia Estyticzny* (1989), forthcoming.

vant, I have tried to center this discussion mainly on the extremely rich and profound work of Roman Ingarden.[2] This work for some years has strongly influenced that of more widely known theorists such as Mikel Dufrenne in France, Wolfgang Iser in Germany, René Wellek in the United States, and Stefen Morawski in Poland.[3] And now the work deserves a careful rereading in the changing contexts of contemporary aesthetics.

It will be useful to begin with some generalities about Ingarden's work in order to situate the much narrower examination into questions about aesthetic structure that follows. I will turn to the exposition of that doctrine in section 2, reserving a long appendix for the key issue of aesthetic objects, then use section 3 to contrast it with the important alternative views of Monroe Beardsley. Finally, I will attempt to defend Ingarden's position against these particular criticisms and alternatives while leaving the general question about the existence of aesthetic objects open for further reflection. Throughout, my aim will be to draw attention to many of the interesting perspectives Ingarden's work opens up on questions that too often continue to be viewed only in terms of either analytic or hermeneutic approaches.

Ontology and Cognition

Roman Ingarden's aesthetics is a phenomenological oeuvre in the sense that it begins from Husserl's critique of antipsychologism, part of which we explored in chapter 8, and goes on with the help of a modified intuitive method to look for some middle ground

[2]The standard bibliography, which incorporates and much extends that of A. Poltawski, "Bibliografia prac Romana Ingardena 1915–1971," in *Fenomenologia Romana Ingardena*, 19–54 (Warsaw, 1972), is to be found in *Roman Ingarden: Selected Papers in Aesthetics*, ed. P. McCormick, 181–262 (Munich, 1985). See also Petsch, "Roman Ingarden's Works Published by the Polish Scientific Publishers," *Dialectics and Humanism* 2(1975): 123–24. A shorter bibliography based on Poltawski is G. G. Grabowicz's in his translation of *The Literary Work of Art* (Evanston, Ill., 1973), 397–403. References here will be to first translations in English of Ingarden's works (sometimes by Ingarden himself) rather than the Polish originals.

[3]Mikel Dufrenne, *The Phenomenology of Aesthetic Experience*, trans. E. Casey et al. (Evanston, Ill., 1973); W. Iser, *The Act of Reading* (Baltimore, 1978); R. Wellek and A. Warren, *Theory of Literature* (New York, 1949); S. Morawski, *Inquiries into the Fundamentals of Aesthetics* (Cambridge, Mass., 1974). A well-informed discussion of the precursors of Ingarden's work as well as its influences can be found in Grabowicz's introduction to his translation cited above, li–lxx. See also N. Hartmann, *Das Problem des geistigen Seins* (Berlin, 1932).

between versions of idealism and realism.[4] Literary artworks for Ingarden are intentional objects—constructions, that is, that are correlative with authorial mental acts of a specific kind.[5] One of the early accounts of Ingarden's aesthetics in English provides a convenient point of orientation.

> As a phenomenologist, Roman Ingarden takes his starting point in the discussion between epistemological idealism and realism, and he finds a pertinent strategy in finding out how the work of art exists. The work of art has a formal structure which is its mode of being, and this mode of being is related to a situation of life. Behind the formal structure or mode of being of the work of art are the intentions of the artist to give the work of art an artistic significance. This significance is interpreted by the reader, beholder, or listener by means of an intentional activity. So the work of art is not the typography of the text or score, the painted surface, the sculptured stuff, the sounds, the human movements and diction, but the interplay between the transmitting artist and the receiving beholder or listener. The aesthetic object is an intentional object.[6]

This summary comment, despite its overreliance on a communication model of art ("transmitting...receiving") that is irrelevant to Ingarden's aesthetics, is nonetheless a useful overview. For it not only stresses the intentional character of the artwork but also calls

[4]On the realism-idealism problem see Ingarden's "Bemerkungen zum Problem Idealismus-Realismus," in *Festschrift, Edmund Husserl zum 70. Geburtstag gewidmet: Jahrbuch für Philosophie und phänomenologische Forschung, Supplement*, 159–90 (Halle, 1929); "Les modes d'existence et le problème 'idéalisme-réalisme,'" in *Library of the Tenth International Congress of Philosophy*, vol. I (Amsterdam, 1948); "Über die gegenwärtigen Aufgaben der Phänomenologie," *Archivo di Filosofia* 1(1957): 229–41; *Der Streit um die Existenz der Welt*, 4 vols. (Tübingen, 1964–74), 65–75; "Die vier Begriffe der Transzendenz und das Problem des Idealismus bei Husserl," *Analecta Husserliana* 1(1971): 35–74; "About the Motives Which Led Husserl to Transcendental Idealism," in *Phenomenology and Natural Existence* (Albany, N.Y., 1973); and J. Siefert, "Roman Ingarden's Realism," *Reports on Philosophy* 10(1986): 27–43.

[5]Ingarden's major works on aesthetics are *Das literarische Kunstwerk: Eine Untersuchung aus dem Grenzgebiet der Ontologie, Logik und Literaturwissenschaft* (Halle, 1931); *Untersuchungen zur Ontologie der Kunst* (Tübingen, 1962); *Vom Erkennen des literarischen Kunstwerks* (Tübingen, 1968); and *Erlebnis, Kunstwerk und Wert: Vorträge zur Ästhetik, 1957–1967* (Tübingen, 1969). An authoritative view by Ingarden's assistant can be found in D. Gierulanka, "Ingarden's Philosophical Work: A Systematic Outline," in *On the Aesthetics of Roman Ingarden*, ed. B. Dziemidok and P. McCormick, 1–21 (Boston, 1989). See also her classification of Ingarden's work in the same volume's "Selected Bibliography," 297–301.

[6]T. Brunius, "The Aesthetics of Roman Ingarden," *Philosophy and Phenomenological Research* 30(1970): 590–95.

attention indirectly to a triple relationship between the artist's intentional object, the physical work itself, and the reader's intentional object. This relationship, of course, is extremely complex. But until recently we have been able to construe intentionalism only in terms of the artist's intentions. Part of the merit of Ingarden's analysis is its persuasive account of why the intentions of the reader must also find some place in the determination of the artistic nature of the verbal artifact.

These analyses, as the Amsterdam lecture of 1969 showed,[7] proceed across an extensive range of problems stretching from a series of issues in ontology finally formulated in his four-volume masterpiece, *Der Streit um die Existenz der Welt*, through the epistemology of critical cognition, and into the very diverse regions of aesthetic problems in the individual arts.[8] This research centers on the nature of intentional objects. Ingarden "returned to the same themes and issues," as Morawski observed, "analyzing them in new contexts and a new perspective. He avoided definitions, afraid of their illusory character. The deliberate flexibility of terms and indetermination of concepts he used corresponded to his indefatigable digging into all possible aspects: interdependence, connections, or disconnections within the frame of analyzed patterns and structures.... what matters in this practical making of phenomenological aesthetics, is the realm of objects to be grasped, not the logical concepts formally structured in smooth axioms and definitions."[9] And it was specifically in this area of the ontology of aesthetic objects and structures that Ingarden is considered to have made his greatest contribution.

Some idea, however fragmentary, of the range of his work may be gathered from the analysis Ingarden gave of the different areas of

---

[7]"Gastvorlesungen von Roman Ingarden, Amsterdam 14. März, 1969," *Bulletin International d'Esthétique* (Amsterdam) 5(1970): 5–7.

[8]Ingarden's epistemological studies are extremely important for understanding the background of his work both on the realism-idealism problem and on the cognitivity of art. See "Über die Gefahr einer Petitio Principii in der Erkenntnistheorie," *Jahrbuch für Philosophie und Phänomenologische Forschung* 4(1921): 545–68; *Über die Stellung der Erkenntnistheorie im System der Philosophie* (Halle, 1925); "Prinzipien einer erkenntnistheoretischen Betrachtung der ästhetischen Erfahrung," in *Actes du IV Congrès International d'Esthétique* (Athens, 1960–62), 622–31; and "De la connaissance de l'oeuvre littéraire," *Archives de Philosophie* 31(1968): 202–63. For background, see essays in P. Graff and S. Krzemien-Ojak, eds., *Roman Ingarden and Contemporary Polish Aesthetics* (Warsaw, 1975).

[9]S. Morawski, "Ingarden on the Subject-Matter and Method of Aesthetics," in *Roman Ingarden and Contemporary Polish Aesthetics*, ed. P. Graff and S. Krzemien-Ojak, 179 (Warsaw, 1975).

philosophical aesthetics in his late and important paper "Ästhetik und Kunstphilosophie," presented at the Fourteenth International Congress of Philosophy at Vienna in 1968.

Die philosophische Ästhetik umfasst folgende Teilgebiete der Betrachtung: (1) Ontologie des Kunstwerks und zwar a) die allgemeine philosophische Theorie des Aufbaus und der Seinsweise des Kunstwerks überhaupt, b) Ontologie der Kunstwerke der einzelnen Künste (Bild, Architektur, literarische Kunstwerke, usw.). (2) Ontologie des ästhetischen Gegenstands als einer ästhetischen Konkretisation eines Kunstwerks. (3) Phänomenologie des schöpferischen künstlerischen Verhaltens. (4) Das Problem des Stils des Kunstwerks und dessen Beziehung zu seinem Wert. (5) Ästhetische Wertlehre (künstlerische und ästhetische Wert, ihre Fundierung im Kunstwerk und ihre Konstitution im ästhetischen Erlebnis). (6) Phänomenologie des ästhetischen Erlebnisses und die Konstitution des ästhetischen Gegenstandes. (7) Theorie der Erkenntnis der Kunstwerke und der Erkenntnis ästhetischer Gegenstände und insbesondere der Erkenntnis der ästhetischen Werte (Kritik der Bewertung). (8) Theorie des Sinnes und der Funktion der Kunst (bzw. der ästhetischen Gegenstände) im Leben des Menschen (Metaphysik der Kunst?).[10]

Philosophical aesthetics includes the following subdivisions for treatment (1) ontology of the work of art, and in particular a) the general philosophical theory of the structure and mode of existence of the work of art, b) ontology of the work of art in the individual arts (painting, architecture, literary artworks, and so on). (2) Ontology of the aesthetic object as an aesthetic concretization of an artwork. (3) phenomenology of the creative artistic activity. (4) The problem of the style of the work of art and the relation to its value. (5) Doctrines of aesthetic value (artistic and aesthetic values, their foundation in the artwork and their constitution in the aesthetic experience). (6) Phenomenology of the aesthetic experience and the constitution of the aesthetic object. (7) Theory of the cognition of the work of art and the cognition of aesthetic objects and in particular of the cognition of aesthetic values (critique of valuation). (8) Theory of the meaning and the function of art (with respect to aesthetic objects) in human life (the metaphysics of art?).

All these different problems arise for Ingarden in related ways. His work not only deals with all these problems, but in addition raises the challenge of attempting to treat these problems precisely in their systematic interconnections.

---

[10]"Ästhetik und Kunstphilosophie," in *Akten des XIV Internationalen Kongress für Philosophie, Wien, 2–9. September 1968*, vol. 4 (Vienna, 1969), 216. See also W. Biemel, "Reflexionen zu Ingardens Deutung des Bildes," *Reports on Philosophy* 10(1986): 5–19.

With these comments about the general associations and specific emphasis of Ingarden's aesthetics in mind, we now need to review briefly the content of his two major works on literary aesthetics, *The Literary Work of Art* and *The Cognition of the Literary Work of Art*.

The Literary Work of Art (LWA) is the first and most important of a series of works and studies that Ingarden devoted to formal and epistemological problems in aesthetics.[11] As such, this book applies an elaborate ontology to a particular domain of inquiry and develops this ontology by taking critical account of the conceptual strains its application entails. The ontology put to work here comes from Ingarden's seminal studies with Husserl and his later decision to reject the transcendental idealism of Husserl's middle period.[12] After his doctoral dissertation and habilitation, Ingarden turned away from the endless Husserlian analyses of modes of consciousness and returned to a preoccupation with questions about categorial structures, the typology and identity of different kinds of objects, and especially the nature of the difference between real and intentional objects. The *LWA* first mapped out the contour and detail of his continuing concern with the ontology of aesthetic works, specifically with the Husserlian problem about the relations between ideal objects and their existence in the spatiotemporal world. Ingarden's emphasis on aesthetic objects is indebted, as he points out, both to Aristotle's primary stress, in the *Poetics*, on the stratified structure of the work of art itself, and to Lessing's attempt, in the *Laokoon*, to set aside psychologistic questions in the interests of general problems of structure.[13] In turn, much European work on aesthetics since the thirties has been indebted to Ingarden. *The Cognition of the Literary Work of Art (CLWA)* is a sequel to the first work and was elaborated by Ingarden in succes-

[11]See "Essentiale Fragen," *Jahrbuch für Philosophie und Phänomenologische Forschung* 7(1925): 125–304, also published separately as *Essentiale Fragen* (Halle, 1925); "Edmund Husserl: Formale und transzendentale Logik," *Kantstudien* 38(1933): 206–9; "Kritische Bemerkungen zu Husserls Cartesianischen Meditationen," in *Edmund Husserl, Gesammelte Schriften*, vol. 1, *Cartesianische Meditationen und Pariser Vorträge* 203–18 (The Hague, 1950); "Uber die gegenwärtigen Aufgaben der Phänomenologie," *Archivo di Filosofia* 1(1957): 229–41; *Edmund Husserls Briefe an Roman Ingarden: Mit Erläuterungen und Erinnerungen an Husserl von Roman Ingarden*, Phaenomenologica 35 (The Hague, 1968); *Innforing i Edmund Husserl Fenomenologi* (Oslo, 1970); "What Is New in Husserl's Crisis?" *Analecta Husserliana* 1(1971): 36–74.
[12]References are to the English translations cited in note 2.
[13]See "A Marginal Commentary on Aristotle's Poetics," *Journal of Aesthetics and Art Criticism* 20(1960–61): 163–73, 273–85. The materials on Lessing have not yet been translated.

sive editions, largely in response to the criticisms his first work encountered.[14] Finally, Ingarden extends and tests these two theoretical works in the detailed analyses of other than just literary works of art in his three-volume *Studia z estetyki*.[15]

If this is some needed background for Ingarden's aesthetics, what is the substance of at least the two major books? The subject of *LWA*, Ingarden says, "is the basic structure and the mode of existence of the literary work, and in particular of the literary work of art"—in short, aesthetic structures.[16] His main orientation is to steer a course between too great a reliance on parallels between the literary work of art and painting and too great a stress on only the linguistic element of the literary work of art. The first extreme is frequently connected with the view that the work of art is identical with our mental experience of it, whereas the second is frequently connected with the other extreme view, that the work of art is identical with its physical substrate. By rejecting both extremes, Ingarden wishes to keep open the possibility both of criticism and of scientific investigation. The motives of the work, however, are more general, since Ingarden is concerned to pursue the problem of realism and idealism in a Husserlian vein by examining, as he says, "an object whose pure intentionality was beyond any doubt and on the basis of which one could study the essential structures and the mode of existence of the purely intentional object without being subject to suggestions stemming from considerations of real objectivities."[17] Briefly, then, Ingarden's *LWA* is about how the literary work of art is structured and in what senses these aesthetic structures are "real."

The subject of *CLWA* is a series of answers to Ingarden's question, "How does the cognition of the work of art come about and to what does it lead?"[18] Again, with reference to those Husserlian orientations Ingarden is concerned to show, once the structure of the literary aesthetic object has been delineated in the earlier work, how this object presents itself in different ways to our consciousness of the object. "Cognition" is at first construed quite broadly. Gradually, however, this cardinal concept is differentiated in terms

---

[14]References are to the English translation by R. A. Crowley and K. R. Olson (Evanston, Ill., 1973).

[15](Warsaw, 1947–70).

[16]*LWA*, lxxi. For a good review see J. Mitscherling, "Roman Ingarden's *The Literary Work of Art*: Exposition and Analysis," *Dialectics and Humanism* 12(1985): 199–220.

[17]*LWA*, lxxiii.

[18]*CLWA*, 4.

of the different kinds of knowledge we may develop of the literary work of art itself, of our reconstruction of such a work, of a particular concretization of such a work, and so on.[19] Hence the aim at the outset of this second work is to focus on the different kinds of cognitive attitudes we can adopt in the presence of the literary work of art. More particularly, Ingarden will be concerned to analyze the essential features of "just three of the possible attitudes: the aesthetic,[20] in which an aesthetic object is constituted, the pre-aesthetic in which we gain reflective knowledge about the work of art, and the postaesthetic attitude of reflective cognition of the aesthetic concretization."[21] Finally, Ingarden orients his second work in terms of two basic preliminary theses: that the cognition of the literary work of art "is composed of heterogeneous but closely connected processes (operations)"; and that this cognition "is accomplished in a temporal process."[22]

These two works are substantial achievements filled with all the distinctions and detail worthy of a student of Twardowski, Husserl, and of the translator of Kant's *Critique of Pure Reason*. We shall have to content ourselves here, however, with a brief summary of the central claims about the literary work of art. Here are ten general assertions. (1) "The literary work of art is a many layered formation" composed of four strata. (2) The formal unity of the work derives from the essential innerconnectedness of the four strata. (3) The work is also distinguished by its ordered sequence of parts, a "peculiar quasi-temporal 'extension.'" (4) The declarative

[19]For Ingarden's idea of concretization see Y. Takei, "The Literary Work and Its Concretization: Roman Ingarden's Aesthetics," in *Phenomenology of Life*, ed. A. T. Tymieniecka, 285–307 (Dordrecht, 1984); M. Glowinski, "On Concretization," in *Roman Ingarden and Contemporary Polish Aesthetics*, ed. P. Graff and S. Krzmien-Ojak, 33–45 (Warsaw, 1975); and J. Kmita, "Work of Art—Its Concretization. Artistic Value. Aesthetic Value," in *Roman Ingarden and Contemporary Aesthetics*, ed. P. Graff and S. Krzemien-Ojak, 109–28(Warsaw, 1975).

[20]See M. Brinker, "Phenomenology and Literature: Roman Ingarden and the 'Appropriate Aesthetic Attitude' to the Literary Work of Art," *Iyyun* 33(1984): 137–55; B. Dziemidok, "Roman Ingarden's Views on the Aesthetic Attitude," in *Roman Ingarden and Contemporary Polish Aesthetics*, ed. P. Graff and S. Krzemien-Ojak, 9–31 (Warsaw, 1975).

[21]*CLWA*, xviii. Note that Ingarden's historical views about aesthetics, though largely Aristotelian, are not strongly developed. Nevertheless, be owes much to a reading of the history of aesthetics that is very different from either the analytic or the hermeneutic one, namely the extraordinary and still largely overlooked work of his colleague Wladyslaw Tatarkiewicz. See his *History of Aesthetics*, 3 vols. (Warsaw, 1970–74), and *A History of Ideas: An Essay in Aesthetics* (Warsaw, 1980), as well as the general essay of Z. Kerderowicz, "Wladyslaw Tatarkiewicz as Historian of Philosophy," *Reports in Philosophy* 5(1981): 3–8.

[22]*CLWA*, 16–17.

sentences in a literary work of art are not genuine judgments but only quasi-judgments. (5) Each stratum of a literary work of art has value qualities of two kinds, artistic and aesthetic.[23] (6) "The literary work of art must be distinguished from its concretizations," its individual readings. (7) The literary work of art is a schematic formation that contains "places of indeterminacy." (8) Individual concretizations remove these places of indeterminacy only partly, so different concretizations remain possible. (9) "The literary work of art is a purely intentional formation," but "it is not a psychological phenomenon and it is transcendent to all experiences of consciousness." And (10) the literary work of art is an aesthetic object. It is of course this last claim, that there are aesthetic objects, that has stirred renewed controversy. I explore its details in appendix 11.

The Structure of the Literary Artwork

Ingarden's account of the structure of the literary work of art includes a negative element and a positive element.

To begin with, Ingarden excludes three features that are sometimes connected with the literary work of art from the structure of that work. These three extrinsic features might be summarized under the headings of the author, the reader, and the nonfictional world.

The author is to be excluded from any account of the structure of the literary work of art in the sense that the author's "vicissitudes, experiences, and psychic states" are taken as irrelevant to that

---

[23]J. Makota, "Aesthetic vs. Moral Values in Roman Ingarden's Philosophy," *Etyka* 22(1986): 183–94; G. Küng, "Brentano and Ingarden on the Experience and Cognition of Values," *Reports on Philosophy* 10(1986): 57–67; L. E. Patrick, "The Aesthetic Experience of Ruins," *Husserl Studies* 3(1986): 31–55. On the central role of values in Ingarden's aesthetics see "Quelques remarques sur le problème de la relativité des valeurs," in *Actes du III Congrès des Sociétés de Philosophie de Langue Française* (Brussels-Louvain, 1947); "La Valeur esthétique et le problème de son fondement objectif," in *Atti del III Congresso Internazionale di Estetica, Venezia, 3–5 Settembre 1956*, 229–41 (Turin, 1957); "Artistic and Aesthetic Values," *British Journal of Aesthetics* 4(1964): 198–213; B. Dziemidok, "Roman Ingarden's Theory of Value of the Work of Art in the Light of Marxist Aesthetics," *Dialectics and Humanism* 2(1975): 123–32; M. Golaszewska, "Aesthetic Values in Ingarden's System of Philosophy," in *Roman Ingarden and Contemporary Polish Aesthetics*, ed. P. Graff and S. Krzemien-Ojak 47–68 (Warsaw, 1975), and idem, "Ingarden's World of Values," *Dialectics and Humanism* 2(1975): 133–46; A. Szczepańska, "Perspectives on the Axiological Investigations of the Work of Roman Ingarden," *Journal of the British Society for Phenomenology* 6(1975): 116–25.

structure.[24] The point here is the noncontroversial one that however important such considerations might be for determining the genesis of the literary work, its structure cannot be determined in the same way.

Readers are also to be excluded in the precise sense that their "attributes, experiences, or psychic states" are also taken as irrelevant to the structure of the literary work.[25] This point is more complicated than it may at first appear. For though most theorists are alert to the danger of construing the value of a literary work of art in terms of a particular reader's response to that work, however enlightened, fewer theorists see the related danger in analyzing the structure of the work in the same way. Indeed, it is not clear even on detailed examination of Ingarden's own account that he himself always avoids this danger. Moreover, any theorist who holds for the existence of such a state of affairs as aesthetic attitudes has difficulty accounting for structure on terms other than readers' experiences.

The last feature Ingarden wishes to exclude is what I will call the nonfictional world, that is, "the whole sphere of *objects* and *states of affairs* which constitutes, as the case may be, the model of the objects and states of affairs 'appearing' in the work."[26] The nonfictional Moscow does not belong to the world called *War and Peace*. Just what the relationship is between these two worlds is not, Ingarden holds, a question that concerns the structure of the literary work of art, although it may well concern the ontological status of that work.

If these three elements are to be excluded from that structure, then just what features are to be included? Or as Ingarden himself formulates the question, "Which, then, are the strata that are necessary for every literary work if its internal unity and basic character are to be preserved?"[27] He answers this peculiar question as follows:

(1) The stratum of *word sounds* and the *phonetic formations* of higher order built on them; (2) the stratum of *meaning units* of various

---

[24]*LWA*, 22. This is an important restriction. See the different views of K. Sasaki, "Idée de la philosophie de l'oeuvre et la structure élastique de celle-ci," in *The Reasons of Art*, ed. P. McCormick, 47–51 (Ottawa, 1985).

[25]*LWA*, 23.

[26]*LWA*, 25.

[27]*LWA*, 30. Cf. the excellent account in A. Szczepańska, "The Structure of Artworks," in *On the Aesthetics of Roman Ingarden*, ed. B. Dziemidok and P. McCormick, 21–55 (Boston, 1989).

283

orders; (3) the stratum of manifold schematized *aspects* and aspect continua, and series, and, finally, (4) the stratum of represented objectivities and their vicissitudes.... this last stratum is, so to speak, "two-sided": on the one hand, the "side" of the representing intentional sentence correlates (in particular the states of affairs), on the other, the "side" of objects and their vicissitudes achieving representation in these sentence correlates.[28]

The first two strata, simply put as sound and sense, are easily recognizable, but we need a word of explanation about the last two.

The stratum of manifold schematized aspects cannot be understood completely without a detailed account of Husserl's theory of perception and his theory of internal time consciousness. But in general the idea behind this talk of aspects is reasonably plain. We are familiar with the distinction between something we perceive and the light in which this thing appears. The face we recognize, for example, is different from the emotion that may accompany the recognition. The point is that things and the properties of things can appear to a perceiving subject in different ways. To the doctor as professional there appears the impersonal visage with the once-broken nose, and to the doctor as brother there appears the loved countenance of the childhood playmate with the broken nose. These different ways of appearing are said to be schematized, in the sense that all the aspects of a perceptible thing are ordered according to definite rules. Such schematized aspects belong structurally to literary works, in the sense that their basis is, as Ingarden says, potentially "in the states of affairs projected by the sentences or in the objects represented by means of the states of affairs."[29] Aspects of the Moscow train station that appear in the film *War and Peace*, for example, are actualized by viewers who have never seen either the actual Moscow train station in question or its cinematic substitute, the train station in Krakow. To the degree that these aspects are actualized in a rule-governed way, Ingarden speaks of the stratum of schematized aspects in a literary work.

The last stratum is that of represented objects. Again, the details of this fourth level can be found in Ingarden's work itself. I think we can identify for ourselves in a rough way what he is talking about, however, if we notice the difference between the features of actual objects in the nonfictional world and those of intentional objects in the fictional world. The table where Dr. Zhivago writes his poems, we all know, is different from the one where Boris

[28]*LWA*, 30.
[29]*LWA*, 264.

Pasternak writes his novel. Notice that both have a determinate size, but that only one can be exactly measured by going to Pasternak's cottage and taking out a tape measure. The latter table is an object, the former is roughly an instance of what Ingarden calls a represented objectivity. His point in making this distinction is to notice a peculiar structural feature of all literary works. Although we transpose to represented objectivities features that are characteristic of actual objects, we often overlook just what is particular to the represented objects themselves. It is a structural feature of a literary work that only some of the features of its represented objectivities are explicitly described. The chestnut tree in the park in Sartre's *La nausée* is importantly different from the chestnut tree in the park outside my window. And this difference is a central feature in one level of that literary work of art.

When we add to this summary account what we have already noted about Ingarden's theory, I think enough has been said about Ingarden's theory without going into the details of criticizing that theory in its own right. Let us turn to some features of a different theory of aesthetic structure that will open up useful contrasts with Ingarden's theory.

An Alternative View: Beardsley on Literary Structure

It is important to note at the outset that Monroe Beardsley's theory[30] is presented in a very large context. Not only is this theory part of a treatment of literature that stretches over three long chapters in his magisterial thematic work *Aesthetics*, but these chapters are very detailed, including twenty-eight subdivisions and more than 150 pages. The theory is also designed to parallel, wherever possible, similar accounts he presents of the aesthetic structure of other arts, especially painting and music. I shall look further on at the particular constraints that this twofold context imposes on his theory. The immediate point is that any brief account of his theory necessarily slights this extensive context.

Before we look in detail at Beardsley's theory, however, a diagram of its parts will be helpful.[31] This will allow both a preliminary

---

[30]Beardsley's publications are many. The major books are *Aesthetics: Problems in the Philosophy of Criticism* (New York, 1958), *Aesthetics from Classical Greece to the Present: A Short History* (New York, 1966), and *The Possibility of Criticism* (Detroit, 1970).

[31]I take Beardsley's theory here from the *Aesthetics* (1958), which is representative of his central views even though some modifications have been introduced in later articles. This book is cited hereafter as *A*.

survey of the theory and a convenient point of reference for the discussion. The diagram, as I make it out, looks like this:

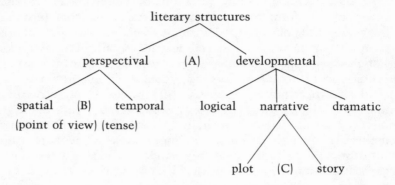

In the diagram, three distinctions have been labeled A, B, and C. I shall be concerned in what follows with trying to explicate just what principles are used to make each of these three distinctions. And my major criticism will be simply this: since these distinctions are central features of the theory, since the same two principles are used to make all three distinctions, and since each distinction purports to be of a different order of importance, central features of the theory overlap in an unacceptable way.

With this summary in hand, we need to begin to get at some of the detail by looking first at just how the cardinal term "structure" is being used in this theory.

Beardsley wants to maintain that the structure of the literary work of art "consists of the large-scale relationships within the work, the major connections."[32] This brief account is designed not specifically with the literary work of art in view, but with an eye on the arts in general. Although Beardsley concedes that "there are many varieties of possible structure," he does not take time to provide us with an analysis of just how such "large-scale relationships" are to be distinguished from smaller ones, or whether such "large-scale relationships" are to be understood in importantly different ways within the different arts. He is content, rather, to take the idea of structure in the literary work of art as more or less clear from the overly brief account cited above and to move on to a general classification of these large-scale relationships in terms of space and time.

[32]A, 247.

The first of these relationships, perspectival structures, are to be understood as spatial structures in the sense that they refer to the "various possible relationships between the speaker and his situation."[33] And the second type of structures, developmental structures, are taken as temporal in the sense that they refer to the various possible relationships, in the changes that occur in the speaker's attitude or situation. Perspectival structures thus seem to be static features, whereas developmental ones are dynamic.

What complicates this theory almost immediately, however, is Beardsley's second set of distinctions between two kinds of perspectival structures, what he terms spatial and temporal ones. The problem is already evident in the terminology. The same features, space and time, are being used to distinguish both between perspectival and developmental structures and within perspectival structures themselves.

Before pursuing this problem, I need to describe the theory a bit further. The first kind of perspectival structure, the spatial one, can be identified with the term more familiar in literary criticism, "point of view." The point of view in a literary work of art is "the spatial perspective from which the speaker observes the events he describes."[34] The second kind of perspectival structure, the temporal one, can also be identified with a more common term. This term, however, is a grammatical one rather than a literary critical one. Accordingly, we say that a literary work has a tense, a prevailing "temporal relationship between the moment of report and the moment reported."[35] A literary work of art, then, is structured so far in terms of perspectives in that it characteristically exhibits both point of view and tense.

Two points should be noticed here. We know, first, that all nonliterary artworks also have spatial and temporal features. Hence these features themselves are not sufficient to specify the peculiar structure of literary texts. We also know, second, that both point of view and tense often change in literary works. Of course there is usually a general point of view and tense that predominates in a particular work. But frequently the peculiar character not of literary texts in general but of a specific kind of literary text—for example, the essential element of recognition in Greek tragedy—depends upon change or lack of change in just those features. So

[33]A, 247.
[34]A, 247.
[35]A, 247.

these features themselves are also not sufficient to specify the particular kind of literary text in question. If we are to differentiate the structure of literary texts from nonliterary ones, then, the literary texts of a particular genre like tragedies from those of another like narrative poems, we require further reflection on developmental structures.

Developmental structures are of three kinds—logical, narrative, and dramatic. Logical structures in literary works are frequently to be found in such texts as sonnets, for example, or didactic poems like Lucretius's *On the Nature of Things*. These structures are identifiable by the presence of systematic relations between sentences of statement form, some of which function as premises and some of which function as conclusions in argument. The difference between such logical structures in literary as opposed to nonliterary texts is that the statements appearing in the former kind of texts are not asserted as true in the real world but are propounded or acted out in a fictional context.

We should note that the well-foundedness of this last controversial distinction between truth conditions for fictional as opposed to nonfictional statements has important consequences. If, for example, it can be shown that the basic distinction here between uttering a sentence in the fictional context and asserting a sentence in the nonfictional one breaks down, as I think it does, then the question arises whether there can be any logical structures at all in literature. But that is another story, part of which we already touched on in chapter 10.

The second kind of developmental structure is narrative structure. Narrative structures in literary works can be taken as the likenesses and differences among the episodes in a sequence of events. Now, all the features in this account are necessary. A sequence of events, for example, appears in many nonliterary texts and in all kinds of literary texts. What distinguishes the narrative structure of a literary text from that of a nonliterary text is the presence of episodes, or scenes and summaries of events. What distinguishes the narrative structure of one kind of literary text from that of another might be taken as the nature of the episodes. And what further distinguishes between the narrative structure of two instances of the same kind, say two novels, is the specific contrast between the likenesses and similarities in the episodes narrated. More, of course, could be said, since the number of variations is great. But, again, two familiar words help to get the major point clear here: the plot, that is, the sequence of events in the order of their occurrence, and the story, that is, the sequence in the order of their telling, are the two essential elements of narrative structure.

Just as in the case of logical structure, so too we find a problem here. The difficulty is not so much in the account of narrative structure itself, which I find instructive, as in the lack of an account of the relations between narrative and logical structure. Beardsley holds that a work cannot have both at once because, he says obscurely, "the movements are different."[36] It is true, of course, that the movements are different, if we take this cryptic remark to mean something like the difference between the relation of premises to conclusion and of one episode to another. But that such relations are different does not entail the impossibility of having both structures in the same text, as Beardsley's own example of Lucretius's poem shows. This poem does include both a narrative and a logical structure. So if I have not misunderstood him on this point, it appears that Beardsley is simply mistaken. If so, then we still need an account of the relationship between the two structures, logical and narrative.

More important, a second problem arises here. For in stressing the sequence of events in narrative structure and also in distinguishing between plot and story, this account seems to rely on the same features already distinguished as perspectival structures—tense and point of view. It is not clear whether narrative structure is properly situated in this theory as a kind of developmental structure or rather as a subdivision of one kind of perspectival structure. This problem raises again a question about the coherence of Beardsley's theory.

The last kind of developmental structure, dramatic structure, involves "the building and relaxation of tension" or, in other words, "variations in the on-goingness of the world, in its pace and momentum."[37] This kind of structure seems omnipresent in literary texts, especially when we notice the differences between poems, plays, novels, short stories, and so on. Moreover, these differences are often a function of various devices like the connection among scenes or the orchestration of emotion or even shifts in the attitude of the writer. The fact of such a structure I do not think is in doubt. Just what such a structure involves in its details, however, is unfortunately not explicated.

[36]A, 250.
[37]A, 251.

To summarize, we may say that there are two basic kinds of structures in literary works of art, each with its own subdivision. Perspectival structures include point of view and tense, while developmental structures include logical, narrative, and dramatic types. The basic problem I have noted in this theory is the overlapping of these distinctions because of repeated appeal to the same principles to distinguish different features. Why Beardsley's theory makes too great a use of space and time is not evident, but it is likely that the overreliance on these two principles alone is one central consequence of the parallelism he wishes to preserve between his theory of structure in literary works of art and a structure in nonliterary ones.[38]

We now must turn to the task of formulating several general questions about aesthetic structures that the differences between these two accounts suggest.

Toward a Theory of Aesthetic Structure

If we look back through Beardsley's theory with at least some of the features of Ingarden's theory in mind for contrast, I think several merits of Beardsley's theory, together with several deficiencies, are plainer than I have made out so far.

One of the positive aspects of that theory surely is the close attention to detail, the attentiveness to the many ways the structure of the literary work continues to resist the simplifications of anyone's theory. Another point in Beardsley's favor is his use of already familiar critical terms such as point of view, plot, and story, but with a greater concern for accurately distinguishing their different senses. Finally, a point my own summaries unfortunately omit, Beardsley's theory is especially noteworthy by reason of the extended examples the theory interacts with.

---

[38]This account could be filled out in much greater detail were someone to investigate systematically the bearing of Beardsley's major articles on the question of structure. For some, but not all, of these articles see, in chronological order: "The Intentional Fallacy" (with W. K. Wimsatt), *Sewanee Review* 54(1946): 3023; "The Affective Fallacy" (with W. K. Wimsatt), *Sewanee Review* 57(1949): 3–27; "The Metaphorical Twist," *Philosophy and Phenomenological Research* 22(1962): 293–307; "The Limits of Critical Interpretation," in *Art and Philosophy*, ed. S. Hook, 61–87 (New York, 1966); "Textual Meaning and Authorial Meaning," *Genre* 1(1968): 169–86; "The Aesthetic Point of View," *Metaphilosophy* 1(1970): 39–58; "What Is an Aesthetic Quality?" *Theoria* 39(1973): 50–70; "The Descriptivist Account of Aesthetic Attribution," *Revue Internationale de Philosophie* 28(1974): 336–52.

More important than these merits of the theory, I think, are the shortcomings. With the benefit of contrast, we notice the lack of any sustained attempt to exclude from consideration nonstructural features of the literary work of art. Of course, it is important here not to overlook the considerable force of Beardsley's comments elsewhere against intentionalism and other extraneous matters that Ingarden alludes to. Beardsley does take up these matters. The difficulty here is not that Beardsley's account leaves something out, but that his account does not show the relevance of his exclusions elsewhere to the actual matter in hand, namely, the question of aesthetic structures in the literary work of art as opposed to other kinds of artworks.

There are some omissions nonetheless. Thus the peculiar and complicated role of the reader's interaction with the text is not adverted to at all in the discussion of literary structure. Nor, for that matter, is there any discussion of the ontological issues that are raised once we concentrate on structure. Again, we need to note that Beardsley has provided elsewhere a more general account of the interaction between audience and artworks and also an account of the disputed status of ontological objects. The point to this criticism is once again the lack of a more particular account of these matters in connection with problems about aesthetic structure precisely in the literary work.

One might object that Beardsley cannot say everything all the time about each of the arts, and that surely what he has already said in general applies to the individual cases. But while the first point is a truism, the second point is controversial. And it is controversial specifically because of the confusions we have already noticed in the overlapping of the different kinds of structure Beardsley's theory wants to describe. Whatever the full explanation for this overlapping, at least one of the central reasons is his concern for parallelism. Wherever we can find a theory that does justice to the parallels in the structure of different arts, we of course should be grateful. But that is quite another matter than using the desirability of parallelism to draw attention to kinds of structure that are supposed to be importantly different but turn out not to be. It may be that Ingarden's own theory makes the opposite mistake of imposing on the structure of all the arts those categories that are discovered in analyzing the structure of the literary work. Be that as it may, we must steer a course between the two extremes. Whatever theory of aesthetic structure in the literary work of art we settle for must, I think, avoid both the weaknesses of an exaggerated parallelism and those of generalizing the peculiar features of an eccentric account.

With these critical comments behind us, are there some general requirements that an adequate account of the aesthetic structure of literary works ought to be expected to meet? I say "ought to be expected" with the idea in mind that this examination of Beardsley's theory in the light of Ingarden's, whatever its inadequacies, should be made instructive. Rather than try to spell out such requirements on the basis of such a particular critical analysis, it seems better to formulate several questions that might provoke us to further examination of literary texts themselves rather than just theories of these texts. I see, for now, four such questions.

The first we can simply take over from the previous comments on parallelism. Hence the question here looks something like this: How can we arrive at a theory of the aesthetic structures of the literary work of art that is sufficiently detailed to account for that structure adequately without making impossible any general extension of that theory to the structure of the other arts? The problem is not only whether a general theory of aesthetic structure is possible but, assuming it is not impossible, just how to formulate hypotheses at, so to speak, the middle level between the structure of all arts and that of the literary work of art only.

A second question might be put this way: What analysis of the concept of aesthetic structure will allow us to do justice to the different layers of complexity in the literary work of art without compromising decisively the presence of a harmonious interrelationship among these layers? This is, of course, simply one version of the great problem of unity and diversity, of the one and the many. But for all its familiarity, this problem should not be left unaddressed in this context. The concept of aesthetic structure continues to preoccupy not just literary critics but linguists, social scientists, theologians, and philosophers. And until we can get clearer on just how this abused term is to be parsed in the specific context of the literary work of art, we cannot expect to make much sense out of Beardsley's perspectival and developmental structures, or of Ingarden's strata either. How, then, can we construe the term "structure" in such a way as to account for the unity in the diversity of the literary work of art?

A third question is still more particular. Both Beardsley and Ingarden continually make much of the temporal component in the literary work. And indeed this element has continued to hold the fascination of literary theorists for a long time, despite the extensive and centrally important work of such critics as Georges Poulet. But again a satisfactory account is still lacking. I would put this third question as follows: What general analysis of the phenomenon of the temporality and historicity will enable us to present a theory of the sequential structure of the literary work that is rigorous in its formal character and yet wide ranging enough not to exclude the central topic of tradition? Beardsley does not seem to have a general metaphysical viewpoint behind his own comments on temporality, though Ingarden does allude frequently to the importance of Husserl's reflections on time consciousness. But in each of these instances there are important problems. Where, then, are we to find a sophisticated philosophical theory of temporality that genuinely illumines the structure of literary texts?

For my final question I return to a very general point of the same order as the first question about parallelism. I have already noted several times the problem of accounting for the ontological independence of the literary work from both its author and its readers, whether in Beardsley's theory or in Ingarden's. The problem, of course, is the old chestnut of psychologism, the attempt to explain the nature of the literary work by appealing to empirical happenings in the minds of authors and readers. This problem again, however, is more general than just the case of literature might suggest, since it continually comes up, as we have seen, in other areas of psychology, such as the philosophy of logic, where the status of logical laws is at issue. This question might best be put at the general level: Can we provide a refutation of psychologism in such a general form that it holds both for logical psychologism and for what I have in chapter 8 called aesthetic psychologism? This is not easy, as the philosophy journals amply show. Either we put down logical psychologism effectively but find intentionalism still on the scene in aesthetics, or we put intentionalism out of action in aesthetics without drawing any consequences at all for the related problems in the philosophy of logic. How to do both is the issue.

Here then are four aspects of the aesthetic structure of literary works of art that may focus some of our continuing inquiry: parallelism, the concept of structure, the general analysis of temporality, and psychologism.[39]

[39]See Beardsley's generous reply to these criticisms in his "Comment on Six Commentators," in Text, Literature, and Aesthetics, ed. L. Aagaard-Mogensen and L. De Vos, 179–87 (Amsterdam, 1986), esp. 182–84.

Ideal Entities and Real Objects

This discussion of structure and especially the argument I detail in the appendix 11 about the status of aesthetic objects underlines, I think, important aspects of Ingarden's treatment that have too often been left without careful enough scrutiny in contemporary aesthetics—namely, the nature of real objects, the idea of aesthetic properties, and the notion of aesthetic perception. Gary Iseminger has gotten each of these points wrong. And his failure can be taken, especially after the care in his approach has been underlined, as symptomatic of wider misunderstandings of Ingarden's work among contemporary aestheticians at large. In light of the discussion so far of aesthetic structures, in this final section I will isolate three distinct interpretations of just what aesthetic objects are.

Iseminger's misconstrual of "real object" as "spatiotemporal entity" shows a symptomatic insensitivity to the idea of possibility. For in fact a careful reading of *Essentiale Fragen*, published in volume 7 of Husserl's *Jahrbuch* for 1925, indicates clearly that for Ingarden "objectivity" is a complex topic.[40] Reacting strongly to Husserl's epistemological preoccupations, even at this early point in his career he tried to enlarge the concept of object to include the realm of possibility. The result was that "object" no longer was used to refer exclusively to actual entities but was applied to all entities that can be thought. Ingarden went so far in this direction as to thematize the ways possibility is originally given to consciousness. Of course this kind of doctrine remains necessarily connected to what is a complicated and sometimes obscure notion of essence.[41] But however nuanced we wish to make our acceptance of Ingarden's view of essence, his texts and his problematic clearly reject construing "object" in terms of "spatiotemporal entity" alone. One of the central concerns of Ingarden's work, from his earlier preoccupation with Husserlian issues through his work on aesthetics and into his culminating reflection on the complex

---

[40]See "Essentiale Fragen," *Jahrbuch für Philosophie und Phänomenologische Forschung* 7(1925): 125–304. Also published separately as *Essentiale Fragen* (Halle, 1925).

[41]See "The General Question of the Essence of Form and Content," *Journal of Philosophy* 57(1960): 222–33; F. Kersten, "On Understanding Idea and Essence in Husserl and Ingarden," *Analecta Husserliana* 2(1972): 55–63; and A.-T. Tymieniecka, *Essence et existence: Etude à propos de la philosophie de Roman Ingarden et Nicolai Hartman* (Paris, 1957).

problems of the existence of the world, is not so much the description of spatiotemporal entities as just how the nature of all possible objects can be constituted.[42] It is this emphasis that distinguishes the "objective" realism of Ingarden, which stresses the preeminence of ontological issues over epistemological ones, from Husserl's transcendental phenomenology with its extraordinarily persistent concern with the primacy of epistemological concerns. In addition to the view of aesthetic object as spatiotemporal entity, then, Ingarden's work suggests the conception of aesthetic object as a possible entity.

A related area of confusion in Iseminger's treatment has to do with the distinction between real properties and aesthetic properties. On Iseminger's reading of the Louvre example, an important distinction is to be made between the properties of the real object such as being stained or being corroded and the properties of the aesthetic object such as being uniformly colored or being uniformly smooth. But once again this distinction itself involves an important set of qualifications that needs to be understood if we are to represent Ingarden's views accurately.

We need to recall that Ingarden has an elaborate technical terminology, very much like Bolzano's and Twardowski's, that is both the context of his concept of object and the major means Ingarden uses to carry this concept. To find an example of this richer context, we might look to the early sections in part 1 of volume 2 of *Der Streit um die Existenz der Welt*, where Ingarden insists on distinctions among ideas, ideal qualities, individual ideal objects, and ideal concepts. Or even better, the distinctions can be found mentioned together in the preface to the first edition of *Das literarische Kunstwerk*. Ingarden writes there the following:

This is the first essential difference: all objectivities which he previously held to be ideal ... Husserl now considers to be intentional formations of a particular kind and in this way he arrives at a universal extension

[42]On constitution here see "L'institution Bergsonienne et le problème phénoménologique de la constitution," in *Congrès Bergson*, 163–66 (Paris, 1959); "Le problème de la constitution et le sens de la réflexion constitutive chez Edmund Husserl," in *Husserl, Cahiers de Royaumont*, 3: 242–64 (Paris, 1959); participation in the discussions, ibid., 66–67, 88–89, 188, 233–34, 269–70, 329–30, 373; "Husserls Betrachtungen zur Konstitution des physikalischen Dinges," *Archives de Philosophie* 27(1964): 356–407; A.-T. Tymieniecka, "Editorial: The Second Phenomenology," in *For Roman Ingarden: Nine Essays in Phenomenology*, 1–5 (The Hague, 1959); and K. Tawowski, "Roman Ingarden's Critique of Transcendental Constitution," *Dialectics and Humanism* 3(1976): 11–119.

of transcendentalism; whereas I today still maintain the strict ideality of various kinds of objectivities (ideal concepts, ideal individual objects, ideas, and essences) and indeed see in ideal objects an ontic foundation of word meaning that enables them to have intersubjective identity and an ontically autonomous mode of existence.[43]

A second construal of aesthetic object thus is aesthetic object as an ideal entity.

Although the notion of ideal entity, as George Kalinowski has indicated, remains sketchier in the rest of Ingarden's actual use of these distinctions, we are still able to see the point of this richer terminology for our discussion of Iseminger.[44] For just how are we to take the difference between being stained and being uniformly colored or that between being corroded and being uniformly smooth? Is the distinction here between real properties and ideal properties, as Iseminger would have it? Moreover, is the distinction between the first pair of the same order as the distinction between the second? Or do we need here still further distinctions between the properties of ideal objects and the properties of what Ingarden calls *Wesenheiten*? Finally, do we also need a distinction between idea and concept if we are to be critically sensitive to the difference here between real objects and ideal objects?

The problem in Iseminger's single distinction is clear: without a more finely calibrated set of distinctions—particularly between levels of objectivities, kinds of ideal objects, and properties of different kinds of ideal objects—it makes too little sense to pin a very consequential argument on a distinction as large as that between real and ideal objects. Briefly, to make Iseminger's argument work we need an expanded ontology, an ontology that requires some clear talk of schematism and aesthetic structure.[45] It is this expanded ontology that makes room not only for a much wider set of distinctions, but for a more adequate conception of aesthetic object in terms of an intentional construction—what Brunius has called "a perspective of experience bound in the matter by means of the intentional form of the transmitting artist."[46] Here, then, is a

[43]*LWA*, lxxiv.

[44]G. Kalinowski, "Ontologie et esthétique chez Roman Ingarden," *Archives de Philosophie* 31(1968): 281–87.

[45]On schematism see J. Fizer, "Schematicism: Aesthetic Device or Psychological Necessity?" *Journal of Aesthetics and Art Criticism* 27(1969): 417–23.

[46]Brunius 1970: 592. For very recent critical essays see B. Dziemidok and P. McCormick, eds., *On the Aesthetics of Roman Ingarden* (Boston, 1989).

third construal of aesthetic object: aesthetic object as an intentional entity.

If we are to settle the issue whether there are aesthetic objects, we still have to do so on other grounds than Iseminger suggests. Part of that task, I suggest, must involve getting clear about the importantly different ways we impute existence to at least four kinds of entities: spatiotemporal entities, possible entities, ideal entities, and intentional entities. And those elucidations, as I have tried to exhibit here, require paying fresh attention to the notion of aesthetic structure.

However we construe it,

> the literary work of art, Ingarden has written, is a true wonder.... If we wish to apprehend it theoretically, it shows a complexity and many-sidedness that can hardly be taken in; and yet it stands before us in aesthetic experience as a unity which allows this complex structure to shine through.... it seems to be completely passive and to suffer defenselessly all our operations; and yet by its concretizations it evokes deep changes in our life; it broadens it, raises it above the flatness of everyday existence, and gives it a lovely radiance. It is a "nothing" and yet a wonderful world in itself—even though it comes into being and exists only by our grace. (Ingarden 373)

The key to Ingarden's view on aesthetic perception, aesthetic properties, and aesthetic structures, however, remains the well-foundedness of Ingarden's claim that there are aesthetic objects. Establishing that claim against its critics involves turning critical attention away from the nature of mental acts and the kinds of mental objects and toward the much different realm of the spatio-temporal world. But this kind of attention requires investigating a set of considerations that, as I have been anxious to suggest in part 2 of this book, derives largely from the realist backgrounds of modern aesthetics inaugurated in Bolzano's critical appropriation of Kant from a different perspective than either analytic or herme-neutic theorists today care to remember in sufficient detail. We need now, however, to step back from these various investigations within the realist backgrounds of modern aesthetics into the many-faceted and problematic notion of the aesthetic and to return in concluding to our contemporary standpoint.

Appendix 11: On Whether Aesthetic Objects Exist

If my account here may be taken as a fair summary of the contents of Ingarden's philosophy as a whole—its range, his understanding of aesthetic structure, and especially the context of his major works on the literary work of art—in what respect is the foundation of this work, the concept of aesthetic object, controversial?[47] Consider one of the most serious challenges to Ingarden.

In an important article, Gary Iseminger has claimed that Ingarden needlessly dulls the edge on Occam's razor by holding for the existence of aesthetic objects.[48] His justification for this claim has two parts, an expository element and a critical one. Before we move to an evaluation of their respective merits, it will be helpful to look at each in turn.

The structure of Iseminger's exposition is helpfully clear. First, a putatively central claim in Ingarden's aesthetics is cited. Next, on the basis of this claim an argument that could generate such a claim is reconstructed. Then, after the key premise in this argument is isolated, the cardinal term of the premise is interpreted. Finally, this interpretation itself is buttressed by an explication of several assumptions that one of Ingarden's examples seems to involve. We need to scrutinize these items in some detail.

On the basis of Ingarden's claim in "Aesthetic Experience and Aesthetic Object" that it is a mistake to hold "that the object of such an [aesthetic] experience is *identical* with an element in the real world,"[49] Iseminger constructs the following argument, here slightly abbreviated.

1. There are aesthetic experiences.[50]
2. Every experience has an object.
3. The object of an aesthetic experience is not identical with any real object.

---

[47]Besides two articles mentioned in note 1, see W. S. Hamrick, "Aesthetic Experience and Aesthetic Object," *Journal of the British Society for Phenomenology* 5(1947): 71–80, and B. Smith, "The Ontogenesis of Mathematical Objects," *Journal of the British Society for Phenomenology* 6(1975): 91–101.

[48]For reference to Iseminger's article, see note 1.

[49]"Aesthetic Experience and Aesthetic Object," *Philosophy and Phenomenological Research* 21(1960): 289, cited in Iseminger 1973: 417.

[50]For Ingarden's notion of aesthetic experience, besides the article mentioned see "Das ästhetische Erlebnis," *II Congrès International d'Esthétique et des Sciences de l'Art*, vol. 1 (Paris, 1937), 54–60. For a recent perspective on this see M. Golaszewska, "Platonic Ideas in Ingarden's Phenomenological Aesthetics," *Diotima* 12(1984): 113–19.

Therefore:
4. There are aesthetic objects (as distinct from real objects).[51]

The key premise, as Iseminger views the matter, is (3), and the cardinal term in that premise, "real object," he interprets as "something like" spatiotemporal entity or physical object.[52] How is this interpretation justified?

Iseminger calls attention to Ingarden's discussion of the Venus de Milo, the statue in the Louvre. He notes that Ingarden wants to hold that an aesthetic perception, although beginning with sense perception of a real object, does not remain within this attitude. On this reading of Ingarden's example, Iseminger goes on to infer the following: "It seems ... that to maintain that we 'remain within the limits' of the real object in aesthetic perception would be to maintain that there are no properties that the object of our aesthetic experience has which the real object does not have."[53] But an examination of Ingarden's example gives grounds for claiming that in fact there are just such properties.[54] The physical object, for instance, has such properties as being stained, being broken, and so on, whereas the aesthetic object has no such properties. So since the properties are not identical, the objects are not either. Hence, besides real objects there are also aesthetic objects.

So much for the expository element in Iseminger's discussion. Now for his criticisms. Here too we find a clear structure. Iseminger's critical strategy turns on his wager "that the facts cited by Ingarden can be accommodated without generating an argument of this kind for (3)."[55] His central idea here is that while the real object remains always the same, our perception of this object can be of different kinds. Here is the emphatic way Iseminger formulates his point: "Nothing prevents us from saying that the *very same object* has both the property *appearing stained to sense perception* and the property *appearing uniformly colored to aesthetic perception*, just as nothing prevents us from saying that the very same thing is both tall relative to one thing and short relative to another."[56] The final move Iseminger makes here is to account for the alleged weakness in (3).

---

[51]Iseminger 1973: 417.
[52]Iseminger 1973: 417.
[53]Iseminger 1973: 418.
[54]But note Ingarden's own nuanced views about aesthetic properties in "Das Problem des Systems der ästhetisch relevanten Qualitäten," in *Actes du V Congrès International d'Esthétique, Amsterdam, 1964*, 448–56 (The Hague, 1968).
[55]Iseminger 1973: 418–19.
[56]Iseminger 1973: 419.

The third premise is weak, Iseminger thinks, because of its dependence on the second premise. And behind *this* premise he senses the doctrine of intentionality and its correlate, the concept of intentional object. Although Iseminger's discussion of intentionality is, I think, seriously mistaken, there is no room here to discuss these issues satisfactorily. Rather, for our purposes we need only note how Iseminger concludes his thoughtful criticisms. "What I have been urging," he writes, "is only that the distinction between aesthetic experience and 'simple sense perception' (1) and the thesis of intentionality in any plausible form (2) can be maintained without commitment to (3) and that the difficulties which (3) appears to be required to solve admit of other solutions. It seems to me, thus, that everything *else* that Ingarden wants to say can be said *without* commitment to (4)."[57] All of this comes down to the familiar but not inconsequential claim that there simply are no such things as aesthetic objects. In other words, on a most fundamental point, and one on which so much of his extraordinary contribution to aesthetics depends, Roman Ingarden is quite mistaken.

It is useful when trying to evaluate these criticisms of Ingarden's view to spend some time examining the general strategy behind them. What Iseminger has done is to isolate what he takes to be a central tenet in Ingarden's view. The argument that Iseminger reconstructs is, as we have seen, necessarily dependent on that claim. What remains striking, however, once we have gone back to reexamine Ingarden's 1961 article that is the context of this claim, is just how many other theses Iseminger could just as easily have isolated. The point is, of course, that several of these other theses (1) could have been generated by arguments with similar conclusions but different premises than the one Iseminger has proposed, and (2) could easily have been construed as theses just as central as the one Iseminger has spotlighted. What (1) and (2) come down to, quite simply, is that the centrality of Ingarden's claim is controversial.

If we grant the availability of numerous other putatively central claims, then we require of Iseminger something more than he has provided. For grateful and interested as we may be for the reconstruction he presents, we must have something more essential— namely, an argument, presumably historical in character—of just why *this* claim among the many Ingarden has made in this *one* article (not to speak of his four books on aesthetics) should be

[57]Iseminger 1973: 420.

construed as central to Ingarden's view. And *this* argument is precisely the one that is lacking.

Suppose, however, we waive the historical issue of whether the claim Iseminger is so anxious to examine is in fact as central to Ingarden's view as he would have us believe. The result is that a further difficulty in Iseminger's strategy quickly comes into view.

We recall that what draws Iseminger's fire is premise (3) of the argument Iseminger himself has reconstructed for a conclusion he takes as virtually the same thing as Ingarden's putatively central thesis. The question that arises, once we put the historical concerns aside, is whether we can reach the same conclusions on premises other than the ones Iseminger suggests. If so, then all Iseminger has shown is that one of the premises in *his* argument leaves something to be desired. But even if Iseminger has been successful in manipulating his own reconstruction, this surely says nothing directly about some other set of premises, this time Ingarden's own, that would lead to the same conclusion yet avoid the difficulties Iseminger has brought against his own reconstruction.

Now we need not immediately start rereading Ingarden's work to find the set of premises that would succeed in showing that much of Iseminger's argument is beside the point. There is a simple procedure much nearer to hand that can accomplish the same purpose. I am referring to the problems Iseminger has in construing the key terms in his third premise in anything like the sense Ingarden most often insisted on. My point comes to this: even if Iseminger is right about the centrality of the claim he has chosen to criticize, and even if his reconstruction of an argument that has this claim as conclusion accurately reflects the central types of argument Ingarden himself has used, nevertheless Iseminger misconstrues the sense of the key term in his own reconstruction. I have been maintaining, of course, that there is serious reason to doubt the truth of both of these "even if" clauses—and now I want to show reason for doubting not the truth, but the sense, of the "nevertheless" clause as well.

How then does Iseminger construe "real object" in the central premise (3), "The object of an aesthetic experience is not identical with any real object"? Iseminger writes: "By 'entity in the real world' or 'real object' Ingarden evidently means something like 'spatio-temporal entity' or 'physical object.'"[58] The alleged justification for this interpretation is twofold, but both aspects turn on

[58]Iseminger 1973: 417.

Ingarden's example of the Louvre statue. Iseminger continues: "For in suggesting how someone might set out to deny (3) he (A) proposes as a possible counter-example the statue in the Louvre in Paris known as the Venus de Milo, and he (B) recognizes that there is considerable *prima facie* plausibility in saying that it is precisely this *one* physical object which, on the one hand, is what we enjoy and appreciate, and, on the other, is located in a certain determinate weight, and so on."[59] I will look briefly at each of these points in turn.

Iseminger himself notes in a footnote to what I have called A that Ingarden's example gives his opponent "the most favorable case possible." He also notes, much more importantly, that where Ingarden speaks of literature or music it is much more difficult to see how the argument would be reconstructed.[60] The reason is clear. In sculpture the carved block of stone itself is the obvious candidate for the real object that the aesthetic experience must depend on, whereas in both literature and music, although with some straining we may come up with a candidate or two, no *obvious* candidates are to be had at all. But this point is just the observation we need to confirm whatever hesitations we may have had about Iseminger's construing "real object" as "spatiotemporal entity" on *this* ground. So on Iseminger's own admission, the first element of his justification for his interpretation of the key term simply fails.

I think the second element, B, fails too, but for different reasons. It simply won't do to cite Ingarden's recognition of "considerable *prima facie* plausibility" as a justification for the claim that Ingarden means "spatiotemporal entity" when he says "real object." The fact that a particular view is plausible has nothing more to do with the truth of that view than the fact that a stick in water appears bent has anything to do with whether the stick *is* bent. All that the plausibility of a view, and, a fortiori, the prima facie plausibility of a view, shows is that such a view is not manifestly absurd. But that something is not manifestly absurd is surely not the kind of

[59]Iseminger 1973: 420.

[60]For Ingarden's work on music see Roman Ingarden, *The Work of Music and the Problem of Its Identity* (Berkeley, 1986); idem, *Untersuchungen zur Ontologie der Kunst* (Tübingen, 1962); A. Lissa, "Some Remarks on Ingardenian Theory of a Musical Work," in *Roman Ingarden and Contemporary Polish Aesthetics*, ed. P. Graff and S. Kzemien-Ojak, 139–44 (Warsaw, 1975), and "Zur ingardenschen Theorie des Musikalischen Werkes," *Studia Filozoficzne* 4(1970): 331–50; and M. Rieser, "Roman Ingarden: Untersuchungen zur Ontologie der Kunst—Musikwerk—Bild—Architektur—Film," *Journal of Aesthetics and Art Criticism* 24(1966): 454.

support we require to justify construing a controversial view one way rather than another. Hence the second element of Iseminger's justification is also inadequate.

So as I see the case, Iseminger fails to justify his interpretation of just how the cardinal term "real object" is being used. Moreover, the grounds of this failure are in the nature of the reasons Iseminger himself cites, not in what Ingarden has himself propounded. These grounds suggest several larger issues that both contemporary Anglo-American and Continental aesthetics have for the most part simply neglected.

A final point that insists on some comment is the distinction, operative throughout Iseminger's discussion, between sense perception and aesthetic perception. We recall that Iseminger thinks that we can save the apparent edge on Occam's razor by construing the distinction between two kinds of objects in terms of two distinct ways of perceiving the same object. "To say that the Venus de Milo is stained," he writes, "then, is in this context, to say something like 'The Venus de Milo presents a stained appearance to sense perception.'... To say that it is uniformly colored is to say something like 'The Venus de Milo presents a uniformly colored appearance to aesthetic perception.'"[61]

But this is a difficult matter just when we insist that there are no aesthetic objects that are precisely what are perceived in aesthetic perception. Here too, of course, just as in the case of talk about objects and objectivities in Meinong, we need a larger and more powerful terminology.[62] But without going that far just now, we can already appreciate the problem of making a distinction between sense perception and aesthetic perception work without some reference to aesthetic objects.

One useful comment on this problematic distinction has been offered by John Fizer and requires mention in this context. After comparing and contrasting older, divergent views of perception by James, Piaget, and the Gestaltists, Fizer writes:

> I think...that the difference between non-artistic and artistic perception lies not so much in the encounter of the perceiving mind with the perceived object or in the absence of such encounter, but rather in

[61]Iseminger 1973: 419.

[62]Such a terminology is provided in part by Ingarden's work *Der Streit um die Existenz der Welt*, 4 vols. (Tübingen, 1964–74). See, however, H. Steinbach, "Ist Ontologie als Phänomenologie möglich? Kritische Betrachtungen zu Ingardens Existenz-Ontologie," *Zeitschrift für Philosophische Forschung* 22(1968): 78–100.

the role these two play. It seems to me that in non-artistic perception, the objects of one's perceptive field seek their actualization, while in artistic perception it is the inner scheme, that seeks its outer actualization, either with the help of its outside correlative, if such is present, or with the help of its own inner dynamics.[63]

Now the point of this comment is its use as a reminder of a distinction that Iseminger and others have overlooked but that nonetheless remains central in Ingarden's aesthetics, the distinction between aesthetic and artistic perception.

Unless we add nuance to our understanding not only of the basis of Iseminger's distinction between sense perception and aesthetic perception but also of Ingarden's own distinction between aesthetic and artistic perception, I do not see how we can go on with concluding against Ingarden that there are no aesthetic objects.[64] Moreover, without a surer critical grasp of Ingarden's polyvalent notions of objects and properties, much of his central importance for contemporary Anglo-American and Continental aesthetics will be simply overlooked.

[63]J. Fizer, "Schematism: Aesthetic Device or Psychological Necessity," *Journal of Aesthetics and Art Criticism* 27(1969): 420.

[64]On whether the existence of intentional objects requires the existence of real objects, see M. Rieser, "Roman Ingarden and His Time," *Journal of Aesthetics and Art Criticism* 29(1971): 443–52.

CONCLUSION

MODERNITY, AESTHETICS, AND THE BOUNDS OF ART

W<small>HEN WE</small> return to our starting point with the conceptual strains among interpretation and history, theory and practice, in distinguished and representative work in both contemporary analytic and Continental aesthetics, and try to view these persistent tensions from our present perspective, we can appreciate how much the two parties have in common. It is true, as I detailed in the Interlude, that within contemporary analytic reflection on the arts there are substantial differences about the structure of taste theories and aesthetic attitude theories, as well as about how to read the eighteenth-century thinkers, that still call for careful investigation, formulation, and adjudication. And substantive disagreements within contemporary Continental reflection are also widespread. We need only recall the debates between Gadamer and Habermas, or Derrida and Gadamer. But as I tried to show in chapter 1 and chapter 2, their similarities seem more important. Once we notice the family resemblances in these different but nonetheless related readings of eighteenth-century aesthetics, we can appreciate how much more dramatic a difference separates these analytic readings from the hermeneutic ones, especially when we turn to the crucial case of Kant. How to interpret Kant's aesthetics in the context of the eighteenth-century thinkers—whether as the culmination of a progressive refinement in the understanding of aesthetics or as the major obstacle to be overcome in a regressive reading aimed at recovering much of the forgotten legacy of these thinkers—seems to be the most general issue on which the analytic and hermeneutic readings diverge. Recognizing this issue brought us, in chapter 4, to a series of reminders about some but not all of the salient features of Kant's aesthetics. These features then lead us to reconsider one of the most important and yet less well known critical accounts of Kant's aesthetics, the work of Bernard Bolzano. In Bolzano's interpretation of Kant, I suggested, we may find the elements for more than a new approach to the Kantian movement in eighteenth-century aesthetics. In an unusual combination of conceptual rigor and thematic perspicuity, Bolzano opens the way to an original rereading of the eighteenth-century thinkers, with a critical yet closely appreciative eye on Kant—a retrospective I have tried to motivate here—as well as to inventorying the richly detailed and often forgotten resources of the realist backgrounds of modern aesthetics.

In this concluding chapter I reflect a bit further on the context of our starting point, one of the guiding historicist assumptions common to both Danto and Gadamer: that how we understand the relations between philosophy and the arts in our modern era is in central ways tributary to our readings of the eighteenth-century thinkers. I will scrutinize this assumption more closely, now that we have newly in mind the main features of divergent readings of that seminal period as well as of the realist tradition deriving from Bolzano, by once again trying to win some distance on these largely historical concerns.

Accordingly, I begin with an attempt to sharpen what is at stake philosophically in such an assumption by returning at the end of our inquiry to another element in the contemporary standpoint from which we began. In particular, I will examine briefly Jürgen Habermas's most recent characterizations of our contemporary standpoint under the label "modernity." For Habermas not only thematizes the problematic starting point of any philosophical reflection today, he also directly addresses the tensions between theory and practice that we discerned in both analytic and hermeneutic aesthetics. After sorting these views critically from the perspective of our present concerns with both the eighteenth-century thinkers and the realist tradition in aesthetics, I turn next to a related but quite different view of Kant's role in this story of modernity, the equally recent work of Hilary Putnam. Examining these two standpoints on modernity, one analytic and the other, if not hermeneutic then certainly Continental, enables me to keep faith at the end of this book with my concern from the very beginning; to respect a plurality—in the eighteenth century, in the realist tradition, and in my own starting point. The critical contrast between these two views of the nature of modernity—its origins and exactly what features of Kant's thought are the crucial ones for modernity—brings me to my conclusion. Here I try to reformulate in only a programmatic way several of the issues we first caught sight of at the end of the Introduction, issues that reassessment of these eighteenth-century readings as well as their realist legacy for the aesthetics of modernity should be expected to address satisfactorily.

Modernity, Rationality, and Communicative Reason

Over a number of years Habermas has gradually developed an increasingly subtle interpretation of what characterizes the modern era. From his early works, though a first synthesis in his 1968 *Knowledge and Interest* and the inaugural lecture at Frankfurt, and into the complexities and nuances of a second synthesis in his two-volume *Theory of Communicative Action* (1981), Habermas has described this interpretation in different ways.[1] For our purposes, however, I will use the term "modernity" to refer to this description in its most recent guises, in the works subsequent to the 1981 synthesis and in particular in his very important "Paris Lectures," now translated as part of a much longer collection entitled *The Philosophical Discourse of Modernity*.[2]

In 1983 Habermas presented four lectures at the Collège de France, where he pulled together much of his more recent reflection on a theme that had preoccupied him almost since the beginnings of his critical work on Max Weber's discussion of modern societies. Although these lectures do not address in any detail the many difficult issues involved with modernism in the arts, nonetheless they are, with several exceptions, arguably the most recent and extended formulations of his view on modernity; moreover, they include important qualifications in the articulation of his ongoing research program.

Habermas's starting point once again is a new statement of how Weber, Durkheim, and Mead sketched the outlines of modernity

[1]For Habermas's works through 1981 see R. Görtzen and F. van Gelder, "A Bibliography of Works by Habermas," in *The Critical Theory of Jürgen Habermas*, ed. T. McCarthy, corrected paperback ed., 442–64 (Cambridge, Mass., 1981).
[2]Trans. F. Lawrence (Cambridge, Mass., 1987). This book first appeared in German in 1985. Hereafter, page numbers in the text refer to pages in the English translation.

and of how some theorists today have styled themselves "postmodern" in their preference for talk of "modernization" rather than "modernity." Habermas is critical of both sets of views. He argues instead in a protracted narrative for a renewed examination of a key historical moment at the end of the eighteenth century, the situation in which the young Hegel, neither Gadamer's nor Danto's, pursued his first sympathetic and then critical readings of Kant.

For Habermas, "Hegel was the first philosopher to develop a clear concept of modernity. We have to go back to him if we want to understand the internal relationship between modernity and rationality which, until Max Weber, remained self-evident and which today is being called into question" (4). In his attempts to understand how "advanced societies" could be seen to differ from their predecessors, Weber called attention, in *The Protestant Ethnic and the Spirit of Capitalism* and elsewhere, to the peculiar link in modern societies between capitalist economies, growing bureaucratic structures, and the methodical conduct of life.[3]

The details of Habermas's interpretation of Weber remain controversial. But he is interested in the larger claims behind this story, the claims about the appearance of modernity at the end of the eighteenth century when a supposedly uniform understanding of rationality quickly fragmented into what Habermas claims are the three autonomous spheres of the cognitive-scientific, the moral-practical, and what interests us especially, the aesthetic.[4] The plurality of these universes of discourse as well as their increasing divergence is characteristic of the modernist era (192). For each sphere we find distinctive attitudes (objectivity, norm conforming, expressive), dangers (objectivism, moralism, aestheticism), and forms of argument (empirical-scientific discourse, moral discourse, and aesthetic criticism (207–9). Habermas sees this process first attracting

---

[3]An excellent overview of Weber's voluminous work can be found in R. Bendix, *Max Weber: An Intellectual Portrait* (Garden City, N.Y., 1962). Some of the larger backgrounds are set out in S. Benhabib's *Critique, Norm, and Utopia: A Study of the Foundations of Critical Theory* (New York, 1986).

[4]Habermas has schematized various "rationality complexes," "basic attitudes," "domains of reality," and so on, in five schemata that appear in "A Reply to My Critics," in *Habermas: Critical Debates*, ed. J. B. Thompson and D. Held, 218–83 (Cambridge, Mass., 1982); cited hereafter as "Reply." Just as in the Introduction, it is especially important when going into the details of contemporary discussions like those of Habermas and Putnam, Danto and Gadamer, to keep in mind the limited scope of these reflections. Thus, when Habermas talks of "three autonomous spheres," compare the very different picture of related matters in, say, distinguished Japanese work such as S. Kato's "*Cor, Praecordia, Viscera*—Bemerkungen zu einigen psychosomatischen Ausdrücken in Augustins *Confessiones*," *Revue Internationale de Philosophie Moderne* (Tokyo) 5 (1987): 109–29.

the scrutiny of the philosophers in Hegel's early work, especially Hegel's quarrels with Reinhold in the *Differenzschrift* in 1801, where "Hegel conceives the sundered harmony of life as the practical challenge to, and the need for, philosophy," and (20–21) even earlier in the first formulations of his system, which go back to 1796 and 1797.

Habermas sees the early Hegel formulating for the first time the characteristic theme of modernity, what he calls the "self-critical reassurance of modernity" (51). At the end of the eighteenth century, Habermas argues, "as modernity awakens to consciousness of itself, a need for self-reassurance arises, which Hegel understands as a need for philosophy. He sees philosophy confronted with the task of grasping its own time—and for him that means the modern age—in thought" (16). Hegel takes the authoritative interpretation of modernity to be that of Kant, whose thorough and effective divisions within reason leave him blind to any need for unification. Together with his student friends from the Tübingen Stift, Schelling and Hölderlin, Hegel moves to formulate the problem of modernity in his Jena writings, the problem of the reunification of a reason whose principles would be found within itself. But on Habermas's view, when Hegel settles in the Jena period on the notion of an absolute knowledge, he betrays the strength of his original critique of Kant. He renders impossible an acceptable critique of modernity by conceiving "the overcoming of subjectivity within the boundaries of a philosophy of the subject" (22).

The key idea for Habermas in the shift from the old era to the new age, the age of modernity, is that the new age creates its norms out of itself instead of borrowing them from elsewhere. The idea first appears, he thinks, in the eighteenth-century quarrel in France, especially in the context of the *querelle des anciens et des modernes*, a dispute in aesthetics.[5] This dispute centered on whether the central aesthetic norms were to be taken by imitation from the timeless

---

[5]Habermas takes this idea from the work of H. R. Jauss, especially his "Ursprung und Bedeutung der Fortschrittsidee in der 'Querelle des Anciens et des Modernes,'" in *Die Philosophie und die Frage nach dem Fortschritt*, ed. H. Kuhn and F. Wiedmann, 55 ff. (Munich, 1964). It is not clear, however, that Jauss would welcome Habermas's discussion here. Compare the disagreement within the hermeneutic tradition, like that between Dickie and Stolnitz, with the analytic view, between Gadamer on the one side and Jauss together with P. C. Lang on the other, about how the classical is to be understood. See Jauss's *Toward an Aesthetic of Reception* (Minneapolis, 1982), and P. C. Lang's *Hermeneutik, Ideologiekritik, Ästhetik* (Königstein, 1981). For background see D. Hoy's excellent book *The Critical Circle* (Berkeley, 1978). For Habermas's more recent interest in aesthetics see J. Habermas and L. von Friedeberg, eds., *Adorno-Konferenz* (Frankfurt, 1983).

values of the classics or to be discovered in the contingent values of the contemporary. Hegel was to meditate the much larger historical context here of the Reformation, the Enlightenment, the French Revolution, the Declaration of the Rights of Man, and the Napoleonic Code as all leading to the primacy of subjectivity in the various senses of individuality, the right to criticize, the autonomy of action, and the self-referential character of self-conscious knowledge.

The modern principle of subjectivity, Hegel thought, reached its fullest articulation in Kant's Three Critiques, where reason was divided into various moments and the unity of reason was construed as formal. Theoretical knowledge, practical reason, and aesthetic judgment become the respective bases for "science and technology, law and morality, art and art criticism" (19), those spheres of knowing all subordinated to an understanding of reason in terms of the principle of subjectivity and the dynamic structures of self-consciousness. Hegel's subsequent critique of Kant's epistemology and metaphysics focused on the question "whether one can obtain from subjectivity and self-consciousness criteria that are taken from the modern world and are at the same time fit for orienting oneself within it" (20). And in pursuing the project of a modernity that can ground itself while repeatedly criticizing the central oppositions and divisions within Kant's philosophy, Hegel tried to reinterpret the nature of reason and rationality not as a principle of self-conscious subjectivity but as "a power of unification" (21).

His motives, Habermas claims, are to be found in the personal crises of the young Hegel at Tübingen, Bern, and Frankfurt, where reason was still understood in connection with the models of the early Greeks and primitive Christians as a reconciling force between the spheres of belief and of everyday life. Hegel searches to reverse the effective Kantian substitution of understanding for reason by reestablishing the "disintegrated totality" of reason (19) with an appeal in the spirit of the *Systemprogramm* of 1796 and 1797 to the reconciling powers of art, a spirit already elaborated in Schiller's work of 1794 and Schelling's 1800 version of his own *System*.

Starting in 1801 with his Jena writings, however, Hegel sets aside this vision of art and turns instead to his elaboration of a philosophy of the absolute. The early idea of an "intersubjectivity of relationships based on mutual understanding" (29) and the traces of what Habermas controversially calls a "communicative reason" (74, 88) give way to a concept of the absolute, of "reason as the reconciling self-knowledge of an absolute spirit" (84), which finally substantiates a new hierarchy for the Kantian divisions. But this new subordination leaves the task reconciling reason with itself on internal rather than external grounds finally unaccomplished.

Habermas's proposal is that we return to this crossroads in the development of modernity, Hegel's wrong turn at Jena, and attempt to rethink the early project of a communicative reason (31). The task is to reestablish at the conceptual level the unity of reason—which already exists, Habermas thinks, at the intuitive level by retrieving "the scattered traces of reason in common practices themselves" (210). The inspiration is Walter Benjamin's, a view Habermas describes by saying: "the anticipation of what is new in the future is realized only through remembering a past that has been suppressed" (12). But the program is clearly Habermas's, one to which he has devoted enormous energy and on which he is still very much at work.

The diagnosis of the modern era that unfolds from a critique of various accounts since Weber of both modernity and modernization, and the extended regressive narrative that takes the story of modernity back to a postulated "crossroads" in the early Hegel's critique of Kant, is the backdrop of Habermas's own theory of communicative reason. Habermas's theory, however, is also informed by a particular understanding of the role of philosophy in the aftermath of modernity, where the modernist substitution of a procedural rationality of a substantive one in the understanding of objective scientific knowledge, moral practical insight, and aesthetic judgment requires continual criticism. In a section from his important 1983 book *Moral Consciousness and Communicative Actions*, Habermas sees the role of philosophy and his own theory of communicative action no longer as that of an usher or a judge but as the more modest one of a stand-in and interpreter.[6] This role, nonetheless, will still allow philosophy to remain as "the guardian of rationality" so long as it remains critically committed to an unconditional element that is "built into the structure of action-oriented-to-reaching understanding."[7]

---

[6]*Moralbewusstsein und kommunikatives Handeln* (Frankfurt, 1983). I cite the chapter "Philosophy as Stand-in and Interpreter" from the English translation as it appears in K. Baynes et al., eds., *After Philosophy: End or Transformation* (Cambridge, Mass., 1987), 296–319. The reference here is to 299, and I cite this work hereafter as "PSI."

[7]"PSI," 314. Habermas's discussion of the appearance of modernity at the end of the eighteenth century needs, I think, very thorough criticism. It is not clear, for one thing, that Habermas situates the "origins" of modernity early enough, whether in Hegel or in others like Schiller, in calling attention to the "crossroads" in Hegel's development. But even if we look closely at Hegel, why is the *Systementwurf* so

Conclusion

Such a philosophy would try to address in a new way the question Habermas derives from his critique of Hegel's philosophy of absolute self-consciousness and its failed justifications in Hegel's different versions of the *Logic*. The question runs: "How is it possible to weaken the claims of statements about totalities so that they might be joined together with the stronger statements about general structures?" (216). In trying to answer this question Habermas insists that philosophy needs to make a new start not from the subject but from what he calls variously "formal pragmatics" or "a pragmatic logic of argumentation" centered on an interpretation of "truth" in the sense of "a pragmatically differentiated everyday concept of truth" (196, 200, 203). Just what Habermas means in detail he still has not been able to work out.[8] But he suggests in this text that the key lies in "the analysis of the already operative potential for rationality contained in the everyday practices of communication. Here the validity dimensions of propositional truth, normative rightness, and subjective truthfulness or authenticity are intermeshed" (196). For Habermas thinks that every instance of communicative action oriented toward mutual understanding presupposes, as a condition of its possibility, "a moment of unconditionedness" (195).

For philosophy to play its new, more modest role, Habermas thinks that it must link its concern with "the unconditional to an ongoing critique of the 'maîtres penseurs,'" a phrase he borrows from some contemporary French work to describe those "magicians of a false paradigm from the intellectual constraints of which we have to escape" (296). Chief among such thinkers are both Kant and

---

important? Much new material is available on these matters that Habermas has yet to consider in print. Key examples are the latest volumes in the new Hegel edition with their very rich documentation, *Frühe Schriften*, part 1 (Hamburg, 1989), which includes materials to the end of 1796, with the rest to appear shortly in *Frühe Schriften*, part 2, *Frühe Exzerpte (1785–1800)* (Hamburg, 1989), and *Vorlesung über die Philosophie der Kunst* (Hamburg, 1990), as well as new volumes in the Schelling edition (Stuttgart, 1990). Moreover, new attention needs to be paid to Schlegel's *Transzendentalphilosophie (Jena 1800–1801)* (Hamburg, 1990), the six-volume *Kritische Schriften und Fragmente* (Munich, 1989), as well as to the earliest materials for Fichte's *Wissenschaftslehre*, the *Grundlage der gesamten Wissenschaftslehre (1794)* (Hamburg, 1988), and the early Schelling materials in the new Frommann edition (Stuttgart). Habermas at times in these historical musings seems more concerned with providing a genealogy of his own theory of communicative action than with opening up the origins of modernity. For just one of many alternative accounts see D. R. Lachterman, *Ethics of Geometry: A Genealogy of Modernity* (London, 1989).

[8]See, however, "Reply," 220, and the references to two recent dissertations on this topic on 311.

Hegel. The central problems Habermas has with Kant are curiously similar to some that troubled Bolzano—his epistemological foundationalism and his claim that the conceptual scheme he would impose on experience, the pure concepts of the understanding derived from the table of judgments, is ahistorical. And despite his penetrating criticisms of Kant, Hegel too is open to criticism, especially for his claims that the succession in the stages of the genesis of autonomous absolute consciousness is logically necessary and his commitment, shared with Kant, to the primacy of a philosophy of the subject. To both thinkers Habermas, together with other contemporary philosophers, would oppose the primacy of a pragmatic philosophy of the speaking subject. Such a philosophy would emphasize not self-reflection but linguistic communication and purposive action, where intersubjective knowledge "is mediated by language and linked to action" while requiring neither self-objectification nor "foundations" (304).

In pursuing these criticisms of the master thinkers while retaining a commitment to some role for an unconditional, Habermas is brought to consider the possibility that philosophy today might witness the birth of a new paradigm for rationality. Such a paradigm would replace the primacy of a philosophy of consciousness with that of a self-critical philosophy of intersubjective speech communities. But for this consideration, he says, he is unable to provide any arguments other than narrative ones (306). Yet while rejecting the various forms of contemporary farewells to philosophy, whether "therapeutic" like Wittgenstein's or "heroic" like Heidegger's or the "salvaging" type to be found in neo-Aristotelian attempts to reappropriate historical claims, Habermas himself calls attention to the ineluctable role in philosophy of "agreement reached by argument." The analysis of what makes possible such agreements among investigative communities is Habermas's project, especially his attention to the emergence of a new kind of hybrid discourse in the work of such thinkers as Freud, Durkheim, Mead, Weber, Piaget, and Chomsky.

The shift in perspective that Habermas is urging, from "solitary rational purposiveness to social interaction" (149), leads to his basic insight, the repeated claim that "we can find in language used communicatively the structures that explain how the life world is reproduced... through the subjects and their activity oriented towards mutual understanding" (143). This understanding of the life world, however, is not Dilthey's. For Habermas goes on to identify the structures of the life world with those necessary conditions that make rational discourse and arrgement possible, with "the universal pragmatic presuppositions of communicative action and argumentation" that are reflected in "the grammatical form of universal propositions" without, nonetheless, their validity being based upon "ultimate foundations" (408, n. 28).[9] Thus Habermas's theory focuses on an internal rather than an external relation between practices and reasons: "It studies the suppositions of rationality inherent in ordinary communicative practice and conceptualizes the normative content of action oriented toward mutual understanding in terms of communicative rationality" (76).

In his 1983 piece "Philosophy as Stand-in and Interpreter," Habermas has provided his own persuasive summary of this theory in its most recent form, a sentence I have already cited. We will do well now, before turning to an alternative diagnosis of modernity and rationality, to put that key formulation back into its very important synthetic context. Habermas writes:

> Every communication makes possible a kind of understanding that is based on claims to validity, thus furnishing the only real alternative to exerting influence on one another, which is always more or less coercive. The validity claims (i.e., of propositional truth, normative rightness, and subjective truthfulness) that we raise in conversation— that is, when we say something with conviction—transcend this specific conversational context, pointing to something beyond the spatio-temporal ambit of the occasion. Every agreement, whether produced for the first time or reaffirmed, is based on (controvertible) grounds or reasons. Grounds have a special property: They force us into yes or no positions. Built into the structure of action-oriented-to-reaching-understanding is therefore an element of unconditionality. And it is this unconditional element that makes the validity *(Gültigkeit)* we claim for our views different from the mere de facto acceptance *(Geltung)* of habitual practices. From the perspective of first persons, what we consider justified is not a function of life styles but a question of justification or grounding.

Habermas's account in his most recent work since the 1981 synthesis in *Theory of Communicative Action* is complicated. But I do not think we risk doing him an injustice if we try to scrutinize

[9]Habermas defines "communicative action" as "that form of social interaction in which the plans of action of different actors are co-ordinated through an exchange of communicative acts, that is, through a use of language (or of corresponding extra-verbal expressions) oriented towards reading understanding" ("Reply," 234; cf. 264).

that account sympathetically but critically under the somewhat artificial headings we have followed so far—those of his diagnosis of modernity, his narrative of the sources of modernity, and the elements of his own theoretical views in their latest guises.

Although he curiously skirts the major figures in what I have been calling the realist backgrounds of modern aesthetics, Habermas brings to the elaboration of his diagnosis of the modern era an extraordinarily wide-ranging command of the central discussions of the problem of modernity both before and after his chief reference, Max Weber. Moveover, his familiarity with a variety of contemporary discussions within the social sciences involving both methodological and substantive issues has enabled him to criticize Weber and his followers from a thoroughly contemporary standpoint. And his own reflections and activities in the struggle to reconstruct social democratic political structures in the aftermath of Germany's protracted defeat and the cold war have provided a rare pertinence and control to much of his work in the social sciences. But these strengths have corresponding weaknesses that I believe affect the coherence and final persuasiveness of Habermas's diagnosis.

Following up on the suggestiveness of Weber's flawed account of modernity, Habermas calls attention to how the modern economic and administrative organization of society has appreciably narrowed the very open domains of argument and debate that obtained in the eighteenth century. These structures in modern society, Habermas thinks, are best construed as "systems of goal-oriented action, and their growth seen as a type of rationalization which threatens to overcome every sphere of life, disrupting patterns of interaction and stifling processes of communication."[10] Accordingly, Habermas comes to formulate his own goal of displacing the modern teleological concept of action connected with a philosophy of subjectivity by a theory of communicative action joined to a philosophy of language and intersubjectivity.

This diagnosis, however, betrays a recurring difficulty. For it seems overdetermined by Habermas's polemic against an understanding of action in the modern era as mainly technological and

---

[10]J. B. Thompson, "Review of Habermas's *Theorie des kommunikativen Handelns*," *Times Literary Supplement*, 8 April 1983, 357. See also A. Honneth and H. Joas, eds., *Kommunikatives Handeln* (Frankfurt, 1986), S. K. White, *The Recent Work of J. Habermas: Reason, Justice, and Modernity* (Cambridge, 1988), and D. Ingram, *Habermas and the Dialectic of Reason* (New Haven, 1987).

reason as mainly instrumental.[11] We may wish to remind ourselves that Habermas is able to adduce an impressive range of evidence to support his characterization of modernity in terms of these interpretations of action and reason. But in the light of contemporary philosophical discussions of action, working through Habermas's repeated formulations of what he opposes shows that his descriptions remain superficial. They do not address clearly the properly metaphysical issues connected with the concepts of action and reason, some of the very resources on hand in the realist tradition stemming from Bolzano.[12] Instead, they remain caught up in the terminological and methodological tangles of disparate discussions in the social sciences only. The result is that Habermas leaves his diagnosis of modernity too general. One consequence is that his alternative account of a communicative action and a noninstrumental reason and rationality is too polarized by its rival's deficiencies.

Before we can appreciate this criticism, we need to sketch the consequences of this overgeneral diagnosis for Habermas's narrative of the origins of modernity. The difficulty here is not with overgenerality. More than most thinkers, Habermas has taken pains to develop a very detailed account, first in *Knowledge and Interests* and then in *The Philosophical Discourse of Modernity*, of the development of modernity since Kant. Rather, the problem is with the status of his cardinal claim that Hegel took a wrong turn at Jena. What made the turn wrong, Habermas explains at great length. But nowhere do we find sufficient clarification of exactly what the ontological connections are between the traces of a theory of communicative action in the young Hegel's preoccupations with reconciling the divisions within Kantian reason and a more than anachronistic, social-scientific notion of what rational actions are. Habermas does call welcome attention to Schiller's various attempts to salvage a coherent notion of "play" from the Kantian talk of "faculties" and from his efforts to work out a satisfactory

---

[11]See T. McCarthy's critique of Habermas's understanding of Weber, "Reflections on Rationalization in *The Theory of Communicative Action*," in *Habermas and Modernity*, ed. R. Bernstein, 176–92 (Cambridge, Mass., 1985), together with Habermas's replies in the same volume, "Questions and Counterquestions," 192–216, esp. 203–11. Unfortunately, Habermas's replies here do not take account of the very important exchanges with E. Tugendhat and H. Haferkamp on the occasion of their critical reactions to his summary text, "Remarks on the Concept of Communicative Action," in *Social Action*, ed. G. Seebass and R. Tuomela, 151–205 (Dordrecht, 1985). Cf. Apel's recent views in *Diskurs und Verantwortung* (Frankfurt, 1988).

[12]See A. Giddens, "Habermas's Critique of Hermeneutics," in *Studies in Social Thought* (London, 1977), 165 ff., and Habermas's discussion in "Reply" 263–69.

understanding of the reconciliations that art and the aesthetic are said to promise, something that neither analytic nor hermeneutic readings of eighteenth-century aesthetics do (despite Gadamer's interest in the notion of play). But even in these fine historical discussions we look in vain for appropriate analyses of the requisite kinds of rational actions and just how their practice can effect such obscure consequences as "reconciliation" and "reunification" of the cognitive, the moral, and the aesthetic.[13] Thus the overgeneral character of the diagnosis leads to an anticlimactic narrative.

This result once again is not without consequences of its own. For Habermas's narrative is propounded as one kind of explanation both for the continued fragmentation of the unity of reason in the modern era (Hegel made a wrong turn at the crossroads) and for the origins of a theory of communicative action that would allow us to reconcile reason with itself without inconsistency (seeing why Hegel's critique of subjectivity cannot rely on a philosophy of absolute self-consciousness). The new difficulty is not with using a narrative as a species of "explanation" in at least some plausible construal of that term, for Habermas has provided more than one persuasive discussion of "explanation and understanding" using Dilthey, his own readings of positivism, and his quarrels with hermeneutics today. Rather, the anticlimactic nature of the narrative Habermas develops—that is, its arguable misconstrual of the sense and purport of where it is made to end—undermines the avowedly self-critical nature of Habermas's own theory.

Recall that one of the claims of Habermas's predecessors in the Frankfurt school, especially Adorno, Horkheimer, and the early Marcuse, was that Marx and Freud invented a new type of theory, namely, "critical theory."[14] These theories were not objectifying theories like those found in the nature sciences but "reflective" ones, and they did not systematize a knowledge already on hand but provided a kind of knowledge not previously available. Most important, "critical theories" were understood to provide a knowledge that enabled agents to determine just what their "real inter-

[13]Cf. H. Ottmann, "Cognitive Interests and Self-Reflection," in the "Reply" collection, 79–98, and Habermas's rejoinder, 241 ff.

[14]For the history of the Frankfurt school and the work of its major figures see P.-L. Assoun, L'école de Francfort (Paris, 1987), R. Wiggershaus, Die Frankfurter Schule (Munich, 1986), and the influential initial overview by M. Jay, The Dialectical Imagination (Boston, 1973). Jay addresses Habermas's view on aesthetics in "Habermas and Modernism," in the Bernstein collection, 125–40. Cf. the excellent collection Die Frankfurter Schule und die Folgen, ed. A. Honneth and A. Wellmer (Berlin, 1986), with essays by Habermas and others.

ests" are (critical theories yield modern enlightenment) and a knowledge that freed agents from self-imposed coercions (critical theories bring modern emancipation). The goal of such theories was to overcome the ideological illusions—that is, those arising from the beliefs, attitudes, and dispositions that members of social groups exhibit in their motives, desires, values, predilections, and so on—that keep such persons from correctly perceiving their social repression and self-repression. Thus the reflective, enlightening, and emancipatory cognitive structures of the practices of critical theory were to replace the objectifying, misleading, and repressive cognition structures of the practices of scientific theory.[15]

Habermas's theory of communicative action is in part a critical theory of this sort. In its diagnosis of the present era it seeks to make its audiences aware of how their present legitimating beliefs, desires, and corresponding patterns of social behavior are neither rationally acquired nor in line with their rational interests. To the degree that this diagnosis raises consciousness to a reflective cognitive state, a nondeluded knowledge of the social world, we come to a new knowledge, an enlightenment and emancipation, that involves our seeing that there are no good reasons to accept our current legitimating beliefs and social practices. This knowledge opens us to consent with far greater freedom than before, through ongoing rational discussion among diverse communities of sincere inquirers, to the establishment of ideologically undistorted institutions and practices.

Now even when we supplement this sketch, as we should, with some of the rich detail in Habermas's readings of the early Marx and the reconstruction of a historical materialist critique of capitalism, his critique of positivism and ideology, and his readings of Freud, Piaget, and Parsons, as well as his general theories of social evolution, socialization, and universal pragmatics as a general theory of ideologically undistorted communication, we must not lose the forest for the trees. The theory of communicative action is a theory of action. But the overgeneral diagnosis of modernity and the anticlimactic narratives in search of explanation and understanding leave Habermas with the unresolved question of exactly how we are to parse the metaphysics of his highly suggestive but finally too sketchy account of the relations between the unity of an

---

[15]Cf. G. Kortian, *Metacritique: The Philosophy of Jürgen Habermas* (Cambridge, 1981).

immanent reason and the transcendental conditions of possibility for communicative action.[16]

This third and crucial difficulty comes down to questions about the ongoing simultaneous development of our standards for understanding communicative action, including our choices of logical primitives and conceptual frameworks, and the variegated forms of our many kinds of putative rational actions within historical societies and cultures. These issues, however, lead us to a different perspective on the modern era, and the contexts of our own philosophies of art today—that of Hilary Putnam. Looking at our current practices in the philosophy of art today from this second perspective will allow us to increase our purchase on the tensions between interpretation and history, theory and practice, we began with in Danto and Gadamer. Moreover, in Putnam's distinctive uses of a version of "realism" derived from a reading of Kant that unwittingly shows some affinity with Bolzano's, we will find another link with the realist backgrounds not just of modern aesthetics but of contemporary philosophy itself.

Modernity and Pragmatic Realism

Very much like Habermas, Hilary Putnam has been at work on a series of problems arising from his quite different interests in logic, philosophy of science, and language, which have resulted in a protracted diagnosis of the modern era. From his early work, on view in various places such as his 1971 book *Philosophy of Logic* and some essays in the first two volumes of his *Collected Papers*, to the more systematic presentations in *Meaning and the Moral Sciences* (1978) and *Reason, Truth and History* (1981), up to his more recent work in the third volume of his papers, *Realism and Reason* (1983), Putnam has been elaborating a progressive critique of the tensions in various formulations of the realism/antirealism controversies, where "realism" is understood more technically than the broader senses in which I have been referring to the realist backgrounds of modern aesthetics.[17] For our purposes here, howev-

---

[16]See McCarthy's difficulties with a transcendental-pragmatic theory of knowledge in the "Reply" book, "Rationality and Relativism: Habermas's 'Overcoming' of Hermeneutics," 57–79, and Habermas's rejoinder, 243 ff.

[17]Cf. note 25 in the Interlude. Early discussions can be found, for example, in his chapters on nominalism and realism in *The Philosophy of Logic* (New York, 1971), 9–33.

er, it will prove useful to confine ourselves to his diagnosis of the modern era as it takes on sharper contours in a series of later papers, "Two Conceptions of Rationality" (1981) and "Why Reason Can't Be Naturalized" (1982), his foreword (1983) to the fourth edition of Nelson Goodman's *Fact, Fiction and Forecast*, and especially his 1985 Carus Lectures, published under the title *The Many Faces of Reason* (1987).[18]

Putnam has been especially concerned with critically examining different contemporary versions of "relativism." Working from a set of interests in the philosophy of science, for example, he has been quick to contest the early views of both Kuhn and Feyerabend about incommensurability, the view that "terms used in another culture...cannot be equated in meaning or reference with any terms or expressions *we* possess."[19] Such a view, or one very much like it, has been the motive for many varieties of relativism, which Putnam sees as characteristic of our modern situation. Against the incommensurability thesis he argues that the usual practices of historical comparison and contrast presuppose the opposite. Thus, "to tell us that Galileo had 'incommensurable' notions and then go on to describe them at length is totally incoherent" (115).

This critique of relativism has led Putnam to stress the importance of certain "implicit norms" within our modern societies that are the bases of both our perceptual judgments and our linguistic conventions. Again like Habermas, Putnam relies on transcendental arguments to support these claims (113, 119, 124,). He goes on to distinguish conceptions of rationality involving positivist notions of justification that rely on institutional norms for drawing the lines between what is and what is not rationally acceptable— that is, criterial conceptions of rationality—and those that try to purge such conceptions of positivism while widening the interpretation of institutional norms—that is, noncriterial conceptions of rationality (110–13). The characteristic relativism of the modern era, and by extension we might argue of contemporary philosophies of art, depends upon an overly narrow understanding of rationality that is inconsistent with our cognitive, practical, and aesthetic practices.

[18]I have not made use of materials in his most recent collection, *Representation and Reality* (Cambridge, Mass., 1988), which I. Hacking, among others, criticizes in "Putnam's Change of Mind," *London Review of Books*, 4 May 1989, 15–16.

[19]"Two Conceptions of Rationality," in his *Reason, Truth and History* (Cambridge, 1981), 114. Following references in the text are to this paper until indicated otherwise.

But if relativism is inconsistent, any kind of dogmatism is equally unacceptable. In exploring the difficulties with any dogmatic alternative to relativism, Putnam marks out most clearly his own position. Thus in 1982 he pursues his critique of relativism by insisting not just on the transcendence of reason but on its immanence as well. Putnam stresses that we inherit certain traditions and at the same time remake them. Both situations, not just one or the other, must be addressed in any adequate account of rationality. Talk of truth and falsity makes sense only against the backdrop of criticizing inherited traditions of such talk; but such criticism itself makes sense only against the backdrop of some contingent interpretation of truth and falsity. Relativism tries to capture the insight that "truth and rational acceptability... are relative to the sort of language we are using and the sort of context we are in."[20] It thereby tries to overcome the difficulties with both evolutionary epistemologies (a belief is rational if it is arrived at by the use of our evolving capacity of discovering truths) and reliability theories of truth (a belief is rational if it is arrived at by use of a reliable method). But in neglecting the interpetations of truth, rational acceptability, and justification that traditions have already built into the very ways we articulate our relativisms, such culturally relativistic views remain contingently self-referential and lead to cultural imperialism (233–34).

Putnam wants to argue positively in these papers that whatever sense talk of "truth" makes is formally dependent on "versions" (223, 227, 234). This term derives from Nelson Goodman's work, which Putnam continued to challenge until his turnaround in his 1983 foreword to the fourth edition of Goodman's 1956 classic. There, in a thorough summary discussion of the continuing pertinence of Goodman's early work on how to describe induction and the problem of accounting for why all predicates are not equally projectable to a population for a sample, Putnam again returned to the characteristic relativism of the modern era, this time to one of its influential logical forms. He stressed how the idea of conceptual relativity behind certain accounts of cultural and epistemological relativisms was linked to the early views Putnam and Goodman shared with their teacher Rudolf Carnap, especially his views on

---

[20]"Why Reason Can't Be Naturalized," in Baynes et al., eds., *After Philosophy*, 222–45 (Cambridge, Mass., 1987). Following references in the text are to this paper until indicated otherwise.

"the way in which a predicate can be disjunctive or non-disjunctive, that is, relative to a language or a choice of primitives."[21]

Goodman provided a mechanism for showing how some predicates, including nonobservational ones, could be understood as acquiring projectability, roughly, through the evolution of a culture. And this view seemed generalizable to the idea that the contingent history of a culture is what determines the critical relations between our standards and our practices. Putnam drew the provisional Wittgensteinian conclusion that, rather than formulations, there are "practices, and these practices are right or wrong depending on how they square with our standards. Our standards are right or wrong depending on how they square with our practices" (ix). This idea, of course, remains full of interest for trying to resolve the split between theory and practice that we explored in Danto's work and Gadamer's in chapter 1.

At this critical juncture Putnam could see the circle in Goodman's mature views—no foundations, just practices; practices not true or false, but right or wrong; rightness and wrongness as functions of our standards; but the standards must cohere with the practices. Yet he saw the circle as virtuous, not vicious, more a spiral than a circle. Standards and practices thus are correlative; they develop together within the contingent historical limits of a culture. The task is not to square the circle but to understand the Carnapian puzzles in the conceptual relativism underlying the modern era. Putnam's own task was to sustain a critique of the strongest versions of a logical positivism to which he himself had subscribed much earlier by working out a fresh understanding of the mysterious correlation of transcendence and immanence he had come to on rereading Goodman. He would do so by moving on two fronts: elaborating, like Habermas, a historical narrative that would move behind positivism and neo-Kantianism to the Kantian critiques of reason, and refining a systematic resolution of the realism/antirealism debate in terms of a pragmatic realism centered on neither metaphysics nor epistemology but ethics. He took up this task in *The Many Faces of Realism*.

Beginning with a sketch of different interpretations of "realism" and showing how each construal relied on a dualistic view of reality with mind and its ideas and impressions (sense data) on one

---

[21]"Foreword," in N. Goodman, *Fact, Fiction and Forecast*, 4th ed. (Cambridge, Mass., 1983), x. Following references in the text are to this paper until indicated otherwise. I discuss some related aspects of Goodman's aesthetics in *Fictions, Philosophies, and the Problems of Poetics* (Ithaca, 1988), 146–51, 261–72.

side and the primary qualities of the physical world on the other, Putnam argues that the central difficulty lies with the notion of an intrinsic property, "a property something has 'in itself' apart from any contribution made by language or the mind."[22] In its modern undifferentiated guise of "disposition," the notion of intrinsic property leads to the denial of objective reality, with a conflation of reality with thought. Putting things right requires avoiding both reductive materialism that explains away the emergence of mind and an extreme relativism that cannot account for the external world.

In place of his own early functionalist approach, Putnam now proposed a view he first called "internal realism" and now prefers to call "pragmatic realism." This view tries to combine a version of realism with a version of conceptual relativity in order to preserve a commonsense realism (tables and chairs really exist) while eschewing a metaphysical realism (tables and chairs are projections only of what really exists, namely, scientific objects). Pragmatic realism, by contrast, holds that terms such as "object," "existence," and even the logical primitives have no absolute meaning but only various uses (19). Pragmatic realism, however, is not a conceptual relativism ("true" is only what persons can agree on) but a conceptual relativity ("true" is what persons can agree on in a consensus dependent on one version within a multitude available). Thus there are no real objects independent of our choice of a language, concepts, and a conceptual scheme, because "there are no standards for the use of even the logical notions apart from conceptual choices" (35–36). But given that such a choice is ineluctable, it follows that there are always real objects—"there are 'external facts,' and we can say what they are. What we cannot say—because it makes no sense—is what the facts are independent of all conceptual choices" (33). Pragmatic realism thus comes to the nonclassical view that there are equivalent but incompatible ways of describing "the same" facts (29), a view that in different guises has a long history.

Central to Putnam's account is his insisting with Chomsky on continua while rejecting dichotomies. In particular, Putnam rejects the splits between a "power" and a property of the thing in itself, between a projection and a property of the thing in itself, between the subjective relative to culture and interest and the objective

---

[22]*The Many Faces of Realism* (La Salle, Ill., 1987), 8. Following references in the text are to this book unless indicated otherwise. Cf. E. Prior, *Dispositions* (Aberdeen, 1985).

relative to culture and interest, and between types of statements in a semantics possessing only assertibility conditions and those in a semantics possessing truth conditions. He also rejects the corollaries— "true" as simply true versus "true" as warranted assertibility idealized, and "exist" in Carnap's version of an existential quantifier versus, for example, "exist" in Stanistang Leśniewski's version of an existential quantifier. When viewed from the perspective of Putnam's pragmatic realism, a world apparently without dichotomies, the world is neither an appearance nor a reality. It exhibits neither a manifest nor a scientific image, but includes tables and chairs as well as quanta and gravitational fields. In short, "we are forced to acknowledge that many of our familiar descriptions reflect our interests and choices" (37). And yet we have no sufficient license for jettisoning the useful distinction between causes and background statements, even when we must free such a distinction from any necesary tie to some fiction called nature in itself.

Now many of these views—and this is our major interest here— share an acknowledged kinship with a particular reading of Kant's philosophy. For Putnam's view is largely a not uncontroversial attempt to tailor Dieter Henrich's reading to his own progressive articulation of a pragmatic realism (cf. 51, n. 7). He does not seem to have studied Bolzano.

Putnam believes that Kant has "two philosophies," that of the *Critique of Pure Reason* and that of the *Critique of Practical Reason*. The first, he thinks, can be read in such a way as to disassociate Kant from the view that a "thing in itself" is an intelligible notion, while the second can be read in such a way as to commit Kant to the view that the notion of a "thing in itself" "makes some kind of sense even if we are unable to say what kind of sense that is" (42). These readings result in the two-worlds view, the world of experience where knowledge is of appearances only (the world of science), and the world of things in themselves where no knowledge is possible (the world of freedom, immortality, and God).

With some others, Putnam rejects Kant's two-worlds view. Yet he finds a clue for rereading Kant in the surmise that the First Critique itself can be interpreted as involving a rejection of "things in themselves and projections," and that the Second Critique involves a different understanding of reason than the first. Accordingly, just as Habermas tries to go back and find a forerunner of his theory of communicative reason in the early Hegel's talk of inter-subjective consensus, so Putnam wants to see in Kant's rejection of a correspondence theory of truth the precursor of his own theory of pragmatic realism. Understandably, Putnam advances this claim cautiously; he uses semicolons. "If Kant was saying that truth must not be thought of as correspondence to a pre-structured or self-structured Reality; if he was saying that our conceptual contribution cannot be factored out and that the 'makers-true' and the 'makers-verified' of our beliefs lie within and not outside our conceptual system; then Kant may properly be called the first 'internal realist'" (43). Putnam focuses this claim on the Second Critique and takes as his task the formulation of an "internal realism" in moral philosophy based on the idea that Kant's moral philosophy "represents, above all, a rethinking of the values that Kant took from Rousseau (and of the fundamental ideas of the French Revolution), in particular of the value of Equality" (44).

We need not follow the twists as Putnam's tries to give Kant's attempts to build liberty into equality a Rawlsian turn (46), or his focus on a deep Kantian skepticism about the use of reason and free will in an Enlightenment rather than a medieval context, where the rationality of morality and religion is inherently problematic.[23] The central claim is clear enough. Kant provides us with, in Henrich's phrase, a moral image of the world, "a picture of how our virtues and ideals hang together with one another and of what they have to do with the position we are in" (51), "a vision which includes and organizes a complex system of values" (62). In this picture the loss of essences and the ignorance of what constitutes happiness as well-being or human flourishing (eudaimonia) is not to be lamented but should be celebrated. And such a picture calls for a new understanding of equality.

Putnam now explicitly addresses Habermas's earlier attempt to derive an understanding of equality from rationality. Relying exclusively on the early work of Habermas (*Knowledge and Human Interests*) and Karl-Otto Apel (*Charles S. Peirce: From Pragmatism to Pragmaticism*),[24] Putnam takes the main ideas to comprise the connections between warranted statements involving implicit references to community, rational discourse involving implicit references to truth, sincerity, and so on, and rational criticism involving implicit references to ongoing communities of inquirers. These

[23]See, however, his 1983 Lindley Lecture, "How Not to Solve Ethical Problems" (University of Kansas).

[24](Amherst, 1981). See also Apel's *Understanding and Explanation* (Cambridge, Mass., 1984) and *Transcendental Semiotics as First Philosophy* (New Haven, 1986), and his most recent book cited in note 11, which Putnam does not mention.

ideas he sees as requiring the principles of "intellectual freedom and equality" (54). Unlike the early Habermas, however, Putnam does not believe that a universal ethic can be derived from truth as "idealised rational acceptability" (55). Pointing rather to situations where one's opponent holds either a noncognitivist view of ethical beliefs or an inegalitarian view of society, Putnam argues instead for weaker connections between rationality and ethics where, without any commitments to a universal ethic, we have strong grounds for holding to "a rich and multifaceted idea of the good" whose parts are interconnected (56), a view that curiously overlaps with some of Gadamer's work.

Such a view involves resisting the two major defects of Kant's moral philosophy as Putnam understands it, a monistic moral image of the world and an unrelieved formal stress on the rigor of duty. Instead, Putnam plumps for a pluralism of substantial "moral images of the world" (Henrich's phrase) and suitable emphasis on feeling that could embrace some interpretations of both Roman civic republicanism and French *fraternité*.

In the last of his four Carus Lectures, "Reasonableness as a Fact and as a Value," Putnam returns to the task of refining his initial discussion of pragmatic realism. He now describes the key to his position as the primacy of the agent's viewpoint over that of the spectator (70). The main problem with the latter is its commitment to there being only one way the world is, to there being *the* world *tout court*, a world that is coextensive with what *the* scientific method shows to be the case. But Putnam's critique of Reichenbach and his pursuit of case studies in various sciences, he reports,have convinced him that "no one paradigm can fit all of the various inquiries that go under the name of 'science'" (72). Consequently he claims that we neither have nor can have any one best version, whether of mathematics or of causality or of ethics. Taking the agent point of view leads rather to a fallibilism, a pluralism, and a version of realism that includes some objectivity—"what we have are better or worse versions, and that is objectivity" (77). In other words, "the fact that we 'make' facts and values doesn't mean that they are arbitrary" (78), for these facts and values can be better or worse, our statements can be more or less right.

For Putnam such comparatives follow from the ongoing, continual historical adjustment within a culture of the reciprocity between practices and standards within a changing, "potentially infinite community of investigators" (83). Here, Putnam says, he can go no further. Alluding to the later Wittgenstein's remark in the

Investigations (sec. 217), he says: "I have reached bedrock and this is where my spade is turned" (85). But even this conclusion he quickly qualifies as provisional, as subject to still further adjustments between his own practices, his own standards.

Now when we look back through this comprehensive and nuanced story in Putnam, we find a number of persuasive discussions. Once again, however, just as in the case of Habermas, though in a different order, I will focus appreciative but nonetheless critical attention on only three elements—Putnam's version of a diagnosis of the modern era and the peculiar problems with practical reason, the prescription for a cure in the guise of a theory, and the narrative and not merely formal justification he proposes for his theory.

Putnam's diagnosis of the modern era turns on a discussion, as we have seen, of the legacy of logical positivism, particularly in the contemporary debates within various philosophies of science of the realism/antirealism issue. The major point here is Putnam's argued conviction that neither an exaggerated conventionalism nor an equally exaggerated commonsense realism can do sufficient justice to this legacy.[25] Thus he contends that the task today is to overcome the central dichotomies of the modern era in such a way as to account for both theoretical entities and everyday, human-scale objects. These dichotomies he understands as arising mainly from Carnap's unsuccessful struggles with the unwelcome metaphysical consequences of his attempts to deal in a new way with the problems of induction as well as from Goodman's working through the projection problem to a metaphysics of neither realism nor antirealism. On Putnam's view, however, such a metaphysics—even if it courageously faces up to the epistemological and ontological demands that in some sense Carnap did not entirely confront—leaves the practical realm, including art and not just ethics, in disarray. For we are left with a finally mysterious account, in terms of an "irrealism" already elusive enough in the theoretical realm, of a central practical distinction between fact and value.

But one might plausibly object that this story of the modern era is far too particular to capture the problematic nature of the very general character of such an era. Granted that making sense of the fact/value distinction in terms of some version of, if not Goodman's "irrealism," then of an "internal" realism, is a necessary sequel to the heritage of a sympathetic account of logical positiv-

[25]See two of his recent papers, "After Empiricism," in *Post-analytic Philosophy*, ed. J. Rajchman and C. West (New York 1985), and "Meaning Holism" in *The Philosophy of W. W. Quine* (La Salle, Ill., 1986).

ism. Still, this task turns out to be far less central an undertaking when we admit, as we must, to the nonexclusive role of logical positivism in the modern period. For our contemporary Western situation also includes the consequences of the fateful split in the 1890s between Frege and Husserl that lead to the separate development of analytic philosophy and of phenomenology. And it also includes the consequences of the still earlier split among Marx, Kierkegaard, and Nietzsche as the critical inheritors of the already divided readers of Hegel. Putnam's diagnosis is articulate, well argued, and persuasive. But in its exaggeration of the role of logical positivism, philosophy of science, and philosophy of logic for understanding the modern era, his diagnosis remains insufficiently general. It focuses on only one division within practical reason as central to modernity while neglecting the more substantial divisions within reason and rationality itself.

The consequences are evident in the account of pragmatic realism that Putnam goes on to prescribe as a remedy. For the recurring difficulty does not lie with understanding the peculiar species of internal realism Putnam is still urging. Rather, even his sympathetic readers are left at a loss to make enough sense out of the difference between Putnam's "correlation" of standards and practices and Goodman's virtuous circle of worlds, versions, and rightness of discourse. In particular, the problem is the unavailability so far of any thorough discussion of how standards and practices evolve together within contingent historical and cultural situations that mysteriously allow some interpretation of "transcendence." The arguments Putnam uses against strong forms of cultural relativism are certainly important contributions to our understanding, but so far we still lack equally persuasive arguments for how his pragmatic realism can accommodate transcendence.[26] Until Putnam is willing to generalize his concerns with the fact/value dichotomy in practical reason to a fruitful discussion of how to address some modern forms of the antinomies of reason *tout court*, I believe that his pragmatic realism will remain a sophisticated theory of only the immanance of reason.

[26]For somewhat different criticisms see H. Field, "Realism and Reason," *Journal of Philosophy* 79(1982): 553–67, and J. Margolis, "Cognitive Issues in the Realist-Idealist Dispute," *Midwest Studies in Philosophy* 5(1980): 373–90. Cf. G. Prauss, *Handlungstheorie in Transzendentalphilosophie* (Frankfurt, 1986), and H. Holz, *System der Transzendentalphilosophie im Grundriss* (Freiberg, 1977). Note that whatever his sympathies may be for Margolis, Putnam is strongly opposed to Field's physicalism, the view that all semantic properties can be empirically reduced to physical ones. See Putnam's article "Three Kinds of Scientific Realism," *Philosophical Quarterly* 32(1982): 195–200.

This need not be the case, especially when we reflect on the suggestiveness of Putnam's supporting narrative. For Putnam sees the interest in the Frankfurt school's attempt to find a version of transcendence within an analysis of the conditions that render sincere argumentative discourse possible inside changing communities of investigators. And while usefully qualifying the universalist pretensions of such a program, Putnam shares Habermas's interest in providing a very general scope for the use of transcendental arguments. Moreover, Putnam also understands in some detail as well as with an attractive critical distance the Kantian antecedents of such strategies. But notwithstanding his own awareness of how the central strands in the problems arising in the contemporary debates of realism and antirealism run back through neo-Kantianism, to Kant's variegated uses of reason in the differences among the Three Critiques and even beyond through Berkeley and Locke back to Descartes, Putnam relies on an avowedly controversial reading of Kant. Yet this reading depends almost exclusively on one contemporary interpretation (Henrich's), without making any sustained attempt to confront Hegel's thoroughgoing overhaul of the Kantian project, which Henrich himself continues to study in detail. Putnam's Kant, for all the promise of understanding newly the recurring ambiguities, strains, and inconsistences in the progressive reformulations of reason and rationality across the Three Critiques, the *Grundlegung*, and the words on religion, finally fails to interest us enough because Kant turns out to be no more than a "forerunner" of pragmatic realism. Very much like the analytic reading of eighteenth-century aesthetics, the narrative argument ends in an appropriation of a controversial "Kant," a reading finally impatient with the complicated detail of Kant's struggles to render reason both immanent and transcendent.

If, very roughly, Habermas's diagnosis of modernity, argumentative narrative, and theory of communicative action relies centrally on an insufficiently detailed account of the immanence of reason within the structure of rational agency, then Putnam's diagnosis, narrative, and theory of "pragmatic realism" rely just as centrally on a still problematic version of the transcendence of reason within the changing dialectical relations of standards and practices.[27] We recognize immediately, however, that such a judgment is too sum-

---

[27]See Michael Devitt's discussions in *Realism and Truth* (Princeton, 1984), and his critical study of Putnam's 1978 *Meaning and the Moral Sciences*, "Realism and the Renegade Putnam," *Nous* 17(1983): 291–301. Cf. also the different picture of Kant in, to take only one example, P. Kitcher, "Kant's Philosophy of Science," in *Self and Nature in Kant's Philosophy*, ed. A. W. Wood (Ithaca, N.Y., 1984), 185–216.

mary. It leaves out a series of genuinely instructive analyses that I now, in the final sections of this Conclusion, review briefly in the interests of inventorying the main elements for a provisional account— of modernity as our present standpoint, of aesthetic agency, and of the eighteenth-century reconstruals of art and reason.

Modernity, Immanence, and Transcendence

We need to pull together in at least a programmatic way the major elements we have been concerned with in this final chapter. My purpose here is not to attempt a diagnosis of the modern era in my own right, nor to put in place a particular narrative, whether progressive or regressive, of the major theories of reason and rationality from the eighteenth century to the twentieth, nor to undertake a systematic discussion of certain issues in one of the arts that would make use of conceptual resources in the realist backgrounds of modern aesthetics. And I do not have any theory or account of such matters as are at issue in communicative action and pragmatic realism. Rather, I am concerned to call attention to how the seminal period in modern aesthetics and the philosophy of art, the eighteenth century, when viewed from the neglected standpoint of the diverse analyses of the aesthetic within the realist tradition, allows of more than one plausible reading, whether analytic or hermeneutic or Marxist. The plurality of these readings, when supported by a critical account of such searching understandings of the modern standpoint from which we undertake such readings, strongly suggests the need to break out of the confines of the most important contemporary discussions of the eighteenth-century thinkers. This applies to the continuing disputes between a Stolnitz and a Dickie on disinterested versus aesthetic perception and their modern legacy as well as to those I have not examined here, between a Gadamer and a Habermas on the claims of universality for a hermeneutic account of understanding.

When we begin with our present standpoint and attempt to gain a critical sense of its historical and philosophical contexts, both Habermas's and Putnam's diagnoses are suggestive. Putnam views the modern era with an eye to the development of modern philosophies of subjectivity. Stretching from Descartes's uneasy epistemological break with the largely logical and metaphysical preoccupations of late Scholasticism, through the development of Continental rationalism in the work of Leibniz, into the consolidation of the early

English empiricism of Bacon and Hobbes in the varied work of John Locke and its different critical explorations in the opposed philosophies of Berkeley and Hume, modern philosophy on this view achieves a reasonably persuasive synthesis in the great and protracted critiques of Kant. And this work continues to dominate our own era in that the agendas of the later neo-Kantian movements, logical positivism, and even much (but not all) of the Wittgensteinian heritage today can plausibly be understood as a development of the Kantian problematic of setting the bounds not just of reason but of language itself.

This account of our present standpoint is helpful in reminding us how situating critically our own reflections on philosophy and the arts requires of us an explicit attempt to deal imaginatively with the very difficult problems of incompatible conceptual frameworks, philosophies of logic, and philosophies of science. But Putnam's view is also too narrow, for it does not allow us to thematize explicitly the larger historical, social, and cultural contexts within which these ongoing struggles with standards and practices are to be negotiated.[28] Moreover, it is dangerously unself-conscious, that is, uncritically content to continue to construe our present dynamic standpoint from the unchallenged perspective of its own neo-Kantian understanding of the modern philosophical canon in the historical works of almost a hundred years ago, those of a Windelband and a Zeller, while neglecting its affinities with the extraordinary work of Bolzano. Putnam's view of the modern era comes to an understanding of modernity in the exclusive terms of a neo-Kantian history of modern philosophy. And this view arguably is also the source of the more restricted history of modern aesthetics we find as the background both to the analytic view of the eighteenth-century thinkers, the Beardsley background to the Stolnitz and Dickie controversy, and to the theory/practice split in Danto's historicist philosophy of art.

Still, if the diagnosis of the modern era in Putnam's progressive reading is overly narrow and insufficiently self-critical, nonetheless this view is accompanied by a penetrating analysis of the tensions between dogmatism and relativism. Putnam's conclusion so far—his shovel has turned on bedrock—may be too fanciful for some, too pretentious for others. But his attempt to move the discussion

---

[28]Putnam does not seem to be aware of the controversial backgrounds of his account of ethics. See S. Benhabib and F. Dallmayer, eds., *The Communicative Ethics Controversy* (Cambridge, Mass., 1988).

of incompatible if not incommensurable logical and conceptual frameworks a step beyond Goodman's very suggestive but finally unsatisfactory talk of radical pluralisms—of rightness of renderings and versions rather than of truth theories and worlds—while at the same time rigorously resisting the sirens of Richard Rorty's radical relativism is impressive.[29] For those concerned with understanding just what possibilities remain to be explored in the interactions between the diverse practices of philosophy and the arts when the modernist contexts of both are put into critical perspective, Putnam's investigations about alternative logics, modal concepts, analyticity and apriority, equivalence reference and truth, on "why there isn't a ready-made world" and on "why reason can't be naturalized"—to cite only a few topics from his 1983 collection *Realism and Reason*[30]—are indispensable aids in seeing through the epistemological fog to some of the genuinely metaphysical and ontological issues involved in the realist backgrounds of modern aesthetics.

By contrast with Putnam's progressive reading of the modern era in the neo-Kantian light of a history of modern philosophy only, Habermas may be understood as proposing a regressive reading of modernity in the neo-Hegelian light of the historicity of the modern era as itself a philosophical problem, a view extremely close to Danto's guiding lights. Habermas, as we have seen, begins with a controversial but wide-ranging critique of contemporary social science understandings of the modern era, moves behind poststructuralist, Frankfurt school, hermeneutic, and neo-Kantian thought to the work of the masters of suspicion—Freud, Nietzsche, and Marx—and then undertakes a repeated scrutiny of German idealist thought from the Young Hegelians back to the work of Fichte and Schelling and to Hegel's mature philosophy, which he sees as a failure. The source of this failure he pursues even further back, we recall, to the "crossroads" in the early Hegel where the insights of his Tübingen friends, Hölderlin and the young Schelling, as well as the essays and drama of Schiller and Schlegel's early criticism, all converged on the task of rearticulating the unity and reconciliation of reason

---

[29]Rorty is an important link between Habermas and Putnam. See, for example, his "Habermas and Lyotard on Postmodernity" together with Habermas's responses in *Reply*, 161–76 and 192–98, respectively, as well as "The Historiography of Philosophy: Four Genres," in *Philosophy in History*, ed. R. Rorty et al., 49–77 (Cambridge, 1984), and Putnam's strictures in his 1982 paper cited above on Rorty's more general views. Rorty has also tried to use Gadamer against Habermas and Apel. See G. Warnke's helpful discussion in *Gadamer: Hermeneutics, Tradition, and Reason* (Stanford, 1987), 137–66.

[30](Cambridge, 1983).

with itself on immanent rather than transcendent terms. And here at last in the earliest criticisms of Kant's aesthetics, especially as we find them transmuted in the *Systemprogramm*, Habermas claims to discern the traces of a theory of communicative action that his present work is designed to explicate.

Once again we may find this account helpful, although in quite different ways than Putnam's. It compels those of us who are interested in philosophy and the arts today to situate our present standpoint in a context larger than merely philosophy. For Habermas's view compromises a distinctive and continuing discussion of the many ways the preoccupation with philosophical knowledge is continually exposed to the subversions of unacknowledged interests.[31] And these interests inform much of the context of our philosophical reflection—they structure in important ways the institutions and practices in which people do philosophy today while practicing and criticizing the arts. Habermas's repeated emphases on the historical, political, sociological, psychological, and even psychoanalytic dimensions of our current philosophical standpoint, as well as his awareness of the challenge to philosophy in "hybrid discourse," give his diagnosis of modernity a breadth and an openness of self-criticism that is often missing in Putnam's much more conventional story. And his critical understanding of Hegel links him closely, despite his interests, with Gadamer's affinities for Hegel—affinities, it must be said, that lie far deeper than Danto's.

Yet Habermas's account is, as we have seen, not without weaknesses of its own. Regardless of the controversial aspects of his narrative, his own theory of communicative action seems to claim a universality whose pretensions he himself had thoroughly criticized in Gadamer's hermeneutics.[32] More important are the as yet unresolved difficulties with working out exactly how we may construe the unity of reason and the reconciled forms of rationality with the aid of a philosophy of language and communicative speech acts that pays sufficient attention to the consequences of radical conceptual pluralisms. If, very generally, we may say that Habermas's diagnosis of modernity is a persistent reminder that any more satisfactory investigation into philosophy and the arts today must look through the contemporary philosophical scene to its larger and mainfold

---

[31]See his *Die neue Unübersichtlichkeit* (Frankfurt, 1985).

[32]See, however, his discussion of different universality theses in "Reply," 256–57. Habermas's original criticisms are to be found in *Zur Logik der Sozialwissenschaften* (Frankfurt, 1970), and in K. O. Apel, ed., *Hermeneutik und Ideologiekritik* (Frankfurt, 1977). Warnke provides a good discussion (1987: 107–38).

nonphilosophical backgrounds, that is not to say that we need buy uncritically into Habermas's concomitant theory of communicative action. And if just as generally we may argue that Putnam's philosophies of logic and language sensitize us to the ineluctable role metaphysics must play in our investigations, we are not by that fact constrained to select and address only those metaphysical issues that arise from the diverse legacies of logical positivism in our philosophies of science today and their continuing disputes about versions of realism, antirealism, and "irrealism."[33] The metaphysical issues that we now suspect render Putnam's pragmatic realism unpersuasive—if we can succeed in formulating them with a greater distance from their inspiration in Putnam's critiques of Reichenbach, Carnap, Quine, and Davidson and draw on the larger realist backgrounds of modern aesthetic, to which I have tried to point here—require our fresh attention. For every philosophy of art is more than an ontology; it is also a historical metaphysics. And the unaddressed linguistic and logical issues we equally suspect of continuing to undercut the persuasive historical and philosophical motivation of Habermas's theory of communicative action—if we can succeed in articulating them quasi-formally with some strong rational independence from historical and narrative supports, perhaps again only by drawing on the same realist backgrounds—also require fresh attention.[34] For every philosophy of art is more than a historical praxis; it entails a rationality as well. And just as Habermas's inviting appeal to the uses and implications of transcendental arguments in the modernist practice of philosophy invites further scrutiny, so too does Putnam's attentive insistence in the limits of systematic philosophy but also on its necessary role in philosophy today. Both merit the renewed attention of philosophers of art, whether those who lean to Danto's work and others like Margolis and Sparshott in an analytic tradition, or those who lean rather to Gadamer's work and others like Ricoeur and Deleuze who are in a Continental tradition. In each case, however, further substantive work in the philosophy of art must address not only its own

[33]See, for example, Putnam's "On Truth," in *How Many Questions?* ed. L. Caumann, 35–56 (Indianapolis, 1983). Cf. R. G. Millikan's criticisms in her book *Language, Thought, and Other Biological Categories* (Cambridge, Mass., 1984), and especially her article "Metaphysical Anti-realism?" *Mind* 95(1986): 417–31.

[34]Habermas recognizes some of the key difficulties here, as his 1976 essay "What Is Universal Pragmatics?" shows. See the English translation in his collection *Communication and the Evolution of Society* (Boston, 1979), 1–69. See also J. B. Thompson's strictures in his "Universal Pragmatics" contributions to the "Reply" book together with Habermas's response, 116–34 and 270 ff., respectively.

context of modernity and the historically overdetermined notion of aesthetics but perhaps the bounds of art as well.

Toward Rethinking the Aesthetic Origins of Modernity

Having in hand these instructive attempts at interpreting our larger contemporary philosophical standpoint on the problems of reconciling immanence and transcendence, theoretical and practical reason, I now return to our concern in part 1 with how to read the seminal eighteenth-century texts in aesthetics. My aim will be to suggest, although not to argue in any extensive rereading of the texts themselves, that understanding the consequences of modernity for philosophy and the arts today requires us to relativize the major opposition between analytic and hermeneutic views. We need to displace its center of gravity from the Kantian texts to those earlier and more obscure exchanges that are part of the larger and more than just philosophical shifts in the early to middle eighteenth century, with the difficult emergence of neoclassical frameworks for mind and the world, a work I have begun to develop elsewhere.[35]

The Stolnitz-Dickie controversy is, as we saw in the Interlude, instructive in its own right. As a case study of a protracted contemporary controversy within Anglo-American aesthetics today on just how our philosophical concerns with the arts are in central ways indebted to the eighteenth-century thinkers, the dispute provides a reading of these thinkers together with a systematic attempt to differentiate the structures of aesthetic attitude theories from theories of taste. Whatever we make of the merits and weaknesses of these extensive exchanges (A tempest in a teapot?), we need only expand our angle of vision to recognize immediately a very different picture of these eighteenth-century issues, the one that emerges from the oppositions between an analytic and a hermeneutic reading of these texts and others. In this larger perspective the central issue is not whether the eighteenth-century investigations are finally to be comprehended in terms of the legitimacy of construing their very complicated discussions of disinterestedness as aesthetic, not just disinterested perception.

---

[35]See my forthcoming paper "Hogarth and the Realist Backgrounds of Modern Aesthetics," in *Hogarth*, ed. S. Shestakov (Moscow, 1989). Careful attention must be paid as well to currents like those W. S. Howell studies in his *Eighteenth-Century British Logic and Rhetoric* (Princeton, N.J., 1971).

Rather, the cardinal issue comes down to recognizing and retrieving the many disparate considerations in these texts of common sense, taste, tact, cultivation, and so on as genuine though indirect forms of knowledge. But here too still more important matters come into view when we forgo mediating this larger dispute not between two analytic readings but between both analytic and hermeneutic ones in favor of turning our critical scrutiny back on our own standpoint at the outset of this book, the standpoint of modernity that in its shared but different allegiances to Hegel and historicist philosophies of art underlies the different tensions between theory and practice in both Danto's work and Gadamer's.

When we undertake such an attempt to relativize these contemporary controversies and try to think twice about both our standpoint and our angle of vision, we come upon deep disagreements about the nature, kinds, and consequences of philosophical pluralism in the work of many philosophers today, especially such representative Continental and Anglo-American figures as I have settled on here with Danto and Gadamer, Habermas and Putnam. The peculiar strengths and weaknesses of these sophisticated views—at least the few I have had to select, without claiming to do any final justice to such diverse, extensive, and penetrating work—suggest at the end of this inquiry at least four issues that rearticulate our concerns at the end of the Introduction and cut across the major differences between a hermeneutic and an analytic reading, while drawing on at least some of the resources of another tradition, the arguable successor to Bolzano.

Habermas and Putnam share with a number of their contemporaries one critical charge against modernity—its institutionalization of an epistemological foundationalism, issuing from the vagaries of a post-Fregean reading of Kant's transformation of a Cartesian philosophy of subjectivity. The key to neutralizing the stultifying effects of this heritage, they both believe, is to substitute the primacy of action for the primacy of knowledge, a fresh metaphysics for a withered epistemology. Thus both Putnam and Habermas insist on reconstruing the problem of how to make a beginning in philosophy with a protracted analysis of the agent and the nature of rational action within historical communities of discourse as opposed to the elaboration of still another foundationalist program from the analysis of the knower and the closed epistemology of the subject. Whatever their differences here, Putnam and Habermas are entirely committed to working through the demands of describing rational agency perspicuously. But such a position, supported repeatedly with all the detail of their very extensive and continuing work, goes just as much against the grain of the Stolnitz-Dickie controversy as it does against that of the analytic-hermeneutic disagreements. Let me put the issue here in the form of a first question for further reformulation and investigation.

1. How should the problems with parsing the complex notion of a philosophy of intersubjective rational agency incline us both to reconceptualize the nature and the elements of such cardinal issues in the philosophy of art as interpretation and history[36] and to reread the seminal eighteenth-century thinkers having in hand not merely epistemological interests but the mainly metaphysical ones arising from the realist backgrounds of modern aesthetics?

But if Putnam and Habermas have certain affinities, they also diverge widely, as we have seen. A second issue becomes clear when we notice how the crucial difference between the analytic and hermeneutic readings of Kant find their echo in a very similar disagreement between Habermas and Putnam. For Putnam, overcoming the peculiar conceptual impasses of modernity and the strong relativisms that are the issue of its various kinds of foundationalism requires returning to Kant, especially to the salient differences in the understandings of reason in the First and Second Critiques, for a fresh way to think about the dialectic within a pragmatic realism between standards and practices. But for Habermas we cannot finally succeed in working out the detail of a theory of communicative action unless we overcome precisely the Kantian fragmentation of reason in all three critiques into the fatefully divided spheres of the cognitive-scientific, the moral-practical, and the aesthetic. And this task in turn requires taking fresh critical insight from the as yet insufficiently ruminated early texts of Hegel, where the possibility of a reunification of Kantian reason was seen, with the help of Schiller's neglected work, in the reconciling powers of art. Like the analytic reading of the history of aesthetics, Putnam's larger reading of modernity gravitates to the need for a reappropriation of Kant, whereas Habermas's reading seems almost a generalization of the hermeneutic concern to overcome Kant's restrictions on what counts as genuine knowledge by rethinking Hegel. This second issue suggests a further question.

2. In rethinking the consequences of our present understandings of the relations between art and philosophy today in view of the

---

[36]Much important work continues to be done on part of this issue in Japan, thanks to the project of T. Imamichi and the Taniguchi Foundation on "Eco-ethica."

realist backgrounds of modern aesthetics, what weight must be given to relativizing the modernist standpoint with a renewed and argumentative rather than merely historical assessment of Hegel's attempt to overcome the Kantian divisions of reason against itself, an assessment centered on the metaphysical issues of adjudicating changing conceptions of rationality?

But as soon as we complement our first question, a systematic one, with a second that reserves a central place for history, we come to yet another issue. For throughout this extended inquiry, whether in the details of the Danto-Gadamer discussions, or in those of the Stolnitz-Dickie controversy, or finally now in the divergences between contemporary neo-Marxist and Anglo-American thought in the work of Habermas and Putnam, the story here has turned on talk of different historical readings or accounts. In each of these investigations we have been concerned with how certain thinkers and their ideas are seen to interact, and with how they are seen to interact from the characteristic standpoint of modernity. But how exactly are we to understand the interests, the aims, the procedures, and the materials of such readings when the very notions of history, story, and narrative are left unaddressed? And how are we to get clear enough about these notions without exploring conceptually their correlations with the ideas of description, explanation, interpretation, and especially "reading"? In this connection, then, turning to the problem of rethinking the relations between philosophy and the arts today raises a third issue.

3. On what argued construals of the conceptual correlations between writing history and reading history, many of which are already sedimented in the realist backgrounds of modern aesthetics, are we to undertake the kind of metaphysical genealogy in the eighteenth-century thinkers of the relations between philosophy and the arts in the modernist era that can genuinely enlighten, emancipate, and refigure the new dynamic understanding we require today?

But once again the formulation of this question, however provisional, calls attention to a further and for now final issue we need to identify. For this formulation simply repeats one of the unspecified phrases that have recurred throughout this book—"the eighteenth-century thinkers." Suppose we were to offer some sustained reformulation and response to each of the three questions so far. A further question would still arise about just what materials would be the proper objects of a fresh philosophical reading from the standpoint of a theory of rational communicative agency that sought to move regressively, unlike Habermas, even behind Kant[37] with the help of reassessing the reflections of art in the circle around the young Hegel, with an eye on their debts to the early Enlightenment.

Since I am not able to deal here at any length with the previous questions, I will not try to specify the materials at issue in other than a programmatic way.[38] Nonetheless, I want to call attention to at least three elements that, despite their relative familiarity in other contexts, none of the philosophical readings before us have even touched on. Thus I will argue for the absolutely central role in the eighteenth-century thinkers not just of kinds of indirect knowledge or aesthetic perception or theories of taste but of the many and complex understandings of nature in its various guises—for example, in the "nature" of natural morality and religion in Shaftesbury or Butler, of the "nature" in the satires of Swift, and of the "nature" Hume pits against reason.[39] Further, philosophers would need to pay much more attention to the interactions not just among theories of art but especially among the arts themselves— for example, among opera, theater, and painting in the critical discussions of Mozart, Marivaux, and Watteau in the *Nouveau Mercure* and other journals of the early eighteenth century. Finally, we would need to reexamine the English eighteenth-century thinkers— their interests, their ambitions, and their texts—not just in connection with the German thinkers of the early Enlightenment or thereafter but especially in their links with the ongoing critical debates in France. Hence we would need to look not just at the literary wrangles, the *querelle des anciens et des modernes* that Habermas keeps citing in the studies of Hans Robert Jauss, but also at the controversy in, for example, painting between the Poussainists and the Rubenists and the influence of Batteux on Shaftesbury, Crousaz on Hutcheson, and the Abbé Dubos on Hume, all of whom

[37]For just one example see C. Seerveld, "Early Kant and a Rococo Spirit: Setting for the Critique of Judgment," *Philosophia Reformata* 43(1978): 145–67. Cf. J. Chytry's discussion of classicism and realism in *The Aesthetic State* (Berkeley, Calif., 1989).

[38]I do this provisionally in the Hogarth paper cited in note 35. For the necessary historical background for the English context see P. Langford, *A Polite and Commercial People: England, 1727–83* (Oxford, 1989).

[39]Consider the detailed discussion M. J. Ferreira provides in *Scepticism and Reasonable Doubt: The British Naturalist Tradition in Wilkins, Hume, Reid, and Newman* (Oxford, 1987). Curiously, the medieval tradition is very important in this story. See, for example, R. Inagaki, "Habitus and Natura," *Revue Internationale de Philosophie Moderne* (Tokyo) 2 (1984): 99–105.

the English thinkers cite generously. Thus a fourth question arises.

4. What kind of systematic view of history and its peculiar logic, one that would draw critically but fruitfully on the realist backgrounds of modern aesthetics, can allow us sufficient warrant for circumscribing the appropriate objects for a fresh reading of the eighteenth-century thinkers in such a way as to capture those critical moments in the reformulation of reason and rationality in the transition from the late baroque to the neoclassical styles in England, without either surrendering the variety of the interactions among the arts and criticism or overlooking the central and shifting understandings of reason and nature?

Here, then, are four issues out of the many that clamor for critical attention at the end of the provisional inquiry into taking the critique of modernity another step toward appropriately relativizing our present all too blinkered understanding of the strained conceptual relations between philosophy and the arts today. Compassing these issues—or related ones in more perspicuous formulations—against the realist backgrounds of modern aesthetics, I believe, will entail thinking twice not just about interpretation and history, theory and practice, aesthetics and modernity, but about why we need to set the bounds of art themselves in more than one way.[40]

[40]One example of such work is the extraordinary article of K. Tsujimura, "Über Yü-chiens Landschaftsbild 'In die Ferne Bucht kommen Segelboote zurück,'" *Revue Internationale de Philosophie Moderne* (Tokyo) 3(1985): 153–67, where the question is how truly distinguished works of art compel thoughtful reflection to assume new orientations.

Index

Index

Index

Index

Index

Library of Congress Cataloging-in-Publication Data

McCormick, Peter (Peter J.)
  Modernity, aesthetics, and the bounds of art / Peter J. McCormick.
    p.   cm.
  ISBN 0-8014-2452-6 (alk. paper).
  ISBN 0-8014-9740-X (pbk.: alk. paper)
    1. Aesthetics, Modern—18th century. 2. Aesthetics, Modern—20th century. I. Title.
BH181.M36   1990
111'.85—dc20   89-71309